Praise for Bob Shacochis and The Immaculate Invasion

"Hard reporting and sharp commentary."
—*Foreign Affairs*

"Shacochis demonstrates that truth is immeasurably stranger than fiction . . . A book about moral ambiguity, about political confusion, about unanswerable questions."
—Michael Pearson, *The Atlanta Journal-Constitution*

"If you only have the time and energy for one serious work of non-fiction this year, do yourself a favor: read *The Immaculate Invasion*, Bob Shacochis's brilliant report on the 1994 U.S. invasion of Haiti. . . . It is a complicated series of events, but Shacochis both personalizes it and makes it fascinating. His sympathies are always with the common people, both American and Haitian, whose nobility and suffering are illustrated with brilliant vignettes the reader will be tempted to read aloud to anyone handy."
—Nora Marsh, *New Orleans Times-Picayune*

"A compelling and highly personal eyewitness account of Operation Uphold Democracy, the 1994 U.S. invasion of Haiti . . . *The Immaculate Invasion* is important historically because it is probably the most honest version of this episode in American-Haitian relations we are likely to get. Aside from its historical importance, however, Shacochis's storytelling talents are spellbinding. His writing is as beautiful as his story is heartbreaking."
—*The Denver Post & Minneapolis Star Tribune*

"A surreal joyride through the history, politics, and culture of Haiti—and through that country's uneasy relationship with the United States . . . A powerfully perceptive portrait."
—*Houston Chronicle*

"A brilliant book full of sharp analysis and superb reporting, mindful of the best reporting to come out of the Vietnam War . . . On a grand scale, Shacochis paints a nightmare of souls in hell, like Hieronymus Bosch with a laptop."
—Henry Kisor, *Chicago Sun-Times*

"It takes a writer as talented as the National Book Award–winning Bob Shacochis to make sense not only of Haiti, but of the role overworked and sometimes befuddled U.S. troops are being asked to take these days. . . . Shacochis tells the sympathetic story of American troops deployed on a not-quite battlefield and makes it clear from the start that he knows Haiti."
—Charles Jaco, *USA Today*

"[A] remarkable account of the most recent U.S. military occupation . . . Shacochis is a master at describing American ambivalence towards Haitian democracy. . . . He shows, with great subtlety and sympathy, how men trained to kill and die, men proud to the point of vanity about their martial skills and group cohesion, were forced to operate in a situation whose complexity they were never able fully to

grasp, let alone master. . . . One of the many admirable things about the book is the way he is able to move, effortlessly, it seems, from the human and operational details to the larger considerations of U.S. policy and the nature of the new role that politicians have been increasingly assigning the military."
—David Rieff, *The New York Observer*

"Shacochis details the violent madness of life in Haiti, the horrible lurching between hope and desperation. . . . This is a curious page turner—curious because it's not the plot but Shacochis's gift with words that keeps things moving."
—John Wilkins, *The San Diego Union*

"Shacochis presents a narrative that at times resembles a hair-raising, humvee ride through the jungle. But what emerges, ultimately, is a potent chronicle of both a Caribbean nation and a U.S. military machine in profound transition."
—*Publishers Weekly*

"Brilliant . . . Shacochis's narrative and character development weave together a stunning comedy of terrors. When reading this, one wants to laugh, cry, and take a shower all at the same time."
—*Kirkus Reviews* (starred)

"*The Immaculate Invasion* is an extraordinary book about an extraordinary event in current world affairs: the best of America's soldiers launched on a humanitarian mission to the poorest and most fascinating country in the Western Hemisphere. As I read, I felt transported to Haiti. I could hear it. I could smell it. At moments I felt moved almost to tears, only to find myself, a page or two later, laughing out loud. This is that rare thing, a book that really is hard to stop reading. It took me on a journey that I wished would never end."
—Tracy Kidder, author of *Old Friends* and *The Soul of a New Machine*

"Read this book whether you're interested in Haiti or not—if you're an American citizen, it's the story of your tax dollars at work. Bob Shacochis has written a gripping, ground-level account of the use and abuse of American power abroad."
—Madison Smartt Bell, author of *All Souls' Rising*

"Furious, intense—a razored illustration of Americans and American policy from what might be called the Angle of Haiti. *The Immaculate Invasion* takes as a subtext the almost sensual violence of our contemporary world and its companion numbing of conscience and political imagination."
—Annie Proulx, author of *The Shipping News*

The

Immaculate

Invasion

The

Immaculate

Invasion

Bob Shacochis

Grove Press
New York

Portions of this book first appeared in Columbia Journalism Review, Conjunctions, Harper's Magazine, Outside, Tropic and The Washington Post.

Grateful acknowledgment is made for permission to reprint
the lyrics "Fey" by Richard Morse. Used by permission of Richard Morse.

Map by Mark Melnick
Design by Betty Lew

The author also wishes to acknowledge his reliance on the following texts and their analysis of the Haitian revolution: The Black Jacobins by C. L. R. James (New York: Vintage Books, 1989) and The Overthrow of Colonial Slavery by Robin Blackburn (London: Verso Press, 1988).

First published in 1999 by Viking Penguin

Printed in the United States of America
Published simultaneously in Canada

ISBN-13: 978-0-8021-4518-5

Grove Press
an imprint of Grove/Atlantic, Inc.
841 Broadway
New York, NY 10003
Distributed by Publishers Group West
www.groveatlantic.com

10 11 12 13 14   10 9 8 7 6 5 4 3 2 1

Glossary

attachés illegally deputized plainclothes police auxiliaries who served the Cédras military junta as hit men; death squads

Barbancourt Haitian Rum

BDU battle dress uniform

Black Ops covert operations

bouki some Green Berets called Haitian peasants *boukis,* a name derived from the Haitian folktales of Bouki and Ti Malice

CA Civil Affairs

cacos peasant guerrilla forces from the nineteenth and early twentieth centuries

Caricom Caribbean community

Chef Chief, headman

Chogee Korean war term, still current use in the army, referring to the new subordinate members assigned to a unit or team

CINC Commanders in Chief

DAO Defense Attaché's Office

dechouké to rebel against macoutes; literally, to uproot, destroy

DIA Defense Intelligence Agency

DOD Department of Defense

Dom Rep Dominican Republic

FADH Haitian Armed Forces

FOB forward operating base

foo Creole word for crazy person

FRAPH Front for the Advancement and Progress of Haiti; a terrorist organization

gourde Haitian currency.

houngan vodou priest

ICITAP International Criminal Investigations Training Assistance Program, established by the Justice Department and FBI to train Latin American (and Haitian) police forces

IG Inspector General

Intel short for 'intelligence'

IPM International Police Monitors

IPSF Interim Police Security Force

JAG Judge Advocate General: the military's legal office

JIB Joint Information Bureau

JTF Joint Task Force

Lavalas grassroots coalition responsible for the election of Jean-Bertrand Aristide to the presidency in 1990; Aristide defined Lavalas as "a river with many sources, a flood that would sweep away all the dross, all the aftereffects of a shameful past"

LBE load-bearing element: a vest worn over BDUs

LIC light-industrial complex in Port-au-Prince, headquarters for the U.S. military

LZ landing zone

macoute derived from Ton Ton Macoutes, a notorious paramilitary force created by François Duvalier to counterbalance the power of the Haitian army, the word *macoute* is now used generically to describe anybody associated with the illegal state created by General Cédras and the Haitian army

mambo a vodou priestess

Marassa a *vodou* spirit, or *loa*, represented by twins

MREs morally repugnant elites; also, meals, ready to eat

NCO noncommissioned officer; an enlisted man

NGO; PVO nongovernmental organization; private voluntary organization

NSA National Security Agency

NSC National Security Council

OAS Organization of American States

PAO Public Affairs Officer

psy ops psychological operations

SAW squad automatic weapon

SecDef Secretary of Defense

sit rep situational report; composed by A teams and sent to command

SOC-C Special Operations Command and Control

SOP Standard operating procedure

tap-tap public transportation, often a colorfully painted truck

TDY temporary duty

UW unconventional warfare

vévé a geometric design meant to invoke or summon a *loa*

vodou (pronounced *voh-doo*) The word means "sacred" in Haitian Creole and traces its origin to the Fon language of West Africa. Haitian *vodou*, the oldest religion of the African diaspora, although based on animism and the veneration of *loas*—African deities—acknowledges the existence of one supreme being and has absorbed many of the saints, and the mysticism, of Roman Catholicism. The denigrative term *voodoo* is often used by non-Haitians to refer to black magic or superstitious beliefs.

Contents

Part Six: Beyond the Mountain

Epilogue

Preface

This is a book about America, the triumphant society, a book about how a nation that dares call itself indispensable goes about its business in a world it in many ways owns yet will never control. Mostly this is a story about soldiers, the Special Forces, although it does not begin or end with these men but with drums—and drummers—on the Champs du Mars, the expansive and somewhat tawdry patchwork park that spreads out beyond the grandiose national palace, an architectural wedding cake, in downtown Port-au-Prince.

Handmade drums, *vodou* drums, heartbeat drums with a rising pulse as furious as hurricane-driven rain. Drums like a deafening cascade of rocks on the tin roofs of oppression. Warriors fly to their beat, come and go, advance and retreat, fight or don't fight, come, go, and are gone. Some stories—war stories—must be told this way, like a wild dance that ends in exhaustion, if they are to be told at all. Some stories must be told this way, with their rules—the logic and expectation and understanding—collapsing under you like a rotten footbridge over a furious crosscurrent of rhythms.

Perhaps such a bridge spans the gulf between a country like the United States and a country like Haiti, or the gulf between the lives of white men and black men, or between war and peace, a foggy, swamp-bottomed no-man's-land the military calls OTW—operations other than war: an empty space in an army's traditional reality, where there are no friends and no enemies, no front or rear, no victories and, likewise, no defeats, and no true endings.

This is a war story in the sense that only the drums contain true order, which is not the same as a plan, not the same as a mission statement or a policy directive. All the rest is an illusion called peacekeeping, and an illusion called democracy—the artifice of order, a thin icy surface layer of rationality earnestly manufactured by presidents, ministers, advisers, spies, admirals, generals, colonels, captains, sergeants, cameramen, producers, editors, and writers.

Of course, writers.

The

Immaculate

Invasion

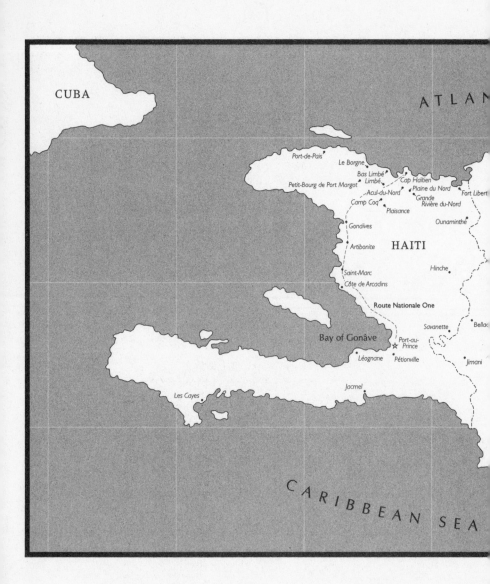

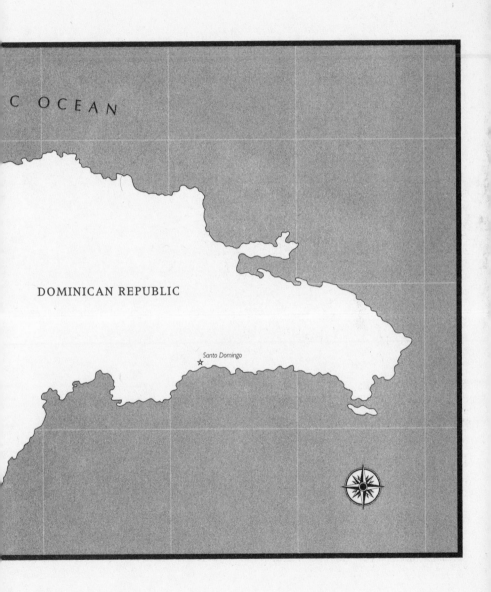

PART ONE

The Day You See Me Fall
Is Not the Day I Die

One black peasant woman fell upon her knees
with her arms outstretched like a crucifix and
cried, "They say that the white man is coming to
rule Haiti again. The black man is so cruel to his
own, let the white man come!"

—Zora Neale Hurston (1938).

VODOU RHYTHMS

The tyrants wanted everyone happy, that first carnival after the coup d'état in September 1991. They wanted celebration and, when it was not forthcoming, set about to manufacture it themselves—because the contagion that had infected Haitian society had been cut away, gouged out with less than surgical precision: the disease called Lavalas was in remission, the malignant Aristide removed, and the status quo revived. No single social event was more important to the Haitian people, high or low, elite or peasant, than carnival, and carnival was the government's responsibility, a once-only chance to exercise its deformed sense of noblesse oblige. But when the tyrants sent the musicians to Champs du Mars to inaugurate the seasonal jubilation, inconceivably, no one came.

There were many reasons for the people's absence, but the foremost problem, the putschists determined, was the music—the music wasn't working. The regime had hired *compas* bands, when what they really needed was a *racine* band, but *racine* was Aristide's music, roots music, the music of the masses. *Racine* was the sound of uprising and revolution; a regime-sponsored *racine* performance would be analogous to Bob Marley playing for the Republican National Convention. But for the moment nobody had the heart for *compas*; its simple upbeat melodies and trivial lyrics were like a funeral dirge for democracy. Nobody much wanted to release themselves to it except the attachés, the killers, the macoutes—the ones who, when they danced, danced in blood.

To control a country as fucked up as Haiti, you had to wrap your hands around the throat of everything—the language, the music, especially the songs and the potent rhythms of the songs, because in the people's centuries-old war against the tyrants, drums were weapons, words were deadly ammunition. And so the generals decided they had to get a *racine* band out on the Champs du Mars, the quicker the better. One Friday afternoon before Lent began, they summoned Richard Morse, a young Haitian-American musician who ran the Hotel Oloffson, to the Ministry of the Interior—the administrative headquarters for Haiti's brutish police and new paramilitary security forces. The duty officer directed Richard to a large room crammed with about fifty or sixty red-eyed attachés—it must have been payday for the assassins—and Richard's thinking, *God, what's going on? These guys have probably been killing people all week and they're waiting to get paid and here I am.*

After about ten minutes, one of the vultures finally said, *Get RAM a chair*—RAM was the name of Richard's band—and so they sat him down and then a lieutenant sauntered in and told him he wanted Richard to do a concert, and Richard said, *Fine.*

The lieutenant said, *If a crowd doesn't show up, I'm going to arrest you.*

Richard returned to the hotel and gathered the band for a debate. Pro-Lavalas musicians were being shot, disappeared; bands were going underground, going into exile. The troubadour Manno Charlemagne had been arrested and tortured before taking refuge in an embassy. In Haiti there was never a good answer, never a right answer. Richard kept soliciting advice until the most logical thing somebody said was, *Play your songs, don't say anything, and get the hell out.*

That night, spreading out from the band shell on Champs du Mars, there were people as far as you could see, ten thousand people, and cars all the way down to the palace. The stage was surrounded by FADH—the Haitian army—a company of helmeted, well-armed soldiers, and two more truckloads of troops were parked on the street. When RAM started playing, anyone in the audience who raised his arms into the air to dance was swarmed by plainclothes cops and dragged away; two songs into the gig, and Richard had counted a dozen arrests. *Good God,* he thought, *I'd hate to leave this party and have them think I'm part of all this.* The intensity escalated, and suddenly everything was quiet, everything was bad, ten thousand faces staring at Richard, the lead singer, the man out front, wondering what he would do next as he stepped back over to the microphone.

He listened to his New York–accented Creole booming, echoing beyond the palace, beyond the Holiday Inn where the macoutes and the journalists congregated, filtering down into the slums, where most of his band members lived. "Join us," he said, signaling to the female vocalists, who began, a cappella, to deliver the band's first of many subversions throughout the years of the regime—an old ballad, a traditional part of Haiti's oral culture of resistance. *Kote moun yo? Pas way moun yo.* Thirty seconds later, realizing what the band was singing—a parable, in a sort of peasant code, about Aristide—the soldiers pulled the plug.

The sun had gone down long before; now there was no power, no stage lights, and it was pitch black in the park. Behind Richard onstage, a row of drummers hunkered over their handmade congas, RAM's *vodou* rhythm section. He turned to tell them to keep drumming, full force, a spontaneous decision that would evolve into a strategy, a method of survival, to be repeated in the difficult years ahead whenever the lights went out and the horror descended. By the time Richard turned back around—fifteen seconds—thousands of people had disappeared into the night. The girls took up the song again, their voices clear and strong in the darkness. The drums were drumming, you could hear their thunderous report throughout the terrified city as RAM played on, drums and vocals, as if nothing were happening, as if this weren't a nightmare and the dream were still alive.

Petro drums, which beat out the rhythms of Haiti's ethos, *maronnage*, the rhythms of the new world, Haitian-born among Indians and slaves— the rhythms of the slaveghosts and *vodou* and insurrection. *Petro* was the percussive language of blackout and embargo. Not *rada* drums—the rhythms of ancient Africa, the mythic Guineé, the lost land beyond the sea—because *rada* rhythms had proved impotent against the French colonials, *rada*'s power had dwindled in the Middle Passage. But *petro*—*petro* lived, thrived. When you heard *petro* drums, what you heard, what you knew you were hearing, was war. *Petro* was the rhythm of war.

Drums and vocals—*Kote moun yo? Where are the people? Pas way moun yo. We don't see them.* Meaning Lavalas. Meaning Aristide. Meaning the multitudes who had vanished into the sea and the thousands who, since the coup five months earlier, were already dead or missing.

Richard Morse counted governments, not years, to measure his time in Haiti since 1987, when he had taken a lease on the most famous hotel in the Caribbean. Fifteen, sixteen? Governments went up and down like tin ducks in a shooting gallery, here at the boneyard carnival that was Haiti.

He had come here by himself from New Jersey, a tall, twenty-eight-year-old, sleepy-eyed, surly-faced Princeton grad, his mother a renowned Haitian dancer and his Anglo father a Latin American scholar at Yale—a kid who had grown up in houses with many, many rooms. He had been playing bass in a New Wave band that worked the downtown clubs in Manhattan—pursuing a vague desire for different rhythms, something like that—when he landed in Port-au-Prince in September 1985, and suddenly they're shooting people everywhere. There's a mass uprising—the *dechoukaj,* or uprooting of all things Duvalier. By February, Baskethead—Baby Doc—was aboard a United States Air Force jet, headed for France to play tennis, twenty-nine years of vampirism and dictatorship out the window . . . then back in again, a phantom, six months later, now in the guise of narcotraffickers and military clowns. Still, a true metamorphosis had taken place during the *dechoukaj,* not from authoritarianism to democracy, but from the bondage of the spirit to the release of the imagination.

Overnight the country seemed intoxicated with possibility, and Richard attached himself to the Hotel Oloffson, a whitewashed, multitiered tropigothic monstrosity nestled within its own private jungle in a high-walled enclave in downtown Port-au-Prince. The Oloffson, by its very architecture and its ceiling-fan ambience, created an indelible vision of faded authority and exotic intrigue, but it was built atop a history that didn't quite match the Kiplingesque groove of the white man's burden.

Instead, the Oloffson was a native hybrid, a reproduction that became authentic through the grind and twist of desperate events. In *The Comedians,* his novel about the Duvalier era, Graham Greene described the grotesque impression the Oloffson, alias the Hotel Trianon, made on one's senses—"You expected a witch to open the door to you or a manic butler, with a bat dangling from the chandelier behind him"—and *New Yorker* cartoonist Charles Addams, a frequent guest, modeled his trademark haunted houses after the hotel. A folly, a travel writer once wrote, "of spires, crotchets, finials and conical towers." The structure was the grandiose vision of the Sam family, who constructed the mansion at the end of the nineteenth century and inhabited it until 1915, when the family's dubious contribution to the nation, President Guillaume Sam, was dragged into the street, shot, his body torn apart by a mob, and the pieces paraded around town skewered on the ends of poles. Waving the Monroe Doctrine and growling about Germany's increasing influence in the West Indies, the U.S. Marines seized the occasion as an excuse to invade. They marched into the capital the next day, the Sam family residence—the future Hotel Oloffson—their hospital until they left, nineteen years later, serenaded by Richard's maternal grandfather, Auguste, a popular resistance singer still remembered for the songs he composed to taunt the American soldiers and their iron-fisted occupation.

Haiti, back in the early seventies, when Baskethead inherited the national palace from his ghoulish father, enjoyed a brief but profitable tenure as an off-the-path destination for the rich and famous (Jackie Onassis, for instance, who became a major collector of Haitian artwork). But once the *dechoukaj* flamed over the countryside, once Club Med closed its doors in 1986, the *blancs*—foreigners, white people—wouldn't come anymore, not as tourists anyway. For generations, there had been the killings, the state-sponsored violence, the crushing and ubiquitous poverty, the incomprehensible polyglot of Creole; now the Centers for Disease Control in Atlanta made matters worse with a bogus AIDS-epidemic alert, although sex tourism had indeed brought the virus to Haiti's shores.

Each of them for their own shameless reasons, Hollywood and the missionaries and the Duvaliers demonized *vodou,* an ancient polytheistic view of the universe based on the idea that everything in one's world, animate and inanimate, possessed a spirit or soul. In 1986, I came across the stationery of one of the island's evangelical missions—*Haiti,* it read, *6½ million souls in witchcraft and Catholicism.* And always there was the racial dynamic, a permanent and insurmountable barrier to the majority of whites contemplating a tropic vacation, and so the tourist trade, never more than a golden trickle, dried up, and Haiti, as was its common fate, fell off the map of civilization.

The Oloffson survived it all by serving as a crash house for bohemian reporters—journotrash—and aid entrepreneurs, some checking in for the sole purpose of carousing with the highly literate chameleon Aubelin Jolicoeur, the hotel's most curious and enduring artifact. Aging spy, former Duvalierist apparatchik, dapper gallant, and gossip columnist for Haiti's only daily newspaper, *Le Nouvelliste,* the spry Jolicoeur was transformed only slightly by Graham Greene into the fictional Petit Pierre. Upon the occasion of the novelist's death, Jolicoeur wrote in 1991 that Greene had enhanced his reputation "to such an extent that some fans kneel at my feet or kiss my hand in meeting a man living his own legend."

Year after year, you could sit on the Oloffson's airy veranda and observe Jolicoeur, his spidery body impeccably suited, a silk ascot at his throat, mount the hotel's diamond vee of steps to hold soirees in the wicker-and-rattan drawing room. Women were often attracted to the gleam of his bald head and gold-knobbed cane, and he stroked the *femmes* with lacy prose, prying himself away from their heavenly perfumes to play backgammon with cronies from the CIA. Jolicoeur had been a fixture at the hotel for decades, just as the foreign correspondents had returned on their migrations, year after year, dining on the veranda at twilight, their collegial discourse interrupted by rude bursts of automatic-weapon fire down the street at the national palace, where, in the long march toward democracy after the *dechoukaj,* coup after coup unfolded, each journalist hesitating with fork in midair, wondering, *Didn't I order a double?*

Bartender, *s'il vous plaît.* Five-star Barbancourt, *encore.*

When Richard signed a fifteen-year lease on the Oloffson in November 1987, the country, snapping out of its post-Duvalier daydream of better times, had fallen apart again. Driving from Pétionville, the elite suburbs up the mountain, down to Port-au-Prince after sundown was considered insane—random shootings, burning tires, vigilante roadblocks, bodies in the street. But Richard was operating on the theory that if there were elections and they went well, there'd be democracy, and tourists would come to the hotel. And if the elections didn't go well, the rooms would fill up with journalists. But the elections, foisted prematurely upon a population forever yearning but ill-prepared for such an exercise by the Reagan administration, were catastrophic. Voters (and journalists) were slaughtered as they queued up at polling stations, and everyone bugged out. The entire nation reeled from one near-death experience to another, everybody's head filled with a kaleidoscopic blur of violent images, while the Americans kept pushing elections, Band-Aids in the trauma unit.

In 1989, George Bush wanted to try the democracy thing again and this time guarantee the result. The White House's handsomely financed candidate, Marc Bazin, an economist and former World Bank executive, was slotted to ascend to the national palace under the sunny skies of Haiti's first free and fair election, which would be overseen by Jimmy Carter, whose own bias for Bazin and antipathy toward Jean-Bertrand Aristide, Bazin's main opponent, was transparent. The subsequent election—in 1990, just as Richard was forming his band—was in fact a triumph for real democracy. The Haitian people, by an overwhelming and euphoric majority, chose for their new president not Bazin but Aristide, a young leftist priest from the slums given to provocative anti-American rhetoric, a disciple of liberation theology, whom the FADH couldn't seem to assassinate, though they burned down his church and hacked to death many of his congregation. What kind of priest will such earthly trials make you, what kind of president?

Inaugurated in February 1991 for a five-year term, Aristide lasted only seven months before the military pitched him into exile and took to murdering anyone who even dared to mention his name—*Titid*, little Aristide, Haiti's apparent messiah. President Bush, underwriter of the island's nascent democracy, swiftly announced that the coup would not stand, then just as quickly receded into embarrassed silence when informed by his staff that his own crew in Port-au-Prince not only had foreknowledge of the putsch but had allowed it to advance without a word. The United States had been Janus-faced in its intentions toward the island ever since, its policymakers split between statesmen who at least professed to support democracy (and its noisy consequences) in Haiti, and the spies and diplomats, the holy rollers at State and Defense with no vision beyond the institutional culture of the American government—still hard-wired for the cold war—who refused to assign any legitimate meaning to the will of the Haitian masses or to accept the fact that Haitians democratically chose Jean-Bertrand Aristide, the only Haitian president who ever attempted to lead his people out of darkness: the only Haitian chief of state who ever seemed to display an ideology beyond self.

Ironically, early on in the coup that deposed Aristide, as the terror began to coalesce into a system, RAM prospered. The band was putting hit singles on the radio even though people were afraid to come to their concerts, afraid to be identified with *racine*, with the politics of the *petro* rhythms. Until the mandarins woke up to the band's agenda, the group had been showcased on the government-run radio and television stations, but then the generals began to censor their tapes, and the military sent attachés out to the Oloffson to interview Richard: *What do you think about what's happening here? What do you think of this situation?*

Uh . . . what situation?

Military coup d'état. And the attachés would take Richard's hand and make him pat the guns tucked into their hip pockets; they wanted payoffs, and Richard would give them RAM T-shirts and twenty bucks.

After the fiasco on Champs du Mars, the macoutes at last understood where RAM stood in their cosmology, and the band was blacklisted by the government. Then filmmaker Rudi Stern's documentary on the coup, *Killing the Dream,* was picked up in Port-au-Prince via satellite, and the generals couldn't believe it. There was this shithead from RAM sitting in his office at the Oloffson, saying the coup looked planned, that the elite families were involved, that they raised the blood money. Saying the military had tried to make it look like Aristide was a man who had to be stopped for the good of the nation because Aristide was a lunatic, a man who talked poetically about the beauty of necklacing, a man who gave a speech advocating crimes against humanity, and so what else could the military do but make it seem that they had whipped up a coup on the spur of the moment. After that, too often when Richard picked up the phone, somebody was calling in a death threat. Then he was summoned down to police headquarters to be interrogated by Evans François, the brother of Colonel Michel François, police chief and prime coup leader, who carefully explained to Richard that there were a lot of people in Port-au-Prince who would be only too happy to waste him for fifty cents. But they let him walk.

What Richard hadn't yet figured out was that he and RAM, by their very defiance, were proving to be valuable assets to the tyrants, window dressing for their faux-democratic posturing—freedom of the press, freedom of speech; subterfuge for the idiot Americans who were trying to bargain their way back toward some gloss of decency and moral rectitude without having to actually go the distance with Aristide. But there were limits to even faux tolerance, and Richard Morse, for whatever reason, seemed particularly slow to get the message.

RAM went into the studio to record their first album, and out it came: *Aibobo,* a *vodou* term equivalent to Hallelujah or Amen. A song on the album—"Fey"—which Richard knew would create a scandal, was positioned at the end of the tape; he released a politically innocuous single—"Ibo Lele," later included by director Jonathan Demme on the sound track of the movie *Philadelphia*—and let the album work its way slowly into the market. By the time the de factos—the coup leaders—discovered "Fey," it was too late. The song was all over the airwaves, people were singing it in the street, and the regime started closing down radio stations—but only outside of Port-au-Prince—and raising the ante on Richard by threatening his wife, Lunise, a beautiful dark-skinned former dancer whom he had made the lead female vocalist in RAM. This was 1993; the tension was vile, unbearable. Aristide's champion in the ruling class, a wealthy businessman named Antoine Izmery, was hauled out of church one morning, during a memorial service for those killed in the 1988 attack on Aristide's church, and murdered in the street. A UN-brokered agreement was being hammered out on Governors Island in New York: Aristide was supposed to come back in October and play the dummy in a power-sharing arrangement with the tyrants. "Fey" was getting played and the rumors were flying: Lunise had been kidnapped, Lunise had been killed.

The band—slum kids mostly, Lavalas diehards—had grown to believe nothing bad was going to happen because Richard had this envelope, these force fields—white guy, American guy—which protected them from harm. Now his phone kept ringing, friends calling to find out if he was dead—*Just checking to see if you're alive, Rich*—and what was he supposed to do? Go away? Go where? Grad school? Some pickup job back in Jersey with a lounge singer? He had Lunise, two kids, the hotel, the band. He had become a strange variation of *vodou* impresario, so wrapped up in the rhythms that they existed within him at the cellular level, they percolated in his blood, and the alternatives were incomprehensible. Life or death—were those the options? What if the options, the true options, were really democracy or repression? He was trying not to get anyone shot, but if you started retreating, where did you stop? Where were the Haitians themselves going to stop, because just about everybody he knew would jump overboard off this festering, floundering slave ship of a nation if they could. Like, *Fuck it, let's just get out of here, two hundred years is enough, let's just go somewhere else.*

Ultimately it would be to the regime's advantage if he left. He understood that, but he had roots in Haiti, old and new, he had insights that maybe Haiti needed. Still, his family, Lunise and the babies—risking their lives was his biggest fear. If anybody hurt them he might mobilize, go down blazing, but he didn't even know if that's really what he would do. He prayed it would never come to that, but it was getting close, getting very close, and like everyone else in Haiti, he was wondering, *Where are the Americans?*

REPRESSION WORKS

To ask a Haitian, *Where are the Americans?* was not unlike asking a grief-stricken child, *Where is God?* Everywhere? Here but not here? Everywhere but with me? It's not as if the Americans weren't in Haiti already, weren't always there in one role or another, as wardens, patrons, carpet-baggers, saints, and thieves. They were like invisible spirits—the *vodou loas*—or like saviors—Jesus Christ was a *blanc, oui?*—like bullies and like big-time fools and like the fountainhead of all good and all evil in the world. America was a steely monolithic turbine on the horizon, which spewed into the air a sickly emission of hope and provided an ominous background hum to the island's tribulations. "Imagine," marveled William Jennings Bryan in 1920, "niggers speaking French." "I don't care if you dress them up and put them in the palace," opined the commander of the earlier Marine occupation, "they're still nigs." John Kennedy and Nelson Rockefeller all but coronated Papa Doc after the dictator cast the deciding vote to keep Castro's Cuba out of the OAS.

"Repression works," John Kambourian told a businessman in Port-au-Prince early in 1993. "It worked in Russia for forty years." A strange acknowledgment of the efficacy of authoritarianism, coming from the embassy's special assistant to the ambassador—a euphemistic title the CIA uses to whitewash its station chiefs, which is what Kambourian was in Haiti from 1992 through October 1994.

Repression works, and especially well, in countries like Haiti. At the expense of the rule of law, innocent lives, and freedom, repression creates order and wealth for an elite ruling class and misery for everyone else. Repression works and has been a not infrequent by-product of American foreign policy ever since the Spanish-American War, when the United States first began modeling itself after the European colonial powers, landing on the backs of the people it had ostensibly come to rescue—in that case, Cuban and Filipino independence fighters and their popular support, described with bitter and intended irony by Mark Twain as those shoeless multitudes "sitting in darkness," yearning for missionaries and a better class of masters. Guys like Colonel Lansdale, the original ugly American. Guys like Kambourian, maybe.

It goes without saying that in a moral universe, repression is abhorrent, but within the shifting moral boundaries of cold war realpolitik, repression was merely another tactic of containment, however distasteful, a tool in the strategic kit to be employed in the service of one's national interests, actual or imagined, economic or elusive, parochial or plural, vital or— especially in the backyard of the Caribbean Basin—vindictive. With the notable exception of the Marshall Plan to rebuild Europe and Japan, between the fall of Berlin and the fall of the Berlin wall American statesmen generally found it more pragmatic to collude with third world strongmen and despots ("He's *our* son of a bitch") than to risk championing the world's downtrodden masses, who in their ignorance gnawed away at institutional structures like termites and seemed congenitally predisposed toward the clumsy deconstruction of society with hammers and sickles.

But the masses have always had bad press, halfhearted endorsements, double-crossing emancipators. In truth, we displayed scant respect or patience for the will of the majority when the majority draped itself in rags and scrawled its name with an X, and accommodated instead the epaulets of absolute control, the fine linen of social rank, the lusty aroma of wealth—in short, the worst elements in a place like Haiti.

On my first visit to Haiti, in the spring of 1986, the heyday of the *dechoukaj,* I had attended a showing of *The Comedians,* a belated premiere of the film adaptation of Graham Greene's previously banned novel about life under the stormy rule of François Duvalier. At strategic corners throughout the capital, movie posters advertised the event, the bloody red lettering stamped on a black background: THE TERROR OF THE TON TON MACOUTES! The film was playing downtown at the Triomphe, a once grand movie house. In the theater's musty darkness, I had my choice of seats. The tinny sound track was dubbed in French, and during the violent scenes, what audience there was—about thirty-five neatly dressed youths and a scattering of whites from the foreign-aid community—remained solemn, even bored. They had seen it all before. The rage had blown through their quotidian lives, jading them to the artifice of the screen. But one scene finally provoked a reaction: when Richard Burton is assaulted by Ton Ton Macoutes, their dirty work is interrupted by a matronly tourist—a bonneted, purse-clutching dowager, a paragon of silver-haired indignation: White Anglo-Saxon Protestant Mom—who makes the blood-thirsty thugs wither by simply mentioning that were the President of the United States informed, he would not look tolerantly upon this sort of low-minded behavior. The audience erupted in laughter—the old white woman's threat was profoundly funny, because everyone in the Triomphe knew the Duvaliers had snookered the State Department, the Department of Defense, the U.S. embassy, and seven U.S. presidents as if they were green schoolboys, with a cynical ingenuity few heads of state would dare to match, crying wolf about communists whenever the White House showed signs of queasiness about its commitment to the Duvaliers, and the audience knew that with the exception of military aid, the open spigot of American taxpayers' money was almost never spent on what it was ap-propriated for but instead gushed rather than trickled into the coffers of the FADH and the macoutes and the national palace, to be squirreled away in Swiss bank accounts, squandered on shopping sprees to Paris, invested in Miami real estate. What the audience didn't yet know, however, was that the future to which they aspired would be indistinguishable from the past; that here in the spring of 1986, on the threshold of freedom, they were en-tering an era that would be described as Duvalierism without Duvalier.

Baskethead and his parasitic entourage had left behind an economy, an ecology, and a human landscape traumatized to the brink of no return, but he was hardly worse than most of the other thirty chiefs of state, strutting chanticleers of misleadership and kleptocracy, who had preceded him. Jean-Jacques Dessalines, revered today as the father of Haitian indepen-dence, crowned himself emperor in 1804 and waged a civil war against the light-skinned mulattoes—the ever-present elites in Haiti's all-important hierarchy of race. Almost without exception, the men who followed Des-salines contributed enthusiastically to Haiti's mythic legacy of avarice and tyranny and, like Dessalines himself, were subsequently assassinated, or deposed by insurrections and shipped into luxurious exile. If any single feature—other than its pariah status—had defined the nation throughout the course of its independence, it was a lack of political self-discipline. On and on, the country marched in place, dirtied and shunned, bearing its perpetually dismal image of *sauvagerie*. The truest aspirations of Haiti's founding fathers, modeled on the libertarian doctrines of the French and American revolutions, failed to conjugate. For almost two centuries, there had been only one overriding point of view in command—singular—and one verb tense—present. *Me, now*. The ideology of infants.

When the movie ended, I followed the audience outside and watched as they strolled toward a line of expensive cars parked along Rue Capois. There was no official curfew, not yet, but almost everyone withdrew behind locked doors shortly after suppertime. On the sidewalk in front of the Triomphe, a coterie of die-hard hucksters and beggars surged forward, enslaved to the tenuous enterprise of survival in this city where tens of thousands of people lived on the streets, in this nation where not even a quarter of the urban population earned a salary.

How's it going? I asked. *Como ye?*

They gave the standard response: *N'ap boule*. We're boiling. We're on fire.

Several days after the premiere of *The Comedians*, I journeyed north to investigate how Cap Haïtien, Haiti's second-largest city, had fared during the upheaval of the *dechoukaj*. Nine years later, after the U.S. invasion, I would come to know this road well, Route Nationale One—this beautiful, perilous road, my nightmare road—the road American soldiers would nickname Highway to Hell, commemorating its misery on what else but a T-shirt. But for its travelers, Route Nationale One was memory lane, the road always hurrying you backward into history.

Its point of origin was the fetid, suppurating, inexplicably inhumane harborside slums of Port-au-Prince, where the hemisphere's poorest families bathed in sewers, slept on dirt, walked daily through pestilence and desperation, surviving solely, it often seemed, on fear and rage, hunted, in the years ahead, by the army and the police and macoutes and attachés and FRAPH, a place where homeless children would one day fight each other for the feral right to lick the gummy residue out of the brown plastic pouches of MREs—spaghetti and meatballs, pork chow mein—they'd scavenged from the U.S. military's exotic proliferation of garbage.

Here the road boasted the world's biggest pothole, dredged out by runoff from the eroding mountainsides—a death trap during storms, as I would learn one harrowing evening, trapped in a long line of vehicles during a downpour, the cars ahead of me swept away one by one into the flooding darkness and the air filled with screams and thunder. Every day, hours-long traffic jams billowed diesel soot—the mucus in your nose turned black with it—and along the quayside it was not unusual to see, throughout the infinite years of the tyrants—white, black, and mulatto; colonial or modern—bodies bobbing in the otherwise tranquil harbor.

Yet everywhere here the roadside was thick with human vitality, thousands of *marchands* and stevedores, teamsters and brute laborers, energetic with need and gifted with tenacious earthy humor, hawking and trading mostly what a world they had never seen had thrown away, a national yard sale of grease-caked junk and tattered hand-me-downs, a Sisyphean economy of rejects, of endless seconds and thirds.

From city center the road slanted west and north, past the walls of the old Fort Dimanche—"the epicenter of Haitian oppression"—where for twenty-nine years the Duvaliers in their madness had murdered friend and foe alike; past the warehouses and the wholesalers and the foreign-owned assembly plants (baseballs, bras, electrical components) and the sugar refinery; past the airport with its derelict fleet of Haiti Air DC-3s.

Past what would one day be the United Nations compound and a newly paved highway—October the 15th Boulevard—commemorating the date of Aristide's return from exile (the best road in Haiti, it would lead past the President's private residence and up the mountain to Pétionville), then, farther along, the Barbancourt rum factory and the roadside artisans—cabinetmakers and coffinmakers, wrought-iron craftsmen and welders and tinsmiths—then past the junction leading to the central plateau—Mirebalais and Hinche—and the Dom Rep border, past the once stately neocolonial Ministry of Agriculture, bigger than a football field, one half of the structure roofless and charred from a fire, the other half still occupied by bureaucratic zombis ... until finally, through the reckless dodge of traffic—eighteen-wheelers and dump trucks and Pathfinders and tap-taps; bicycles and donkeys and pushcarts and an unbroken stream of peasants all clogging the two-lane highway—the road arrived at the leafy outskirts of town, a small village called Tintayen, near an enclave of descendants of Polish soldiers who had fought for, and then against, Napoleon. Tintayen was also the name of the vast coastal plain nearby, mostly methane-whiffy mangrove swamp, where the Haitian military would dump its cargoes of victims, the corpses eventually shrouded by land crabs and consumed by free-ranging pigs.

The capital and its singular degradations left behind, Route Nationale One arrowed ahead, the road pinched between an impressively barren ridge of arid mountains and the nearby but inaccessible coast, past the former Duvalierville and the tawdry lure of its absurdly grandiose cock-fighting pit, like the flared concrete canopy over the entrance of a cheap Las Vegas hotel; past Archaïe, where the *blanc*-hating Dessalines, both the George Washington and the mad King George of Haitian independence, tore the white from the French tricolor to create the island's sovereign flag; until, an hour northwest of Port-au-Prince, Route Nationale One passed the Côte de Arcadins, Haiti's all but deserted beach resorts—Club Med kept its local staff on retainer for nine years after the *dechoukaj,* re-opening as a duller, politically correct version of China Beach for American GIs.

Skirting amethyst-blue shallows, you steered around dripping young fishermen, who stepped into the road holding lobsters or a string of pan-size fish. Occasionally you glimpsed crescents and commas of empty golden beaches, and high walls enclosed the *ti paradis*—little paradises, the seaside hideaways of Port-au-Prince's oligarchy, its shoulder-board putschists, its drug kingpins, the commissars of trade and terror. Beyond was the once lovely port of Saint-Marc, occupied by the British during the French Revolution. Here, as you left town and traveled inland, you began to notice in the palmy hamlets and bare hills the frequency of *hounfours*—*vodou* temples, identified by their gay high-flying flags and crude or magnificent wall paintings of the spirit world, bright cartoons of mythic good and evil—and then the road flattened out through the Artibonite valley, vivid green rice paddies from horizon to horizon.

Beyond the fecund Artibonite, the cactus and thorn acacia of the *savanne desolée* spread up and through and past Haiti's Philadelphia—the port of Gonaïves, city of perpetual rebellion and elusive independence, a dusty decayed ugliness so extreme it seemed a prototype of Hollywood's vision of the postapocalyptic. Here in Gonaïves, after twelve years of slave insurrection, French republican revolution and counterrevolution, foreign invasion, civil war, and homicidal anarchy, during which the Black Jacobins repelled and defeated two major expeditions from the two greatest powers of the day—the British and French both lost more soldiers during these campaigns in Saint Domingue (as Haiti was then named) than at Waterloo—Dessalines declared independence for the colony in 1804. He rechristened it with the Amerindian name Haiti—*Ayiti*—and, at the urging of three Englishmen in attendance, who offered the British Crown's trade and protection in return for French blood, committed himself to Haiti's greatest and most enduring tragedy, branding himself, his people, his newborn nation, and its future with the indelible stain of racial genocide: the bitter, purposeless extermination of all remaining whites on the island, save for a handful of British and American agents and a few skilled craftsmen.

"Haiti," the historian Robin Blackburn wrote in praise, "was not the first independent American state but it was the first to guarantee civic liberty to all inhabitants," an achievement made much easier once you erased the *other* from your midst. No matter that, after generations of the most obscene and unspeakable atrocities, the whites had it coming. The French had gone berserk in Haiti, devolved into beasts, spiritually infirm and twisted by uncontained greed. Then came the French Revolution, and the insanity escalated to a new level, the whites and freedmen splintering into murderous factions and dueling atop the powder keg of a half-million slaves, mostly African born, unable to speak two words of French: *gran blancs* battled *petit blancs*, merchants intrigued against planters, royalists shot populists, the colony wrestled with the metropolis, *ancien libres* executed *nouveaux libres*, the white/black north and east warred against the mulatto south and west, the Spanish and British monarchies assaulted the French revolutionaries, alignments swirled and mutated and about-faced and re-formed, and each faction armed the slaves against its enemies and promised a hierarchy of freedoms to black and half-caste officers. Then the powder keg exploded, until the slaves were forever liberated and the whites were forever gone.

The pitiless Dessalines, himself a barbarian, a mirror to slave owners' inhumanity, abandoned the moral heights so painfully won by the true father of Haitian statehood, Toussaint-Louverture, one of history's great makers of war and peace, a former slave (and slave owner) with the military genius of Hannibal, the world-altering statesmanship of Nelson Mandela, the righteous eloquence of Martin Luther King (Louverture's proclamations were composed with the aid of white secretaries on his staff, since the governor general's French was "vigorous but ungrammatical"). Black Spartacus, Black Consul: "From the First of the Blacks to the First of the Whites," he wrote Napoleon Bonaparte.

Toussaint battled slavery and, however ambivalently, the ancien régime to the point of collapse. Napoleon—to the relief of Thomas Jefferson (the "annihilation of black government," the French Consul promised the British and Americans)—destroyed Toussaint and with him the ideology of reason and enlightenment that had fueled the French Revolution. Dessalines slaughtered the whites and—also to the relief of Jefferson—France's dreams of a New World empire. Yet ultimately what Dessalines's vendetta most dismantled was the nascent integrity and ideological discipline of his own nation, making Haiti anathema to the Western powers, who would forever after hold the island, its tragicomic leaders, and its emancipated but exhausted people, sworn to liberty or death, in contempt.

On Gonaïves's northern perimeter, its Nevada-like arroyos and rocky brown mountains were a shock, here in the balmy tropics. A few miles past the city, though, you began the radical ascent into the mountains of the north, greeted at the summit pass by chilly winds, grounded clouds, and burned-out wrecks, the road a continuous challenge of switchbacks and plunges, blind curves, and dizzying views into the impossibly rugged interior. The road slalomed past packs of uniformed schoolchildren on their daily vertical treks to and from literacy, the busted pavement attenuated by swaths of drying coffee beans, diving toward transparent rivers, their stony bars quilted with laundry, and up again toward a bowled horizon of overcultivated slopes and lush shadowy ravines, until it wound through the village of Plaisance, once considered a center for "more advanced" (French-speaking) slaves.

During the American occupation, it was always in Plaisance that I'd start getting the war zone vibes, a feeling of menace that would only increase as the road roller-coastered another thirty or so miles to Limbé, which had the reputation of being the unfriendliest town in Haiti. It would not be much of an exaggeration, or historically inaccurate, to say that everything bad that had happened in Haiti had started in Limbé and its surrounding areas.

A few miles past Limbé, Route Nationale One crested a final ridge and foreshadowed its terminus on the tranquil shores of the Windward Passage between Hispaniola and Cuba. Straight below, to the north and east, spread the idyllic vista of the coastal savanna—the Plaine du Nord—and its ghostscape of atrocities, of long-destroyed plantations, the fertile land that once made Haiti France's greatest and most lucrative colony, responsible for two-thirds of its overseas trade. The road quit at Cap Haïtien—Le Cap—certainly the most exhausted, depleted city in the Americas. Even in its heyday, when its grand theater could seat twelve hundred of the world's wealthiest planters and merchants to enjoy a continental melodrama, Le Cap's streets were sewers, strewn with shit and garbage, a barnyard where livestock roamed through a maze of gambling dens, brothels, and dance halls, and where violence was too commonplace to draw any but the most prurient forms of attention.

For the owners, slavery was a type of spiritual sugar; they gorged on it, and it rotted their character and decayed their conscience. The founders of the colony of Saint Domingue had been buccaneers, convicts, renegades, warriors. A century later, their descendants, by then handsomely dressed and finely housed, had devolved into one of the most decadent, soulless societies ever to inhabit the earth. A German traveler noted in his journal that he sat down for dinner with a colonist's wife, "beautiful, rich, and very much admired," who earlier, irritated by the mistake of one of the kitchen slaves, had ordered the hapless cook pitched into the oven.

I want an egg, a colonial child announced one morning at breakfast. There were none. *Then,* answered the child, *I want two.*

From the crest beyond Limbé you could also see, to the northwest, the pendant-shaped bay where Columbus first dropped anchor and praised this once most Rousseauan of isles. Setting foot for the first time in the New World in what would later be known as the Bahamas, Columbus asked the Amerindians there the one question that would soon obsess Europe: *Gold?* The aboriginals answered, *Ayiti.*

In less than twenty years, hundreds of thousands of Haiti's Amerindians were dead from forced labor, murder, disease, and deliberate famine, the near total destruction of a society during one generation, the genocide slowed by the only European in the New World who might seem at first to qualify as a human being, the Dominican priest and self-appointed conscience of the conquistadores, Bartolomé de Las Casas, who in 1517 convinced Charles V of Spain to take the pressure off the sixty thousand Indians still alive in the colony by importing fifteen thousand African slaves. "Thus," wrote historian C. L. R. James, "priest and King launched on the world the American slave-trade and slavery." By the eighteenth century, Negro slaves had been shipped to the New World by the millions.

The Spanish word *cimarron* meant "wild, unruly," and the French adopted its derivative, *maroon*, to refer to both slaves and livestock that had broken loose from the sugar plantations. Thus the fugitives had a name and a brutish stereotype, and by the latter half of the eighteenth century, tens of thousands of runaways had taken possession of the Haitian highlands. Only once in the century preceding the French Revolution did the maroon bands manage to organize themselves and rise up against the whites, but the revolt—led by the maroon chieftain Mackandal, a Guinea-born slave from Limbé—had a profound and lasting impact on the already addled psyche of the colonists. For six years in the mid-eighteenth century, Mackandal, the maroons, and their co-conspirators throughout the plantations of the north pursued the torment of their collective dream, the massacre of every white in Saint Domingue, building a network for a mass uprising, poisoning whites as well as traitors in their midst. Poison was the great weapon of the maroons, a legacy of Africa, bush medicine, and the animistic rituals that were known and practiced on both sides of the Atlantic. Mackandal's island-wide rebellion was to commence with the poisoning of every white's household water supply, but before the plan could unfold, Mackandal was betrayed, captured, and roasted alive.

"The Negroes," reads a planter's memoir published in 1789, "are unjust, cruel, barbarous, half-human, treacherous, deceitful, thieves, drunkards, proud, lazy, unclean, shameless, jealous to fury, and cowards."

"The safety of the whites," wrote a colonial governor of the same era, "demands that we keep the Negroes in the most profound ignorance. I have reached the stage of believing firmly that one must treat the Negroes as one treats breasts." But beasts were in fact treated better, and the colonists had little regard for the blacks even as purchased property. It amused whites "to burn a little powder in the arse of a nigger." The decapitated heads of rebellious slaves, jammed atop stakes, had once lined every road in the north. By the time the Parisian revolutionaries had stormed the Bastille, every heart in Haiti had turned to stone. The colonists, wrote the historian Mirabeau, slept on the edge of Vesuvius.

The economy of prerevolutionary France and the livelihood of millions of its citizens depended almost entirely on the colonies and slavery. "Sad irony of human history," wrote Jaurès. "The fortunes created at Bordeaux, at Nantes, by the slave trade, gave to the bourgeoisie that pride which needed liberty and contributed to human emancipation."

As in the motherland, so in the colony: The revolution in France was a catastrophically divisive event, setting into conflict contradictory forces and irreconcilable interests: the monarchists against the so-called patriots, the great whites against the small whites, civil bureaucracies against military administrations. The beginning of the end for Saint Domingue began in Paris, when the revolutionary assembly began a self-serving debate over the rights of man. Abolition was not seriously entertained, but well-educated, propertied mulattoes argued persuasively for an end to their murky legal status. Were they not citizens of France? Were they, or were they not, entitled to political rights?

The colonists followed the debate with an increasing sense of horror and outrage. They had meticulously constructed a classification system to identify and control the offspring of blacks and whites, based on 128 divisions of skin shade and ancestry. The *sang-mêlé*, despite containing 127 parts white to one part black, was still a colored man, a nigger, and thus voiceless in the political life of the colony, although he could, as could all mulattoes and Negro freedmen, acquire wealth and property and own slaves—which many did. The mulattoes and slaves in fact loathed one another, the former arguing for their rights in order to unite with the whites to keep the slaves in line, and the whites conscripted mulattoes to join the *maréchaussée*, a civilian militia, forerunner of the macoutes and attachés, whose job it was to track down fugitive slaves and fight the maroons. Mulatto women were destined for an equally unsavory service: of the seven thousand half-caste women on the island in 1789, five thousand were either prostitutes or kept mistresses.

As the parallel revolution on the island evolved, property became the common bond between the mulattoes and big whites in a counterrevolution against the slaves and the little whites, until the mulattoes, with arms and ammunition purchased in the United States, revolted in 1790. The white revolutionaries and white counterrevolutionaries immediately reunited to murder, lynch, and mutilate the mulattoes, no matter that the crushed and dismembered leaders of the rebellion would be regarded as heroes when news of the action reached Paris. "It was the quarrel between bourgeoisie and monarchy that brought the Paris masses on the political stage," wrote C. L. R. James. "It was the quarrel between whites and mulattoes that woke the sleeping slaves."

Of the half-million slaves in the colony in 1789, two-thirds were African born, which meant that fourteen years later, when, after eradicating the whites, Dessalines declared the independence of the Haitian state, he had created not just the first free black republic in the world but the world's first multiethnic pan-African nation, its precolonial Africanness sealed into a time capsule of neglect and isolation and delivered to the twentieth century. In 1791, it was Africa that went to war with imperial France, with imperial Britain, with imperial Spain, and it was Africa that won.

By the end of 1789, the French Revolution had seriously fractured the structure of Haitian society, propelling its contradictions and divisions to the forefront of daily life. At night, slaves had begun holding mass meetings in the forests surrounding the Plaine du Nord. By 1790, the mulattoes themselves had split into opposing factions, and by the new year, the slaves throughout the north had organized into clandestine cells, sworn to death in a conspiracy against the whites.

Vodou was their medium of communication, and a *houngan* named Boukman, the physically immense headman on one of the sugar plantations, was their leader. Secrecy and solidarity were the cornerstones of Boukman's genius. His organization was vast, his intent devastatingly simple: On a given night, slaves on the outskirts of Le Cap would set fire to the plantations, and upon seeing the flames, slaves in town and across the savanna would massacre the whites, and Boukman and his corps of warriors would seize the colony. Command and control were essential to success, coordination and discipline vital, and "isolated efforts were doomed to failure."

In early August 1791, the slaves in Limbé jumped the gun, "rose prematurely," and were swiftly decimated. The roads into Le Cap swarmed with bands of slaves, haphazardly attacking whites. Boukman could wait no longer, and according to Haiti's most potent legend, on the night of August 22, he assembled his men on Morne Rouge, the mountain overlooking Le Cap, in the midst of a violent storm, to conduct a ceremony that would inaugurate the twelve-year war. In a lightning-blasted, rain-swept clearing in the forest, thunder rolling out across the plain, a green-eyed *mambo* slashed the throat of a pig in offering and drank its blood, summoning the *loas* of destruction with her prayers, which Boukman called the voice of liberty.

By the time the sun rose, the north was a whirlwind of flames, the plain a vortex of fire. The slaves, James wrote, destroyed tirelessly. For three weeks, the people of Le Cap could barely distinguish day from night, while a rain of burning cane straw, driven before the wind like flakes of snow, flew over the city and the shipping in the harbor. Regardless of their eternal prejudice against the blacks, young mulattoes began to join the uprising against their common enemy, and soon enough the insurrection controlled the countryside. One month after the revolt had begun, the uprising, exhausted by the very wantonness of its destruction, paused to collect itself and reorganize, and when it started up again, one of its many new leaders was Toussaint-Louverture.

"Like their more educated white masters," wrote James, "the slaves hastened to deck themselves with all the trappings and titles of the military profession. The officers called themselves generals, colonels, marshals, commanders, and the leaders decorated themselves with scraps of uniforms, ribbons and orders which they found on the plantations or took from the enemy killed in battle, . . . yet, despite these absurdities," the leaders of the uprising were men born to command; "nothing but an iron discipline could have kept order among the heterogenous body of men just released from slavery," many of whom went into battle entirely naked, or draped in pieces of silk and satin pillaged from the plantations, armed with only a hoe, a sharpened stick, a piece of iron, a rusty sword. Early on in the conflict, the slaves couldn't even use the cannon they captured, applying the match at the wrong end of the barrel.

There developed a grisly competition between the two sides, to see who could display the most heads atop their stockades or on pikes along the roadside. This was a game Boukman lost, his own head stuck atop a pole in Le Cap. The colonists, in their panic, began to slaughter all black men, women, and children on sight. In a few weeks, ten thousand slaves rebelling became one hundred thousand. The south and the west joined the fray, and one hundred thousand became everybody. Alliances formed and melted in kaleidoscopic patterns, until it seemed the entire white world had come to Saint Domingue to murder itself, after it had annihilated the slaves. Whites against whites. Whites against mulattoes and blacks. Whites and mulattoes against blacks. Blacks, mulattoes, and whites against whites. Blacks and mulattoes against blacks. Blacks against mulattoes. blacks against blacks. The Spanish and the blacks against the white French. The Spanish against the blacks. The British against the French against the blacks against the revolution against the counter-revolution. Everyone took a turn as Judas.

The atrocities were endless and unimaginable and mutual: a fetus cut from a pregnant mulatto woman and thrown into a fire; black children deliberately infected with smallpox; white children impaled on pikes and carried as standards into battle. They fought and they fought, on and on, and when they had finished, when the blacks had defeated what was then the Western world and won their freedom, even then they had not truly finished or truly won, and they replayed the struggle among themselves, an endless loop of fighting from which there was no escape, no respite, and no glory. They fought on, surrogate masters, surrogate slaves, and it never stopped.

"I fly to vengeance," wrote a mulatto leader early in the rebellion. "Long live liberty, long live equality, long live love."

COWBOY HEAVEN

Shortly after the coup in September 1991, the U.S. military, pairing up with the CIA, its fraternal twin and frequent dance partner, began running black ops missions into Haiti—small teams in civilian clothes engaged in recon and site surveys. Once or twice a submarine slipped into Haitian waters and disgorged a SEAL team onshore to evacuate "unnamed assets," Haitian and American, whose time on the playground had run out. Yet no matter how many players you benched, the sport went on, with a new cast of rogues and star-spangled cowboys; apparatchiks and wonks and theorists; drug barons, crooks, and murderers. And, occasionally, an honest and decent man.

Lieutenant Colonel Mike Jones fit a post-coup pattern of U.S. military involvement in Haiti. He was one of the first to come ashore in uniform, in support of a publicly announced mission, and by the time the invasion became an imminent reality he had digested a bellyful of Haiti, enough firsthand swill to be honestly able to tell the troops he commanded in the Second Battalion of the Special Forces Third Group, even the ones who thought the operation was a bad joke, why they were going in and why it was a good mission, a righteous mission.

Jones, a towering, big-voiced, balding man who had played football for Louisiana State, had helped put together an FID recon element—a Foreign Internal Defense survey team—to reevaluate the FADH for the United Nations, ascertain their training needs, and figure out what everybody wanted. He came first on the initial assessment, then returned with the pilot team, moving into the Villa Creole on the mountain above Port-au-Prince, on orders to stick around and convince the FADH leaders they really wanted what they were being offered, that they wanted to do what they had signed up for in July 1993, at the Governors Island accord, a ten-step plan to return Haiti to democratic rule. At the heart of the accord, International Police Monitors (IPM)—Royal Canadian Mounted Police, French gendarmes, and law enforcement officers from other French-speaking nations—would establish and train a professional civilian police force, independent of the Haitian army. At the same time, Joint Task Force Haiti, composed of 599 U.S. Special Forces, Civil Affairs (CA), and psy ops personnel and 110 Canadian soldiers, would conduct humanitarian programs and nonlethal training for the Haitian military: light infantry drills that would center around disaster relief; coastal and frontier security; patrolling techniques; operations in darkness; rappelling; combat lifesaving training; how to load up patients; how to cultivate a thought process that included human rights, discipline, and pride—skills these lunkheads, who hadn't mounted a serious training exercise since 1983, needed; things the FADH could do to help the country, to serve and protect society, instead of swooping down on the population like birds of prey, terrorizing people at gunpoint. Cédras, Biamby, Duperval—the junta generals and their staffs—Mike Jones worked extensively with all of them, sure that given the opportunity, his Special Forces soldiers could convince the FADH of the benefits to be reaped from committing itself to the process.

"If you're going to build an army," said Jones, "let's talk about the failure of your army and why you need an army to do what you do. The first question is what is your perceived threat?"

"Internal instability," replied the tyrants.

"Okay," said Jones, "how is this internal *insurgency* designed? Does it have weapons, tanks, artillery?" Of course the answer was no. Jones asked, "Is the Dominican Republic a threat to you?" No, but the putschists weren't interested in sensitivity training, they weren't interested in rehabilitating themselves into good Samaritans, or in living without constant fear if it meant abandoning power, profits, and privileges. They wanted attack helicopters, they wanted self-propelled artillery and tanks, they wanted patrol boats and fighter bombers. If the UN wanted to modernize the FADH, let them hand over more and better lethal weapons systems. The FADH generals knew how to stonewall and baffle—they were masters of stall. Agreements would evaporate from one meeting to the next. Delegates would filibuster, daydream, withhold information; they played to the U.S. military's distaste for globalism, ridiculing the UN, trying to convince the Americans doors would swing open if only they dissociated themselves from Boutros-Ghali's mission. Plenty of FADH were CIA "assets," on John Kambourian's payroll, and they tried to work that angle too, the we're-all-in-this-together scam. It was an endless repetition of a farce, and between the foreground and the background was an ocean of distrust. Jones would start with General Biamby on a Monday and be handed off down the line, down through the ranks, and by Friday he'd find himself in a room with Hear No Evil, See No Evil, and Speak No Evil, exchanging banalities in the fog, the general's flunkies politely apologizing for their lack of authority to do anything beyond sit at the table and glance at the clock. It became clear, the mission leaders would later report, "that the JTF was operating in a political climate that the diplomatic strategists had neither predicted nor planned for."

It had infuriated General Raoul Cédras, being pressured at Governors Island to "professionalize" his army. He'd been cornered by the politicians: *Sign,* they demanded, *so you do not completely piss off the entire world.* But now here he was, bolted to the floor, back in his own headquarters and mightily offended by the assertion that he somehow lacked a professional military. How could that be? His staff was salted with West Point graduates, Young Turks direct from the Naval Academy, guys who had rotated through the School of the Americas at Fort Benning. What were the Americans talking about? Americans had been "professionalizing" the FADH themselves for years, decades. It was one of their many little projects in the Caribbean Basin; they were the FADH's fairy godmother, the FADH's Daddy Warbucks. And why, Cédras demanded to know, after so many years of being obsessed with communism in the region, and after they'd helped keep communism out of his country, why did the Americans suddenly want to bring socialists into power in Haiti? What was going on? Was this all about Clinton, that draft-dodging, faggot-loving traitor? Cédras had plenty of sympathetic contacts in the American government. He had a great Washington lobby; they told him, *Right. It's about Clinton. It's about liberals and the goddamn Black Caucus seizing control. We're working on it. Just hold tight and it will blow over.*

"Hey, look," Jones told his Haitian counterparts, "your form of government's not quite getting it here," but they didn't want to hear that sanctimonious crap. It was a major disconnect, Lieutenant Colonel Jones traveling back and forth between FADH headquarters and the embassy and the Villa Creole, amazed and bewildered by the stifling degree of oppression the people endured, by how life itself had been reduced to a cautious whisper. At nine o'clock at night, you could drive down the street and not find a soul except for attachés out with the anti-gang units, you could hear a pin drop all the way from central Port-au-Prince up to Pétionville, and he began to feel that going into Haiti hard was something his country needed to do. Somebody had to step in to rescue these people, and where else could they turn? He knew as well that no one would readily understand who hadn't been there during the de facto regime, hadn't interacted with the vermin, the misguided hacks and deadly psychopaths in charge, and lacked the insight that Haiti was not a divided nation, Haiti wasn't even a sovereign nation. *Haiti was a country kidnapped by a small group of uniformed bandits, self-important drug dealers, and unscrupulous businessmen.*

One day, Lieutenant Colonel Jones watched a crowd gather in front of the legislative assembly building. The police arrived and almost immediately opened fire, five or six demonstrators fell over dead, and Jones finally began to realize that was the way it was. This was the regime's preferred method of dispersal—shoot people down right in the street, without warning, without cause. Another day, he was driving down the mountain, en route to negotiate with the FADH, when he and his companions heard shots and saw a group of people running to beat hell. By the time he pulled up and stopped in front of the Sacré Coeur Church, Antoine Izmery and another man were lying in the street, bleeding to death. Jones stopped, but there was nothing he could do except call an ambulance to collect the bodies.

This was the summer of '93. Aristide was coming back, Aristide was not coming back, the Americans were bringing him home. Yes? No? Clinton had checkmated the tyrants at Governors Island, but he wouldn't act. The embassy was divided over whether the negotiations were too hard on the Haitian military or too hard on Aristide. The CIA, in collusion with elements in the Defense and State Departments, Congress, the INS, and the national press, was openly working to subvert the White House's stated policy. It launched a smear campaign against Titid's mental health with fabricated evidence recycled by Brian Lattell, a senior analyst at the agency, quietly boasting that the bug-eyed little priest would never again set foot on Haitian soil, and, most damagingly, the agency functioned as the behind-the-scenes architect of FRAPH, a paramilitary terrorist organization run by a media-slick, cocaine-snorting, self-infatuated madman named Emmanuel "Toto" Constant.

FRAPH evolved out of a series of discussions between Constant and Colonel Patrick Collins, the U.S. Defense Intelligence Agency's attaché to the embassy, shortly after the coup, the colonel urging Constant to organize an effective counterforce to Aristide's base of popular support among the masses. Collins left; Kambourian and Collins's replacement, Lieutenant Colonel Steven Lovasz, took over the asset. They gave Toto a high-tech walkie-talkie—his code name was "Gamal"—and seven hundred dollars a month. He had regular, sometimes daily meetings with the CIA station chief, delivering full accounts of his political and paramilitary activities. It was a big party: the junta leaders were on the payroll as well, and the CIA's pet project—the Haitian Intelligence Service, established by the agency— had gone seriously awry, its agents deep into narcotrafficking, attacking Aristide's supporters. Whatever was going wrong in Haiti, whatever atrocities were sucking American troops closer and closer to a hard-entry invasion, the CIA and the DIA were inside it, whistling "Dixie."

Rogue elements? In style, perhaps. But in substance—the behind-the-scenes consensus in the U.S. government to develop mechanisms that would limit Aristide's power—absolutely not. Whatever your political bent, if, since the ouster of Baskethead in 1986, you worked for the American government in Port-au-Prince and had a behavioral propensity for blood sport, to be a freewheeling saboteur of this or that agenda, then Haiti was your cowboy heaven, but you could always gesture obliquely, up the chain of command, to a happy patron.

Then the United Nations dispatched the USS *Harlan County* to enforce the Governors Island agreement, more than two hundred soldiers aboard, mostly American Special Forces in their friendly-neighbor mode, masquerading as medics and engineers. It was meant to be the spearhead of a UN mission that would eventually, and peacefully, build to thousands. But when the *Harlan County* sailed into Haitian waters, the mission—Joint Task Force Haiti—came unstitched.

On October 4, 1993, eleven days prior to the scheduled resignation of General Cédras, twenty-six days before the scheduled return of Aristide, the American task force commander and five staff personnel arrived in Port-au-Prince and moved in with Mike Jones and his detachment of Special Forces trainers. At night at the Villa Creole, the attachés would make probes, trying to intimidate the negotiating team, gunfire popping in the surrounding darkness. Everybody on the team took turns standing watch; they had no weapons except their sidearms. The tension was getting extreme—Cédras had blustered in public that he considered the imminent arrival of the *Harlan County* a hostile act, an "invasion." A psy ops unit was supposed to be on the ground (psychological warfare had been General Cédras's area of expertise when he taught at Haiti's military academy), but U.S. Secretary of Defense Les Aspin had delayed its deployment, fretting about "perceptions." All they really had was an e&e plan—escape and evasion—if something happened.

The task force's lifeline was US/ACOM—Atlantic Command in Norfolk, Virginia—and of course the embassy, especially the Pentagon's military attaché, Lovasz, who spoke French with a native's fluency and had the connections in Haiti to get you to the right people. Lovasz and his guys in the Defense Attaché's Office had bonded with the Haitian military and were known to treat the FADH command with great respect. Lovasz's swashbuckling deputy, Major Frank Keene, would occasionally go scuba diving with Cédras—who liked to brag that Haiti would be rebuilt with the treasure he personally salvaged from sunken galleons—and Major Keene rarely hesitated to voice his opinion that the FADH was getting a bad rap.

A lot of times, Lovasz and Major Roland "Spence" Lane, the military liaison between the American embassy and the FADH, were the only Americans with access to the tyrants. Lovasz and Lane could hook up the task force to sources who delivered on the information they needed, and in most cases, when Lovasz said things were going to happen, they happened. Which is why Lieutenent Colonel Jones thought it odd, when Jones reported to Lovasz about something going down with the *Harlan County*, that Lovasz didn't appear to believe him.

The task force team was trying to get the acting prime minister, Malval, to grant them the use of a facility for a UN operational base, and they were trying to secure docking rights for the *Harlan County*. Jones prepared a memo to Cédras describing the *Harlan County*'s mission, took it to Malval's residence for approval, then back down to FADH headquarters, where he seemed to be expected.

Cédras had disappeared. Jones was informed that no one of high rank was in the building. The colonel said bullshit, he had seen one of the command staff officers looking out the window as he walked up from his car. He spotted someone he knew, a U.S. Naval Academy graduate who worked in the building. Jones told him he needed to take the letter inside. Everyone behaved as if he were the colonel's great friend, but nothing happened until finally General Biamby came out, took the letter, glanced at it, and pitched a fit, throwing up the smoke of sovereignty.

That night, one of Jones's own intel sources came to him and warned of a coup: the generals, feeling that the Americans were trying to legitimize Malval's position, make it look as though a civilian authority was in charge of the country, weren't going to abide by Malval's directive. So the military was going to take him out, and they weren't going to allow the ship to dock.

Jones told Lovasz, "It's going to go down."

"Nah," Lovasz said. "There's no way."

"Look, I'm telling you," Jones insisted. "A good friend of mine who's reliable and trustworthy said he just came back from a meeting where Bi-amby, Cédras, the whole crew, were at the El Rancho, and they decided they're not going to let this thing dock, they're not going to pay any attention to our law."

"We'll see," said Lovasz. "We get rumors down here all the time."

Early the next day, Jones drove past FADH headquarters and, alarmed by what he saw, tracked down Lovasz. "Hey, something's going down," he said. "Every car at FADH headquarters is there on a Sunday morning."

The following day, October 11, the *Harlan County*, flying a UN flag and loaded with Special Forces and Canadian soldiers, construction equipment, and matériel to establish a base camp on shore, tried to dock. On board was Alpha Company from Jones's own Second Battalion. From the deck, they watched with mild concern as a Haitian gunboat approached, a fifty-caliber in its prow, a weapon that could at best put a few holes in an LST. One of the commandos focused his sniper scope on the guns and said, to anyone who wanted to listen, "They don't even have bullets!" Still, the jumpy captain of the *Harlan County* told the Special Forces company commander to prepare his men to defend the ship. This was not bad news to the Green Berets. Roger that, sir—let's rock.

But there was more than water between the *Harlan County* and the dock. Eight days earlier, eighteen army Rangers and Delta Force operatives had been massacred in Somalia, and now you had a very nervous Department of Defense, which had never wanted to get dragged into the Haiti imbroglio in the first place. The Pentagon, the National Security Council, and the White House would never quite see beyond those dead Rangers. The *Harlan County* and everything after would be viewed through the optic of Somalia.

Jones was in his vehicle near the embassy, listening to the radio traffic, when the debacle commenced, and he raced down to the dock. He knew some of the potbellied FRAPH guys in the crowd—grandstanding hoodlums, make-believe warlords. The diplomatic crew was there: the White House's special envoy, Lawrence Pezullo, a man born to negotiate; Stan Schrager, the embassy spokesman; Vicki Huddleston, the deputy chief of mission, who was running the embassy between ambassadors; the short, burly John Kambourian. The gates to the port were locked; all the berths just happened to be taken, and there was no place for the *Harlan County* to tie up.

The FRAPH goons went into mau-mau overdrive. This was their coming-out party, and they began to kick and bang on Huddleston's car until Kambourian plunked himself down on its hood, forearms crossed atop his bodybuilder's chest, and that was all it took to encourage the troublemakers to back away. Huddleston drove off, then the rest of the crew headed back to the American compound, and by the time they arrived in their offices, President Clinton had been on the horn to his advisers, and the *Harlan County* had swung around, steaming toward deeper water. Toto Constant was in cokehead heaven. He had finessed a cock strut into a showdown, live on CNN, signaling to the world that it was still possible, even if you weren't Fidel Castro, to make a mockery of American supremacy in its own backyard.

Somalia! FRAPH threatened on the docks that day, a word of almost mystical portent. *Somalia! Dead American soldiers.*

Convinced the ship could have docked without incident, Schrager and Pezullo couldn't believe what they were seeing, or begin to comprehend the apparent lack of resolve at the highest levels. Washington had turned the *Harlan County* around without notifying the embassy's chain of command or seeking the counsel of the diplomatic staff. The agency and DAO intel rats had sat on the hot line, exaggerating the threat, and the Pentagon and National Security Council had deferred to the spooks' assessment. *Harlan County? Yeah, we were all in on that,* one of Kambourian's underlings, a spook who traveled back and forth to Haiti from his post in El Salvador, would later tell an acquaintance of mine. And inside the embassy, someone who had worked closely with Kambourian and Lovasz would confide to me that throughout 1993 and '94, "people were working openly to subvert U.S. policy, and that was happening with the CIA and the DAO." Huddleston, the DCM, who acted like such a victim on the docks that day, knew the day before what was going to happen and never warned Washington. Huddleston herself had not objected to the creation of FRAPH, but now, on this day of reckoning, she and Kambourian and Lovasz lost control of the terrorist organization. Given the ground reality in Haiti, the level of cooperation between the regime and the anti-Aristide team at the embassy, Cédras found it impossible to believe that the U.S. would actually invade. The *Harlan County* wasn't the first occasion of in-house subversion, nor would it be the last, but the humiliation of a U.S. Navy ship was a defining moment in the history of the whole adventure, and the public emergence of Toto Constant and

FRAPH would haunt the political and military process for the next two years.

USS *Moron,* the Green Berets renamed the ship.

The fate of the *Harlan County* weighed heavily on Lieutenant Colonel Jones, but he thought, *Okay, maybe she'll come in tomorrow.* He had heard talk of taking the ship down the coast, away from the cameras and the theatrics, but then the White House terminated all official contact between the two militaries, Haitian and American, the ship was ordered back to Gitmo—Guantánamo Bay, Cuba—on Tuesday, and the mission dissolved before Jones's eyes. On Thursday, October 14, U.S. Navy Seabees, Canadian and Haitian military engineers, and laborers from the public works department were to have begun the renovation of a boys' high school, to showcase the humanitarian side of JTF Haiti. Instead, a few hundred feet from the school at the Ministry of Justice next door, attachés from the Port-au-Prince police force machine-gunned Justice Minister Guy Malary and two of his staff, the tyrants' farewell gesture to the Governors Island agreement, and that night the Special Forces team at the Villa Creole hunkered down in a high state of alert, listening somberly to the sound of constant gunfire throughout the city. Members of the civilian side of the mission began catching flights out or convoying overland to the border. On Saturday morning, a U.S. Navy C-9 Nightingale landed and, after off-loading a couple dozen well-armed Marines to reinforce the American embassy, flew away with Mike Jones and the advance party of JTF Haiti. The colonel felt that he had seen the last chance to turn this thing—the *situation*—around peacefully come and go, and that eventually he'd be returning to Haitian soil, with attitude, and with a lot of ammunition.

TALKING HEADS: SWING

Ambassador William Swing arrived in Haiti from his previous posting in Nigeria three days after the *Harlan County* affair, the day after Justice Minister Malary was assassinated, and on the day that General Cédras was supposed to have retired. "It was hardly a propitious beginning," he later told me.

Ambassador Swing: This embassy has never been in any doubt as to who FRAPH is, and I had as a standing policy here that no one of my team here could have any contact with them. . . . Now, it's possible, I always can't exclude, that somebody may have had some contact, but if they did it, they did it against standing instructions and without my knowledge, and to this day [April 1995] I've never seen anybody do that kind of thing.

BS: Your team includes the defense attaché and the CIA?

AS: It includes everybody but the commanding general and the multinational force. . . . I always knew what FRAPH was. And I also knew that FRAPH would fade like the dew in the morning sun, if you ever got rid of the army and the paramilitary structure.

BS: There's something else on the grass that will fade.

AS: Right. Exactly. And we knew that . . . we have actually said publicly a number of times that FRAPH has never been a political party, it's been a terrorist organization, loosely held together by the military.

BS: But are there elements on your team that don't have a legal obligation to tell you about certain things?

AS: No. People are required to tell me who their contacts are.

BS: Central Intelligence is required to tell you who its sources are?

AS: Everybody on my team is required to tell me who their contacts are, and we have made it very clear to everyone who they should and shouldn't be in touch with, and FRAPH is one of those who [they shouldn't be in contact with].

BS: You know, a lot of ambassadors have gotten burned by that gap. Maybe they're supposed to tell, but I've heard a Central Intelligence administrator say there's no obligation for—

AS: Well, on that I'd have to say to you again, I don't comment on that, I couldn't comment on that. The point is, I'm saying that on my team there's an understanding that I know who the contacts are, and that in cases like this they've got to hew the line. So I'm satisfied on that case that we did the right thing. . . .

BS: But wouldn't you want some members of your team to have contact with a group like this, on some level?

AS: I never wanted to. No. Zero. Because they were not a legal organization, they were fomenting violence. It would be the absolutely wrong thing to do, it would send the wrong signal to them and to people who oppose them.

BS: You know about all this awful stuff in Guatemala these days, and for the past week before I came down here you have the CIA all over the television, spinning it: Look, we've got to associate with bad guys, there's no way around it; if we want certain information we've got to cozy up to them.

AS: Not my philosophy, not my approach.

BS: Okay.

AS: If you do anything on intelligence, leave that out for me. I mean, I don't deal with intelligence on the record. But my philosophy is, certain groups are beyond the pale, and to deal with them brings nothing in and you do so at enormous risk.

BS: And that's hard and fast?

AS: With FRAPH it was throughout. Oh, yeah. Oh, absolutely.

Several days after my interview with the ambassador, I ran into one of his team, who asked me how it had gone. "He told me that the CIA had no relationship whatsoever with FRAPH," I said. "Yeah," said the embassy staffer, who apparently had been debriefed by Swing about the conversation. "I don't know why he said that." But it was well known inside the embassy that the ambassador was a man who hated confrontation.

CRACKDOWN

After the generals assassinated the minister of justice, the wholesale killing began again, nothing working in the now embargo-suffocated country but state-sponsored terrorism despite the presence of OAS human rights observers. Richard Morse wondered what they were doing to earn their six grand a month, other than hanging out at the Oloffson, glued to the chairs on the veranda. The capital seemed to be operating on ever more poisonous energy. Smelling a showdown, the foreign media poured onto the island and began to drive the story. Meanwhile, scores of Haitian journalists were menaced, beaten, and arrested, among them Radio Tropic FM's Colson Desamir, who, while attempting to report the arrival of UN special envoy Dante Caputo, was rifle-butted to the ground by a FADH soldier, bound, blindfolded, taken into custody, and incarcerated in the hellhole known as Fort Dimanche. Radio Tropic FM, the only station in Port-au-Prince to broadcast news updates on the half hour, began using the airtime to plead for his release, putting his family, friends, and fellow journalists behind the microphone, none of whom could have imagined they were colluding in Desamir's misery. For two days, with the sound of his wife or father crying in the background, or a familiar voice demanding his freedom, the soldiers, with a radio tuned to Tropic FM, would torture him during newscasts, every thirty minutes. When they got tired of that, they dragged him outside into a courtyard and attempted to cut off his arms.

RAM started doing regular Thursday-night gigs in the acoustically rich cavernous rear half of the hotel lobby, its back wall the bare limestone face of the hillside. The house was packed, everybody coming to blow off steam. The bourgeoisie were there, the MREs—Morally Repugnant Elites, so called by embassy wags; the MREs themselves called Aristide "the little monkey." These beautiful, beautiful women from up the mountain in Pétionville, La Boulé, Kenscoff came, Valium and coke and handguns tucked into their purses; the attachés came, the macoutes, even some low-profile Lavalas, foreign legionnaires from France, the Christians In Action spooks, military guys from the embassy in their civvies, the international press, and of course the human rights observers, until one night, after the attachés started smashing bottles and smacking around one of the band members, the OAS banned the observers from the Oloffson. Attachés coming to an American-run business, beating up Haitians, making them bleed, *and the people supposedly there to monitor human rights violations* were being pulled out. If that was happening at the Oloffson, Richard dreaded to think what sort of awfulness was washing over the rest of the country.

"Fey," meanwhile, wouldn't go away. Stations were still slipping it onto the air, and the band heard stories of people singing "Fey" in crowds, the police coming out of nowhere, swinging their batons; apparently the regime, in its duplicity, would permit RAM to sing "Fey," at least for the time being, but no one else could.

The violence swelled with a life and momentum all its own, one long crescendo of wretchedness into 1994. The embargo was crucifying everyone in the country, destroying for years to come what little was left of the economy, while up on the border with the Dominican Republic, the army extorted bags of money from the contrabandistas. On the diplomatic front, after a series of mini-*Harlan Countys*, the Clinton administration canned special envoy Pezullo and replaced him with Bill Gray, a former member of the Black Caucus, who had no intention of negotiating. *Bad guys out, good guys in,* said Gray. Unfortunately, there was no consensus in Washington on who was which.

Everyone thought Clinton had no choice but to slap Cédras down. In May, the President refused to rule out the use of force, but an early-summer invasion never materialized. Cédras and his guys would simply call Clinton's bluff—he's a chickenshit, there's no congressional support, no public support—and as the big-bad-wolf rhetoric escalated, American credibility became inextricably braided into the process.

The island was infused with despair, hordes of people flinging themselves into the sea. Coast guard cutters couldn't handle the outflow—on July 4, they picked up 3,200 boat people; on July 5, 2,800. Stan Schrager, the embassy's spokesman, was flipping out at his press conferences, with the dump of numbers and what it all meant. The Haitian army was sexually mauling the wives and daughters of Lavalas supporters, a campaign of intimidation that inspired a counterterrorism expert at the embassy, political officer Ellen Cosgrove, to compose a memo arguing that the military regime's use of rape as a political weapon was exaggerated by the press and no big deal anyway, since, according to Cosgrove, rape itself seemed innate to Haitian culture, somehow a quasi-acceptable form of expressing one's Haitianness.

RAM kept playing at the hotel. The attachés would come around, liquor up and flaunt themselves, then disappear after midnight, headed for the slums, and in the mornings the bodies would be there on the streets, strategically placed at intersections, trussed and mutilated and fly-blown, the regime's version of Thought for the Day. (Stan Schrager: "It was an interesting experiment in the nature of repression. The idea that, you know, you didn't have to kill that many people to have a totalitarian aspect to the city and to the country. . . . All you had to do was kill certain people in certain places at a certain time, and you had it. And it was, in the most draconian, evil sense, a magnificent expression of the regime.")

The Champs du Mars became the frontier, and the band members were terrified to cross it at night. They'd sleep on the floor of the hotel, or sometimes journalists would take them home, speeding through the deserted streets. If they'd had their way, the musicians would have left; the airports were closing at the end of July, and they wanted out. RAM had been invited to perform in New York, but if they went, the airport would shut down behind them, and Richard said no, he had a hotel to run, he didn't want to get stuck in New York with the band, playing daddy to eighteen people. In truth, he couldn't bear the defeat, knowing the Duvalierists and the macoutes and the elites would love it if everyone left—everyone with an education, everyone with an open mind, everyone who lived in the twentieth century. We'll stay, he told the group, and see this thing through to the end.

Every day now on television, the tyrants were broadcasting a Creole-dubbed documentary about the Panama invasion, the Americans plunging out of the sky like the Last Judgment, shooting up Panama City, the slums afire and reduced to ashes, the rows of civilian corpses. Usually you could get through the day without feeling crippled by fear, but every once in a while the paranoia came in waves. Richard would wonder what the hell he was doing; was he out of his mind? The band had become a symbolic target and he asked himself, *What's the thing we haven't done yet, the thing that takes it to the next level, and are we on track for doing it?*

Up in the heights of Pétionville there was a club, The Garage, owned by Michel Martelly, a popular singer who had a band called Sweet Mickey, and Sweet Mickey was *the* macoute band, Michel François's favorite group, and so The Garage was a thug hangout, a playground for macoutes and prostitutes and dealers, the second-most-nasty joint in the capital (first place awarded to a downtown bar called the Normandie, next to FRAPH headquarters, its walls pasted with trophy snapshots of the terrorist group's victims).

It was August, no one knew which way the "situation" was going to go, Sweet Mickey had left the country for New York, and Martelly's wife was running the club. The Garage was no place for a band like RAM, but Richard was Michel Martelly's cousin—that's Haiti—and Michel's wife had been trying to book Richard into the club for a year. Richard had fended her off, but now she sent her father down to the Oloffson, and the guy wouldn't leave until Richard agreed to bring the band up the mountain the following Saturday.

That Saturday night, the crowd in The Garage had a predatory reek— Haitian military and police, French gendarmes, the bodybuilder types from the American embassy, a table full of journalists too prudent to mingle. No Morally Repugnant Elites—none. *Here we are,* Richard thought, *in Babylon.* While the band opened with their introductory number, Richard walked through the crowd, checking out the genetics, making a mental note of two heavyset dudes, each with a whore, their tables next to each other. They had that look, military big shots in civilian clothes— *chefs.*

The gig was flat. It was customary for Richard to remain backstage until the third song, when he would amble out like a Corsican pirate, scrutinizing the audience with his heavy-lidded eyes, his skull wrapped in a *houngan's* scarlet scarf, a skinny rat-tailed braid of his wiry hair flopping down between his shoulder blades. For Haitians, he was an odd sight; his appearance onstage usually stirred things up, but tonight it seemed to make little difference, which meant he had to reach into his bag of tricks. Trick number one: If it's not happening, send the girls—the backup vocalists—out into the audience. The first two bounced out, little queenies pulling guys off their seats. Richard was about to send a third girl down when, glancing over to the side entrance of the stage, he saw two cops in uniform and thought to send the girl after one of the cops, get him to dance; it would be like a semi-coup, just bring them all in and get everyone cooled out. So the girl went over to one of the cops and asked him if he was happy, took his hand and brought him across the stage to the dance floor, then Richard started fretting about what he was doing and looked at one of the two guys he had noticed earlier in the crowd and mouthed, *Is it all right if he dances?* and the guy mouthed back, *Yeah, that's all right.* Richard had guessed correctly, because the cop went straight for the guy's table, whipped off his hat and gaily placed it down before the *chef,* then danced away with the girl. The crowd warmed instantly, even the journalists were jumping up, and then the band went into "Fey" and the trouble started.

Six macoutes—military in civilian clothes—plowed through the front door. One of them beckoned at the cops and demanded they arrest the band, but the cop who'd been dancing balked, protesting that RAM had done nothing wrong. The guy shoved past him, hopped onstage, focusing on one of the dreadlocked musicians, and said, *Stop playing now.* As if someone pulled the plug out of the wall, the music died, and Richard was furious.

What the hell's up?

You can play any song, but you can't play this song.

Richard told him if he had a problem, go talk to the club owner. The guy went off and came back with Sweet Mickey's father-in-law, who said, *Rich, what's wrong with the song?*

I dunno, said Richard, thinking, If you can play dumb, I can play dumb. Martelly's wife's father said, *Well, shit, skip it, don't play it, and we'll talk about it later.* Richard said, *Fine,* the owner nodded gratefully and walked away, but it wasn't fine. He was sick of the pathology, the compromises and subterfuges and obfuscations and games, sick of being a caged prop for the generals and their reptilian smiles, the blather they fed the Americans about democracy. He remembered the job RAM had played the month before in Jacmel that had gotten way out of hand, how the *militaire* who rescued the band had identified himself as the officer du jour, so he stepped back to the microphone now and asked, *Is there an officer du jour here?*

To his bewilderment, somebody answered. *It's me*—the heavyset guy who had let the cop dance.

Nooo! You're kidding. It's you? Richard said, not even certain what an officer du jour was, but he gambled on it anyway. *Can I play the song?*

The man hesitated for a second and said yes, looked for confirmation to his twin at the next table, who shouted out, *Play the song!* so Richard turned around to the band and said, *Gimme the song.*

Which was stupid. The band started playing the opening bars of "Fey," and Lunise, the song's lead vocalist, looked at Richard and said, *I'm not singing.* Richard waved the band silent. There they were onstage, tête-à-tête, arguing in restrained voices, the band huddled around. Richard was proud of himself for coming up with the whole officer du jour bluff, but Lunise had dug in her heels, telling Richard he was out of his mind to even think about playing "Fey" in the middle of a macoute pissing contest, and the discussion continued on until Richard deferred to her; they played two more songs and went home. But there would be a price to pay for Richard's brinkmanship at The Garage.

The next day, the story got back to police headquarters. Michel François considered the incident an affront to his almighty power and personally reprimanded the army's officer du jour for interfering with the cops. He went so far as to question the officer's sympathies: *Perhaps,* François insinuated, *he was Lavalas, eh?* Now the fellow had no choice but to prove himself loyal to the fraternity.

The band held meetings, fire drills, about what to do if the shit went down, and Richard kept telling them to stay on track, focus on the music. *We're playing music, music, music, music—that's it, period.* But of course there was more to it than that. Every day, the band members would duck into the Oloffson's enclave with fresh horror stories. Richard himself had lost half a dozen close friends since the coup . . . you lose one, you lose another. The attachés were taking over neighborhoods wholesale, you couldn't walk past Cité Soleil or La Saline without spotting gore, some poor disemboweled soul, someone slashed into grisly chunks, headless people, shotgun-blasted brains. The city had turned gangrenous, rotting on the hoof, and stank of death and dying. Still, the band's Thursday nights proceeded, an eerie bubble of grace.

That Thursday night after The Garage, there they were back at the Oloffson, the same officer and a selection of goons, and the plan was, when RAM goes into "Fey," bust up the joint. From the stage, Richard scoped the crowd, as was his habit, checking for weapons. He noticed his ally the officer du jour and didn't think anything of it, but suddenly he's surrounded by a creepy throng of attachés, clamoring for him to play "Fey," hissing, *Play "Fey," play "Fey," please.* Guys were walking across the stage, whispering, *I hear they're giving you a hard time about "Fey." Don't worry, I've got your backup,* and everything's backward, the people asking for "Fey" were the people who shouldn't want it.

The band finished "Ibo Lele," the crowd was at a high pitch of doomsday wildness, screaming, singing, at the point when, normally, RAM would segue into "Fey" and send it over the edge. Instead, Richard walked off the stage. Everything was too backward, so he just left. One of the goons blocking the exit grabbed him, but he twisted away into the crowd, and now the entire audience was chanting, *Fey! Fey! Fey! Fey!* The soundman, sitting across the room at the mixer, had overheard the conspiratorial mutterings of three macoutes and, realizing the band was in jeopardy, preemptively shoved a cassette into the deck. Richard, still deluding himself about the possibility of an encore, heard *compas* pump through the system, looked at the soundman, and thought, *Damn, he blew it. We could have done "Fey" and gone off into rock-and-roll ecstasy.*

One by one the band slipped away and regathered at the family residence attached to the Oloffson. Half the members were in a rage over skipping the encore, saying, *We're punks.* Richard himself fell into a fury. One of the backup singers had cut his dreadlocks in the aftermath of The Garage, afraid he had been singled out by the cops, and Richard, whipping off the guy's cap, suspended him on the spot. He thought the singer was endangering the band, because in Haiti, if you buckled to the pressure, they came after you hard; if you were scared, it meant your conscience wasn't clear, that you were doing something wrong. *If you die, you're guilty*—that was a Creole proverb.

Richard was on the phone daily with the embassy, telling one of the political officers, *Hey, man, you've got to get people over here,* and the guy was saying, *Well, have you thought about not playing, have you thought about switching songs?* It was the first week in September, the airport was closed, you couldn't get in or out, the Americans had ceased being coy about an invasion, the FADH were pretending they could handle it, FRAPH was boasting they'd kill GIs à la Somalia, Father Jean-Marie Vincent, a prominent Catholic priest and a close friend of Aristide's, had been murdered on August 29, and the tyrants' puppet in the palace, President Jonaissant, was saying, *We're going to fight this down to the last man.* The country felt like it was being microwaved, cooked from the inside, incubating lunacy, and here comes another Thursday night, RAM's onstage, standing room only, two hundred people crammed front to back, half of them armed but not all for the same reason, the band's in the middle of a song, and the lights go out.

It's pitch black. Richard expected little yellow-blue flames of gunfire any second. The attachés were frantic, thinking Richard maybe doused the lights to hit *them;* the CIA guys were backing up against the walls (they're big, they're bad, they're embassy—but it was dark); people were waiting to get stabbed, people were waiting for shots; pants were being stained, it was so god-awful scary inside the Oloffson. Then the drums started, *petro* rhythms battering through the hysteria, Champs du Mars déjà vu, the weirdest thing, because there was Richard in the middle of the stage without the slightest idea what was going on, nobody could see him, but the drums were lifting him up, lifting him beyond the vortex, and he spread his arms like some deranged healer and started singing. He figured the girls had disappeared, because that's what they were supposed to do if something happened, but they were behind the stage, tucked into a corner, and suddenly there were their voices, harmonizing, it sounded to Richard, like angels. They were singing what were called "points"—messages—old *vodou* songs, very meaningful, very antagonistic to the regime despite their beauty, very fuck-you: war drums and vocals resonating supernaturally—spiritually—in the pitch pitch black.

People started lighting matches, the staff found candles, the hotel's handyman finally cranked the generator, and Richard's thinking, *If the macoutes don't have the balls to get us in the dark, we're just going to give it to them,* and off they galloped into "Fey." The audience exploded, rapturous, reeling, and nothing whatsoever happened. Later, the band celebrated, giddy and drinking and horsing around, ready for next Thursday, thinking everything was over, they'd passed through the thing, the trial, whatever it was, and now they were invincible, the artful dodgers. Untouchable.

The officer du jour from The Garage, however, who had been to every RAM gig for three weeks straight, still had a big, big problem, still had to prove to his superiors that he wasn't Lavalas. Journalists began to shadow Richard, reasoning that when the macoutes offed him, it would trigger the invasion. A British photographer was advised by the embassy not to take pictures around RAM concerts because she'd start a huge brawl and get herself killed. More prudent members of the press were simply avoiding the Oloffson, moving up to Pétionville to the well-guarded Hotel Montana—a safer place to be anyway, when the Americans started bombing the capital.

That final Thursday, the officer du jour was dressed all in black, like a gunfighter, and when the band launched "Fey," he removed a shirt tied around his waist to wave in the air. Richard saw him do it and thought, *This guy can't be dancing.* The malevolence in the officer's eyes was too intense, *too intense,* and Richard followed his gaze to a man sitting at a table; the men's eyes were locked, a diabolic telepathy between them like a red current. The political officer from the embassy split; uniformed cops, jigging with excitement, were scurrying out. Richard could feel everything slipping, sinking, and he spun around to the drummers and said, *Switch songs now.* Which they did without skipping a beat—a little roll, and they were in another song—but here was the officer du jour onstage, bellowing, *Stop playing! Stop playing! You can't play this song!*

Richard feigned innocence. *What song?*

The officer appeared dumbstruck, taking a second to realize what had happened, and then started hollering back out to the audience, *It's not "Fey." It's not the song. Stop! Stop!* Now, this wasn't Champs du Mars, this wasn't Jacmel or The Garage, this was Richard's home, and it was out of bounds. He'd had enough bullying and crude intrigue, and decided to find out once and for all who was behind this thuggery. Cordless microphone in hand, he worked his way through the dancers to the veranda. Someone behind him was saying, *Go around the corner,* so he walked down the veranda, turning left toward his office and head-on into a snakepit. There was a nest of vipers—two uniformed cops, two lieutenants in the police, two slick guys in civilian, probably higher ranking, and a tribe of nasty-looking brutes with Uzis and riot guns.

Everyone was surprised, everyone's blood was running high. The band was onstage, playing, and Richard just stood there staring recklessly at Michel François's assassins, until one of them said, *Rich, what are you doing here?* and Richard answered, *What do you mean, what am I doing here? This is my house.*

Nothing's wrong, man. Everything's okay. Go back onstage.

I am onstage, Richard told him, raising the microphone to his lips. *Yeaaahhhhh*—his voice rumbled through the sound system. Suddenly he was off his feet. The officer du jour had come up behind, grabbed him low and started walking with him, Richard's shoes off the ground. They struggled and he broke free just as one of the lieutenants flipped a table, smashing bottles and glasses. Cops were roughing up a photojournalist to get his camera. The officer grabbed Richard a second time, wrestle-walking him down the veranda as the band played on, and Richard didn't know what to do but start singing.

Kadja bosou a ye ma prale.

These were mystical lyrics. *Kadja bosou* was one of the *loas* of the crossroads, and Richard had asked the spirit for safe passage, implying he was leaving, which so unnerved the officer du jour that he let go. The band couldn't see Richard, but they heard. RAM was singing one song, and here was a disembodied Richard singing the song they always finished with, and they figured it out, brought the music to a slow stop and vanished. They'd gone into an automatic Haitian thing: *Everything's falling apart, let's just be nobody and disappear.* Richard's aunt had vanished, his mother, who often helped at the gate, had vanished, half the waiters were hiding in the charcoal pits, the crowd started mobbing the stairs down to the parking lot, and the attachés had grabbed a young man sitting at one of the tables, the muzzles of their Uzis shoved under his chin as they dragged him toward the steps. A girl with terrified eyes behind her glasses clutched at Richard, pleading for help because the macoutes had taken her brother, and Richard thought, *My God, maybe the embassy warned them not to grab me, so they just grabbed anybody to get me to stop.* That was the tyrants' gamble—as long as they didn't harm an American citizen or diplomatic personnel in Haiti, the big bad wolf would never materialize.

He'd been making decisions all along designed to keep people from dying, at the same time trying not to compromise what the band did, their essence, the rhythms and the old roots songs, but now it seemed someone *was* going to get hurt, and he was responsible. In a world gone mad, he had used, however impetuously, however narrowly, his position of privilege to challenge the tyrants, and they, in return, had let him buzz about like a bumblebee tied to a string. But now, if ever a party was over, it was this one at the Oloffson, Haiti's only DMZ throughout the time of the de factos. RAM was going on ice, and there was nothing left for Richard to do but take the deep breaths necessary to bring himself under control and walk down the steps to the fragrant palm-lined drive, where his guests negotiated for their lives.

There was no music at the Oloffson that next Thursday night. Richard sat at the bar, watching Clinton on CNN calling the regime the worst in the hemisphere, and when it was over, you could almost hear the entire country praying for salvation and yet fearing salvation's wrath.

Outside, American planes droned over the city, parachutes fluttered and popped, and out of the balmy sky fell not troops but transistor radios and psy ops cartoons.

Several months later, I was talking to the British photographer who had been warned by the embassy not to take pictures during RAM concerts at the Oloffson. "Can I tell you something about 'Fey'?" she said. "It was in October. The Committee Commes il Faut had organized a *manifestation* down south in Grand-Goâve, so we went there for that, and it was basically a demonstration against the FADH that were still in Grand-Goâve. The *manifestation* went around, and we were all getting very nervous as it got closer to the police station, and everyone thought, *Oh, God, if it goes down there, it's really going to be a blowout,* but it didn't, and then the people broke out into absolute glorious song—'Fey'!—and I couldn't believe it, they went into that glorious chorus. And I just thought, *Fucking A,* because I had always thought RAM was just a phenomenon at the Oloffson, but no way, *this* was RAM, it's everywhere, and 'Fey' was an anthem for the movement, for freedom."

> *I'm a leaf.*
> *Look at me on my branch.*
> *A terrible storm came and knocked me off.*
> *The day you see me fall is not the day I die.*
> *And when they need me, where are they going to find me?*
> *The good Lord, and St. Nicola,*
> *I only have one son*
> *And they made him leave the country.*

That was "Fey." Nothing much really, eight lines, a harmless arrangement of folklore, traditional *vodou* lyrics for *petro* rhythm. Twinned parables of death without dying and the hope of resurrection; the divine voice of a woman singing in ever fluid darkness, the necrotic skeletal hand of evil reaching for her throat.

That was "Fey," and that was Haiti—a paradox, a riddle: a song to sing if you wanted to live, but, depending on who you were, if you sang it, you died.

PART TWO

Our Work Is as Old as Our Country

[T]he idea of a "just war" could be summed up in three
parts. First, a war to be considered just had to be waged
by public authority rather than by private individuals.
Second, it had to be waged with "just intent";
that is, in order to avenge an injury, or inflict punishment,
or redress a grievance. Third, the extent of the damage
inflicted on the enemy had to stand in rough proportion
to the cause for which the war was fought.
Thus, in theory at any rate, just war resembled a
punishment administered by a benevolent father.

—Martin Van Creveld, The Transformation of War

THE GREAT VOODOO WAR

September 13–16, 1994: Washington, D.C./Port-au-Prince

Maintain gravitas, please.

In the paramagnetic subatomic fifth dimension of the spirit world, the first and perhaps greatest battle of the voodoo war for the soul of the Haitian people has been enjoined. Into the early-morning hours, Make-Believe President Émile Jonaissant, a former *houngan* and self-promoting mystic, roams the national palace in Port-au-Prince, hurling curses northward, badgering the *loas* to mount up, gallop their ethereal stallions to Washington, to sow still more indecisiveness throughout the American government. Tell Clinton, Jonaissant urges the gods, we don't need weapons to kill his soldiers. A plane crashes into the White House, supernatural flames erupt from light sockets in the East Wing offices, staffers complain of migraines, a fluish sap of energy, and, for a few hours at least, press secretary Dee Dee Myers gets fired. *Top that, blanc.*

In the Oval Office, there's a perceptible *whoosh*, the clawlike swipe of Jonaissant's mojo coming within inches of the President's celebrated groin, and without further delay, Clinton summons his inner circle, the head priests, the Zombi of State, the *mambo* empress, the National Security nihilists in need of better, stronger, blacker magic than has so far been provided by the increasingly enfeebled oracles and squeaky-voiced guardians of his pacific youth. However Clinton achieves this end—sacrifices a goat? enlists the services of an exiled Cuban santero?—his administration manages to break free of Jonaissant's crude enchantment and counterattack with some potent hocus-pocus of its own.

Overnight, dissimulations reverse themselves, money reverts to its original form of blood and tears, and tens of thousands of economic refugees are transformed into tens of thousands of political refugees. General Raoul Cédras, yesterday's reluctant putschist and democratic man of reason, a guy the Pentagon regards with some measure of paternalistic respect, a real soldier, et cetera, is today's bloated, drooling vampire, an emissary of unvarnished evil, as big a dirtbag as the Duvaliers. Bolstered by a new in-house human rights report from the State Department, which essentially paints the Cédras regime as a pack of murderous thugs, Clinton appears on television to play, somewhat dispassionately, his public opinion trump cards—graphic pictures and horrific anecdotes of Haitian victimhood (See! See!)—and the sorcerer's wand of statesmanship grows spikes and becomes the big stick of universal democracy. One, two, three, and—poof!—the gods of war spin into being.

The following night, on his Thursday show, Rush Limbaugh has pictures too, which he shoves into the collective face of his television audience as a grisly counterpoint to the President's belated photographs of atrocities in Haiti.

Rush's congregation cranes forward to see the gory details, gasps, then recoils from the glossy image of Reginald Denny, his skull bashed, his face pulp. "Why not invade Los Angeles?" Limbaugh harangues his titillated viewers. "Why not invade D.C.?" Things are a lot worse in our own cities than in Haiti, he asserts, confirming for millions of dittoheads—Yo, white folks, listen up—that in the hemispheric neighborhood, Haiti is after all the nigger of nations, the spear chucker in the backyard, and not worth one American's life—presumably one Anglo American's life.

Back in the palace, Jonaissant is not intimidated. He had been thrown in there by the Generals—Wear a suit, they probably had to tell him, a clean tie. Maybe they gave him some Visine to squirt into his empty, alcoholic eyes. Even as figureheads go, Jonaissant was ridiculous, blustering in grandiose French about the soveriegnty of a nation in whose destruction he himself had colluded. This is our dungheap, these are our sacred miseries, you expected to hear him sputter in nationalistic intoxication. You have no right! A thousand upwardly mobile reincarnations would barely deliver Jonassaint to the threshold of what he fancied himself to be— politician, visionary, patriot—but, bottom line, he was not a fellow without a few tricks up his sleeve, and he prided himself on being a pretty fair conjurer. Now, his expression frozen in the scowl that had apparently been carved into his face at birth, he set about propitiating the spirits, seducing them with cakes and sweets and beaucoup bottles of *clairin* rum, after their tiring jaunt up inside the beltway. He prostrates himself finally before the great *loa* Ogoun, lord of the battle.

"Fly north," Jonaissant rasps, commanding the god. "Fetch me Jimmy Carter."

PRELUDE TO AN ASS WHIPPING

At the U.S. Atlantic Command in Virginia, Admiral Paul David Miller, one of the military's new generation of leaders, couldn't recall ever being so red-faced angry as when he received word that the USS *Harlan County* had failed to dock in Port-au-Prince. Joint Chiefs of Staff Chairman Shalikashvili and SecDef Aspin—that's where that puppy rested, as far as the admiral was concerned. It was pure, disgraceful horseshit, no more a military operation than the man in the moon. The muck-a-mucks had even wanted to paint the ship white, and Miller had told them straight out they were nuts.

Contretemps, however, had become part of the daily texture of life at US/ACOM. The admiral didn't care who he pissed off these days, not since he had finally gotten to a job where nobody could tell him no except the man he worked for directly, the secretary of defense, and the SecDef wasn't going to tell him no. As for Shally, he was out of Miller's chain of command—shit, if it weren't for the flower girls on Aspin's staff, who had torpedoed the admiral off the President's short list, he would have had the little man's job. And screw the Pentagon. Minions up there in Alexandria who had never even seen the crease in his pants were quick to call him divisive, flamboyant, transparently ambitious, abrasively self-confident, self-righteous, self-aggrandizing, all because he and Colin Powell were on the same wavelength about what the changing security environment would look like in the post–cold war world.

Adaptive joint-force packaging—Miller had introduced the concept more than a year earlier at his first CINC conference, only to be met with muttering resistance from the unified command, all the commanders in chief of the various theaters, General John Shalikashvili—at the time the admiral's European counterpart—included. Four years after the Berlin wall crumbled into history, the Pentagon was calcified in the successes of the past, deploying its battle groups and squadrons and corps the way it had for decades. Miller had argued tirelessly for each service to funnel its huffing and puffing into a single chimney of integrated capability, responsive to a single command, which could wring out all possible utility from the taxpayers' investment. Can't be done, said Miller's detractors, who were many.

His career—as the media enjoyed reporting, a fast track somehow synonymous with character flaw—had been charmed. Little orphan boy from southern Virginia, at forty-nine one of the youngest people ever to make admiral. He'd bypassed Annapolis, entering active duty in 1964 as an ensign with a master's degree in economics from the University of Georgia. Vietnam, where he earned a reputation as a surface-warfare expert. Harvard Business School's executive management program after the war. In the early eighties he took up residence in the Pentagon, top aide to John Lehman, the secretary of the navy.

Afterward he commanded a destroyer group, worked for Frank Kelso off Libya, took his dreamboat—a nuclear-powered aircraft carrier—around the Horn of Africa when the Egyptians declined to punch his return ticket through the Suez Canal. He commanded the Seventh Fleet in the Pacific for two years, until destiny brought him home to Norfolk to command the Atlantic Fleet. Then in June 1992, they promoted him to kahuna—supreme allied commander and commander in chief, U.S. Atlantic Command, with domain over all services in the continental United States, Europe, western Asia and the Near East, Africa, and the Southern Command. Overnight, Miller had planted himself on the summit of an unprecedented centralization of military power. Authority and ambition had become one with god. Alexander the Great commanded diddly-squat compared to what the admiral had been given.

Before he had even unpacked in his new office, Miller commenced firing shots over the bow of military tradition, requiring the different services to mix and match their forces in an exotic, and unproved, manner. Take two navy squadrons off the USS *Teddy Roosevelt,* he ordered the Atlantic Fleet commander, and fill the empty space with Marines. Heresy. The navy balked, and so did the Marines—*What are you doing to our carrier? What are you doing to the corps?*—but Miller had seen operations from every angle except upside down, and despite the controversy and the whining, he got his way.

He wired the entire command with a secure video teleconferencing technology, the mother monitor right on his desk, and anytime he wanted, he could slip into cyberspace, drop in on any of his service commanders for a face-to-face, wherever they were, whatever they were doing. And these commanders—oh, boy, they were *really* upset. Europe, the Southern Command, Western Asia—if they wanted forces, they had to come to him. Every sailor, soldier, airman, and Marine, Miller had caught them all, gathered them into his net.

Which meant that although it was clear that the Clinton administration seemed determined to exhaust all remedies, spend beaucoup dollars and eat up a lot of time trying to resolve the Haitian crisis peacefully, Miller understood that after the folly of the *Harlan County* and the demise of the Governor's Island accord, to stop the hemorrhaging of refugees would take some kind of action. So he began planning in earnest for whatever contingency might develop, and by the summer of 1994, Admiral Miller had created a fully integrated task force, trained and tailored for the invasion of Haiti.

Miller was in the catbird seat to watch the whole thing unfold. He was Atlantic Fleet commander, and his disengagement from Desert Storm coincided with the coup in Haiti, so that suddenly, in 1991, he found himself feeding and caring for fifteen thousand refugees at Gitmo. Back then, Haiti as a strategic issue was in its infancy. Neither the SecDef nor the White House was providing the admiral with any direction, but like Cuba, Haiti was a hot spot, always there on the periphery, and in the CINC you always had a cell going, the joint staff brainstorming up contingency plans, nothing spotlighted but you had to keep updating tactical approaches, just in case the whistle blew and the NSC said, *What's your plan?* Because the last thing you wanted to do was show them a blank sheet of paper.

The admiral advocated using U.S. military capability for tasks other than those with a strictly military application, especially for the Haitis of the world. Somalia notwithstanding, deploying a force for humanitarian reasons was good training—great training—that took you all the way up to pulling the trigger. In January 1994, Miller issued his first white paper on the crisis, summarizing the planning and examining the reformulation of goals and objectives. "Our current approach to restoring democracy in Haiti," wrote the admiral, "will shortly drive us to a choice among some bad options. 1, Increasing sanctions. 2, A strategic retreat, whereby we sort of cast a pox on both Aristide's and Cédras's houses and withdraw from active engagement in the Haitian dilemma." The problem with this second option was that it was morally unfit, you still had refugees pouring through the door, and the United States had just cut and run in Somalia. Once is a mistake, twice is an ugly, disastrous habit. The third option, Miller wrote, was military intervention, and since the political stalemate was likely to drag on, the pressure for a Grenada/Panama scenario would only increase.

Starting in January, the White House planning cells were also meeting more often than not, and everybody—the NSC, the NSA, State, the CIA, the SecDef, the joint chiefs, every deputy they could throw a rope around—was involved in it. For the longest time, Miller and his crew were backed up into a reaction mode, and when you were on the implementation side of an event, you grew weary of the constant outside tinkering, the perpetual changing of course by a degree or two, and with each degree of variance came one hell of a lot of motion at Miller's end.

Eventually Miller set four joint task forces cooking simultaneously: JTF 120, the interdiction outfit; JTF Gitmo, picking up "migrants" and bringing them to Cuba; JTF 180, the contingency task force that would be the end of this nonsense; and JTF 190, basically a walk-on force if the politicians started pulling out rabbits.

Hugh baby!—General Henry Shelton, commander of the Eighteenth Airborne Corps, out of Fort Bragg—was tapped by Miller for the driver's seat on JTF 180, the hard entry. He summoned Shelton to Norfolk for a "four-eyed summit," the two of them alone in Miller's office for the sake of plausible deniability. The admiral offered Shelton the job: "a clear and direct line of command able to exchange information in a real-time manner, televised real-time to the entire world, with the capacity to adjust instantaneously to a changing strategic environment." The only hitch was, Miller couldn't have some guy running the show who's jumping out of a plane and waiting six hours to set up a tactical command post, so he wanted the general to work off the USS *Mt. Whitney*, the flagship for the fleet commander.

No deal, Shelton replied. He was army, he didn't sit out fights on a ship, having his butt powdered by the navy. Miller was bucking the culture—joint task forcing made everyone uptight. Finally, Miller tired of the protests and gave the general thirty seconds to make up his mind. Shelton acquiesced, as did the fleet commander, although he wasn't happy about Miller's plans to move army equipment—helicopters and armor—onto his ship. The military had never gone that far before; branch integration wasn't refined to the point where you could rely on the communications ability of any of the services to interact seamlessly; but Miller was going to pay the price, and he was going to rehearse with an assumption of jointness.

Over the next few months, Shelton began piecing together the overall plan, so heavily biased toward airborne that even Miller was compelled to say, "Hold on, something's wrong here." Airborne troops were ideal for Port-au-Prince, Haiti's center of gravity and major population center, but the countryside presented a more subtle array of challenges. To address those subtleties, they made SOFCOM—Special Operations, Special Forces—integral to the plan and brought Generals Downing and Scott into the cabal. General Potter, the man responsible for Operation Provide Comfort in northern Iraq, was put in charge of the Joint Special Operations Task Force. JSOTF would be staffed by the officers in the Special Forces Third Group—which in the SF's regional land grab had dibs on two Caribbean islands, Cuba and Haiti.

By August 1, the unconventional warfare planning effort would rest entirely with the SF's Third Group and its commander, Colonel Mark Boyatt. From the beginning, however, there was an immediate disconnect, a systemic warp that left a lot of holes in the JSOTF support staff, officers assigned to both Shelton's and Boyatt's commands, leaving the SF colonel with too many empty desks. The staffing problems never quite got straightened out, foreshadowing the increasingly contentious competition that would evolve between the conventional and unconventional forces deployed to Haiti.

Third Group worked four or five different plans continuously, including one where the Special Forces became the only show in town, but the option Boyatt found most compelling—more a concept than an actual plan—was to sideline the invasion in favor of a sequel to the Bay of Pigs. Go totally unconventional, grab four or five hundred gung ho Haitians already in the States or Gitmo, establish training bases and build a Haitian army in exile. Nothing covert or clandestine, mind you—we'd be supporting a legitimate president, an ally, a government in exile that enjoyed universal diplomatic recognition. Boyatt wanted to advertise the operation, split it wide open, carefully explain what they were doing and why. Aristide could vet the force himself, choose its leaders, then Boyatt and his Green Berets would teach them how to kick ass, transport them back to the island—not unplug these guys, like we did with the Cubans—provide them with a little aerial platform fire support to ensure success, and *voilà*—a total win-win scenario! It made the crisis a Haitian problem with a Haitian solution. Ironically, a cadre of trusted and willing FADH military officers and enlisted men had followed Aristide into exile, soldiers who passionately believed in Boyatt's concept, as did Aristide himself. The colonel proposed it to General Potter, ran down an outline and showed him some slides, and that was the last he ever heard of it.

The two commanders, Miller and Shelton, worked through iteration after iteration of JTF 180, but it soon became evident, as they watched the convoluted politics of the situation evolve, that they would need what Miller called another bookend ready to go—a hard entry paired with a soft entry. Soon US/ACOM had two contingency task forces coalescing—180 and 190—and two (and a half) invasion plans rolling: 2370, the hard entry; 2380, the soft entry; plus a hybrid, 2375, the yin-yang/love-hate alternative, which no one wasted much time on, although it most resembled what they ended up doing. Everybody's energy was focused on 180/2370, but you couldn't soft-entry with a prized combat group like the Eighteenth Airborne—you just didn't do that; it wasn't the signal you wanted to broadcast to the world, or to your troops. So Miller had people reviewing what regular army capability was available for JTF 190/2380. Major General David Meade and his Tenth Mountain Division, out of Fort Drum, New York, topped the list. All the commonsense ingredients seemed to be there: Meade and the Tenth had somehow managed to survive Somalia, where the general had earned high marks for his ability to bridge the shoals between the political and military sides of the operation.

The final difficulty was to decide how best to position the package, but it just wasn't coming together. They were going to fly troops across from Florida to staging bases. Miller asked why. The offensive would come at the time of his choosing, and the tactical situation was a cakewalk. The FADH had had no combat training since 1983; its elite units carried M-16s or Israeli Galiels, while the rank and file toted rusty World War II M-1s, or Garands—"an arms collector's dream and a fighting army's nightmare," according to one of Aristide's own military experts. Morale had been shredded by purges, nepotism, whimsical vetting, a parasitic officer corps, racketeering, narcotrafficking, and internecine shoot-outs. The patrol boats that constituted Haiti's pipsqueak naval force were mostly inoperable, cannabalized for parts, entire engines pilfered and sold to private buyers. The island had about as much artillery as a VFW hall in Iowa, the vast majority of its resources moldering in Port-au-Prince, and it had no air support—no air force, basically: a half-dozen unarmed planes and no radar—and posed no surface or subsurface threat. It had taken a better-trained FADH and its paramilitary militias three months to stamp out the "invasion" of thirteen young Haitian exiles trying to overthrow Papa Doc in the mid-sixties. When a half-dozen exiled patriots invaded the island of Tortuga, off the northwest coast, in 1983, Baby Doc sent his best counterguerrilla unit, the Leopards, to kick them back into the sea, but rather than face combat, the troops deserted or shot their weapons into the air and withdrew to the mainland, claiming they lacked sufficient ammunition for the mission. In conventional terms, the immediate tactical problem an American invasion force would face, beyond friendly fire and bumping into each other—that sort of thing—was formulating the logistics of how to traffic and pen prisoners once the FADH surrendered en masse.

Find me an aircraft carrier, Miller told the fleet commander. A carrier was 4.1 acres of astronomically expensive real estate, to be used, as far as the admiral was concerned, in whatever fashion to execute a mission at hand. *Hell, make it two, and strip off their jets.* Instead of starting a fight the usual way, by bringing in troops to a secure airfield aboard large cargo planes, Miller was going to put grunts, MPs, logistical and civil affairs personnel, on the USS *Eisenhower,* and put the Rangers, the first guys to be pushed ashore during the invasion, aboard the USS *America,* which they would use as their forward staging base and training platform.

Admiral Miller was ready to launch when, early in the summer of 1994, the President called US/ACOM and ordered him to execute a forcible entry into Haiti, but the operation was deferred at the last minute, preempted by still more diplomatic posturing and interagency catfights. If you want to come back to it, Miller told the commander in chief, cut me ten days to pull the trigger.

Clinton called the admiral back at the beginning of September and said, *Pull the trigger.*

THE WAY IN

They were always going off, these men; they were always kissing their wives goodbye, always committing tiny sins of omission, telling the little white lies of patriotism. This time, they were headed for California, they said, for more training, which was a good enough story, because however well they knew their jobs, there was something still to learn, a skill to hone to perfection, tactics that required endless rehearsal, a more profound layer of understanding to grasp about teamwork, about logistics, about mission analysis, and so they existed in a perpetual state of training— of *becoming*—here in the sand hills and pinelands of Fayetteville, North Carolina, or out in the western deserts, with their allies in Europe, all over the world. However untested by combat, they were already warriors, mentally, physically. What they most strove to *become*—the last lesson—was survivors.

Their leave-takings had become routine, but even the fact of their regularity wasn't enough to keep Joanne Miatke free of anxiety, going weepy on her husband, Bill, every time she saw him off on another mission. *SF wife,* one of the T-shirts sold at Fort Bragg's Green Beret museum read. *The toughest job in the army.* It was late, past eleven o'clock, on the night of September 12, when she put her three young daughters in the family's minivan to ride with their father over to the base and deliver him to what had been until yesterday—at least for her—a great mystery. For Fayetteville, it was a typical late-summer evening, the air conditioners humming throughout the neighborhoods, a cooling stillness bringing relief from the humidity, the darkness perfumed by the lovely heaviness of honeysuckle and pine.

Halfway there, Bill pulled into the all-night Hardee's for coffee, one of those things they always did, and french fries for the sleepy-headed girls, to help them stay awake. Try as she might to keep her fears from rising to the surface, Joanne knew that something serious—something bad—was happening. A month earlier, Sergeant First Class William Miatke had apparently been *read in* to the operation, whatever it was, and almost immediately he had just disappeared for several days on some black ops don't-breathe-a-word-of-this mission. Of all the arrangements they had made as husband and wife to preserve domestic tranquillity, all the understandings they had negotiated to provide for the irregular rhythm of his absences, fair warning was not a guaranteed part of the deal. Then he was back home, making cryptic references to "the boat," but he wouldn't say anything more than that, and there was a tightness to his mood, an increasing preoccupation, that she couldn't penetrate. That's when the deception about California started.

They were from the same place, the cornfields of northeastern Illinois, and she had met him in high school. Bill had disappeared then too, enlisting only days after graduation in 1979 to become an army combat engineer, and it took him a year and a half to come back home to marry her and whisk her away to Germany. Those were the best years, exciting but steady, predictable, the three good years in Germany. But once Bill had moved her and the kids to Fort Bragg, after he had donned the green beret of the Special Forces, he felt the necessity to remind her constantly, in the strictest, most uncompromising terms, about the nature of security. Security was everything, he'd say. Security could make the difference between his coming home alive or vanishing into harm's way. I'm never going to be able to tell you what's going on, he would warn her, although she had known well in advance about his deployment during the Gulf War, where he had sat at a desk at Joint Special Operations Command headquarters in Saudi for two months and then come home. You're just going to have to trust me and trust the people I work with, he had told her, and keep your eye on the news if shit like this ever happens. You're smart, he'd say. You'll figure it out.

And now it was happening. What you never wanted to think about or say—*the shit*: not games, not exercises, not training, not school. She could read it in her husband's flinty silence, the stress compounded by his new assignment, the quantam leap in responsibility. On August 1, he had been selected for promotion to master sergeant and slotted into another team—A-Team 311—in Alpha Company, First Battalion of the Third Special Forces Group, where he was now known as Top: top sergeant; the highest-ranking NCO on the team, second in command. If Joanne Miatke could have read her husband's mind after he returned from his secret mission to the boat, she would have known how shocked he was, initially, once he learned exactly what it was he and the other teams from Third Group would be doing, come the middle of September.

Even after fifteen years in the military, Sergeant Miatke had never shot at anybody, never been shot at himself—which was a blessing, certainly, but to a professional soldier it was a deprivation too, a flaw not just in your experience but in your psyche, the wiring of your metaphysics, and it left you with a gnawing sense of incompleteness. The Special Forces were primarily teachers, advisers; they hadn't participated in full-scale direct action since Vietnam.

In 1994, there were about two thousand Green Berets dispersed in small six-to-twelve-man teams throughout more than sixty countries—not a secret, exactly, although you could hardly call the scope of the Special Forces involvement around the world public knowledge. Sometimes they did their job too well, as in Sierre Leone, when their students exercised their newly acquired skills by overthrowing the government. Sometimes they were farmed out to the unsavory side in a civil war, as in El Salvador and Guatemala, and abandoned by the politicians who sent them there to drown in the irony of the Special Forces motto—*De Oppresso Liber.* To free from oppression, free the oppressed. And sometimes, as in Operation Provide Comfort in Kurdish Iraq, they actually went somewhere and did something that made the planet a better place to live on, however temporarily. In the Persian Gulf, they had functioned as CSTs, coalition support teams, keeping all the different nationalities on the same sheet of music. A few teams stepped in shit on recon missions across the border, others trained Kuwaiti soldiers, but for the most part they didn't fight, they were muzzled by General Schwarzkopf, who, like many conventional commanders, hardly bothered to disguise his contempt for Special Operations Forces. He regarded the SOFs as renegades, unscrubbed scofflaws, self-important grandstanders forced upon the purists in the regular army and sopping up appropriations.

The Quiet Professionals, the Green Berets took to calling themselves, spinning the Nam image toward a softer light. The Peace Corps with guns. Not Caesar's legionnaires, running around the map hurting people. More like a professional sports team, the exhibition squad, only heavily armed, dazzling the farm leagues, operating clinics, making buddies, setting standards, Liberty's own ambassadors on the best of days, a bloody moral and diplomatic nightmare on the worst, sharing the expertise of the United States Army's elite troops. They were altruists in uniform, missionaries in the shadows, ennobled souls echoing the government's own shibboleths about social justice, the optimistic face of what presidents and pundits wanted to describe as the New World Order, its vanguard, the military's easy-to-apply contribution to the quixotic but simultaneously ambiguous crusade for global democracy, the mythic Arcadia of free-market capitalism, unfettered by wrong-thinkers.

Joanne Miatke asked her husband how long he thought he'd be gone. Six months, he answered, which only heightened her feeling of alarm. They pulled into the battalion's parking lot at Fort Bragg right on schedule at eleven-forty, one of many families dropping off men, and got out of the van to say their goodbyes. Sergeant Miatke hugged his drowsy girls, then kissed Joanne, who had already started to bawl. "Watch the news," he said, still working the subterfuge, stepping back away from her, toward some far-off edge she wouldn't dare imagine. "Just watch the news, hon."

Third Group had been packed up for ten days and had spent the interim in intense planning sessions, trying to visualize, clearly and precisely, each step, each second, of what they were in for, all variations and degrees on the theme of success. And escape and evasion scenarios, should it all end in disaster. Each team had been given its target intelligence packets, the DOD maps and ultraclassified National Security Agency satellite photographs, and their missions. Infil, for *infiltrate*—is what the military called it: going in, crossing the physical and mental span between peace and war. The operation was going to be a forced entry, meaning they'd really be shooting at people, and people were going to shoot back. Seven days from tonight, on September 19, at H hour plus, the Eighteenth Airborne Corps would slam into the capital of Port-au-Prince, the Marines would launch into Cap Haïtien, Haiti's second-largest city, and the Special Forces would scatter through the rest of the country, A-teams taking down the FADH garrisons in the provincial towns and cities, a dozen men often going up against ten times that many. Nobody on the teams was saying they couldn't do the mission, but some of them had already come to the conclusion they were going to be shot.

The parking lot was a swarm of camouflage. Hundreds of men were drifting away from their families, then gathering in their individual team rooms to get down to business. Like the newly built battalion head-quarters themselves—the clean slant of the roofs, the brick-and-glass facades—they were the improved and modernized Green Berets, the mature low-profile geniuses of unconventional warfare (UW). Nobody here from central casting—plenty of them weren't even six feet tall. They were beyond John Wayne, scornful of all frauds and fantasies, that Rambo silli-ness, beyond the hurt and stigma of Southeast Asia. And on September 18, when the sun began to set over the Windward Passage between His-paniola and Cuba, and the conventional forces began to smear on war paint, these SF teams would sit back on their heels, disassociating them-selves from the kids and bad-ass killers who would compose the bulk of the direct-action strike force. In Haiti they'd be the hearts-and-mind repertory road show, "white-faced people here to fix up things," one of the white faces said, even if they had to administer a low-intensity whirlwind of dread and pain to get the message across.

In 311's team room—part storage space, part office—Miatke found thirty-year-old Captain Edmond Barton understandably edgy, spitting a steady stream of brown tobacco juice into a Styrofoam coffee cup. Not only was Team 311 Barton's first command, but his wife had given birth to their first child, a son, only six weeks earlier. The rest of the members wandered in—Sergeant First Class Ernie Brown, their weapons specialist, who seemed particularly sullen, grumbling about the timing of the deployment—his girlfriend had arrived from South Carolina only a few hours ago. Staff Sergeant Bill "JC" Collins, the medic, the team's youngest member, who had waited through four years of inopportune missions be-fore ever getting the chance to be home for his son's birthday.

Sergeant First Class Bob Fox, a former drill instructor, and Staff Sergeant Walt Plaisted (the only noncommissioned officer on the team with a college education—a bachelor's degree in American literature) were 311's engineering specialists. The communications—commo—man,

Staff Sergeant Jim Pledger, was a tall, lunky-looking blond Californian who had an abiding love for combat aircraft, Rush Limbaugh, fishing, cheap bourbon, and his beautiful born-again Christian wife. As they lugged their rucksacks out to the parking lot to board the transport that would take them up the road to Pope Air Force Base, they cracked jokes about deer season, which would open in a few weeks. All of them had bought hunting licenses, *but hey, brah, the Prezdent, what's he care about my forty-five bucks.* They were not well-paid men.

Like so many nights they spent on duty training, humming with the bad energy of sleep deprivation, this one turned fast into something execrable, god-awful. Ernie Brown wouldn't even admit to himself that they were actually deploying until they were on the plane and gone, because a year ago, too, they'd been activated to go to Haiti, but "the people in Washington hemmed and hawed and sucked their thumbs and nobody in command wanted to make a decision until somebody finally said, Fuck it, we're not going, and after that everybody figured they had as much chance of being dropped into Haiti as Clinton had of being reelected." Now, however, they had no choice but to sit on the Green Ramp, where the Eighty-second Airborne would launch in six days, and wait while the L1011, a commercial charter, was loaded up with gear, which took forever, until, half awake but wired into the huge spiderweb of commotion that was the operation—Admiral Miller's "ten day cascade" to H hour—they clambered aboard and flew out at four in the morning, jetting south toward Gitmo, the United States naval base in Cuba.

Somewhere within the Bermuda Triangle, everybody on the plane became mortified, the pilot stammering, ordering the attendants into their seats, as the aircraft was surrounded by white blasts of lightning and shaking like some B-movie special-effects sequence, pummeled by an unimaginably ferocious tropical storm. Everybody was trying to be cool about it but, white-knuckled, held on tight. Under the circumstances, what you never tried to think about—death—became unavoidable. Looks like we don't have to die in Haiti after all, someone joked. Miatke gripped the armrests, certain the tempest was going to slap the plane out of the sky. Bracing himself against the violent loss and recovery of altitude, Ernie Brown tried to empty out his mind, but a prayer looped through his thoughts, a grunt's prayer, one of those fragments of language that just kept buzzing in your head, because somebody back at Bragg had told them that if you get shot, as long as it burns and stings you're all right, brah, and now he couldn't stop saying the mantra, as an imaginary bullet entered his flesh: *Burn, just burn, just keep burning.*

He had no doubt whatsoever about what would happen when the team infilled into Haiti, into Cap Haïtien at H hour plus 15, when they would helicopter down to Limbé (pronounced *limBAY*), the largest town in the 53rd Northern District, a six-hundred-square-kilometer area in the rugged mountains below Cap and the coastal plains, land on a soccer field at Limbé's outskirts, and attack the FADH's district headquarters, neutralize the garrison, the casern's hundred-man contingent, and hold the compound until further notice. And if they had to fight their way in, there was going to be a wicked mess. Many people were going to be hit, point man first, and Ernie Brown was walking point. At thirty-seven, he was Team 311's senior citizen, too old for this shit but two years from nailing down his pension. *Man,* Ernie said to himself, *this sucks. This sucks bad.*

By dawn, over the turquoise waters of the Bahama Banks, they had passed beyond the turbulence. The L1011 did a slow, come-back-around bank toward the crooked finger of southeastern Cuba and by seven-thirty had landed safely at Gitmo, where the teams were trucked away from the center of the naval base and its overcrowded holding pens, stacked with refugees. On the western perimeter, up against the border with Fidel's once impressive revolutionary army, they were given tents to pitch alongside the Rangers, the U.S. Army's custom-made barbarians, their quick-reaction strike force (whose all-purpose mission statement boiled down to a bloody essence: *We're here, we need to get there; kill everything in between*). The forced entry was on, and everybody was charged up and lusty, programmed for destruction, the iron scent of blood and glory blowing in on the prevailing winds. The aircraft carrier *America* anchored offshore, loaded up with more jaw-clenched hoo-ah! Rangers and the phantoms from the officially nonexistent Delta Force that General Potter had helped put together.

Top Miatke shook everybody out of the tent at five-thirty the next morning for PT—calisthenics, jogging—and he pushed on Barton, who had a tendency, Top felt, to sleep in. Here in close quarters, he was starting to look at the captain with more unforgiving eyes. Officers were only summer help anyway, temps, transient workers—eighteen months and they were off the team, slotted into staff, a desk job from which very few would ever find a foot up the sheer slope of an ever narrowing pyramid. From an enlisted man's point of view, officers *pinged* too much, bounced off the walls, while the NCOs made nests, settled in for the duration of their careers, and the tops anchored the teams, ran the show.

To Miatke, Barton seemed confused, panicky even, and he was pissing people off by spitting tobacco juice on the floor of the tent. We gotta do rehearsals, Miatke kept telling Barton; we gotta plan air support. He tracked down the pilot from the AH-6—Little Birds, Miatke called them; small helicopters with mounted cannon—who was slated to accompany them on the ground and call in their air support. No one on the team had mastered this particular task well enough to do it under a lot of stress—at least not do it rapidly—and they were going to have a Specter gunship in the air, a flying beast that spewed death, vomited it down in an unending red-hot splash, thousands of rounds a minute; and a DAP package, Black Hawk helicopters with rockets and guns and AH-6s swooping around like raptors to help out if the mission started to come apart. Miatke didn't know what the letters in the acronym DAP stood for; as far as he was concerned, all it meant was bad-ass helicopters, annihilation by air.

So now, with the pilot among them, they refined their course of action, walked through rehearsals with the meticulousness of a troupe of Shakespearean actors, walked through them again, day after day, broiled by the sun, drilling themselves into a state of exhilaration, and as the weekend neared and they bunked down on the cool concrete slabs of tent city, it was almost as if they had to restrain themselves from cheering.

We are ready, point man Ernie Brown kept blurting out. Get the fuck out of the way.

THE PRICE IS RIGHT

If ever there was a showcase for a mastermind, this futuristic war council out of some space trekkie's fantasy was it—the first preinvasion closed-circuit teleconference in history, the National Command Authority all in one room of virtual reality—produced and directed by Admiral Miller, the far-flung guests and supporting cast linked up and poised to brief the commander in chief, who was prepared, this Saturday morning in September, to lead his troops, via video, into battle.

In the Pentagon's war room, Bill Clinton and Al Gore sat casually at the head of a long conference table, dressed in sports coats and open-necked cotton shirts, tieless and young and brightly attentive—president and vice president of the Kappa Alpha alumni association, in town for the big game, not leaders of the most sophisticated and lethal military force ever assembled on the face of the earth. Also at the table, flanked left and right, were the men the President most relied on and trusted—Shally, SecDef William Perry, Secretary of State Warren Christopher, National Security Adviser Tony Lake, White House chief of staff Leon Panetta—and in the rear of the room, like a jury or chorus, sat the top echelon of their respective staffs.

No President Aristide. This wasn't the little priest's party.

Miller, in Norfolk, welcomed Clinton and his entourage to the Pentagon. "Just a few days ago," the admiral reminded the President, "you authorized the forces to act. Today these troops and ships are nearly in a fighting position," closing quickly and simultaneously, a modern campaign defined not merely by jointness but by multiagency and international cooperation, as well as potential for unprecedented media impact. Nearly one hundred journalists in the DOD pool were already on their way to Guantánamo, Miller reported, where they would embark with major units, their stories embargoed until the main activity had been completed. The media already hunkered down in Port-au-Prince was a different story, warned the admiral—Washington was still finalizing policy with the news organizations—but the forces had been alerted to the factor of real-time down-your-throat coverage.

The admiral was particularly sensitive to the capital's slums going up in flames. Fearing a repeat of the conflagration in Panama, or acts of arson by the FADH, Miller explained that he had folded a firefighting capability into the operation—a huge fire bucket, two fire trucks, C-130s loaded with chemical retardant. Also, as of this morning he had learned that all the combat surgeons had arrived aboard the USS *Comfort* hospital ship, which was steaming into the AO, the area of operation. Besides essential support equipment, the first two ships to unload in Port-au-Prince would be carrying Bradleys, to provide the troops with immediate armor coverage in addition to the armor brought in through heavy drops, and field engineers would be on hand to make temporary repairs to bridges and roads.

"And finally," Miller summarized, "this is sort of the pre–H-hour picture. Strategic surprise isn't there anymore, of course. You've seen lots of details on the TV and print media. This operation is based on execution. We'll get as much tactical surprise as we possibly can, and then rely on the expert ops of the commanders and troops you're going to hear about now."

Miller began to beam in the commanders of the package for their assessment, conjuring them up from across the hemisphere. Occasionally the transmission would freeze as it bounced back to earth from its satellite relay, and bursts of feedback from the encryption process would squiggle the voices, making the cameos sound watery. The transportation commander outside Saint Louis explained to the President how he believed the military's mobility had improved since the Persian Gulf. Lieutenant General Bob Johnson from Camp Lejeune reminded the President that Marine amphibious forces had been offshore Haiti for several months. The commander of the invasion's air components checked in from Langley Air Force Base, and the Atlantic Fleet commander reported from the *Mt. Whitney* in Haitian waters that his naval forces numbered fourteen thousand personnel aboard forty ships, his flagship was preparing to enter the operating area, and he was standing by for General Shelton's arrival in the morning.

Rear Admiral Bill Wright and Marine Colonel Tom Jones were aboard the USS *Wasp,* patrolling the Haitian coastline. "Last night shortly after midnight we had a SEAL insertion," they told Clinton and Gore. "We covered all four of the possible beach landing sites." The SEAL units, undetected, were extracted at four in the morning and brought back to the flagship for a full debriefing. Next, the video spotlight tagged Gitmo, where Brigadier General Dick Potter had just completed rehearsals for his special operations forces. As the President thanked General Williams for managing the refugee camps, Miller interrupted him to switch over to Fort Bragg, where a technical problem had kept General Shelton off the air. "I was hoping he hadn't bailed out of this operation," joked Clinton as Shelton, perhaps the most granite-jawed man on earth, smiled tightly and reported.

"Currently we have over three thousand two hundred troops—predominantly here at Bragg, out of the Eighty-second Airborne—that are in their marshalling areas," said Shelton. "They're going through their final preparations now, to include extensive training in the rules of engagement." He explained that General Meade, who would be his deputy force commander if the President implemented the JTF 180 kick-in-the-door option, would arrive in North Carolina that afternoon. "We usually sign off from Fort Bragg, as you're aware, with a big airborne *All the way, sir!* but today, to show you the jointness, we'll sign off with *Under way, sir!*"

Now it was President Clinton's turn to speak. He introduced his lingering concerns into the discussion, on the assumption, he emphasized, "that we will not be successful in this peace mission [the Carter negotiations]—or even if we are." What would happen, wondered the President, after the initial success of the military operation? "Most people," he said, "predict that if there is any substantial resistance to this effort, it will be in the form of small groups of people, lightly armed, perhaps individuals alone who might in effect operate as snipers and otherwise just try to pick off people." Clinton worried that such a threat was difficult to prepare against and posed an enormous challenge in terms of ROE, the rules of engagement, thereby increasing the likelihood that the military would be obliged to do some things that could undermine civilian support for the mission. (Nobody asked, *What civilian support?*) Were the rules of engagement absolutely clear? Was there a clear distinction between the military imperatives of the mission versus the vortex of domestic police work that might suck in the troops?

The chairman of the joint chiefs of staff fielded the question, allowing that the issue of ROE had been uppermost in everybody's mind. The staff had wrangled it back and forth, adjusting and readjusting the rules past the point of sensibility until Admiral Miller stepped in. After the initial phases, Miller had argued, the ROE could be adjusted as the climate permitted, but he refused to sign off on anything that was not lucid and unencumbering while bullets were flying, anything that would require a soldier to stop and say, *Wait a minute, do I have to figure out the ABC and D of this before I fire?*

He and the SecDef had done some last-minute tuning, the chairman of the joint chiefs told the President, particularly in regard to groups of armed civilians. "As you know," said Shalikashvili, "there are many, many weapons there. We keep hearing more and more reports that FADH members are taking off their uniforms and disappearing into the population."

(The reference here was to Cédras's so-called vaporization strategy, described at length on CNN by a straight-faced Peter Arnett: the FADH would shed their uniforms, melt into the population, and wage a costly counterinsurgency campaign against U.S. forces—a hilarious proposition, since the chances of the FADH engaging in protracted guerrilla warfare were nil, given their cowardice, ineptitude, and, most important, utter lack of popular support.) Any civilian armed with machine guns, rifles, or shotguns would of course be considered hostile and confronted with deadly force. But, Shally acknowledged, civilians armed with pistols or machetes would not necessarily be hostile, and here the rules were less clear.

Military commanders loathed having several different levels of ROE, but Miller begrudged that Haiti appeared to demand them. Buffoons with crew-served or automatic weapons or rifles, forget it, but a person with a shotgun trying to protect his store had to be looked at differently, and that was going to be tough on the troops, especially under the press's eyes.

The solution seemed to be ROE by phases: three different ROE cards had been issued to the troops to serve as a ready reference, each card stressing a set of responses tailored to a stage of the operation. The staff had likewise prepared vignettes—ROE drills—to train the soldiers to use restraint. Miller had a comprehensive disarmament plan for the Haitian population when the dust settled, and an aggressive weapons buyback program, which, everyone hoped, would get them all off the hook.

Despite these reassurances, Clinton kept worrying away at it. "Now, if we were in the United States," suggested the President, "we'd know what the difference was between a demonstration that turned into a riot and whether somebody robbed the corner 7-Eleven," but he wasn't sure Haiti would provide an environment that would readily allow such distinctions, as a practical matter, on the ground. Miller asked his deputy, Lieutenant General Bill Hartzog, who had grappled with the same issue in Panama, to address the President's concerns.

"I think," said Hartzog, "that it is reasonable to expect a potential for looting or large-scale events that would threaten the continuation or the buildback of President Aristide's government." It was not reasonable, however, either by structure or by intent, to get tied in to daily police work, "and by organization," Hartzog continued, "we've attempted to keep that distinction and build, or have the capability to help in the building of, a

Haitian police force capability early in the game," the bridge between the U.S. military and the Haitians to be provided by a multinational force of police monitors, the IPM.

The best prescription, Miller added, was speed—narrow the window for lawlessness as swiftly as possible. Get the FADH vetted pronto. Get the Haitian police recruits in Gitmo on station with all due haste, and apply diplomatic and intermilitary pressure on the countries pledging police monitors to put their guys out there on the mean streets. Clinton had a final question about the collection of weapons and the buyback program. "I think we'll get the bulk of them within one or two days, sir," a staff officer asserted. Such optimism—or perhaps hubris—would never quite match the hard truths of disarmament.

SecDef Perry offered concluding remarks, and Shally spent a few moments brown-nosing the President, who returned the favor. "I have done my best to clarify this mission," Clinton told his commanders on the eve of his inaugural invasion. "Our work is as old as our country. We are committed to putting an end to the most brutal regime in our own neighborhood. We are committed to restoring a democratically elected government. We're committed to preventing a further explosion of immigration in an effort that can destabilize democracy in other areas and compromise our own future. It's also important to remind all Americans that these people came to our country and signed an agreement to leave, in return for which we made certain commitments, and we keep our commitments in the United States and I think we have to expect that those who make commitments to us to keep them as well. These are very important interests but, in the end, of course we pray, we hope, that the Carter-Nunn-Powell mission will succeed today, and then we can have what you call a soft landing, or a soft entry, but if it does not, the whole weight of these interests and these commitments will fall to you, and all those under your command.

"Godspeed," said the President.

Take Haiti when ordered, establish a stable environment overnight. . . . All those words, Miller told himself, that's what they meant. Establish sanity by morning and roll on into phases one through five. Bring in the necessary troops, the agency support; create a climate for the expeditious return of Aristide. Emphasis on *quick*. Then get the hell out of that god-forsaken place, redeploy, have everybody back home by November, for the admiral's retirement party.

"Our prayers will be with the youngsters who are actually going to take the operation ashore," said Admiral Paul David Miller, and then he closed the electronic curtains, immensely satisfied.

Eight months later, I spent an afternoon with Miller in Charlottesville, Virginia, where he now ran Sperry Marine, which built gyroscopes for weapons guidance systems and jets. The admiral had read my cover story for *Harper's* magazine and phoned to chew me out. "From a military standpoint, your piece was NQR," he told me—Not Quite Right. You better come up here and sit down with me and let me straighten you out, he said, so I did. "We had our shit together for this," Miller boasted, and rightfully so. As the author of the unorthodox strategy that endowed the military with the flexibility to slam the brakes on a large invasion force already at full throttle and, using his fancy videoconferencing equipment, transform it, overnight, into something loosely resembling a peacekeeping operation—a remarkable feat, by all accounts—the admiral was MR.

Mostly right.

TALKING HEADS: SCHRAGER

Aspiring poet and former Peace Corps volunteer Stanley Schrager became, from the perspective of the regime, the most hated man in Haiti in the eleven months between the *Harlan County* affair and the military intervention. The walls of Port-au-Prince bloomed with anti-Schrager graffiti, there were threats on his life, a bodyguard was constantly by his side. Haiti personalizes everything, and Schrager, the embassy spokesman, became the face of American pressure for Aristide's return. Pro-regime newspapers called him a pointy-headed moron, mentally deficient. One article claimed he stalked young girls in Pétionville and that he corrupted the morals of foreign correspondents by taking them around to pick up underage prostitutes. The weekend before the invasion, the intel branch at the embassy intercepted a radio transmission that said, Okay, let's start killing whites, and let's start with Schrager. He had been through a lot of the same stuff at his previous diplomatic posting in the Philippines. Maybe he was just being naive or fatalistic, but the threats never particularly stressed him out. "A damn good way to provoke an invasion is to kill an American diplomat, baby," he once told me. He was short, dark-haired, liked wearing madras shirts, liked vodka martinis, liked romancing women (though not underage prostitutes), and talked with an idiosyncratic snort.

Stanley Schrager: Clinton gives his speech the middle of the week before, the fifteenth, outlining the reasons, showing pictures, the whole thing. . . . They called me and said, "We need some photos of human rights abuses," and I talked to the AP people, said just call the AP people in New York and tell them what you want and you'll get it. So he uses that. An interesting aside: CNN broadcast his speech live, nine o'clock at night. Afterward they invite me to be interviewed. Since they invite me, for balance they invite Mireille Durocher-Bertin [an attractive, English-speaking Haitian lawyer, often used as a spokesperson by the Cédras regime]. You know, her side. CNN was very nice to her. Politically she was a fascist, and obviously you regret anybody's death, especially in those circumstances, but this was a mean lady. Her rhetoric was fiery, it was insensitive. She was clearly a right-wing fanatic in that sense.

BS: A perfect representative of her crowd.

SS: Exactly. And an articulate one. A lot of them are not so articulate. So after the speech CNN interviews me, interviews Mireille, we're both watching the speech together, and we've been through this before, against each other, and we're avoiding eye contact and ignoring each other, as if neither one of us existed. . . . The next day, a rumor started about a last-minute Carter mission, and sure enough, Carter ends up here on Friday, and what looks like it's going to be a tough thing, Carter in his own negotiating style—You know, people have commented on this, whether it was a sellout or whatever it was. Carter knows how to ingratiate himself with tyrants and dictators. It's a very smart way of negotiating, which seems to me that Carter senses how insecure these totalitarian dictators really are and how much they really want to be loved.

BS: [Laughter.]

SS: It's very strange. I mean, what is Carter? He goes to Cédras and he says, "General, I'm sure you have a story to tell, you must feel misunderstood, you must be an honorable man, you've done a lot for your country, you know. I want to hear your side of the story." I mean, he did it in North Korea, he just did it in Sudan, he's done it elsewhere, and he did it here. And Mrs. Cédras even more so—"My God, somebody's finally listening to us. A man of stature and honor thinks that we have something to say." Instead of being bombarded. It's a fascinating kind of two days with Carter, with Mrs. Cédras of course being the pivotal figure, like Imelda Marcos—the power behind the throne, literally. The way to get to Cédras was through Mrs. Cédras. How to say publicly that Cédras is an honorable man. Inviting Cédras to come and speak to his Sunday school class in Plains, Georgia.

BS: Very inflammatory.

SS: But very effective. All of a sudden, somebody listens to me [Cédras]. We would never have used that tactic, because we thought it was hypo-critical, and I don't know whether Carter ever thinks it's hypocritical, but that's the way he operates. Even to the extent of catering to Jon-aissant, the puppet president, who we refused to recognize. Carter's convinced that hey, the only way we can get it is for him to sign an agreement with Jonaissant. He apparently then calls Clinton, and Clin-ton says no, we don't recognize that guy, you can't sign an agreement with him, and Carter says hey, it's the only way. You want it or you don't want it? And Clinton says all right, sign the goddamn thing, but hold your nose while you're doing it. Very embarrassing. And you know, it says, *"For the President of the United States, Jimmy Carter. For the Re-public of Haiti, Émile Jonaissant."*

THE WAY IN—ACT TWO

On Sunday, September 18, Operational Detachment A-Team 311 made ready their mondo rucks, packed for combat with well over a hundred pounds of "beans and bullets," and sat out on the sweltering tarmac at Gitmo, ecstatic that their time had come.

War fever. Let's get it over with, everybody was saying. Let's go, we've got a job to do. Then, at the last possible moment before penetration, with the first-wave assault troops like the Eighty-second Airborne already launched off the Green Ramp back at Fort Bragg, the word buzzed through the ranks, leaving in its wake a rejection almost sexual in the way it completely collapsed the mindless, molecular rev of anticipation, the sense of incipient climax. Even the jargon of invasion encouraged the parallel imagery of fornication.

Stand down.

No fucking way.

Gone was the forced entry, the hard entry. In its place, the "permissive" entry, the "soft" entry. Warfare's version of date rape. Men could die from friendly fire; governments could be undone by "friendly" occupation.

Stand down.

Don't cocktease me, sir.

Sergeant Miatke called it "a letdown from hell."

Unkind things were said about Jimmy Carter. There was something immoral or at least amoral about the way he conducted business, smarming up to dictators. All right, maybe not immoral, but you'd have to say cowardly. Liberalism as appeasement. Was Carter being outrageously clever in his accommodation of the tyrants, sugarcoating a bitter pill with New Age Baptist sensitivity-speak, snookering everybody with this messianic defense of the Generals, softly preaching that it wasn't, or shouldn't be, the United States' intention to violate anybody's basic human rights, despots awash in blood included? Or was Carter the ultimate mutation of some trend that had broken the surface of the culture back in the sixties, the sanctity of the individual and the squishy moral tenets of political relativism and correctness? Was this shameful mollycoddling by a man with an absolute belief in his own earnestness and good intentions? Or were the negotiations in Haitian Army Headquarters on the Champs du Mars in downtown Port-au-Prince simply a favorite and familiar waltz, a classic good cop–bad cop psychodrama, empathy and menace, weakness obfuscating aggression, clouds of perfumed rhetoric concealing sudden lightning bolts of forthrightness? As when Colin Powell, speaking soldier-to-soldier, general-to-general, asked the Haitians to imagine the one true and lasting alternative to Jimmy Carter's pained benevolence: If you don't abdicate your power, Powell told the Haitian generals, we're coming in here and we're going to kill you all.

"That sonuvabitch Carter," the men in Guantánamo grumbled. Aristide and his government in exile were muttering identical sentiments.

Cédras cut the deal but refused to sign, playing out the final act in his grand masquerade as Servant of International Law, champion of the inviolable rights of nationhood. Jonaissant signed—to "save" Haiti, he said. The two hostile armies—one real, the other farcical (yet decidedly unfunny and brutal: feral clowns)—would "cooperate" in the dismantling of the regime and the subsequent "restoration" of "democracy." Despite its life—and face—saving design, the agreement was generous only in its use of euphemism and obliquity.

No one would really surrender, no one would really attack: a recipe for endless uncertainty, reversal, promiscuity, and evasion. "Get on the ground first," Colin Powell told the Pentagon. "Don't worry about the details." Aristide himself was dismayed by the Carter accord, and Clinton dispatched Tony Lake and a three-star general to calm him down. Last week, the junta leaders had been "thugs"; this week, they were gentlemen deserving of "military honor."

By early Monday morning, after the fever and the disappointment receded, nothing much about the overall mission of the Special Forces had really changed except its pace. In all likelihood, no one would be returning home with a combat badge, but their operational space, the environment which virtually begged for the SF gestalt, had been preserved. By daylight, Third Group joined the airlift to the tarmac in Port-au-Prince. It was one of the most awesome sights Lieutenant Colonel Mike Jones had ever witnessed, dozens of Pave Low helicopters lifting off the ground in Cuba, an armada of iron dragonflies headed for Haiti.

Third Group had a total of thirty-two operational detachments—ODAs, or A-teams—and five administrative B-teams. Only the A-teams in Second Battalion's Alpha Company had drawn missions in Port-au-Prince (PAP), where Jones's battalion HQ was posted. The bulk of the force was warehoused at the airport in a building that was pestilent and rat-infested—rats eating holes in battle dress uniforms, rats falling out of the rafters. General Potter was working closely with Joint Task Force headquarters—Shelton and Meade—and the FADH, trying to determine what locations the Special Forces would enter first. The premise was the SF would notify the FADH where they were headed so there'd be no miscommunication, nobody killed.

The first night on the airstrip in PAP went on forever, and Potter, who had laid out his bedroll atop a desk inside the terminal, contacted Jones in the middle of it, telling the colonel to get a company of men together to get into the FADH garrison Camp d'Application, up the mountain on the outskirts of Pétionville, where the Haitians had stockpiled whatever heavy weapons they controlled. Jones said, "Hell, General, I thought you were going to send the Rangers in there, make sure things were squared away." "No, you're going," said Potter, which made the colonel light up.

Camp d', with its heavy-weapons company and its garrison of two hundred fifty men, had been one of the principal targets of the invasion, and Jones thought it was a pretty ballsy move to just hustle his men straight out there, but Potter was a no bullshit guy, he made things happen; Schwarzkopf had had to rein him in during Desert Storm to keep Potter from starting the land war prematurely. So here was Alpha Company staring down the FADH, their eyes scanning the parade ground, strewn with weapons—157mm cannon tank guns, mortars, machine guns mounted on tripods—an entire football field filled with armaments, some of it clearly junk, like the World War I vintage tank, but all in all a legitimate threat to the security of the mission.

Alpha Company established a perimeter and bedded down for the night and in the morning started recovering weapons and getting them inventoried. The SF were under the impression that after they'd wrapped up the count they were free to destroy the stockpile. The teams prepared all the breeches for disabling, then word came down from Potter saying hold off, we don't have authority on that from JTF HQ, and thus the first of many food fights broke out between the conventional and unconventional forces in Haiti.

Later that morning, a column of Meade's Tenth Mountain Division infantrymen came bulldozing into Camp d', like a scene out of *Westward Ho!* We're saved—the cavalry's here. The Greenies were so unimpressed they did the Wave—*Whoa, brah!*—welcoming the riflemen with a rolling two-armed salute and snickering cheers. It was an amusing but impolitic moment. Jones got his ass chewed by Meade and then, reluctantly, by Potter. General Meade was enraged by the SF's mockery of his troops and by the Green Berets' decision to go in soft, leaving their helmets and armored vests back at headquarters.

Meade hated the SF and was always finding reasons to try to embarrass them, repeatedly dressing down General Potter and his field commander, Colonel Mark Boyatt, for invented transgressions. Meade ordered Potter, who tried to buffer his troops on numerous occasions from the Tenth Mountain commander's caprice, to order Lieutenant Colonel Jones to conduct an investigation of himself and his men. But they were a good group of guys, just blowing off stress, and Jones hated to see them in a general's crosshairs. *You're in command, you're out there making history, do you want to do that or go home?* Jones stood before the dour Meade and the humorless Potter, defended his troopers as best he could, took his licks, and drove on.

Over at FADH headquarters, General Shelton sat down with Cédras and the Haitian high command, initiating what would ultimately amount to divorce proceedings between the two armies. Meanwhile, across the street, Boyatt and Jones moved a couple of A-teams onto the grounds of the national palace, which housed, along the back wall of its compound, the equally palatial Dessalines Barracks, manned by a three-hundred-strong contingent of FADH soldiers. The face-off was weird. The Haitians were under the impression that the Special Forces had come to give them more training. Some of the older FADH whispered conspiratorially among themselves, trying to decide whether to just shoot the American soldiers when they turned their backs, and the two armies began an awkward routine of simply watching each other.

The Green Berets took up quarters in the compound's dispensary, with no alternative but to cook, eat, sleep, and use the toilet in the impossibly cramped two rooms where they lived. The biggest threat they faced, the A-teams felt, was against their health. The FADH had a genius for neglect, and there was shit and filth everywhere you stepped. The FADH's sergeant major turned off the water to the building so they couldn't shower. Human remains and skull fragments were scattered throughout a trash pile in front of their quarters. Too lazy to walk to the overflowing latrines, the Haitians were pissing in their helmets and dumping them out the windows. Any unoccupied room in the cavernous Dessalines Barracks was layered with feces. The occupied rooms were strewn with eclectic garbage: drug paraphernalia, syringes, plastic panties, condoms, cheap running shoes, playing cards, dirty clothes, women's purses, rum bottles, ammo belts, toothbrushes, bare foam mattresses, boxes of rat poison. A plaque on the Dessalines Barracks, dated 21 Oct. 1934, commemorated its builders, the U.S. Marines. Walking through the casern, the Green

Berets were afraid the first casualty they would suffer would be from someone falling through the rotting floorboards.

Outside the door of the dispensary, a "guard" goose lived in a derelict van, and the SF would throw it crackers from their MREs, currying its favor, because it would honk at night if anyone approached. Peacocks also roamed the palace grounds; the FADH asked the teams not to hurt the birds, which they considered pets, claiming that Aristide had killed and eaten the last flock.

The SF observed the FADH passing guns from the barracks out to the streets—they knocked holes in the walls to shove weapons through like a rat line—and tried to put a stop to it, but the Green Berets were limited in what they could do: *Just walk around and look; don't confiscate.* It was all too strange for words. The teams had been geared up to kill these jokers, but once they got here, it was: *The FADH's your friend.* Three days later it was: *No, these are not your friends.* The ROEs would change in hours. You thought you were doing things right, but somebody would come and tell you you had it all wrong.

Finally, permission came through the chain of command to clear rooms of ordnance and begin collecting weapons. In the basement of the palace, it was as if they had thrown back the doors of a museum containing Haiti's weapons history, from nineteenth-century Remingtons to Israeli Galiels. There were 1918-vintage .45 pistols, Mausers, a gold-plated Thompson machine gun, crates of Uzis, the Haitian weapon of choice: *spray and pray.* They found a room inches deep with armor-piercing rounds, rooms piled with Sam Browne belts, fifty-five-gallon drums full of CS gas, gas masks, LBEs, mounds of military paraphernalia, grease guns and scabbards, piles and piles of ammo turned white with oxidation, ammo crates rotting. In the armory were enough unassembled pieces to build twenty Browning automatic rifles, eight hundred M-1s. Box after box of M-14 stocks, Galiel parts, and documents identifying who had signed out what weapons and when. It became immediately apparent to the teams that, like the Germans, the Haitians were avid record-keepers—interrogations, arms sales, payrolls, arrests, duty rosters, and more, thousands of documents the team swept together and sent up through channels. From the Haitian soldiers themselves they confiscated six thousand weapons and a plethora of fragmentation grenades.

After four days, the palace band started playing "The Ballad of the Green Berets" instead of reveille in the mornings.

◻   ◻   ◻

From September 20 to 23, most of the teams at the airport bivouacked right out in the open, in public view, without toilets, showers, or tents, isolated from the Eighteenth Airborne Corps and its ever increasing support as the transport planes and choppers landed, one after another, and disgorged the Tenth Mountain's infantry. They were not happy living out of their ruck-sacks in the killing heat, sun-ripened and soured, ordered to keep their Kevlar helmets and body armor strapped tight, the conventional dicks get-ting bossier and more paranoid by the hour. Generals went after anybody in their path, flaying SF troopers for wearing "catch-me fuck-me" Oakley sun-glasses. Meade's second man, General Close, upbraided Team 311 when he found them chatting up locals out by the gate. Maybe brushing up on your French was now going to land you with a letter of reprimand, an Arti-cle 15, the beginning of the end of your career. It was a depressing message, an old story: If you were SF, you were doing something wrong. President Kennedy himself had defied the wishes of the conventional army back in the early sixties, when he allowed the commandos to wear green berets.

All that energy, the turbinelike roar of the event, just to dig in against an imaginary counterassault. The A-teams had heard rumors about a fi-asco down at the port, American soldiers standing only a few feet away while Haitian police freely and without mercy beat innocent bystanders who had gathered to watch the troops and equipment come ashore. ("I am doing my job," one of the stick-swinging cops told a journalist. "What's your job?" the journalist asked. "To intimidate the people," said the cop.) And here the teams were, locked in behind the perimeter, furious that American soldiers were being ordered to stand back from the action. The conventional army prohibited its troops from going beyond the wire, com-mand afraid to send them *out there*.

"The Special Forces," Top Miatke would sometimes tell civilian friends, "they all want to do good in the worst way," but standing here on the air-field in Haiti, hanging around waiting for the Forward Operating Bases, the hubs, to be established in the three provincial centers—Gonaïves in the middle of the country, Jacmel in the south, Cap Haïtien up north—was like punishment, the end of romance, operational purgatory. The team could feel its finely honed edge turn brittle and begin to flake off: "Maybe the airflow's been thrown out of whack by Carter's 'Kumbayah' plan, but why are we being so pussy?" said one of the A-team captains.

Finally, on the twenty-fourth, SF detachments from the First and Third Battalions were airlifted to Cap, the U.S. military's second base, where the Marine Corps jealously hosted the party, doing their own thing, not to be eclipsed by the dog-and-pony media show down south, their feathers already ruffled because they believed the entire operation, top to bottom, should have spelled Marine. Haiti was all ports and shoreline, not even worth bombing, you know. This cockamamy mix-and-match Joint Task Force cross-dressing blurred the line between services, putting airborne infantry on ships, for chrissakes. What did the army think it was anyway— the Marines?

Miatke and Team 311 were confined again in an isolated section of the airfield, straitjacketed by the same trifling restrictions they had suffered in PAP, shunted aside to watch teenage Marines scurry around in frightful self-importance. Sometime after dusk that evening, everyone heard the staccato splurts of automatic-weapon fire coming from town. A red flare, the signal for reinforcements, streaked into the sky and was promptly answered by the Marines at the airport, who fired a white flare straight overhead, illuminating the camp with raw light. Stupefied, troops throughout the compound dived for security in the shadows, and the Special Forces watched the flare drift back to earth, setting the air force's air-conditioned command tent on fire. Radios hissed and squawked, and the news was head-clearing, either chilling or fabulous, depending on how anxious you were to rock and roll: a Marine patrol had opened fire on police headquarters in downtown Cap Haïtien. Operation Uphold Democracy now had a body count. Ten.

THE WAY IN—PARALLEL UNIVERSE

A handful of government-selected pool reporters had come in with the troops privy to the secret life of the assault, issued Kevlar helmets and flak jackets and helicoptered ashore; submersed into the sea aboard landing craft; thrown, intimately but anonymously, into whatever midnight pain or glory awaited the landing force.

Everybody else—hundreds of journalists from around the globe—

were fending for themselves, playing a heads-up game of unforseeable consequence—part treasure hunt, part commodities market trading, part mugging—and finding their way onto an island ostensibly under a red alert, its air and sea routes severed, its mountainous border with Dom Rep patrolled by uniformed criminals, and its countryside controlled by militias armed with machetes and guns.

By September 17, the travel agencies ferrying the media across the island from Santo Domingo to Port-au-Prince, an infernal daylong journey, were overwhelmed, the sun-baked border crossing at Jimani clogged with legions of harried reporters, photographers, cameramen, technical crews, fixers, and producers, their gear measured by the ton and fought over by bands of screaming porters, the road gridlocked with convoys of vans and flatbed trucks hauling satellite dishes, generators, warehouseloads of footlockers packed with electronics, lighting and sound equipment and videotape and bottled water, everybody slick with sweat, aggravated and verbalizing in a half-dozen languages, peeling hundred-dollar bills off their bankrolls—ten grand in hard cash, minimum, if you were working for a major news organization—and each one of them determined to be the next guy to pass through the looking glass into the surreal, topsy-turvy world of war.

From whatever angle, with whatever motive, you approached the border, Jimani was a wild, unfriendly place. Even for the adventurous with an expense account, acquiescence to extortion is neither a happy nor a noble occasion, the ad hoc redistribution of wealth never so threadbare of illusion, the last absurd thread of civility to be entertained this side of armed robbery. Given the financial clout and amoralism of the networks (who had greased the border so thoroughly that even the Dominican soldiers were wearing CBS bill caps), the media rip-off warranted scant sympathy, but imagine the sinking feeling, the awful chagrin, of the three Agence France-Presse reporters who, after bribing the Haitian guards a thousand bucks each to cross without *laissez-passers* (all bribes by nature nonrefundable), were blithely turned back at the first police checkpoint on the road to Port-au-Prince.

If, on the other hand, you were Ed Barnes, *Time* magazine's seasoned war correspondent (persona non grata to Haitian military brass), nobody was more useless to you than an honest person. When Barnes and two other journalists were nabbed sneaking over the border at Perdanales, a more porous and obscure crossing on the island of Hispaniola's south coast, their escorts returned them at gunpoint to the guard post, where, for twenty minutes, the Haitian soldiers discussed the pros and cons of accepting Barnes's offer of massive payola before marching the trio back across no-man's-land. "You've got to be kidding," Ed protested. "The most corrupt country in the world, and we can't buy our way in? This is fucking outrageous!"

Barnes resorted to Plan B, hoping to circumvent the border outpost and interior police checkpoints at Jimani by trekking forty-some miles over goat paths and mountain trails to the central plateau city of Hinche, then hiring a taxi onward. When he arrived at Jimani, though, a tour operator introduced him to a Haitian, a man of some influence, relaxing in the comfort of an air-conditioned Mercedes while he waited for a couple of *U.S. News & World Report* correspondents whose papers weren't in order. The driver, George, claimed he could get them across the frontier, no questions asked. George, it so happened, was a candidate for the new Haitian senate that was scheduled to be elected in December. One carload of journalists anted up a six-thousand-dollar contribution to his campaign.

Some journalists—Susan Benesch, for instance, of the *Miami Herald*—were already in Port-au-Prince and had been for months, chained to the reeling, spitting creature that was the never-ending story. Thursday, I phoned Susan from Florida and she said *yeah, it's happening, everybody knows, the embassy has been dropping very serious hints, this weekend, early next week, better get down here quick.*

So after a day's-long delay in Santo Domingo, waiting for my *laissez-passer* to be approved, I shouldered my bags and walked across a barren lot from customhouse to concrete guard post, empty inside except for a single Dominican soldier dressed in camouflage fatigues, snatching five-dollar donations from the herd, a gratuity for the protection he claimed to have provided. I stood now on the broiling terrain of geopolitical limbo where, by definition, one should expect to be delayed. The porters grew surly, jostling for advantage with a motley pack of their Haitian counterparts.

I stowed my luggage on the Chatelain Tour bus and introduced myself to a fresh set of traveling companions. The porters suddenly swarmed on us, snarling like dogs, the big ones slapping the small ones aside, yelling, *Paga! Paga!*—pay us more, give us a bucket of money—and the film crews paid more but to no effect, and the porters blocked the bus with their bodies, pounded on the windows as we snapped them shut, trapping us in the steam room of their greed, until finally, their pockets crammed with hundreds of dollars, they drifted away. *Thank God,* you could imagine them saying, *thank God for this little war.*

Cruel sun, beautiful sea-blue lake. We edged our way toward Haiti, and at a second barrier, after another wasted hour, we were permitted to further enrich the Haitian army, its representative du jour a wiry officer in civilian clothes, jeans, and an unbuttoned rayon shirt, his sockless feet squeezed into canary-yellow vinyl loafers, like a barrio pimp. The only clue to his military association was the belt he wore, and alternately fierce and jovial, he flipped through our passports, took five hundred dollars, laughed at the joke we seemed to be for him, and released us into the violent disarray of his country.

In the smoky twilight of late afternoon, we arrived—weary, hungry, and dehydrated—at the postapocalyptic outskirts of the Republic of Port-au-Prince, as it is derisively called by Haitians who resent the centralization of power and privilege there. We had traveled the breadth of the Haitian countryside without spotting a single sign of the U.S. military occupation, not yet a week old.

At first glance, nothing much had changed, I thought, since 1986. The capital was a relentless urban labyrinth, propagating itself, one mutation after another. Vast areas of the cityscape seemed constructed of shortcuts, stopgaps, and makeshift solutions, erected by the homeless for the homeless, every structure either half built or half destroyed, impossible to tell which, creating the smoldering architectural temperament of a dream constantly solicited and constantly deferred. Competing chronologies of decay were overshadowed by the random paternalism of the government ministries, imposing neocolonial facades flaking mustard-colored paint chips onto unkempt lawns.

In the Caribbean, Port-au-Prince was unrivaled in the dimension of its maladies, the scale of its roasted, treeless slums. The city's million and a half citizens seemed to subsist on streets congested with traffic and fumigated by raw exhaust. Wood smoke billowed from cook fires, threadbare laundry flowered on hedges and walls. Port-au-Prince was the ultimate village, a hive of wasted labor buzzing with penny commerce and nickel enterprise. Unlike Havana, Port-au-Prince had not been rewarded by neglect with its own aesthetic, so thoroughly impoverished even decadence could not flourish here. Yet still the city possessed a survivor's élan and mesmerized—blasted—a traveler with the vividness of its hallucinatory images, its dense strata of realities.

As we neared the international airport, connecting dot to dot potholes, the bus seemed momentarily swallowed by a poltergeist, pitching and vibrating with a concussive rhythm churned down on us from a covey of Black Hawk helicopters dawdling above. Up ahead, the roadside flow of pedestrians had coagulated along a cinder-block wall, and there was now an unfamiliar weight in the air, a strange tension of violently mixed emotion—suppressed hate, rapture, disbelief, fear—and here, finally, were the troops, armed to the nines and hunkered down beneath sandbag igloos along the perimeter of the airfield, their helmeted faces nervously scanning the crowd, which stared back with hyperfocused inertia, hypnotized, as if the soldiers were walrus and this was what a movie was. I stared too, never having seen an American infantryman in full battle dress, let alone twenty thousand of them deployed in a theater of operation, and I didn't know quite what to think, not yet, beyond the unfamiliar impulse to shout *Hurrah!*

We passed on into the downtown neighborhoods, eerily empty, the streets banked high with rotting garbage, wandered by pariah dogs and untended pigs, then we turned away from the harbor and its flotilla of warships to ascend, with nightfall, the incongruously named Avenue John Brown toward the sweeter air of Pétionville, the notorious suburb of privilege, carved into the mountainside above the darkening city. Within ten minutes, I stood in the illuminated lobby of the Hotel Montana—space-warped into an après-beach party in the Santa Monica hills—gawking at the throng of media celebs, the Eddie Bauer tropique fashion show, the crush of boyos at the bar in walking shorts and network bill caps, looking as if they'd spent their day playing softball for the corporation. On the patio, CNN was feeding snacks to a satellite; in the lounge, a big-screen TV broadcast the Michigan-Colorado game. Reporters for the dailies queued up at the phone links, computers in hand.

When I found my way downstairs to the apartment rented by the *Miami Herald*, where I had been offered sleeping space on the floor, Susan Benesch and her colleagues, Yves Colon and Peter Slevin, were seated around a messy dining-room table, hushed and intent, squinting at their glowing PC screens, striving to make deadline. I dumped my bags, stole a cold beer from the refrigerator, and sank wordlessly into a cushioned chair, listening to the mouse patter of their keyboards, to Susan's CD player, from which the soprano Montserrat Caballé infused the room with the oddly soothing passion of a Bellini opera. Dulled by the radical trajectory of my journey, I felt submerged in an exquisitely fecund yet hazardous plane of unreality. I'm here, I kept saying to myself, I made it, even though I could not possibly say I understood just where exactly I was on the metaphysical map. After a second beer, I had recovered my senses enough to shower and change into clothes that did not reek of my anxiety.

Reservations for dinner were made. The embargo's impact on one's opportunity for fine dining in Pétionville was zero. Souvenance, the restaurant of choice for the capital's aristocracy of crisis (the politicians and millionaires, the well-heeled gangsters, the diplomats and upper-echelon journalists), was booked up, and so we settled for the gastronomic artistry—langouste creole, entrecôte à la moelle, rack of lamb—of the chef at La Plantation, where the clientele could fill their goblets with the best French wines to toast the continuing—and in some cases karmically inexplicable—miracle of their survival.

We rendezvoused in the noisy Montana bar, joining up with three compatriots—Philippe Diederich, a Haitian-American photographer for the *New York Times*; Ed Barnes from *Time* and his colleague Miami bureau chief Cathy Booth (who before the week was out would be medevaced home to Florida, gravely ill with typhoid and malaria). I rode with Yves and Peter through the blacked-out maze of streets, slowly resigning myself to the paralyzing fact that I was terrified to be moving about the city's corpse-strewn nighttime. Except for the better hotels, the military caserns, central police stations, and homes flush enough to afford a generator, the entire country had been living in darkness, without electricity, for months. We became lost, made a wrong turn, and ended up on the concrete apron of what seemed to be a police substation. Someone in a uniform lurched forward into the yellow cone of our headlights, raising a rifle. "Fucking Christ, *back up!*" I heard myself pleading, but Yves calmly rolled down the passenger window and asked the gunman for directions, defusing the tension with an artificial tone of normality.

The bare Mediterranean elegance of the restaurant, the refinement of the cuisine, the good-natured collegial self-importance of our conversation, the apparent gentility of the local crowd at the other tables—how marvelous, how glamorous, how familiar. We could have been in Coral Gables, Saint-Tropez, the Seychelles, Macao, but instead we were in Haiti, where the ruling class could not seem to grasp, either in 1986 or in 1994, that if, after a coup d'etat, the incoming regime had exhibited one trait more mature than the insatiable egocentricism of children, one guiding principle more enlightened than avarice and venality, if they had only bothered themselves to do one good thing for Haiti more constructive than reenact the despot's bloody panacea of law and order—just *one:* fixed a pothole, picked up the trash—then Aristide, unloved by the U.S. government, would be history, Cédras wouldn't be scouting real estate in Panama, the Marines would be back at Camp Lejeune, and the tyrants would be riding high, still in the saddle, robbing and killing to their hearts' cold content; running drugs; stowing millions into offshore accounts. *The imbeciles, they could've gotten away with it,* but no lust is as beguiling, no mistress as treacherous, as unmitigated self-interest.

Up in the north, flares arch into the sky over Haiti's second-largest city. Out on the airfield, atop the roof of what used to be a morgue, the members of ODA 311 hear the Marines dug in to the right and left of the building call urgently to one another in the brightening darkness: Take position! Take position! *They could hear the M-60s clicking down in the foxholes, bolts going forward, the rusty-hinged creak of adrenaline prying open the door of the night. They could hear the reports come in on the squad radios.* Firefight! *There's been a firefight, a patrol has stepped in shit and they need help, and Captain Ed Barton, watching the flares whoosh up and hang over the city like biblical stars, thinks,* Well, here we go, it's the Somalia thing. It's going to get nasty.

INFIL

On Monday, September 26, ODA 311 received final orders: that afternoon, they would be infilled from Le Cap into Limbé, and because reconnaisance flights reported large demonstrations in the town center, the team would be reinforced with personnel from two other detachments. Top Miatke collected the unit—now seventeen strong—and rehearsed, one last time, the course of action scenario, which seemed to have an amazing isotopic propensity for change. Now they were supposed to "tap first"—a graduated response—Miatke explained, unfolding his well-creased map of Limbé. When they got to the casern, they'd set up a support position, then Captain Barton was supposed to go forward with one man and attempt to make contact with the FADH commander—go up and say, Hey, I'd like to talk to you, we're not here to hurt you, last thing we want to do is hurt you, we want to talk sense to you, come on out a minute and talk. Then Barton was going to give him the conditions: All your weapons and equipment out front in a pile, all your men in back in a formation. Those were the rules. That's where they were going to start. If the Haitians said no, then Barton would back off and the team would hose down the building from the support position—bullets striking against the walls, something the men inside could see and dread. Then Barton would try again.

The old plan had been for command to contact Cap Haïtien, talk to the FADH colonel—Josephat—in charge of the northern region, and tell him to call all his garrison commanders throughout the countryside and inform them that the Special Forces were coming in. (If the forced entry had ever gotten the green light, the teams would have come so fast they fully expected to capture entire garrisons intact; no one would have had the opportunity to flee.) The word would go out through PAP's chain of command, then the A-teams would overfly the caserns on their infils, ideally able to observe the weapons clearly laid out on the ground, the Haitian soldiers clearly in formation in the back of the compounds, and a white flag flying nearby. And all the Haitian commanders were supposed to have done this before the teams ever came in.

It all turned into wishful thinking once the Marines had smoked the fellows at Le Cap's police headquarters. Even if the garrisons had been linked up by phone or radio, which they were not, there was no

Commander of the North to make the calls. Lieutenant Colonel Josephat had vanished into the night, and now the Marines were hotdogging it, conducting surprise raids throughout the mountains without telling anybody, poking a stick into the hornet's nest, disarming the caserns but leaving behind sufficient rifles and ammunition for the beleaguered Haitian soldiers to defend themselves against the emboldened masses.

So now Team 311 was going to be stuck with a walk-in. A gunship, Specter, was supposed to be up there somewhere—maybe, maybe not. Nothing was that well wired together under walk-in as it had been with the forced entry. You could feel the rhythm becoming haphazard, the mission get garbled. And this graduated response: Shit, Top knew it all came down to *You set the conditions and you set the responses.* They were required to ask for the guns—*Your weapons, please, gentlemen*—rather than use their heads. Command didn't want them tapping, kicking, and shooting all at the same time, so a lot of guys were saying, Well, let's see, I have to knock first, then I have to announce my presence, then I'm allowed to shoot, then I'm allowed to hit them with a grenade, then I'm allowed to blow them up with the DAPs. . . . *Well, hell, I'm going to do all five as fast as I can.*

When urged to slow down, to try to manage a peaceful solution first, plenty of guys were balking: *You ain't the one gonna get shot at.* If shots went off from the inside of those caserns, God help whoever fired, because even without the DAPs, even without Specter, they still had SAWs (large machine guns), they had M-16s, they had M203 grenade launchers with 40mm rounds, they had hand grenades, they had claymore mines and light antitank rockets, so who needed air support anyway, because at the first sign of trouble during the walk-in, the teams were going to envelop those caserns with a swirl of ordnance, a shit storm of blinding hurt, nothing left of the buildings but sizzling rubble, and they'd sing a Fort Bragg lullaby for the poor stupid fuckers mangled underneath it all.

Around two o'clock in the afternoon, the reinforced team boarded three CH-46 Marine Sea Knight helicopters and lifted into the air. Ten minutes later, they were circling Limbé, peering over the shoulders of the door gunners to stare down at the FADH casern—which occupied the west side of the town's marketplace—trying to determine the compound's defenses, though they could see no soldiers below in uniform. What they saw instead were thousands of people jammed into the market square, the pulsing core of the crowd concentrated along the high wall fronting the barracks. Captain Barton gave the order, and the choppers veered off to the landing zone, a fifteen-minute walk from the marketplace.

Two helicopters touched down on the soccer field: one disembarked the infil unit, one remained poised to provide landing zone (LZ) security. The third—command support—hovered overhead, then followed the fourteen men on the ground as they moved into town, their M-16s on lock-and-load, 40mm grenades chambered in their 203s. The team jumped out of the back end of the bird, fanned out, and established a perimeter around the helicopter. When Captain Barton yelled for everyone to move out, point man Ernie Brown looked up from where he crouched, and his mouth fell open. Hundreds of people had swarmed onto the soccer field, and Ernie thought, *Either they're on our side or we're going to expend some ammunition right here.*

He stood up straight, looked at the crowd, looked over his shoulder at Barton, who seemed glassy-eyed, and starting walking forward. Then everything became strange. The people combusted into song, thunderous, deafening song, and they swaddled him like a heat pack, swarming around him, their bodies raising the air temperature to 98.6, their feet churning yellow dust into the humidity. Two or three men in rags attached themselves to him, babbling loudly in a language he figured was Creole but that sounded like nothing he had ever heard, and he tried to maintain his composure, not get sucked away in the fraying unreality of the moment, not overload on the fire-hose blast of stimuli. Caught in the crowd's rapturous momentum, being led away—he hoped toward the marketplace and casern, but he didn't know; this wasn't the route they had rehearsed in Gitmo—he didn't know, once they were off the soccer field, where he was. The men were babbling at him and they were moving ahead, more and more people joining the insane parade with every turn they made onto another street.

Ernie looked back for JC Collins, the medic, the second man in the file, but could see only the top of his head, because people were packed that close between them, singing, chanting, bunny-hopping, wild as dervishes. They came through a maze of wattle huts to a graveyard and a street that seemed to lead to the center of town. Ernie saw the market opening up ahead of him, but he didn't have his bearings and kept trying to imagine the aerial photograph in his mind. *We gotta talk, man, we gotta talk,* he said to himself, looking behind him for the other members of the team. The mob was singing, the sound of their voices was a roar, a fury, and the mood in the streets and alleys was spooky, tight, ready to snap. Some people who saw them coming just cleared out pronto, their faces inchoate with fear, and then the crowd swung right, into the dirt plaza of the market and its sea of narrow tin-roofed stalls, which messed him all up, because they had planned to come into it from the other side, the Catholic church side, and now he could see that the market stalls were open-sided buildings, and they hadn't known that from the aerial photographs, they hadn't planned for that. You couldn't take cover behind them. When you walked into the market, there you were, exposed.

Swallowed by his own crowd, he didn't immediately notice the thousands of screaming people already in the marketplace. His personal crowd took him past an old machine, a broken-down street paver with a big iron roller, where someone ran up to him, yelling in English, *Damn damn he shoot he shoot!* Ernie looked at him with a puzzled expression and said, "Oh? When?" About thirty feet behind Ernie, Sergeant Bob Fox called over his shoulder to Captain Barton, "Guess we're not going in as planned, sir," meaning *hot,* but no sooner had the words left Fox's mouth than he turned a corner past a row of shops and found himself in the market on the edge of a mob that appeared to be storming the casern, its gate less than a hundred feet away from where he stopped, leveling the SAW it was his job to carry. Then the air cracked with a volley of rifle shots, discharged from within the casern.

"Oh," said Ernie. "*Oooohhh!*"

Above, in the command helicopter, the reserve medic, Sergeant First Class Tom Milam, watched dismayed as the crowd in the marketplace almost magically disappeared and the team members scattered into firing positions. On the second chopper, which had moved from the soccer field to the cemetery closer to the middle of town, the radio reported what was already obvious to the medic, and the door gunners started shouting their heads off: *Shots have been fired! Get into the air* now! *Shots have been fired!* Back in the marketplace, the detachment spread out in front of the casern, tucking themselves as best they could behind the slender posts of the stalls. It dawned on Ernie that whoever was shooting was using

PART THREE

Liberation

"Violent deaths are natural here.

He died of his environment."

—Graham Greene, The Comedians

INSIDE THE MANIFESTATION

Sunday morning 9/25: From the balcony of the apartment at the Montana, I gaze across a jungled ravine to stucco villas and million-dollar estates—a private Haiti that is celestial, undisturbed, and obscene. No point questioning the rich, however; the answers are always the same. One three-story mansion boasts crenellated towers at each corner, a Norman castle domesticated by white paint. Its front entrance is approached by a palatial upsweep of steps that, if you stood at the top, looking down, lead nowhere, as though the mansion expected its most important visitors to crawl up out of a bushy hole.

After a week's occupation, the capital had not yet afforded itself the highly combustible luxury of imagining it had been liberated. Just what were the Americans up to, everyone wanted to know. It was as if the United States believed the mere presence of its armed forces was somehow therapeutic. For months, the Pentagon had been pumped up for an invasion, high-tech slaughter, another victory for the microchip, and at the last conceivable second it had been told to change the software, uncock the gun—but go ahead anyway and try not to break things. That the Atlantic Command might need a few days to reshape its thinking to this unprecedented circumstance was certainly understandable.

But what was the causal relationship between role and pace? Why, as the timetable expanded, did the mission seem to shrink? Even post-Carter, wasn't this still Operation Uphold Democracy? No one was asking

General Cédras to fall on his sword, let alone beat it into a plowshare, and the immunity granted his various legions of thugs seemed, inexplicably, unlimited, as long as no one pointed a gun at a kid from Kansas. The Americans, it appeared, were practicing an abnormally benign form of co-ercion, as if finesse alone would win the day and the dictatorship would dismantle itself because it was the right thing to do.

Port-au-Prince just squirmed. The generals remained unscathed on their thrones, the FADH inhabited their mango-colored caserns, the police played dominoes in their stations, and the Front for the Advance-ment and Progress of Haiti—the flatulent-sounding FRAPH—owned the streets. FRAPH was to the regime what the Brownshirts were to Hitler, though the comparison begs the questions of scale and purpose, if not effectiveness.

Meanwhile, the Americans drove past in their Humvees without stop-ping, the Eighteenth Airborne Corps seemed to be locked down at the waterfront and airfield, and you never saw a soldier after dark, when the attachés and macoutes materialized like vampires to stalk their prey. Haiti seemed suspended in volatility, neither what it was nor what it intended to be once Aristide returned, if he ever did. Saying his name in public could still get you killed.

Down the hill we went—Yves and I and two other reporters—into Port-au-Prince, to track down a Catholic priest, Father Gérard Jean-Juste, who, after three years, had supposedly come out of hiding to say mass. We found him in a tiny courtyard behind his namesake's church—St. Gérard's—wearing his jaunty woven-grass pancake beret, and he held a cassette recorder, an object of prudence, to tape himself as he gave inter-views. Jean-Juste, since his days as director of the Haitian Refugee Cen-ter in Miami, had always been a media darling, a well-lighted stop on the tour of Haitian activism, and he customarily talked in carefully measured sound bites. We sat down by his side along a concrete bench and let him vent. *Maybe the murderers should be sent somewhere for reeducation,* he says, *maybe we should give them some medication. They were sick. When they brutalized people in front of the international media, they proved they had no brains at all.* What medicine is that, I wondered, that would cure no-brains disease?

We descended farther into the city, its festering heart, the slum of Cité Liberté, home address of many attachés. The neighborhood was an odious honeycomb of colorless blocks connected by a grid of dirt alleyways, wide enough only for foot traffic, where lethal games of hide-and-seek were a nightly occurrence. Spotting a large crowd ahead, we accelerated toward its edge. How deep in did I really want to go? How would I know when I got there?

My level of apprehension, however, seemed moderate compared to what we now observed on the faces of a platoon of Eighteenth Airborne infantrymen, one of the first foot patrols dispatched into the city—flybait trying to walk down the unpaved street. Escorted by the noisy crowd—hundreds of people—the soldiers rotated their bodies, some skip-walked backward, some moved like automatons straight ahead, their eyes stark, alternately expressing fear and intimidation and sparkles of bravado, their rifles leveled for firing, and everything about this dance said Somalia. Yesterday's scenario with the Marines in Cap Haïtien, the lightning strike of violence, became easy to visualize. "Have you seen anybody carrying weapons around?" one of the soldiers naively asked the crowd, not realizing that the question itself was a form of incitement. Yes! everybody screamed in unison. The names of the guilty tangled in the air.

We got back into our car and drove to the United States Information Service building near the embassy, which had been turned into the Joint Information Bureau. There we'd be entertained by the public affairs officers, the PAOs, the military's homegrown breed of spinmeisters. The daily reporters wanted to attend a press briefing, and I needed to obtain my military accreditation, essential for passing through concertina wire or begging a seat on a helicopter. In the JIB briefing room, the Pentagon's songbird, Colonel Barry Willey, updated the Cap Haïtien shoot-out: Dunno. Dunno. Dunno. A fragment of news slipped out: Last night in Gonaïves, American troops disarmed two attachés, who were taken forthwith to the cleaners by a mob, ten thousand strong. GIs in Gonaïves? However incrementally, the occupation of the Haitian countryside had begun.

Outside on the street, Ed Barnes and Susan Benesch had their heads together, quietly engaged in a strategy session, trying to stay a step ahead of the shifting action. Ed's best bet was Gonaïves—stage for the original rebellion in the nineteenth century, costar of the *dechoukaj,* and a perennial troublemaker—for the explosion of anarchic retribution from the masses that everybody could smell on the wind. The Marines up north, by killing the ten policemen, had opened the door for it, which explained why Susan was determined that whatever story she filed the next day would carry a Cap Haïtien dateline. Road trip à la inferno, a pilgrimage toward a wildness absolute. Got room? I asked, quite ready to take no for an answer.

An hour later, I found myself crammed into the backseat of Ed's four-wheel-drive Mitsubishi (rented for five thousand dollars) with Gary Metellus, our Creole interpreter, a big, soft-voiced man in his mid-thirties with close-cropped hair, a round face, and shy mannerisms. Gary and I had exchanged self-incriminating looks—*What are we getting ourselves into?*—and left it at that.

"Do you have a shirt with epaulets?" Ed asked, turning to look at me, his Irishman's eyes audaciously blue and wide. He was wearing such a shirt himself, khaki-colored.

"Nope. Why?"

"It makes a nice impression," he said. The mischief in his voice put a knot at the center of my stomach. Then, more somberly, he made a general announcement: we wouldn't be stopping for roadblocks, we wouldn't be stopping for police. We stared ahead out the windows. I started a silent argument with myself, weighing the pros and cons of Ed's recklessness as he accelerated like a stock car racer late for his own wedding, passing on blind curves, on the shoulder, in the face of oncoming traffic, roaring past sluggish military convoys.

Our masochistic daylong drive north coincided exactly with the collapse of the Haitian state, invisible from within Port-au-Prince yet increasingly evident and animated as we motored farther and farther into the country's exorcism. Rounding the shoreline of the immense blue gulf—the Bay of Gonâve—responsible for the opened lobster-claw shape of Haiti, we passed a mangrove swamp, with its reek of muddy decay, to our left; sad denuded highlands on our right, eroding into the sea.

Except for an infrequent tap-tap, draped with clinging passengers and overpiled with cargo, we soon had the road to ourselves, though the roadsides were another matter, funneling an arterial stream of farmers astride toy-size donkeys, women with pans and water buckets balanced atop their heads, bicycling teenagers, children wrapped in rags, scab-backed paso fino horses, a free-range strip of chickens and goats and cowering dogs. At one dip in the two-lane highway, pairs of boys stepped into the road and waved for us to stop, hoping we'd buy the songbirds they had trapped and strung like live fetishes, six or more to a cord, a jumpy blur of wings dangling from their outstretched hands.

For a few miles, the road hugged the coast and we raced past postcard beaches that once hosted a long-defunct tourist industry. Then the road returned us inland to the more familiar and ubiquitous habitations of the masses—mud-and-wattle huts with thatched roofs, densely built in tribal clusters; two-room cinder-block houses roofed with tin; clapboard shanties with ornate fretwork. Entering Saint-Marc, we could see barrels ahead in the road, a police station off on the left. As we drew closer to the station, I watched a uniformed policeman come off its stoop to intercept us. Ed looked him in the eye and saluted smartly. The cop stepped back with a look of puzzled but nevertheless reflexive respect for a *blanc* of seemingly high rank, and we barely slowed to weave though the barrier of oil drums positioned across the checkpoint.

"Wow," said Gary, and then none of us dared say anything more, lest we unnecessarily encourage Ed. He was the journalist hundreds of Iraqi soldiers had surrendered to during the war in the Persian Gulf, Sarajevo was his favorite place in the world, and he was going to either get us killed or save our lives, hard to say which, but it was becoming clear to me that when you hooked up with Ed Barnes, you had signed on for the advanced course.

Susan punched a tape of classical music into the Mitsubishi's deck, and we all exhaled. On the opposite side of town, the highway rolled us out into the Artibonite valley, Haiti's breadbasket and cradle of *vodou,* its vast expanse of malarial rice paddies harvested by the peasant collectives, who labored at the mercy of *zeglendoes*—bandits who roamed the countryside, burning down granaries, slitting throats. The Artibonite was so overtly primitive that the Special Forces who would soon be patrolling its flat expanse dubbed it Dinosaurland, and its industrious inhabitants, mud people.

The richness of the land, however, existed in inverse proportion to the impoverishment of the road, Route Nationale One, the sole overland link between Port-au-Prince and Cap, constructed by the U.S. Marine Corps in the 1920s, and vital to Haiti's rural economy, its internal flow of people and goods. Earlier that morning, a CBS film crew had flipped their vehicle trying to swerve through its splatter of axle-breaking craters, pits, and chuckholes. Nowhere in the world had I traveled a surfaced road in greater disrepair, its bed so severely exposed that the pavement appeared to be the victim of low-altitude cluster bombing.

Where the irrigated plains ended, the arid, treeless *savane désolée* began, a Nevada-like vista of desolation surrounding the equally destitute ugliness of Gonaïves, a city impossible to imagine ever being beautiful. Approaching Gonaïves's central crossroads, we found the intersection blocked tight by a large crowd, a *manifestation*, several thousand people. Unable to go on, we parked and got out, only to be mobbed by cheering demonstrators, the heat of their jubilation pressing in on us. I was momentarily unnerved by their crush, the passionate intensity of their dancing, of which we alone seemed to be the catalyst. *We are liberated!* the crowd sang in a single, chanting voice. *Long live the Americans! Long live Aristide!* I scanned the side streets, half expecting the FADH to materialize and start dropping people.

We returned to our vehicle and inched ahead, the *manifestation* doubling in size before we were able to park in front of the FADH casern, where, to our surprise, out strolled a poster boy for America's new and improved volunteer army—Major Mark O'Neill, the commanding officer of the one hundred and five soldiers who yesterday had taken over the town. Susan, despite her ingrained skepticism for the military, perked up. Relaxed and debonair, Hollywood handsome, Gonaïves's new king of carnival, O'Neill had to shout to be heard above the crowd, which grew more raucous by the second, taunting the unarmed Haitian soldiers who stood sullenly at the entrance to the barracks.

"So who are you guys anyway?"

"Special Forces."

"Special Forces?"

"Yes, sir. Green Berets."

Oh, I thought. Vietnam—though that set of references didn't seem to fit anymore.

O'Neill was buoyant. He had that cowboy-come-to-town beam on his square-jawed face, even as the crowd grew bolder, more frenzied, and he sent a combat-ready trio of his men out front to pacify them. Right now he was ready to sleep with the devil, O'Neill said, to maintain order, and you had to figure he'd find plenty of opportunities to crawl in between the sheets. You could almost smell the soap on the major, he was that clean, that fresh and healthy, out here in the third world being of use to mankind. When two Black Hawk helicopters suddenly appeared low overhead and began to land a couple of blocks behind us, the joy of the crowd soared to a new and higher range. The volume of noise made even our shouting inaudible, and I felt as if I had been pile-driven into the center of a fabulous though potentially fatal eruption, battered by euphoria.

Nor did this sensation wane as we ascended into the spectacular mountains of the north; instead, it was renewed again and again, at the heart of each village and town we entered, each successive population thronging the road to cheer us, as if it had fallen to us to ignite the fires of their celebration, as if *we* had somehow saved them. Crowds roared at the sight of us, the effect like spontaneous combustion, a house bursting into magnificent flames, and the air throbbed with drums and homemade trumpets—*ra-ra,* the primitive atonal music of the *bands a pie,* like elephants carousing in syncopation.

But the mood of the mob inside the colonial gates of Cap Haïtien—a metropolis touted by the eighteenth-century French as the Paris of the New World but now a virtual junkheap—was not so gleestruck, not so gay. Several blocks before the first roundabout, we came to a halt on the edge of pandemonium, a large agitated crowd. At its convulsive core, a knob of berserk men screamed in Creole: *Lie down flat! Lie down flat!* Susan and Ed climbed up on the roof of the Mitsubishi for a better look. The people had caught an attaché and were ripping him to pieces. We could see the red cap of his bloody skull, distinct among the dark sea of angry faces, the man lurching forward like a deer being brought down by a pack of wolves. *Lie down flat!* the crowd demanded, savoring its power to say these chilling, heartless words, customarily the same command given by attachés before they opened the back of your head with a bullet. Ahead, across from the roundabout, were three armored personnel carriers, in T-formation, manned by a platoon of clench-jawed Marines, their M-16s leveled. The carriers' mounted machine guns were trained on the crowd, the gunners round-eyed as the mob rocked ever so slightly forward toward their position, cordoned off with razor-sharp loops of concertina wire, clubbing and pummeling its victim, swiping at him with machetes until he managed to stumble to the brink of the wire, where the troops yanked him in and he collapsed to his knees, raining blood.

The light, as they so often say in Rome, was beautiful.

Viv le demokracie! the people crowed. The scene slowly marbleized into a tableau, and the city's ambience couldn't possibly have been more sublime or profound. Old gods, like gargoyles crowbarred off the walls of the nation, toppled into the dirt.

Surging with newfound exuberance, hundreds pressed around our vehicle, removing pictures of Aristide tucked away inside their Bibles and wallets, locking elbows to shout their depositions. *A policeman actually made me eat my own shit,* said a student who himself seemed baffled by the fact. A man grabbed my arm, sputtering, *There's an attaché named Champagne. He has weapons. You must go get him.* Their hope was so thorough and consuming, it frightened me, this transfer of responsibility.

For now, the crowd seemed sated by its victory over the nameless attaché, dying on the other side of the wire. Traffic began to move again, and we drove deeper into the lawless city, its void of civic amenities, its locked gas stations, an open-air market selling every bicycle ever thrown away or stolen in Miami, the grim warehouses and shuttered shops, its broken streets depopulated by the uncertainty of dusk. A few blocks from the harbor, we parked inside the high walls of the Hotel Roi Christophe, a former governor's palace, inhabited by Pauline Bonaparte when Napoleon ordered his brother-in-law, General Leclerc, and an army of 35,000 men across the Atlantic to put down Haiti's slave rebellion.

The ride north had been not unlike six hours on a mechanical bull, and now we wanted to walk. Susan and I slipped around the corner, heading in the direction of a nearby seaside plaza, one side of it bordered by the FADH garrison, which had been overrun by a mob earlier in the day. Its five-hundred-man contingent panicked, tearing off their uniforms, and disappeared into the slums, fearing the Marines would come here, too, on the heels of the crowd, as they had the previous night at police headquarters, and shoot them dead. And come they did, but too late for body counts and too late to prevent the demonstrators from trashing the casern. Anticipating nightfall, the American guards behind the barred wrought-iron gates were twitchy, antisocial. Throughout the afternoon, people had been bringing in weird booty: officers' uniforms, straight from the dry cleaners; baglike hoods used during torture sessions. "Take this down," growled an unhappy Marine. "We haven't showered in six days."

Shouts and cheers from around the side of the compound lured us to a soccer game, half the crowd its spectators, the other half yelling up to the second-story windows of the casern, filled with Marines. A shoe came sailing down and into the outstretched hands of a mechanic, who had lost it inside earlier during the day's mayhem. It was a curious thing about shoes, how terror made them jump right off your feet. Empty shoes and pools of blood: the lingering traces of a massacre. Thunder blasted the waterfront. People ran away, shrieking with genuine fear: *The devil is coming!* Indeed, cloaked in a fury of geysering spray, a strange machine, throwing a froth of water thirty feet in the air, flew toward shore to beach itself, more like an oceangoing Veg-O-Matic than any commercial hovercraft I had ever seen.

Susan and I continued on, hoping to encounter the FADH commander of the entire northern cantonment, the oleaginous Lieutenant Colonel Josephat, who resided in the pretty, unpretentious estate house on the opposite end of the square. The twilight, like a Flemish painting's, seemed golden brown and heavy. I began to notice an occasional piece of trampled sheet music, yellow with age, in the street, but the oddity didn't quite register with me. We made a right turn onto the lane that passed in front of Josephat's digs and slowed to a stop, dumbfounded by an extraordinary roadblock constructed out of dented tubas, a disassembled trombone, a trombone case, and palm fronds. Behind the iron spears of Josephat's fence, a Marine hunkered down in a pod of sandbags, manning a machine gun set on a tripod.

"Keep moving," he said. "You can't stand there."

Who, *us?* Correspondents—infosluts—operate on the premise that they can stand anywhere. "Where's Colonel Josephat?" we called back innocently. "We want to talk to him."

But he wasn't there; he wasn't anywhere; he had slithered away, a serpent in the bush, betrayed, he would later say, by the entire universe. We ignored the gunner to stare for another minute at the roadblock. A kid sidled up to us, casting a wary glance at the Marine. "Who made this?" we asked him, pointing to the tubas in the road. What native Dada?

"I made this."

"You! Why?"

"To help."

Of course, we nodded, turning away to wander into the dreamscape of the plaza's tree-shadowed park, its lawn whitened by a snowfall of sheet music, a blizzard of clef notes, thousands and thousands of delicate hand-ruled pages, increasing in density until we waded through them ankle-deep, arriving at a bandstand in the center of the green, a wooden closet spewing antique scores, folios dating back to the 1870s, and plenty of Sousa. I stooped to pick up a handful: "That's My Hap-Hap-Happiness" (I attempted to sing to Susan); "Anchors Aweigh" for alto saxophone; the "U.S. Field Artillery March," lovingly penned in browning india ink.

Night brought total darkness—no electricity, no phones, no city water. We grabbed the last two rooms at the Hotel Christophe, packed with un-shaven media types, and ordered contraband beers from the candlelit bar. We drank in silence, dulled by the day's fast-paced madness, then retired to our rooms to shower cold, before Henri, the French proprietor, turned the taps dry. A generator coughed into operation, bringing juice until ten-thirty. The journalists on the upper floor had removed the louvered slats from their windows to crawl out on the roof, where they had set up trans-mitting dishes, but we were on the ground floor, and Henri found an alu-minum ladder for Susan so she could climb up and use her satellite phone to call in stories to the *Herald*.

From month after month of zero customers to a full house overnight: the staff exuded gratitude, handing out menus with apologies, as if we might enjoy looking at them even though the embargo had rendered them moot. That morning at breakfast, our fellow diners told us cheerily, gun-fire had erupted outside the gates of the hotel and everybody hit the deck. Also, the police had run away from the main penitentiary, and the prison-ers had decided this was a fine opportunity to check out. Outside in the darkness, the air began to compress, fold in; the ice water in our glasses trembled. A helicopter that seemed to originate in our subconsciousness was suddenly close above us but unseen, an airborne locomotive with an American voice—some kid, a psy ops wizard—broadcasting a reverberat-ing screech of comforts and warnings in Creole: *All is well. We have*

*come to help you. Stay in your houses. If you hear noise in the night, don't
come out!*

A while later, Ed appeared at my side in the bar, that mad-dog Colonel
Barnes look in his eyes. He'd just been out on the streets, strolling around
in the dark. It calmed him, he swore. There was something lovely and
peaceful about being out in a city after curfew. I couldn't understand what
that desire was all about—Ed didn't just like taking risks, he throve on them.
"Listen," he confided. "I've just heard they're burning the casern in Limbé."

I wanted to say, *I don't want to hear it, Ed.* Where the hell was Limbé?
What about the curfew? What about Susan, who was back up on the roof,
whispering into space at the rate of sixty bucks a minute? It was almost
eleven. Maybe Barnes wasn't as bone-weary as I was, but we were simi-
larly intoxicated. Couldn't this wait until morning? Apparently not. Susan
chose to remain with her satellite, but we grabbed a drowsy Gary and as
many of our equally foolish colleagues as we could possibly fit into the
Mitsubishi.

Out beyond the walls, lifeless black streets; even dogs and Marines
knew better than to flirt with the midnight of Haiti's trauma. In the
countryside, the breeze was cool and wet. Short bursts of rain pelted
the windshield as Ed sped recklessly across the coastal plain toward the
southern uplift of mountains, the scent of wildness on the wind blowing
through our open windows. Thirty klicks later, Limbé was likewise deserted, spooky with toxic vibes, and I hated the place from the moment
we entered its outskirts. Wherever the location of the garrison, it certainly
wasn't on the main road, and, searching, we lost not only our way but our
enthusiasm, our night riders' confidence. Our headlights finally seized two
men on the ground, attempting to repair a broken-down truck, their expressions sharpened by terror as we pulled over to speak with them. There
was a *manifestation* in the afternoon, one of them recounted, visibly relieved that we hadn't stopped to harm them; but now everyone was asleep.
"Turn around," I urged Ed, but he had the scent of trouble in his nose—
we all did—and had to be badgered to give up the hunt.

I kept telling myself, *I'm not really like this, I don't do stupid things like
this, I'm the goddamn voice of reason.* One day in Haiti, and I had reverted
to an incautious self, the wired college boy. Still, I was learning that an
empty road was an uncommon pleasure for a traveler in Haiti, the soothing night air jasmine-scented and delicious.

In the morning, there was a corpse in the street outside the hotel, someone beaten to death during the night.

FLAMINGO

Let's go to the prison, someone said, so we went to the prison, an open house in the aftermath of the Marine shoot-out. In the courtyard of Cap Haïtien's penitentiary, a column of smoke rose from a mound of documents and files. I picked up a narrow blue card, the record of a prisoner named Delian Petit-Homme, Mister Little Man, a cultivator, age unknown, 120 pounds, arrested on the 17th of September, 1962, for the crime of stealing bananas. Townspeople shepherded us from cell to cell, pantomiming the miseries endured: *Here they would burn you alive, here they would beat you with batons until your ears leaked blood, here they would cut you many times.*

The tiny cement rooms were windowless, smelled of urine, and contained sad curls of shit. Graffiti—mostly prayers and day counts, names of lovers—were scratched into the grimy walls; drawings too, crudely executed with a lump of charcoal. The *vodou* dandy, Baron Samedi, with top hat and frock coat, lord of the cemetery. The parade ground was scattered with rubbish, junked cars, things smashed long ago. Behind the intimidating walls of their caserns, the Haitian military and security forces existed in their own exclusive pigpens of indifference, a preferred and long-practiced style of dissolution.

Inside the barracks and administrative offices, people were tearing out every last piece of wood for their cook fires, ignoring the staccato harangue of a Lavalas partisan who appeared on the scene. "Don't do *dechoukaj*," he excoriated them, "because Lavalas gets blamed for it. If you *dechouké* the prison, you're the same as the attachés, you put a bad image on Aristide." Then, as if he were a comic book supervillain, a notorious macoute named L'Overture sauntered forward to threaten the crowd. His muscle-bound hubris was breathtaking to observe. People stepped back from his challenge, their faces averted, their eyes gone blank. "He's too strong," someone muttered. *Too strong.*

Across town at the police substation adjacent to the city gates, the doors were askew on their hinges, windows unshuttered. Street kids had the run of the building, and we watched their matinee performance, a spontaneous opéra bouffe. They donned calabash-shell helmets, brandished make-believe rifles and wooden-stick guns. They strutted imperiously, barking absurd orders. Pounding a desktop with his fist, their "commander" raged into a toy phone, making flamboyant gestures of intolerance. His arrogant aide-de-camp transmitted from an imaginary radio, while on the veranda the troupe conducted mock beatings, to the general amusement of the crowd watching from across the street. In a tyrannized population, it was the felicitous spirit of the imagination that first sprang free, giddy and victorious, in the dawn of liberation.

All morning, the Marines had remained out of sight. Whosoever should desire the city, it was theirs, with no guarantees, but no one was daring enough to assume authority, an act analogous to pinning a target on your chest. The Marines, following the pattern of the Eighteenth Airborne Corps and the Tenth Mountain Division in Port-au-Prince, were bivouacked at the waterfront and dug in around the airport behind head-high arabesques of concertina wire. The teenaged Marines who checked us over at the field's entrance were bulked up like camouflaged snowmen in their combat gear, melting in the sun. As we walked to the terminal down the unpaved road, dehydrating Marines sprawled in foxholes questioned us about what was uppermost on their minds—college football scores. Various species of gunships and transports were continuously landing or taking off; I wanted a laminated card, like the type snorkelers have of reef fish, to identify these exotic creatures.

We located the JIB at the airport's open-air "welcome center," although what its courtesies had been, and who, other than drug dealers, gunrunners and smugglers, had enjoyed the service these past three years, was anybody's guess. It seemed the jolly Marine Corps Public Affairs Officer would rather shoot himself than disseminate a morsel of news. Too readily bored, we marched back to the civilian side of the perimeter, our pockets fat with cookies and miniature bottles of Tabasco sauce from MRE discards—Meals, Ready to Eat, the modern army's version of C rations. Standing near the Mitsubishi was a group of men, two of them bird hunters on their way to market. One cradled a small blue heron with his arm, snared in the coastal swamps. The other held a pink flamingo, half alive, its elegant neck barely able to support the weight of its large, clownish beak. None of us tried to talk her out of it. Susan bought the flamingo for two hundred gourdes. Twelve, thirteen dollars. At the right time and place—somewhere quiet and isolated, where the flamingo might have a chance to recover its strength—she figured to set it free.

Before gaining elevation and twisting up toward the mountains, the route out of town led us through a vast, flat expanse of sugarcane, the crop that virtually invited slavery into the hemisphere. Coffee, a less labor-intensive crop than sugar and requiring abundant shade, had saved much of the island's north from ecological ruin. Despite omnipresent cultivation, the sloping land was lush, paradisaical, luxuriant with citrus groves, stands of bananas and plantains, the roadside canopied by cocoa trees, coconut palms, leafy avocado and mango trees. For some time, we paralleled the course of a blue-green river, bare-breasted girls bathing in its pools, women spreading laundry on white rocks, young boys swimming in the transparent water, naked and happy, their slick brown skin diamonded with light. But because Haiti is a place where people are everywhere, a culture where solitude is nonexistent, we were confounded in our auxiliary mission to release the flamingo. In the back of the vehicle, it lay listless in Susan's lap while she held its head erect, and as I dribbled water down its soft, long throat, a length of pink rope, I tried not to think of how ludicrous we would seem if we were stopped at a roadblock.

Forty-five minutes southeast of Cap, on the dirt road to the village of Grande Rivière du-Nord, attack helicopters swooped low overhead, casting dragon shadows on the green hillsides, rising and dipping with the contour of the land. There's going to be trouble, we said to ourselves, knowing only that teams of Marines were doing quick-strikes throughout the northern countryside, disarming the caserns. We were moving through a war zone without the war—more than an exercise, less than combat—an ill-defined game between superior American forces and a mercurial network of inept terrorists holding a nation hostage.

Something strange was happening as we entered GR du-Nord, but we couldn't tell quite what. The street suddenly swarmed with agitated townspeople—a confused crowd not yet cohered into the common purpose of a demonstration. Beyond the business district, we turned gradually uphill into the central plaza—a tranquil park shaded by towering hardwoods. At its high end was a promenade; behind it, from left to right, a rectory separated by a wall from the yellow casern, and then a cathedral. Until now I had not seen Haitian soldiers in uniform, but here they were, perhaps a dozen poised on the veranda of the garrison. An officer was on hand, wearing his peaked cap and sunglasses, seemingly in repose (yet nevertheless imposing) in the driver's seat of a new sport utility vehicle, parked out of the sun. Captain Yvonne Jean-Jacques, commander of the FADH garrison here in historically rebellious Grande Rivière du-Nord, was an alumnus of the U.S. Army's School of the Americas at Fort Benning, Georgia, where despite other intentions, many a guest murderer has improved his technique.

How's the weather? we asked, and the captain jutted his chin downhill, back toward the center of town. I turned to see a white Toyota pickup truck swing into the plaza, a Haitian soldier at the wheel but its bed packed with Marines, who were not at their friendliest. Scornful, with ample sighs of persecution, Captain Jean-Jacques explained: "We have been *disarmé*." The Marines had come only a short time before in their helicopters, emptied the casern's arsenal, stacked the weapons in the Toyota, and ordered one of the captain's subordinates to drive them back to the landing zone. The garrison had been left with only sidearms. "To defend ourselves," the captain spat, then smiled sardonically. "To defend ourselves!" he repeated, making sure we shared the joke. From the center of town, the sound of chanting resonated up the hill to where we stood, the beginning of a *manifestation*.

"You're not worried?" we asked.

"These people li-like me," he said. Captain Jean-Jacques's upbeat arrogance was fascinating—the soldiers had taken his bullets but left him his balls. He was a little wired, stuttering in English. "They-they-they respect me. There's no problem." (*Pwobwem* is how Haitians pronounced this word—like Elmer Fudd. *Pas pwobwem*: No problem.)

The stone-faced Marines escorted the FADH driver back to the relative safety of the casern, hopped out of the rear of the truck, and moved briskly back down the slope toward town, spinning warily, prepared to open fire. Nothing was out of bounds in Haiti, and what *we* were doing now struck me as patently insane—trotting alongside extremely edgy combat-ready soldiers as they plowed through a nascent riot toward their landing zone, we engaged them in banal chitchat: *Hey there, where you from? Where you going? How old are you, man?*

One moment they seemed invincible, then their vulnerability began to scare you. An idiot with an M-1 could take any one of them down, and then there'd be death as far as the eye could see. Death's proximity, its kinetic crackle, was deafening, and this wouldn't be the last time I would suddenly awake to the obvious in the experiential world—in this case, three Cobra gunships circling directly overhead, so much an integral part of the sensory texture of events that I had failed to notice them covering the Marines' retreat. We broke into an opening, a soccer field protected by still more Marines, down on one knee and aiming at the crowd. The foot patrol sprinted ahead to a waiting CH-53, and one by one the troops on the perimeter disappeared up its ramp until the last defender was aboard, the machine lifted off, and we were suddenly, alarmingly, alone with a cityful of well-incited citizens, dancing and singing as if this were how they planned to dance and sing on the graves of the FADH, the dozen or so who remained in the casern, disarmed, with nowhere else to go.

In the throb and swell of the *manifestation,* I became separated from Susan, Ed, and Gary and found myself another anonymous human particle in the universal muddle, unable to extricate my body from the slow but inexorable flow backward toward the center. This was Lavalas unbound, the zombi resurrected. Like bandits, people tied bandannas below their eyes against the dust storm of their stamping feet. Now there were drummers, now the forest of celebration sprouted the leafy branches called *koujei,* the symbols of renewal, and someone glued a poster of Aristide to the stanchion in the middle of the town's crossroads. The crowd generated its own corporeal heat, and like everyone else, I poured sweat, my senses drugged by the humid swelter of flesh, and I truly dreaded the power that was beckoning us toward the hill, the seductive force of vengeance, which was God's very own romance with evil.

But what in fact happened was this:

The demonstration parted ranks and closed again around a pickup truck nudging its way stoically toward the plaza and its cathedral. Standing erect in the back of the truck, six men in business suits balanced, on the roof of the cab, a coffin upholstered in iridescent blue velvet, gripping its handles tight to keep it from bouncing off and catapulting into the street. Guerrilla theater, I thought for a moment, but no, someone had

died, someone was being buried, such was fate. With this, as on many occasions in Haiti, death took life in tow.

Together and indivisible, the funeral and the *manifestation* spilled into
the plaza in a jumble of anguish and ecstasy, a confusion of mourners and
celebrants, of burial and resurrection, requiem and carnival. I clawed my
way, finally, to the now dented roof of the Mitsubishi, which stood like a
boulder in a current, and watched the outlandish casket carried up the
wide steps of the church.

The drums ceased, replaced by the wails and shrieks of grief echoing
within the vault of the cathedral, the church bell clanged without restraint, and everyone began to Congo dance (a style of rhythmic steps an
American during the 1920s occupation had described as "petulant, hacking, hysterical"). The demonstrators shifted left, directing their attention
toward the casern, daring to approach, singing taunts at the FADH soldiers lined up along the veranda who, in either contempt or fear or both,
turned their backs on the citizens of Grande Rivière du-Nord. With marvelous impudence, the crowd danced for some time in front of the military headquarters before withdrawing back toward the cathedral. For my
own sake and theirs, I rejoiced that nothing bad was going to happen, that
this was a great uncapping of the silence held tight within the Haitian
people for so many years, a ritual of catharsis that uplifted and restored—
but restored to what, no one could yet imagine.

Gary, Ed and Susan had made their way back through the chaos and
hauled themselves up atop the vehicle, which we were slowly destroying.
Captain Jean-Jacques, still in his vehicle, had been biding his time
throughout the affair, but now he stepped out and waded into the throng.
The people challenged him: "Why couldn't we protest before?"

"It's different now," he said wryly, and smiled, a comedian. Then he ad-
monished them, his children, to be good, and I wondered if he and his
men would survive the night.

When we climbed back into the Mitsubishi, we discovered what we
had half expected. The flamingo was dead, a small tragedy that we managed to make surreal, a pathetic gag. On the road out of town, we had a
hell of a time—we frightened people—trying to give the bird away. A carload of whites coming suddenly to a stop, Ed holding the big floppy
flamingo out the window . . . people just took off. Finally, we pulled up
next to a stoop-backed old woman, toothless and frail. Gary called her

over. "Are you hungry, grandmother?" *Oui.* "Would you like something to cook in your stew pot?" *Oui.* She took the flamingo, the color of a little girl's purse, and hobbled onward with the bird tucked under her arm.

IMMACULATE INVASION

In Cap Haïtien, we checkpointed through to the wharf where Marine command and control had nailed up its shingle. What do you want to call this event, this thing the USMC is doing in Haiti? we asked Colonel John McGyre, who met with us in a communication post tented with camouflage netting. Its proper name, said the colonel, was an "administrative landing." So . . . who are you administering? The elected mayor had been in hiding since the coup. Except for one fool, the entire FADH garrison had followed its man Josephat into the ether.

Yeah, there's a void, McGyre admitted. He had spent much of the week trying to locate the Haitians in charge of the city's defunct power and water systems, but they were all allegedly in Port-au-Prince. This morning, the de facto mayor had told him, *Colonel, you're the government here,* which was a rotten turn, actually, since the Marine Corps had never bothered to develop an especially nuanced or civically applicable definition of authority. Neither had they given much thought to the stagecraft of politics or to the art of the deal. They were high-gear guys, meatheads with brave hearts, and the colonel was loath to turn them into sensitivity trainers settling civil disputes out on the street.

Nevertheless, McGyre anticipated he'd be called upon to rebuild Cap Haïtien from the ground up, which was why he'd brought to the island the phone book from his hometown, as a guide for what a city of sixty thousand people needed in the way of services. There it all was in the blue pages, the master plan, listed under *City Government:* Water Department, Sanitation, Fire Department, Sheriff, Education, City and County Police, Dogcatcher. But here in Cap, all he could do was look around and say to himself, *Boy, this isn't the way it works back in Bryant, Texas.*

We left the pier to inspect police headquarters, where, as McGyre told the story, the firefight at the station ignited when a Haitian cop lowered

his Uzi at a foot patrol. There had been a daylong *manifestation,* which the
police had laughed off, even playing cards on the front stoop. The
Marines, though, had been prowling the street, suspense incarnate, getting high on the tension. One would expect to read "Sheer idiocy" under
"Cause of Death" in the coroner's report, if there was one, but the bodies
had been buried hastily and Cédras, who had flown to Cap the day before
with General Shelton, would have the corpses exhumed as a grisly gesture
of protest. Honor, Cédras angrily declared, demanded it.

The facade of the station, especially in an arc around the entrance, had
been jackhammered by automatic-weapon fire. A crowd urged us across
the threshold, pointing like Florentine tour guides to smears of blood and
ghastly handprints on the walls. These had not been noble men who died
for love of country and it was difficult to pity them, but their deaths had
clarified a central truth of the intervention: that regardless of the Carter
negotiations, no challenge to the United States armed forces would go
unanswered. Dead, the ten policemen insured the future, perhaps saving
many lives—Haitian and American—by example: a most indirect form of
patriotism. A legitimate representation of Big Boy Games, Big Boy Rules,
Big Boy Pain. But the message, we were about to learn, was one-sided.

A transistor radio cupped to his ear, a man in the crowd exclaimed he had
just heard a report of shooting in Limbé. We returned immediately to our
vehicle and sped south, delayed only by the celebrations, hamlet after
hamlet, that we encountered on the road. By now, late afternoon, clouds
had obscured the sun. The mood of the elevating landscape degenerated
with the light, became sulfurous and foreboding, and I no longer enjoyed
the sight, the hack irony, of so many white doves fluttering into the trees
along the highway. It seemed that entering Limbé, we crossed a boundary,
moved outside an illusory envelope of grace and safety and into a realm of
tangible danger, an environmental characteristic you could taste and in-
hale, with a numbing weight you could actually feel, there on your shoulders, in the muscles of your legs, radiating back at you from the empty
streets, so acutely did the city telegraph its stress and ferment. Con-
sciously or not, we had conjured trouble, and here it was.

Halfway into the center of town, we encountered a ridiculous warrior,
a very loose interpretation of a *mujahid,* Haitian style, who appeared to be

single-handedly guarding the road. Small and sinewy, he wore army boots, civilian pants, a lime-green tank top, and, looking as if it had been chewed by a goat, the remnant of a peasant's straw hat. Whatever he lacked in physical stature or sartorial costuming was well compensated by the panache with which he had adorned himself with weapons—an M-1 rifle in one hand, bandoliers of ammunition strapped across his chest, a dagger tucked into his belt, alongside two Russian grenades that resembled Christmas tree balls. Ed pulled over next to him and rolled down his window.

"My, don't you look lovely today."

"Cool it, man," I said. I was afraid Ed would antagonize the great hero, but he instead perceived us as arbiters. He was a beleaguered soldier—a FADH sergeant and grateful for our presence. Yesterday, he explained, the Marines had shown up unannounced at the casern and, with nary a conciliatory word, confiscated the garrison's heavier weapons—mortars, fragmentation grenades, automatic rifles, et cetera—and vanished back to Cap Haïtien. Naturally, this created problems. An unruly crowd formed, provoked by Lavalas radicals and hooligans, of which Limbé had plenty. The crowd turned into a mob, the mob attempted to *dechouké* the casern, but the generous Marines had let the soldiers keep six M-1s. The FADH had fired back at the crowd, the people retreated, then regathered, newly emboldened, and charged again and again, only to be driven back throughout the afternoon and into the evening, until everyone was exhausted. So far today, things were quiet.

"Only a few are left, mostly officers," said the sergeant, answering our question about the rate of attrition inside the casern, and then he disingenuously summoned us forward into the storm. "Come, I'll show you."

He escorted us off the main road and into the center of town, where the narrow street dumped into a ramshackle and seemingly colorless open-air market, flanked on three sides by ratty shops, sorry-looking two-story houses, a Baptist church and its decrepit rectory, and on the fourth side by the vivid, mustardy headquarters of the casern, a rectangular concrete building with an arched but doorless entrance, casement windows, and a backward-sloping roof of corrugated zinc. Separating the casern from the marketplace was a shoulder-high cinder-block wall, a sentry post guarding a four-foot-wide opening that allowed access to the walkway and steps leading into headquarters. Parking outside the wall, we grabbed our notebooks and began walking into the casern, oblivious of the suction drawing us inward.

We were in an altered state, no longer capable of reading the signals. Perhaps it was simple resignation, muffled in the subconscious, or perhaps we had become so accustomed to the drama of the milieu that familiarity had glazed our senses. A harsh resonance energized the thick air, but we failed to connect it to the Sea Knight helicopters whipping overhead in ever tightening spirals. Indeed, we were unaware of the skies overhead and whatever forces seemed to churn them. The atmosphere I remember was one of hushed apprehension; in reality, the marketplace had become a coliseum of thunderous reverberating noise. Something was about to happen, but we could not grasp it.

In the gloom of the casern's spartan interior, we began questioning its huddle of defenders, an ensemble of enlisted men, officers, and, apparently, macoutes with too much history behind them to expose themselves to the mercy of the people. A dozen men or less—we never had time to make a proper count. During the night, the majority of soldiers in the garrison had stripped off their uniforms and abandoned their post. Propped against the inside wall of the duty officer's bull pen were four M-1s, a fifth rifle in our escort's hands. The room smelled of damp concrete, workmen's sweat, and fear, which seems to have its own olfactory clarity, like snow, and rivets the senses.

The headquarters' butterball commander sat on a metal folding chair just inside the entrance, pointedly ignoring the scene outside, the bad-tempered crowd that had collected in our wake. But his composure, you could see, was flagging, and he wanted very much to plead his case with us, the injustice and humiliation he and his remaining men now endured, thanks to the imperial presumptuousness of the Marines. "Who gave them the right to come here and take our weapons?" he asked, but his indignation was unconvincing, since his own generals had thrown open the FADH's door, and the alternative—a hard entry—would have been many times worse.

"Why aren't you in uniform?" we asked the commander.

"They burned our uniforms," he replied, and gestured toward the crowd outside, which, I registered with alarm, had clogged the ungated entrance to the compound. "They throw stones at us," the commander fretted, squirming in his chair. From the rear of the building he summoned Exhibit A, an injured soldier in shorts and T-shirt, an oozing circle of blood staining the crown of gauze bandage on his shaved head.

Then, *boom!* and all of us jumped a foot as a rock landed on the tin roof, its report echoing like a shotgun blast. The commander sprang out of his chair. "See," he complained. "They want to kill us." Again, a stone—*boom!* In a flash, the commander's expression turned from crybaby desperation to desperate resolve. The soldiers' eyes narrowed. I looked at Susan and Ed, their own eyes huge. An electrical bloom of adrenaline made me momentarily light-headed, a sensation quickly replaced by what I want to call Darwinist lucidity, which slapped me awake to our predicament.

"Maybe we shouldn't be in here," Susan said softly, stepping aside from the entrance.

"Too late for that," I said, the most I could say. *We should have known better,* I thought, mad as hell—and then everything boiled over. The press of humanity bulged through the open gateway, and a soldier rushed to greet the breach, swinging a machete with all his might. "Jesus!" said Ed. "He's really putting his arm into it." The roar of the mob achieved a terrifying pitch, a tornado of noise, and suddenly we were under siege, trapped in the riotous heart of Haiti's redefinition. Stones clattered on the roof in a deafening barrage, pelted through the windows, and when a grapefruit-size rock grazed the side of my knee, I announced, "That's it," to no one in particular and started edging backward toward the casern's rear exit.

My heart sank as I saw the soldiers hoist their rifles, saw Ed and Susan sliding into crouches against the wall, heard the command to fire, and the last thing I saw before I slipped outside was the clownish road warrior unhooking a grenade from his belt.

I could feel the concussive puffs of the first volley of gunfire against my skin. My mind stopped, but my legs kept moving me out farther onto the parade ground of the walled compound, as I searched instinctively for a place to climb over, unable to decide if I was better off inside or outside the garrison. The back wall seemed too high to scale anyway, so I turned to my right, toward a cluster of outbuildings, looking for somewhere to take cover and hide. As a second volley ripped the air, I turned in my tracks, realizing that I had little idea how to handle this. Then Gary was beside me, and the sight of him restored me to an utterly bizarre state of calm, as though I had been able to call *Time out* and make everything stop to enable the two of us to pull ourselves together.

"Man, I don't like this shit."

"I feel the same," Gary agreed. The shock in his eyes must have mirrored my own.

We'd been knocked silly by our fear, hopelessly plumbing the absurd like two characters on one of hell's more existential street corners. Where were Ed and Susan, why hadn't they followed us out? Before the question even formed on my lips, Gary and I watched dumbstruck while the Haitian soldiers flew out the back door of the casern, wings on their feet, sprinting across the parade ground without disturbing the silence that had fallen upon us, the terrible elongated seconds that seemed to preface greater disaster.

What I didn't know was that as the crowd scattered in panic, Ed, peering over the windowsill, was stunned to see American troops fanning out through the market square, readying their guns. Everyone in the compound was still alive, a Green Beret would later tell a Reuters correspondent, because Ed Barnes, without thinking, had leapt through the doorway, screaming at the Special Forces not to fire. What we next observed, however, was even more astonishing. As the Haitian soldiers bolted out the back, Ed popped out the front of the casern, his face drained of blood, his hands raised above his head. A moment later, Susan did the same, supernaturally pale, surrendering to the unseen, and then they both disappeared through the perimeter wall and out of our line of vision. This was a stupefying turn of events. Who for Christ's sake could they be giving themselves up to—the mob?—yet here they were again, turned back by an invisible authority, still surrendering as they came out back to find us.

"Where'd they go?" Ed called out to me, meaning the FADH.

"They're gone, they hopped the wall."

"Come on," Ed urged gravely, his chest heaving. "Put your hands up and follow us. We've got to get back out front. *Right now.*"

The Special Forces were in the marketplace, he said, stammering with excitement—a piece of information that did not immediately jell or enlighten. The Green Berets were *here?* Unschooled as I was in the unpredictable drama of military conflict, not to mention its etiquette, I couldn't fathom why it was we were surrendering to our own troops; but surrendering, I discovered once my hands were in the air, brought tremendous relief, akin to placing one's faith in a higher being. Absolved of responsibility for myself, I cheered up. The sharp smell of cordite hung in the casern as we marched back through and down the steps into a scene I had no cultural or historical reference for except Vietnam. Palm trees, soaking heat, stark-eyed villagers who spoke no English, uptight American soldiers fingering the triggers of their assault rifles. No reference other than Vietnam *movies*, I mean.

The first GI I encountered was a huge, and hugely displeased, Haitian-American infantryman, who scolded me as I moved past his position.

"You're goddamn lucky we're not Marines."

"Why?" I asked, watching him bristle at my stupidity.

"You'd all be dead."

Which begged the question *Why weren't we all dead?* given the script we were working with, identical to the one staged at the police station in Cap Haïtien, yet without the bloody denouement. But as much as I wanted to stop and process the day's incongruities, I wanted first to obtain my surrender, which would apparently not be forthcoming until I was outside the walls of the compound.

Where I went straightaway, into the marketplace, only hesitating at the casern's threshold for a queasy moment before stepping over an unexploded grenade—one of the Christmas balls with its pin pulled; a dud, I guess—that the dirtbag had lobbed into the crowd. Outside the gateway, an American soldier squatted behind the wall, poised to turn and fire back through the entrance, should reason arise. "Hey," he said amiably, nodding, and it was odd, under the circumstances, to be treated with such an innocuous smile. Nice guy, I thought, walking past him, with new insight into just how friendly friendly fire might be. A ring of SF troopers lay flat on their stomachs in the muck of the mostly deserted marketplace, deployed for battle, the quizzical look on their faces saying, *What next?*

"You can drop your hands now," I was told by one of the sergeants, less an order than a kind suggestion. Now that we were safely out, the detachment moved in to secure the casern, and for a few minutes, at least, the four of us were intoxicated with gratitude not to be flat on our backs in triage, wondering if the bleeding would ever stop.

We leveled off in our excitement, but still there was a skewed exhilaration, as if we were at a party where a bomb had gone off but everyone was okay. The war gods, however, kept pouring fuel into the engine of sur-reality. Suddenly the marketplace was engulfed in an artificial typhoon, as a boxcar-size Chinook helicopter made an unsuccessful attempt to set down in the inadequate space in front of the Baptist church, intending to off-load the team's gear. Soldiers tried frantically to wave it off but then curled themselves into protective egg shapes, the chopper's blades per-ilously close to a snare of power lines. A steady blast of grit embedded it-self into my scalp, my notebook flapped into the air like a white hen and sailed away, vendors' tables tumbled end over end, sheets of tin ripped from the market sheds and flew, scythelike, through the plaza. At the last moment before catastrophe, the pilot had the sense to abort the landing and lifted away toward the cemetery across town, and I found myself en-listed, ten minutes later, to head over there with the Mitsubishi to ferry material.

The sky blackened, and rain showers drenched Limbé, without signifi-cantly cooling off its emotions. During my absence, the SF commandos had handcuffed and jailed six detainees: two FADH soldiers they'd fer-reted out of hiding inside the back of the compound, two who'd hopped back over the wall to escape the unforgiving wrath of the mob, and two captured and severely beaten by vigilantes, one with machete wounds that the medic, JC Collins, closed up with sixty stitches. A fat macoute in a brown leisure suit was trying to ingratiate himself with the casern's new commander, Captain Edmond Barton, offering the SF a car. As twilight approached, the crowd surged and flowed at the gate, Lavalas at flood tide, singing and dancing with abandon, passing in weapons to the sentries—a shotgun, two ancient pistols, helmets, pieces of FADH uni-forms, canisters of CS gas—and by nightfall the marketplace was end-to-end madness, yet the Special Forces were in an almost mystical groove, beautifully composed even on this darkest of rainy nights, outnumbered, theoretically, a hundred to one. Or a thousand to one, depending on who you thought your enemies were.

"We can take care of ourselves," they said, no swagger to the claim. "Man, the folks around here really needed to blow off some steam—guess they had it pretty bad, huh?" "Man, it gets dark quick around here, doesn't it? How these people live without 'lectricity?" "Who wants to vol-unteer for foot patrol? Hold on now—everybody can't go."

Wow, we said to ourselves, what was going on at Fort Bragg? Here we were, your regulation-issue bleeding-heart media types, standard-bearers of cynicism, and we *liked* these men, and not just because they'd had the presence of mind not to reduce us to hamburger. Ambiguity didn't seem to cast them off balance or make them weird. We appreciate, they said, not in so many words, the complexity of difficult situations. *Shit*, we kept saying to ourselves, *these guys are from Mars*, and mentally we sat back, waiting for the sometimes treacherous and deceitful history of the Special Forces to float to the surface and gag us. *We'll see*, we kept telling ourselves, *we'll see*. But they had yet to arouse in us any emotion more querulous or troubling than pride.

In the darkness out beyond the compound's walls, it sounded like some major-league sports event gone wrong, the fans wilding through the neighborhoods. Casualties were being deposited by the gateway at a steady rate. The Special Forces remained in a state of high alert, whirling with esprit de guerre, which they seemed to enjoy immensely. As if it were a fun thing to do, one of the captains of ODA 311's reinforcement detachment— blond-haired Captain Bruce Rohn—announced that he was going off into the night to track down a presumed ally and a town notable, Doctor Hodges.

Hodges was an American who had lived in Limbé for thirty years, a physician and a Baptist missionary, the administrator-owner of the district's biggest, most reliable, and always profitable hospital. Hodges had also drilled wells to provide the town with the cleanest drinking water in Haiti and, until he got fed up with nobody's paying for it, had supplied the population with electricity. He was a world-renowned amateur archaeologist to boot, constantly scraping up artifacts to hide away in his barricaded museum, and in the process staking out claims to subsurface mineral rights throughout the northern mountains. One does not accomplish such things in Haiti without submitting, at least through charade, to the status quo.

You wanted to sit Captain Rohn down at a table, give him a glass of milk and a slice of pie, and tell him, *Look, killer, you've had a big day, better get some shut-eye*. It banged against my vestigial countercultural perception when nice guys went to war. Then again, this wasn't war.

"Why do you want to see Hodges?" Susan asked dryly. She had interviewed the patriarchal doctor several times and was disconcerted by the captain's mission. The doctor considered American journalists to be emissaries of the Antichrist. And his opinion of the U.S. military wasn't even that positive.

It was one of those SF things: make contact with town leaders, co-opt the local power base. Besides, they needed to score gasoline for the casern's generator, and Hodges, a humanitarian entrepreneur who had meticulously constructed his own little kingdom in the region, was at the top of their intel mooch list. Bad intel, Susan forewarned.

We drove straight north to Cap, pummeled by rain showers. There was a young American nurse, a Hodges runaway, at the Christophe bar, who whooped and clapped her hands and jumped in the air when Ed told her the Special Forces had taken down the casern in Limbé. *"Yes! Yes! The fucking bastards—I hope they all get what they deserve."* The nurse was AWOL, sick of life among missionaries, headed for the capital with a stringer for National Public Radio, Cameron Brohman, a Canadian up from Port-au-Prince, where he was employed as caretaker of Habitation Leclerc, the once glamorous resort that had been transformed into a dance school and botanical park by the legendary American choreographer Katherine Dunham.

That morning at breakfast, both Susan and Ed wondered if I'd yet bumped into Cameron. "No," I said. "What's he look like?" They chuckled, trying not very hard to keep from smirking. That Cam's quite a character, way, *way* out there. You'll know him when you see him. "He's here with Micah," said Ed. Micah was a Haitian crackhead Ed had once hired as a fixer before the invasion, another guy off the charts. One day months later, when I checked into the Hotel Oloffson, the topic du jour would be, Where is Micah's head? because somebody had chopped it off and carried it away.

I did know Cameron when I saw him. A lanky, rope-muscled blond strutted into the room and sat down on the other side of the horseshoe bar, nodding at Ed and me. He had burning eyes and a con man's charm, the face of a cutthroat surfer from Malibu, and a mouth like a furnace stoked with amphetamines. "How goes it with the Immaculate Invasion?" he asked, smiling wickedly. Cameron had christened the beast, freeing it from the weight of original sin.

FIELD NOTES

In April 1995, during an interview with Mark Boyatt at Third Group head-quarters in Fort Bragg, I asked the colonel if I could see his field notes and fireside chat transcripts from Haiti. Boyatt, making a grudging face, al-lowed that a field commander's notes were the rope that would eventually be used to hang him, but nevertheless agreed to provide me with a copy of the transcripts in his possession, dated from late September until early December. "Where's the rest of them?" I asked. "Still in Haiti," said the colonel, but promised the balance ASAP. When I received the second half of Boyatt's field notes, a year and a half later, the transcripts were heavily censored by the S-2s, the army's intelligence personnel, which didn't come as a great surprise. The surprise was Boyatt's willingness to hand them off in the first place—a command officer who would dare to stand, unprotected by the system, behind his words and deeds.

26 SEP 94

Cap Haïtien: Mr. Paul Hodges, runs airfield, 36 years in Cap Haïtien. Uses brick radio to commo with FADH.

29 SEP 94

Jacmel: Trying to arrange to escort Dutch food relief. Convoy from PAP to Jacmel. ———lady runs program. Says if we escort her convoy, which keeps getting looted, she will provide names of attachés and others who issued Uzis. She seems to know what she is doing. Maj Schwalm provide list of top 10 FRAPH personalities in Jacmel.

Cap Haitien: People are cleaning up town on their own. City town hall has pictures of Lincoln, Roosevelt, USA Bill of Rights.
—People have such high expectations: Food, medicine, jobs 80–90% un-employed. Disarm FADH and attachés.
—Press around: Time, Reuters, Harper's, Miami Herald
—Prisoners found: One 10 to 12 year old they took out and put in the hos-pital. Boy in prison for 7 months for poisoning his aunt. Team leaders checked prisoners every day, had cells cleaned. Need a judge to hear cases. Some have been there 2 years with no judge.

—Expect eventual trouble with Ton Ton Macoutes, Lavalas, FRAPH and attachés with weapons.

Limbé: Know about caches and cannot get there and also reports of beatings in outlying village.
—Attachés/Ton Ton Macoutes are anyone who has property. Aristide rhetoric has convinced people that anyone who has something is bad.

30 SEPT

Cap Haïtien: FADH lt. in civilian clothes was recognized by people, who started to attack him. He tried to pull his pistol from his waist and accidentally shot himself in the stomach. He died from a self-inflicting wound.

HERE'S MY ASS (COME BEAT IT IF YOU CAN)

We cruised the fuel black market, dozens of vendors hovering over their plastic jugs of gas, smuggled across the border from Dom Rep. A transaction customarily involved at least three entrepreneurs: while a primary seller negotiated price, another vendor would begin funneling her own gas, unsolicited, into your tank (which the primary seller must then pay for or replace) and a third would position a cup under the spout to catch and claim whatever's spilled. From beginning to end, everybody yells. Our diesel cost eleven dollars a gallon.

Understandably, we felt proprietorial about the Green Berets in Limbé and drove down to see how they'd fared. Doctor Hodges had met with them earlier that morning, wasting no time in accusing the Special Forces of decapitating the civil authority. With the head gone, Hodges had declared, the body is out of control. That's the way it is, the Top—Sergeant Miatke—had commiserated: "Whether it's good or bad, the established order is gone," although in their own self-interest, the Americans were trying to leave as much of the system intact as possible.

After the doctor left, Captain Barton had convened a powwow with the town's notables, at least the ones he could locate, in an attempt "to set these people up to be problem solvers." Twenty groups butting heads meant another Somalia, said Barton, and he was trying to avoid that. "What'd they have to say?" we asked. The captain deadpanned for a second, then rolled his eyes as he walked away.

During the night, the radio traffic from the SF's Forward Operating Base at the airport in Cap Haïtien had cautioned all troops to be on the lookout for a local mafia drug dealer, Bobby Lecord, one of Cédras's ninjas, the general's private detail of bodyguards. (The ninjas liked to wear black pajamas and jabber to CNN.) Lecord, said the FOB dispatcher, was alleged to be organizing drive-by shootings against American personnel.

The fat-ass macoute cowering inside the casern had donned a wig and a blue dress a co-conspirator had thrown over the wall and sashayed his way out the gate and into hiding. Four of the remaining detainees were FADH soldiers, who were deeply depressed to hear the SF order them back into uniform. The arsenal refilled with weapons that the population had grabbed during the past two days, although most of the casern's Uzis and a truckload of munitions were still unaccounted for.

Late in the afternoon, Susan, our deadline slave, had to report for roof duty back at the Christophe. Ed, Gary, and I thought we might check on Grande Rivière du-Nord, see if the pattern held. U.S. Command, we surmised, was being clever, sending Marines to each district headquarters to confiscate a casern's armory, quick in, quick out, letting the pressure cooker simmer for twenty-four hours unattended, then dropping SF teams into the ensuing havoc to "rescue" the besieged garrisons and manufacture an awkward alliance with whatever FADH remnants they were able to exhume. (The Marines, we would later learn, were not coordinating their raids with the Special Forces; the pattern we thought we had discerned was in fact fateful coincidence and seriously unappreciated by the Green Berets.)

The unease we sensed in GR du-Nord was not entirely overt. People were in the streets but disorganized, hailing us with a now familiar mix of reaction: our presence exhilarated, angered, and instigated. Captain Jean-Jacques and the remainder of his contingent lounged on the veranda of the casern in deceptive reverie, seeming to savor the end of a beautiful afternoon, a beautiful dominion. They were still in uniform, a choice now synonymous with a death wish in northern Haiti.

The captain sauntered out for a bit of palaver, his ruse of confidence intact, though beneath the parabolic peak of his officer's cap his dark eyes jumped, and you could see him grinding his jaw. I felt Ed nudge me. "Look who's here," he said cheerily. Three rifle-toting SF soldiers had sidled up behind us, bright-eyed with interest and, in this case, the tacit but strange assurance of bystanders that they're not really there, that they won't interrupt.

Their leader, Captain Trent Suko, twenty-seven years old, had wheat-colored eyebrows beneath a head as bald as a turnip; a photogenic farm boy's face; and a corn-fed smile as unwavering as transparent plastic. Yesterday, after the Marines and we journalists had left, Suko's team had moved quietly into town and taken up residence on the second floor of the church rectory, separated from the casern by a ten-foot wall. When Suko paid a call on his Haitian counterpart, he found Jean-Jacques and his crew sitting inside the casern with shotguns, Uzis, and grenades and—second time's the charm—disarmed them again.

Jean-Jacques was cracking us up. "Before the American soldiers got here," he sputtered in baritone English, "we didn't have any pwobwem with the people."

Suko couldn't keep it to himself anymore and started butting in, though he refused to talk to Jean-Jacques directly and instead spoke through an intermediary, who seemed to be me.

"Tell him I want him to resume his regular duties."

"You're kidding, right?" I said to Suko, staring at the smile that wouldn't go away. "How's he supposed to do that?"

The two captains couldn't bear to acknowledge each other. "These guys don't understand the concept of peaceful demonstrations," Suko thought it necessary to explain to me, though not for my benefit. "You have to have a graduated response. You don't start out by beating people on the head."

Now it was Captain Jean-Jacques's turn to confide in me, ignoring Suko ignoring him. "I was at Fort Benning. I know American soldiers. They had no respect for me, first because I was Haitian"—meaning black—"and because Americans think Haitians are empty-headed."

"He is still the commander," said Suko, unable to relax that tightly wound grin, while his eyes seared with threat. Jean-Jacques twirled in place, scoffing at Suko's specious proclamation. The problems in Haiti, he said, were being created by people from other countries. "I don't feel happy when I have to give my weapons to foreigners and I don't even know why."

"The guy's not happy," I said to Suko.

"Tell him the government's changing."

"Captain Suko says the government's changing." Two armies engaged in vaudevillian discourse over matters of life and death.

"In the meantime," Jean-Jacques hotly replied, "my soldiers are losing their lives, their children, their homes. I feel very sad. If there's a problem, I want to die with all of them."

As a matter of fact, there was a problem. "Here we go again," said Ed, his eyes dilated—all the better, it seemed, to sponge up the wildness. The population had rallied in the center of town; now we watched wordlessly as the lead cadre of the mass demonstration rounded the corner into the lower plaza, drums and voices like an approaching wall'of water, growing in intensity, and then a flood of humanity resolutely defied the gravity of its former powerlessness and lapped slowly up the hill in the fading twilight, a spectacle of petrifying majesty, rumbling the earth.

Captain Jean-Jacques folded his arms across his chest and planted his feet, the adamant professional, apparently willing to risk his hide to garner a little respect from the Americans, but his men weren't so foolhardy. They gravitated toward the tenuous security of the casern, and with spellbinding nonchalance, the three Green Berets took a step forward to confront the roiling endless crowd, clicking off the safeties on their M-16s. Ed tapped my shoulder, pointing toward the rectory, where the rest of Suko's team deployed along the balcony into firing positions. The horde swelled and crested onto the apron between the garrison and the park, a mere ten or fifteen feet away, luminously pulsating, churning a gauzy, diaphanous veil of dust in the air, which spread a sepia-toned timelessness over the scene, blurring the heave of bodies to a dreamlike softness. It was one of the most beautiful, terrifying sights I had ever witnessed.

Suko yelled to us, something impossible to hear in the uproar of a thousand lungs. He sidestepped closer to repeat himself. "Slide right!" he shouted into our faces. I was fascinated by the potency of his youthful composure, the kid-next-door sangfroid: *Now we are throwing the ball. Now we are killing people.* This, I thought, was the point in making soldiers professional—they didn't have to anguish over transitions, trip across the psychological and emotional and especially the moral gaps between peace and war, between living and dying. You held your ground and you survived, and everything beyond that was somebody else's problem. "Slide right!" he shouted. "We're firing left. You slide right when we do, toward the wall."

It was part of his duty, Suko explained, red-faced from shouting, to protect the lives of Americans, journalists included—a small wonder. "It's an explosive situation," Suko said with ineffable calm, "and it can go anytime."

But it didn't. In the eternal bloody pageantry of revolution and uprising, Grande Rivière du-Nord's populist mobilization was a triumph, quite literally, of cheek. The storm of noise coalesced into an intoxicating tribal chant, the chant framed the rhythm for collective dance, and the dancers edged forward three times, each surge terminating a few feet closer to the casern, at which point the entire mob pivoted, bent at the waist, exposed their buttocks, and repeated with glee:

> *Here's my ass—*
> *Come beat it if you can.*

In the days ahead, Captain Yves Jean-Jacques would become a beacon for deserters throughout the north, and the casern at Grande Rivière du-Nord a haven for many FADH soldiers and officers who lacked the nerve to stay at their posts. More than seventy men straggled in, and Jean-Jacques would plot with them to poison Suko and his Green Berets with "voodoo" powder, a lethal organic toxin extracted from toads and puffer fish. Eventually Suko would tire of Jean-Jacques's intrigues, arrest the whole casern, and ship them off to Port-au-Prince—a feat that would earn him a teleconference with President Clinton and a reputation throughout the Special Forces in Haiti as the mission's boy wonder.

So far, the Haitian citizenry had been playing a high-risk sport, each *manifestation* flirting with the edge, careening out over the lip of the abyss and then jitterbugging away at the last moment. We, too, were seduced by the daily arc toward violence, the centrifugal sensation of escape, of being flung out beyond the harm, yet however real, it was a burnout game, and catastrophe never seemed genuinely aborted or foiled but was deterred, rescheduled on the luckless calendar of the future, and Friday, September 30, would mark the third anniversary of the coup d'état. Aristide's supporters were planning nationwide demonstrations, widely expected to test Lavalas's oft-stated commitment to nonviolence and reconciliation.

"There are no people in the world as nonviolent as the Haitian people," I remember being told by Bernard Diederich, the godfather of all foreign correspondents on the island and one of Graham Greene's drinking buddies. "They've never been able to get rid of the stigma of 1791," the year of payback—the slave uprising, the massacre of whites. This was a nation whose revolution caused the Americans and French to stumble on their pretty words: of, by, and for the people. *Liberté, egalité, fraternité.* Slaves had made themselves free, but their freedom was unforgivable, and despite the accumulating evidence, not many people really believed the masses would behave themselves much longer.

The Marine Corps was going home, we discovered on Thursday morning, handing over its operations here in the north to the Tenth Mountain Division, the army's hapless urban-warfare specialists, recent graduates of the University of Futility, Somalia campus. We, too, packed our bags and began the long miserable drive south to the capital, to attend the large *manifestation* scheduled for Friday.

Stopping in Limbé to pay our regards to ODA 311, we arrived to see a Chinook helicopter hovering fifty feet in the air above the casern, attempting to lower an eighty-pound bale of concertina wire. The prop wash was blowing the marketplace to pieces. An old woman rolled like a tumbleweed in the ferocious gush of wind. The team leader, Captain Barton, looked as though he'd been reassigned to hell and appointed referee.

A band of Lavalas students had been conducting vigilante raids, collaring alleged attachés one by one and dragging them into the casern, "whipping their ass every step of the way," said a tousled JC Collins. In the detention room, the walls were flecked with blood. People scheduled to meet with him had been threatened, said Barton, who would have liked nothing better than to go out and arrest some of the Lavalas firebrands. "These so-called leaders," he snorted. No matter its affiliation, each faction in town perceived the captain as siding with the enemy. It had become clear that the success or failure of Operation Uphold Democracy was going to be carried on the backs of the Green Berets, and that the best way to experience the occupation would be to attach myself to an A-Team, whichever one would open the door and let me in. Barton was the first team leader I asked, and since he had no objections, I made plans to return to Limbé alone four days later. Then we headed for Port-au Prince, where that same morning Cédras confederates had chucked a pair of grenades into the midst of a demonstration celebrating the reinstallation of the city's mayor. Six people were dead, forty-three wounded by shrapnel. U.S. troops chased the attackers into a warehouse, M-16s blazing.

TALKING HEADS: MILLER

April 1995: Charlottesville, Va.

BS: Let's talk about September 30 for a minute. You recall our conversation about the *Harper's* article?

Admiral Paul David Miller: Yeah. There were several things in there that pissed me off.

BS: On the ground, there was all this ambiguity, everybody trying to figure out what are the Americans doing here? And now, on September 30, the journalists are coming down Avenue John Brown, and for the first time they're seeing Sheridan tanks. You mentioned to me that you brought fire equipment.

AM: Oh, yeah. I mentioned that the degree of planning had gone through such granularity that we were afraid that if we went in hard, there would be fires in the slums, and so we had the capability—the 130s to drop the chemicals—to put it out, and we had the big buckets on the carriers from the forest service. When does a contingency plan go into putting out the fires that were started?

BS: It's nice that you were thinking about the slums, but on this particular day, September 30—this is when you called me up and said, "This is bullshit."

AM: What did I say was bullshit?

BS: Well, journalists are coming down now; the Haitians on the street are seeing, for the first time, tanks. And there's your fire equipment too; it's parked right behind the tanks, not to put out fires but for crowd control—Fort Drum fire engines there. This is the day of the anniversary of the coup d'état.

AM: Oh, that anniversary!

BS: And the pro-Aristide forces are going to show that they can demonstrate nonviolently—very important for them to prove that to the
American troops.

AM: The pro-Aristide crowds, *crowds.* Not forces. *Crowds* are going to
demonstrate.

BS: And in fact they do, and it becomes messy. They pass by FRAPH
headquarters, and FRAPH opens fire on them.

AM: One portion of it became messy. One little side street. That's where
it became messy. The whole security thing didn't break down. There
was one little street—I watched it on CNN.

BS: I was there. A photographer I had worked with got shot in the head.

AM: One street! One street!

BS: Absolutely, but we're talking about perceptions, and also about what
sort of signal the military was—

AM: Is the photographer all right?

BS: If the USS *Comfort* weren't there, he would have died.

AM: Well, tell him to send me a thank-you note.

INSIDE THE *MANIFESTATION*— ACT TWO

Until the morning of September 30, the nature and intent of the American crusade was something of a riddle, its posture nothing if not oblique.
Haiti's unique pathology seemed to have stumped, or at least divided, the
policy gurus and strategists back in Washington, and in Port-au-Prince
the popular belief in rescue-by-superpower was severely dampened by the
U.S. military's ambivalence about its mission. More than twenty thousand
servicemen were now in situ, almost exclusively in Cap Haïtien and Port-
au-Prince, occupying not the cities themselves but their entrances—
harbors, waterfronts, airports—and shuttling convoys back and forth between the encampments. With increasing frequency but little effect (except for the incident in Cap Haïtien), foot patrols, and then motorized
platoons, had begun to probe into the city in a show of force, but the state-

ments were too localized and transient, and the bigger show remained meek and halfhearted, seemingly without a macrocosmic purpose. Which is to say, the signs of improvement in Port-au-Prince were too subtle to recognize and the situation was basically unchanged. As interventions go, this one, so far, was another Hamlet gig.

Descending Avenue John Brown from Pétionville into the city, however, Susan and I were quickly required to think otherwise. Port-au-Prince was definitely occupied, bloated with tension, and the objective of the U.S. military now seemed rather conclusive—to protect the well-heeled elites up on the mountainside from the wrath of a million poor people in the slums below, whom the troops had ostensibly come to liberate. Driving off the slope separating the privileged heights from the rotting commercial center of the city, we came to a halt at the first intersection, our way blocked by three Sheridan tanks nested in concertina wire, fortifying a checkpoint barricade. Tanks on urban street corners have a mammoth and sinister presence, in this instance lovingly articulated by the inscriptions I saw painted on cannon barrels: BAD KARMA. HOUSE OF PAIN. Nonsense ended right here. Parked off to the side were two fire engines from Fort Drum, New York, home of General Meade and his Tenth Mountain Division. Meade was now the field commander of Operation Uphold Democracy, taking over from General Shelton and his Eighteenth Airborne Corps.

A dozen blocks farther down the avenue, we were waved past another tank position, and after that nothing—no checkpoints, no troops. In the volatile heart of the city, no security beyond that which the U.S. command had deluded itself into believing the Haitian police force would provide. *Deluded,* however, was perhaps an incorrect characterization. From the looks of it, the American military, ever resistant to finding itself caught in the middle of Haitian-on-Haitian violence—vis-à-vis Somalia—had decided that today in Port-au-Prince hell would break loose, the masses were bound to rampage, and that to attempt to prevent the tempest was imprudent but to contain it divine, so they had cordoned off the city, dividing it unabashedly between the haves and have-nots, and were waiting for the place to blow.

Along the waterfront and its row of warehouses, a crowd of several hundred looters were ripping apart a Cash & Carry wholesaler owned by a Cédras bodyguard. In the middle of this frenzy, a Reuters film crew stood on the roof of their four-wheel-drive vehicle, casually going about their business, the looters as compliant as movie extras. This went on tediously for hours, every network in town swinging by for footage, each celluloid loop identical (pillage by nature being repetitious), until it seemed to stateside audiences that the capital was being torn apart top to bottom.

Downtown, at the Basilica of Notre Dame, the national cathedral, after a requiem mass in remembrance of the four to five thousand people murdered throughout Haiti during three years of military rule, the pro-Aristide demonstration would begin its march across town to the city cemetery, to release a cage of white doves, symbols of peace and reconciliation.

"*Veye yo*"—Be on guard—the crowd milling on the cathedral steps advised one another. In the aftermath of the *dechoukaj*, attachés had developed an especially wicked habit of assassinating Aristide's flock during, or immediately following, church services. Lavalas marshals frisked us as we passed through the doors. In the pulpit, a priest gazed out through a thicket of hand-held boom microphones. A herd of cameramen prowled the aisles, their attention flitting from bloom to bloom in a garden of imagery. Instead of incense, I smelled whiffs of sewage leaking in from the street. Undercover security agents on loan from various embassies were posted at strategic points throughout the pillared hall, whispering into their shirt collars.

A young man distributed handouts urging the establishment of a truth commission. A tiny peasant woman, wearing a simple housedress and a camouflage head scarf, threaded her way down the central aisle, carrying a placard heartbreakingly constructed with a piece of cardboard box and packing-crate sticks. Pasted to its surface were pictures of her savior Aristide and of her two sons—one of them lying in a terrible pool of blood; the other at his funeral. A man approached us, an Aristide organizer who used to courier press releases to news organizations until one night someone came to his house and shot him at point-blank range. He loosened his necktie and, unbuttoning his shirt, showed us the visible length of his suffering, a vertical scar running from the bottom of his rib cage into his pants. In the back pews, a fellow stood up and let loose a long, piercing cock's crow, which was answered by the celebrants with a rousing cheer: the logo of Lavalas was a rooster, and cockfights, political or otherwise, were the national pastime.

I stepped outside for a smoke and noticed Black Hawk helicopters circling overhead. Rick Bragg, a *New York Times* correspondent, was there as
well and mentioned that he recognized some attachés mingling with the
crowd out front, posing as Lavalas supporters. What the people were doing inside the church would have gotten them slaughtered just two weeks
earlier, and you couldn't help but worry that not enough had changed to
remove the risk today.

After communion and a final benediction, the congregation, hugging
one another tightly, began filing out the vestibule to commence the march,
five thousand or so strong, only a fraction of what organizers had expected,
yesterday's grenade attack keeping many people home behind closed
doors. The *Miami Herald* team split up along the route. I drove off with
Yves Colon, planning to jump ahead of the marchers somewhere along
Rue de L'Enterrement. Turning back uptown toward the national palace,
we parked in front of the penitentiary, one block over on a street parallel
to the parade. A cluster of uniformed policemen hung around the prison
entrance, Lieutenant Colonel Michel François's men, directly responsible
for much of the state-sponsored violence in the capital and its environs
during the regime. Only now, as we walked to the corner and made a left
on Rue de Champs du Mars, did Yves fully realize where we were.

"Oh, shit," he said, frowning, "this is a FRAPH street." FRAPH's office
and adjacent hangout—the Normandie Bar—were one block up, just past
the intersection we walked toward, where it seemed the march had
stalled.

We slipped into the river of demonstrators packing the intersection,
which was about to become, in a few minutes, no-man's-land. Several
hundred marchers had already passed beyond Champs du Mars, but not
before a FRAPH thug had grabbed the cage of doves and wrung the birds'
necks.

Where the rocks came from I couldn't say, but suddenly the taunts
turned to stone and the sky above the intersection darkened with a hail-
storm of rocks pitched by brazen demonstrators. Many landed on tin
roofs, banging too much like gunshots. Then a more distinct crack
echoed, a real gun being fired. Yves and I cringed, seeing the bullet skid
along the pavement, kicking sparks. I looked up Champs du Mars toward
FRAPH headquarters and saw men with pistols advancing on the intersection, toward us, rocks jumping off the street like popping corn, and still
they came.

A burst of gunfire sent everyone dashing for cover. Yves and I ended up hunched behind a waist-high wall on someone's front porch, panting. "Look," said Yves, "let's get around the corner so we can talk to the gunmen." Come on, he prodded, but I told him he was out of his mind, that I wouldn't go, that I wouldn't let him go either. I began to shake uncontrollably; my reservoir of courage, so rarely drawn upon, seemed terribly inadequate for the situation.

How I hated being at that intersection, yet hated even more getting *used* to being at that intersection, on that block.

The demonstrators began to edge back to the corner, picking up rocks strewn throughout the battle zone. Like everyone else, Yves and I edged forward with them until, a few yards ahead, at the nucleus of the crowd, another blast of gunfire sent us running, panic-blown, back down the street. I ducked behind a tree to catch my breath, spooning my body against those of people who had beat me to it. On the opposite side of the street, the police watched the scene from the top of the prison wall, waving at us, shrugging. The crowd surged back toward the intersection, and now the firing was continuous, crackling down the street. The next thing I knew, the people had retreated so far that Yves and I found ourselves in its front ranks. Shots exploded only a few yards away, and I was swept into an alley by the crush around me, fifty or sixty of us falling like dominoes into a narrow darkness between houses. When it was quiet again, the pile unfolded, and when I pried myself free I was outraged to find a thief attached to me, his hand trapped in my pants pocket. I grabbed his wrist and snatched my money out of his clutch, cursing this poor fellow as if he were the most evil man in the world.

Turning away from the pickpocket, I saw a man being beaten to death a few steps in front of me. I didn't know who he was, and I didn't understand this, the spray of blood from his head as sticks smashed his skull, the hyena whirl of the mob around its victim, the way he faltered and fell and then leapt to his feet and ran a few steps and died. Then, like a gust of wind, the mob was pummeling another man, blood streaming down his bewildered face, then pummeling an NBC cameraman trying to protect him as a CNN cameraman pressed so close to the action that blood splashed across the lens of the camera, across television screens around the planet.

By the time I crossed the street to do I don't know what, the two victims were hyperventilating, trapped against a chain-link fence, the NBC fellow's arm wrapped around the bloody shoulders of the Haitian, who was trying to explain something—trying to explain why he should not be killed. Finally, the mob let both men go, but too late for the Haitian. He stumbled around the corner and collapsed in the street, dead. Someone told me the first man beaten to death was an attaché who had charged the crowd, firing his pistol, but then his bullets ran out and the crowd closed back in on him. I stared hollow-eyed at a combat photographer I knew from Miami. He was clicking off pictures of the other cameraman's bloody face, and when he saw me, saw how horror-stricken I was, he smirked. "So you wanted to be a journalist, huh?" If the mob had gone ahead and killed the network cameraman, I can't be certain that neither of us would have done much of anything about it besides document the moment on film, in memory, and move on, like buyers at an exhibition. Or maybe not. Maybe we would have been brave, stupid and brave.

Now shooting broke out all over our area of the block. Two people near me were wounded, one a boy who couldn't have been more than ten or twelve years old, who seemed to have been hit by birdshot. I looked back toward the intersection, which was empty except for the wounded, and saw a woman in a red-and-white shirt dashing in a crouch over the hot zone. There was Susan, skittering audaciously across the crossroads for no apparent reason, and suddenly she was at my side. I wanted to know where Gary was, since she had taken him with her from the cathedral. "They're whacking fixers," I said. "I don't know why."

"I made him stay in the car," she said in her whispery voice. She seemed far away and dazed, thinking about something else, and just as she told me this, we lost each other. FRAPH gunmen launched another assault up the street, firing away, the puffs of smoke from the muzzles of their weapons hanging in the air, and I saw Susan fly into an alley as I ran and dived through the open back window of another journalist's car. It sped forward, down to the next intersection, where I got out and was able to see that the attachés now had control of the block. They were trashing the march organizers' flatbed truck, hacking at its loudspeakers with clubs and machetes, shooting out its tires. One FRAPH guy wielded, of all things, a barbecue fork.

"Where are the American soldiers?" people the length of the street cried. The demonstrators carelessly reasserted themselves and charged again, and then the street erupted in cheers, because behind us a motorized American patrol had arrived. The vehicle stopped one intersection away, the gunner standing in the hatch of the armored Humvee scrutinizing the bloody scene, but in fact they'd made a wrong turn, this was not where they wanted to be, and so they drove off. People wailed at this betrayal. "The Americans and FRAPH are twins," people cried. It was too much for anybody to swallow. The soldiers, by their mere appearance, provoked a twenty-minute lull, the attachés not daring to shoot for fear the troops remained in the vicinity.

I had made my way back to the Lavalas truck, searching for Susan and Yves, when the fracas started up again, a man up at the corner in a crouch, firing his rifle right at us. I had no choice but to throw myself with dozens of others into an alley. Shutters banged closed as I sprinted back to where the alley opened slightly into a maze of shanties. I stopped there, afraid to go farther, unsure where the path would lead me, and finally inched my way back to the alley's entrance—no wider than my outstretched arms—which several kids had blocked off with a sheet of tin.

Directly in front of the alley, the street appeared deserted, but when I summoned the nerve to peer around the wall, there was the third member of the *Herald*'s news team, Peter Slevin, hurrying past. I kicked away the tin and hurdled behind a porch stoop wall, Peter ducking in beside me. He had just cut and run from another alley, where two young men had sheltered him (both now dead in the dirt, executed at point-blank range).

Deciding that the coast was clear, we stood up and walked briskly toward the end of the block, where we found Yves and a little kid getting on with his life, selling ice-cold sodas out of a bucket. Time out. We bought three Cokes and stepped around the corner, out of the line of fire. There was Bob Simon, the CBS correspondent, alone, severe, and silent, leaning against the wall, staring straight ahead with a fed-up look on his face. After a while, he went back out to the main street to consult with his crew, nervously checking the faces of nearby Haitians. "Are these guys okay?" he kept asking, his head swiveling. *Are these guys okay?*

The three of us finished our drinks and walked back toward the intersection. Before long, there was another flurry of shots nearby, so loud our ears rang. Cameramen hustled to their vehicles to strap on flak jackets, and then a kid ran up to us, shrieking through the tears rolling down his face. "They shot an American journalist! They shot him in the head!" he wept, and fled erratically down the street, side to side like a jackrabbit.

The news was too much for the demonstrators. There was a final clash. A ball of blue smoke floated to the street from atop the walls of the national penitentiary, where police had fired a volley down onto our heads, and then a lasting stillness, the people's incredible courage broken, its great heart defeated. The Red Cross ambulances arrived to haul off the casualties: eight dead, twenty more wounded. Lee Celano, a photographer who had been with us up in Cap, would be going out to the USS *Comfort*, the military's hospital ship anchored offshore, for brain surgery.

At the afternoon's military press briefing, a roomful of smelly, frazzled journalists collapsed into their seats. Entering the building, I had told a female PAO that an American journalist had been shot. "Well," she said, barely lifting her eyes from her paperwork, "that happens in Los Angeles too." "You left, man," one CBS cameraman was telling another. "You ran like a chicken."

Everyone hollered at the spokesmen, Stan Schrager from the embassy and Colonel Willey from the Pentagon. "Our mission is not to serve as the police force," Willey kept reiterating. Security for the march was the responsibility of the Haitian police force, he emphasized. "Who is in control of the Haitian police force?" a reporter demanded. Schrager shrugged and told the truth. "Nobody," he admitted.

"The mission today was to contain the crowd as they moved inland, to maintain a presence," Willey continued, undaunted. "Our intention all along was to provide a cordon. Work the outer perimeter. The Haitians were responsible for the inner area."

People shouted back at Willey, demanding to know why U.S. forces didn't respond, why FRAPH continued to shoot people with impunity. Transformed into words and images, the bloodshed was already on the air, being delivered stateside to the dinner table of national opinion. The next day, of course, the military's policy toward FRAPH gunmen would be reinvented, to satisfy the imperatives of public relations rather than principle. Stan Schrager's big mouth had something to do with it too—you can't have an honest man out front, one step ahead of the spin.

By Sunday, the better hotels would begin to empty out as the networks reassigned people to the O. J. Simpson trial, which had bumped Haiti as the lead story.

Later, at the Montana, Bernie Diederich happily recounted a scene he had witnessed earlier in the day at one of the Sheridan tank checkpoints. "They took down Boastful Bob!" Bernie said. "Made him get down on his knees in front of the crowd and handcuffed that son of a bitch." Boastful Bob, Bobby Lecord, had been nabbed with a Pathfinder full of heavily armed comrades, headed downtown to join their buddies who were shooting up the demonstration. Drive-by shootings, street fights, ninja duty, drug transactions—Bobby Lecord was a busy guy.

That night, nursing a drink at the Oloffson bar, I happened to glance up at the television screen during a satellite broadcast of CNN. There was the attaché being beaten to death again, and as the wash of blood coated the cameraman's lens, I was mortified to see myself enter the frame, circling behind the ring of murderers to sidestep the mechanical horror of their business, which was vengeance. My knees and body were bent, barely upright, in a primal crouch that made me say to myself, *Australopithecus*. I stared hard, nauseated, at the look of terror on my face and then turned away, back to my drink, ashamed, as if I had done something wrong, something hateful. If someone had stopped me during the street battle and said, *What are you doing?* I would have answered simply, the bottom line. *Well, we're running back and forth, and they're shooting at us.* If someone had asked why, I don't know what I would have said.

TALKING HEADS: MILLER

Admiral Miller: There were two incidents that caused us to review, and adjust, approaches. One was, I got tired of seeing looting in the stores on CNN.

BS: Okay, but CNN just stood there at one store throughout the day—

AM: [Laughs.] I'm glad *you* said that. I got tired of listening to it. So we said, Close that place down. I just got tired of listening to it. I don't know the exact state of play of the intel that they had on FRAPH before that demonstration. Everybody was anxious about what somebody might do with crowds of people. So the attention turns toward protecting, and controlling, the masses.

BS: You're not protecting the masses, but protecting a certain segment of society that—

AM: Nope, nope, nope, nope, nope, nope. That never entered my fucking mind!

BS: Well, you didn't protect the masses. It looked like you were doing exactly the opposite.

AM: Well, that's what it was. What looked like we were doing the opposite?

BS: If you want to protect the masses, why do you park your tanks on the street leading to the elite neighborhoods?

AM: I wasn't there. I don't know if all the tanks were parked on the streets leading to the elite neighborhoods.

BS: They were. It was a cordon. Look, when you cordon off downtown, everything outside of that area is up the hill, and it's where the rich people live.

AM: Uh, I think we might be victims of the geography of Port-au-Prince, okay?

BS: Okay. Nevertheless, when you say cordon off a city—and that's how the military was explaining it: we're to set up a cordon, right? to contain any violence that might break out. . . ?

AM: We don't want to contain it; we wanted to prevent it first.

BS: Negative, sir.

AM: Then after we've prevented it, then we can contain it.

BS: Absolutely not.

AM: By the show of capability of both— Well, I don't know what you heard, but I'm telling you what the— The demonstration we knew was going to take place. First, we wanted Aristide to send messages to his crowd to be nonviolent and to demonstrate in a very peaceable way and just to show . . . [Admiral Miller asserts that the commander on the ground was in full control of the situation.]

BS: This is Shelton or Meade?

AM: On the thirtieth of September, it's got to be Shelton still, I think. I don't know, I don't have the calendar, but I think it was Shelton. [His responsibility was] to work up a plan that put U.S. capability in the field, the field being Port-au-Prince, working and putting as much of the FADH police arm into the field as you could, but then to protect the yellow house, right?

BS: [Gesturing] This is how much they put there.

AM: Around the yellow house?

BS: None.

AM: None around the yellow house?

BS: Zero. Period.

AM: There were some out. I saw some on TV.

BS: The FRAPH headquarters? Zero. You saw them on TV after it was all over.

AM: After the demonstration was all over?

BS: After the shootings had taken place.

AM: That shooting was one isolated event!

BS: It was *the* event!

AM: But still, you had a million-plus people in Port-au-Prince, okay?

BS: You weren't protecting a million-plus people. And this was the only thing going on, it was the only thing scheduled to go on, and the only thing to contain whatever did go on. [Drawing a map] Here's downtown Port-au-Prince, here's the parade route, here are the slums out here, and here's the waterfront—

AM: [Pointing] Now, there's slums out here too.

BS: [Pointing] Well, there's slums this way too, and you had tanks here, here, and here, and here's the mountain above Port-au-Prince, and you had a cordon that went like this, and there were no troops down here whatsoever. Nobody was there [downtown] except the demonstrators and FRAPH.

AM: I think Meade the whole time was in a command helicopter there, to be able to call quick reaction capability wherever it was needed.

BS: Why didn't he, then? Because there was nothing else happening in all of Port-au-Prince except that. And if he was watching it from a helicopter, it went on from eleven-thirty in the morning until one-thirty in the afternoon. Why didn't he?

AM: There wasn't a fight for two hours there!

BS: The hell!

AM: What kind of fight was it?

BS: I was there!

AM: What kind of fight was it?

BS: It was rock throwing—

AM: Aww . . .

BS: —answered by gunfire.

AM: For two hours?

BS: For two hours.

AM: How much gunfire?

BS: Constant gunfire. Pow-pow. Pow-pow. Pow-pow-pow.

AM: Into the air, or shooting at somebody? A lot into the air.

BS: Sometimes into the air. There were twenty people wounded, eight killed. It was for two hours. And then when you go into the briefing at the JIB, after it was all over, and Colonel Willey wants to get out there and say, *Today's been a success from a military point of view.* . . .

AM: Uh, what's the— Eight people? Anytime that you have casualties, it's not a success, right?

BS: Anytime it can be stopped so simply, it's not a success.

AM: Well, it's—it's, uh—the "simply" aspect of it is easy, looking at it after the event took place. But because I wasn't there to observe it as you were. . . .

BS: Well, when you're talking about cowards who don't shoot at people with guns, that only shoot at unarmed people, if a tank was just parked in front of FRAPH headquarters, as a scarecrow. . . .

AM: I don't— Talk to Meade.

General Meade and his staff stonewalled my requests for an interview.

THROUGH THE WIRE

Before the night of September 30 was over, two more actors—American soldiers—were destined to appear on the darkened set of the national penitentiary in downtown Port-au-Prince. One, with a self-acknowledged flair for melodrama, would be dragging a lot of baggage—that would be Rockwood. The other protagonist, the handler, would be Spence Lane, the defense attaché from the embassy. The performance, more a backstage vignette, walk-on roles almost lost in the greater tragicomedy, would end in a court-martial.

Captain Lawrence Rockwood, an intelligence officer from the Tenth Mountain Division, had been raised—like his commander, Major General David Meade—in a family with a long and distinguished military tradition. Rockwood men had taken up arms against slavery in the Civil War and against genocide in World War II. History seemed to have a propensity for bringing, and keeping, families like the Meades and the Rockwoods together—both great-grandfathers had fought at Gettysburg, one as a Confederate officer, one as a common foot soldier.

Captain Rockwood was thirty-six years old and had grown up in Germany, Turkey, a few other places. Both parents were air force officers. His father, who had helped liberate a concentration camp in Czechoslovakia, took young Lawrence to visit Dachau and told the boy something he always remembered: that such cruelty, on such a scale, didn't happen because of a few sadistic people; it happened because of blind obedience and cynicism. At his court-martial, Captain Rockwood would reinterpret his father's observation in his own defense: "Blind obedience and cynicism happen when you turn values off to save your own career."

Rockwood had a master's degree in history, had openly declared a spiritual allegiance to Tibetan Buddhism, and often criticized other officers for being slack on moral and human rights issues. He wore steel-framed eyeglasses and was dark-skinned—the Mediterranean in his blood—but he was dark also in his moods, his morose sense of the world. Sometimes his family called him Gloomy Gus, and in the spring before the invasion he started taking Prozac for mild depression.

Operation Uphold Democracy was a mission tailor-made to Rockwood's twin obsessions—human rights and war crimes. It was enormously uplifting to watch the president on television explain his agenda for going into Haiti—number one, said Clinton, was "stopping brutal atrocities"—and know you were going to be there on the ground, an intimate part of this huge mechanism of redemption.

Upon his arrival in Haiti, Captain Rockwood learned that Meade had distilled the President's directive to a single goal—force protection. The captain applied his own commonsense formula to the order: force protection *equals* stable and secure environment *equals* stopping human rights violations. Proceed with mission.

He began to collect daily reports about atrocities being committed in the prisons. He also began to gather intel on human rights situations in the slums—individuals who talked with Americans during the day would be murdered later on that night. Intel officers were frequently criticized for keeping their intel to themselves, but Rockwood began disseminating his reports to everyone he could think of, issuing updates on a daily basis. The attitude on the JTF staff was *So what?* It's not our priority, it's not our job, he was told.

By now the Americans had been in town for over a week, and no one had stepped inside a Haitian confinement facility in Port-au-Prince. Rockwood paid a visit to the task force chaplain. It was the captain's understanding that chaplains had a duty to report human rights violations and to deal with morale problems resulting from soldiers witnessing such violations. The chaplain told the captain to keep him informed, but he didn't want to get wrapped into any political issue.

Frustrated, Rockwood began to let his feelings be known, telling other captains that he thought the mission was being undermined by the headshop, but they told him to chill, step back, and he began to believe that some of them wouldn't be unhappy if the mission unraveled into an embarrassment for the President. It broke down on partisan lines—anti-Clinton people were anti-Lavalas. The U.S. military had been asked by the President to go in and support a side it historically opposed. Haitian-on-Haitian violence left his fellow officers unmoved, although Atlantic Command always asked for follow-up inquiries on threats of violence against the elites and the information they were getting from their own people was biased against Aristide, the embassy claiming that the real focus for a Somalia scenario was Lavalas, the awakening masses.

There was no book of bad guys and good guys (despite the long lists the defense and intelligence agencies had composed before the invasion). Now there were only old friends and new friends. The FADH were "our" Haitians, they were our old buddies, and the two armies were ordered to work in a spirit of cooperation. Rockwood got into an argument with his warrant officer over the weapons registration program—disarming the FADH and its auxiliaries—the warrant officer saying it stinks, this was the policy that got people killed in Somalia. Focus on protecting U.S. forces, not Haitian civilians, the captain was told by his CO.

◻   ◻   ◻

Earlier in the week, a company of Mike Jones's Special Forces down in the southern claw, on orders from General Potter, busted into the FADH prison in Les Cayes and were stunned and outraged by its barbaric conditions. Rockwood told his superiors, "If we discover the same conditions in Port-au-Prince, we're going to be held responsible for that." The captain felt it was time to bring the issue directly to the attention of General Meade. He sat down and typed up a report expressing his concern that under international law and convention, American troops were in danger of being judged criminally negligent for ignoring human rights abuses despite the military's direct knowledge of such violations. When the captain came off night shift on the morning of September 30, the high-priority intel he had requested six weeks earlier from the Pentagon had arrived on his desk, confirming everything he'd been saying about the prisons.

Later that morning, Rockwood took his own report to the JTF's inspector general, who scanned it with consternation. Basically, Captain Rockwood had lodged an official complaint against Caesar—professional suicide for an officer with fifteen years in the bank. The IG asked if he'd prefer to submit the report anonymously, but the captain told him that would be inappropriate. Well, said the IG, you've done everything you could by the book, but anything further would be over the line.

Rockwood returned to his unit and confronted his immediate superior with a zinger—command was criminally negligent for sidelining President Clinton's directive of U.S. interests and priorities. "Get off your high horse," the officer told him, and Rockwood retreated to his cot, grabbed two or three hours of restless sleep, and woke up wondering if he himself could be held criminally liable because he had not done everything possible to save people's lives inside the prisons. Except for the prisons glitch, so far he'd been gung ho on the Haiti mission. It was the greatest moment of his life, like going through liberated Poland, except this time they had arrived at the gates of the concentration camps and decided it was none of their business.

The captain lay on his cot, meditating in a rank drench of sweat, and tried to calm the charge of emotions through his body. He sat up and read awhile from a Buddhist text, sticking on a pair of lines from the Dalai Lama: *It is not enough to be compassionate. You must act.* Rockwood's conclusion was inevitable. "I am personally responsible for carrying out international law," the captain would state at his court-martial. "That is the Nuremberg principle."

Then, by any rational standard, his mood went into a zone and turned weird. He rose to his feet and suited up in full battle dress, grabbed his M-16, and went through the wire, leaving behind on his bunk a disjointed note implying that he probably wasn't going to make it back alive. He would tell the court, "I was compelled to do what I did because of the moral and physical cowardice of the chain of command. Lawyers aren't executed at war criminal trials. Soldiers are."

Rockwood was at war, if nobody else was.

Outside the fenced perimeter of the JTF compound at 1700 hrs., Rockwood convinced a man to stow him away in his utility vehicle and take him anywhere in the vicinity of the national palace for forty bucks. By the time he was dropped off, the sun was setting and Rockwood moved west below the palace through deserted streets, disoriented and freaked out but unwavering in his solo mission. A truck filled with wary FRAPH gunmen slowly cruised past and then disappeared around a corner. A wretched fellow with a gunshot wound to his shoulder grabbed him with a rush of aggression. Rockwood pried himself free and fled into an alley to hide, waking an old woman unconscious on the ground, who jumped to her feet and grabbed him too. He spun wildly out of her hands and kept moving down through the mean streets, drawn by an inner compass to the gates of the prison. About twenty attachés filled the sidewalk, but he walked through their midst looking straight ahead and pounded on the door, which was cracked open by the warden himself. The captain made his little speech. He was there, he said, to inspect the prison and seek an accountability. The warden told him to get fucked, but Rockwood planted his boot in the doorjamb and pushed his way in.

The warden, Major Serge Justafor, and Captain Rockwood, both armed, squared off, the captain anxious he'd be overpowered by the score of guards surrounding him and lose control of his weapon. But the major, another Fort Benning alumnus, spoke English, and Rockwood calmed down and collected himself. First on Rockwood's plan of action was to make contact with JTF. Under the rules of engagement, they'd have to deploy people to come and pick him up, then when the soldiers arrived, he had only to say the magic words, *human rights violations*, and the Tenth Mountain would be legally required to seize the prison.

The warden became respectful, inviting the American captain into his office to phone his superiors back at JTF HQ. Rockwood had no experience with Haitian telephones, or perhaps he would have known better. No matter how many times he dialed JTF, he couldn't get patched into the number. Okay, forget it, he told the warden. I want to see the prisoners in the main cell block. The warden said, Sorry, no keys until ten the next morning. Okay, said Rockwood, I'm staying here until tomorrow. Then he marched out of the warden's office toward the infirmary, where he found about thirty prisoners, a survival-of-the-fittest situation, everybody emaciated, some collapsed on the floor, no longer ambulatory.

Rockwood naively asked the warden to relay a message to the CO of his unit, Lieutenant Colonel Bragg at the JTF intel center, and remained in the courtyard, patrolling back and forth as if he were on guard duty, for the next two hours. But the warden didn't call Colonel Bragg, he called Major Spence Lane at the embassy, explaining he had some lunatic intel officer camping out on his turf.

The next thing Rockwood knows, here's a pumped-up American in plain clothes—Lane—flashing a military ID in his face, playing the macho fixer. He jeered at the Tenth Mountain captain, saying, *You couldn't take this, could you? You let this Haiti thing get under your skin, eh? Shit like this goes on all over the world, don't you think?* Lane, who thought the captain was in a free fall and might decide to open fire, ordered him to unload his M-16.

"We dragged the American flag through innocent blood," said Rockwood. Whatever its truth, the captain's response wasn't altogether clear, given the moment. They talked for thirty minutes, the major explaining to the captain that the warden was one of "our" Haitians. We know how to deal with him, said Lane, and you don't. Out of patience, he commanded the captain to come with him, and after so many years in uniform, Rockwood couldn't bring himself to disobey a direct order. The major took him to the embassy, then back to the JTF compound and the intel hooch, where Colonel Bragg asked him if he understood the significance of his actions. Rockwood soon found himself in a shouting match with his commander, then Bragg, having had enough, charged his junior officer with insubordination and read him his rights.

"Do you realize you could go to jail?" the colonel bellowed, but Captain Rockwood had already considered that likelihood and wasn't worried—Lieutenant Calley had spent less than seven months in the stockade for the My Lai massacre. Bragg ordered Rockwood to undergo immediate psychiatric evaluation. The medical unit's psychiatrist gave him a bunk and put the captain under observation, talked to him, and the next day proclaimed that in his opinion, Captain Rockwood had an ethical dilemma and made a controversial decision, but his judgment was not impaired. Rockwood released himself from the hospital and returned to his unit, where Colonel Bragg, who'd been telling everybody that the captain was a "psychiatric casualty," exploded in a rage.

"Do you want me to put you in handcuffs?" the colonel seethed. "Do you realize who you are?"

"I'm a soldier," said Captain Rockwood. "But I'm an American soldier, not a member of the Waffen SS." You don't stop being a human being because you're a soldier, he argued.

Rockwood was forthwith escorted back to the hospital. Three hours later, his superior, Major Munn, appeared with an armed squad of soldiers, read out a list of charges against the captain, and informed him that he was to be shipped back to the States immediately.

TALKING HEADS: JONES

Lieutenant Colonel Mike Jones: I got a call from one of the teams out in Les Cayes that they were having problems with [FADH] Colonel Gideon. Colonel Gideon was a pretty bad character. I got a call from Potter, and Potter said, "Pack your shit. You're going to Les Cayes." He said, "I want a battalion commander on the ground." So I said, Okay, I got it, packed it up, flew out there in a helicopter with Potter, who gave me some guidance on the way down—basically, "You're going to straighten this situation out." Honest to God, I felt like Wyatt Earp in the Wild West. . . .

Potter said, "Jones, you're going to be in charge here, I want you to clean this thing up. We gotta straighten this thing out quick." I said, "Okay, I got it." He said, "If Gideon comes back, arrest him." He said, "He's a human rights violator."

Anyway, we got out there, gave the [FADH] garrison a speech about why we were there, what I expected out of them, and in the course of that we found some photographs, pretty damning photographs. People being pulled apart with chains, people being beaten. We went into the jail that day I got there with General Potter. It was the damnedest thing I'd ever seen in my life. Thirty-six people in a tiny cell, one guy lying on the ground with his spine exposed, one guy with a gonad the size of a basketball—had to carry it when he went to take a leak. Lice-infested. I've never seen anything like it in my life.

Had a lady come see me the day after I got there. Said she'd been looking for her husband for two years, had been there to see Colonel Gideon, who said he wasn't there. I had just drawn up a list of people in the prison. They had no system for feeding them or anything. The bottom line is, I told her, "Well, we'll take you back there and we'll see. I've got his name on this list." She said, "Colonel Gideon told me he'd never seen him."

I took her back there, and she broke down crying. She said, "That's my husband; he's been here for two years." Those type of things kinda make you think that what you're doing does make a little sense. Like I said, we were the judge, we were in charge, we told the local government what to do. I basically found the mayor and told him, "You get the judge, you get the son of a bitch out of here and get him bailed." I mean, he was in there for stealing corn! Ridiculous.

We got the jail cleaned out and got that straightened out.

At Fort Drum, Captain Rockwood was given the chance to resign from the army, but he refused. He was ordered to submit to a second psychiatric evaluation: "No acute distress. Very self-assured, well-spoken. Thought process clear, logical and goal-directed. Affect is appropriate to thought content. Free of suicidal or homicidal ideation. Cognitive function intact." The report also mentioned the captain's use of Prozac and claimed he was narcissistic. When the prosecutor tried to make something of this diagnosis at the trial, Rockwood replied, "I guess integrity has a price."

Three months after Rockwood, Dan Burton, a Republican congressman from Indiana, visited the national penitentiary in Port-au-Prince, a handkerchief held over his mouth to prevent his breathing in the stench.

In the common cell, about five hundred prisoners were standing in six inches of excrement, some with their feet rotting off. "Conditions were horrendous," said Burton. "Subhuman. The place was a living hell." The court rejected a defense motion to admit Burton's testimony at the trial, nor was any talk about human rights violations allowed.

On May 14, 1995, Captain Rockwood became a felon, convicted of conduct unbecoming an officer, sneaking away from his post without permission, disobedience and disrespect to his immediate superior, leaving a hospital without permission, and endangering his own life and the life of Major Lane. He was ordered dismissed from the service, pending appeal, fined three thousand dollars, and required to forfeit all pay and allowances. On February 9, 1998, Rockwood's appeal was rejected by the Army Court of Criminal Appeals, although the military's highest judicial body, the Department of Defense's Court of Appeals for the Armed Forces, has agreed to hear the case in 1999. General Meade, by the way, opted for an unscheduled retirement shortly after the court-martial; his successor threw out the captain's most serious conviction—conduct unbecoming of an officer.

Retired Army Colonel David Hackworth, the most decorated living veteran and a columnist for *Newsweek,* writing about Rockwood's court-martial, recited the old saying: "Military justice is to justice what military music is to music."

On December 19, 1994, soldiers from the Tenth Mountain Division finally inspected the national penitentiary. Conditions at the prison would become a top priority of one of General Meade's replacements, General James Hill, deputy commander of Hawaii's Twenty-fifth Infantry Division, who would be shocked to learn of Meade's indifference to daily suffering experienced behind the penintentiary's walls.

A lot of people I talk to about the case—journalists, soldiers, politicians, civilians—still feel Captain Lawrence Rockwood is a screwball. The Prozac, the Buddhism, hiring Ramsey Clark to defend him—not the stuff from which we make American heroes. But consider this: The prosecutors asked General Potter to testify against Rockwood at his court-martial, and Potter refused. The SF general had made sure that his A-teams cleaned up the prisons in their areas of operations. Under Potter's command, Captain Rockwood would have been performing his duty. Under Meade's command, Rockwood was a criminal.

"Please God," prayed a Haitian woman attending Rockwood's trial at Fort Drum, "let the judges see this man through the eyes of a Haitian."

WHOSE SIDE WHEN

Admiral Paul David Miller had told me: "There were lists and lists of people, and you could go to different sources to get the different lists to decide who was on whose side, but the difficulty was, Whose side *when?*"

The morning after the street battle and Rockwood's appearance at the prison, the city slowly decompressed, pulling back from Friday's terror. Over at the embassy, Ambassador Swing allowed that these were days of "emotional whiplash." Peter Slevin's fixer, Margaret, reported that the FRAPH hadn't slept all night; they were scared. "You can buy any FRAPH guy right now," she said, "and make him pro-Aristide." Hell, why not? The CIA had bought FRAPH, the media had bought FRAPH; now that there was a fire sale going on, maybe Aristide would try to pick up a few bargains as well. The U.S. military and the American embassy were already planning their own exclusive shopping trip, buying another pony for the circus.

Peter and I cruised FRAPH headquarters—they'd erected a jumble of half-assed barricades but otherwise were in high spirits—and then we drove to the Pétionville market, resupplying the apartment with beer and Pringles. I ran into one of the correspondents from a wire service, who told me of fabulous private sales going on up the mountain. She was buying antique gilt mirrors from an MRE's collection. The elites, neither shy nor witless, had added MRJ to Haiti's bitter lexicon—Morally Repugnant Journalists, media *blancs* with a chameleon-like propensity for blending into convenient realities, who never seriously questioned their own blithe patronage of the best hotels, the toniest restaurants, the hippest art galleries, and who relied on the MREs for modern amenities, social access, and self-incriminating quotes. Guilty as charged, to some degree, every single one of us.

Back in Washington, Aristide, slow to express his much-solicited gratitude for the "intervasion," had been hinting that Operation Uphold Democracy was a farce unless the U.S. disarmed the paramilitaries, the sixty thousand civilian allies of the Cédras regime, collectively armed with an estimated two hundred thousand operable weapons. The newly inaugurated weapons buyback program, its pay scale far below the black market value of reliable firearms, was a predictable joke, netting a few dozen pieces of junk. Somebody even walked in with a nail gun and the Tenth Mountain bought it.

The Pentagon stated bluntly that the Carter deal had preserved the potential for disorder in Haiti and, despite congressional pressure to withdraw, the army would be increasing its troops in the theater of operations beyond original estimates because of the escalating turmoil. With pressure from all directions, the generals made the decision to start raiding arms caches. The first major raid, however, would not be on the attachés or FRAPH, both still operating against the population with relative impunity, but on National Public Radio's recently unhired stringer-fixer manqué, the perpetually ripped caretaker of Habitation Leclerc, Cameron Brohman.

During his interrogation by military intel after his takedown at the Tenth Mountain checkpoint on Avenue John Brown, Boastful Bobby Lecord, one of the all-stars of the *Harlan County* debacle, had a hot tip for the soldiers who had thrown him to his knees. Lecord had a prank in mind, a practical joke he wanted to play on the soldiers and a loudmouth *blanc*—Cameron. The Canadian caretaker, Boastful Bob told his interrogators, had a Lavalas arms cache somewhere on the grounds of the old resort, where a horde of revolutionaries were being trained in guerrilla warfare tactics by an American commando mercenary, who turned out to be none other than retired Colonel David Hackworth. Hackworth, the military's homegrown gadfly, had been using the plantation as his base of operations while he covered the invasion for *Newsweek*.

Saturday afternoon, a Tenth Mountain Division convoy—several hundred infantrymen, Sheridan tanks, APCs, Humvees—rumbled past FRAPH headquarters through Carrefours and into the Martissant neighborhood to Katherine Dunham's thirty-acre compound: former residence of French colonial governors, botanic garden, failed jet-set resort, dance school, and, so the soldiers were quick to believe, a Lavalas terrorist training camp, with heaps of weapons.

The tanks maneuvered into position, the troops deployed behind the walls, while, inside the Habitation, a dance troupe practiced for an upcoming tour. Cameron was on his way back from a stroll through his own private jungle when he was surrounded by combat-ready soldiers. There was Micah, in handcuffs. "Who are you people?" barked the chagrined warriors to the dancers in leotards. "What are you doing here?"

"We don't have guns, we have drums," said Micah, Cameron's space cadet helper. "We dance here."

Cameron gave some of the infantrymen a lecture on botany. Others at the goofy estate led the soldiers on a treasure hunt to the decrepit resort's bricked-up casino and then into a *vodou* temple, knocking on the threshold to warn the *loas* they were coming in.

"Don't step on the flowers," the dancers told the soldiers. There was no arms cache, and Colonel Hackworth was already back in the States, excoriating General Meade as a Perfumed Prince who had plummeted the morale of the men under his command "to whale-shit depth."

It was time to close the distance between the bluff and the reality and commit to the mission's primary objective—Cédras out, Aristide in. Yet back inside the beltway, the administration remained wary about cutting the Haitians a break. The end of repression, one Clinton administration official told a *New York Times* reporter, means things can turn ugly. The White House noisily prayed it could somehow keep the troops out of the muck of day-to-day law enforcement, still counting on the FADH to disarm the attachés and FRAPH. "We are not the Haitian police force," said General Shelton, "and we are not rent-a-cops."

Well, maybe. But his men were beyond a doubt warriors, and it was time to let them break something. Meade, responsible for daily ground operations, had the belated good sense to let that something be FRAPH headquarters and the Normandie Bar. He even threw a bone to his second in command, Brigadier General Close—another micromanaging maniac, who seemed to think the most important aspect of the mission was how pristine his soldiers looked on television—allowing Close to supervise the attack. Lights, action, camera-ready warfare: one would think that the army of the future would be issued makeup kits.

◻   ◻   ◻

The raid was a cakewalk, given the terrorist group's résumé and its rightful claim to victorious precedent with the *Harlan County*. According to FRAPH's CIA-anointed sultan, Toto Constant, the organization had twenty thousand armed members, offices in nearly every Haitian city and town, and a hard-core nucleus of five hundred gunmen in Port-au-Prince. Whether Constant's numbers could be believed or not, FRAPH was a killing machine, and it was true that the FADH had issued thousands of Uzis, M-16s, and shiny new pistols to the attachés and FRAPH in the months before the not-so-secret invasion, when Toto had also threatened to incapacitate American soldiers with a powder made from HIV-infected corpses.

Anyway, on Monday, the Tenth Mountain boys took down FRAPH, and then the real fun—the perverse spin—began. The infantrymen followed a half-dozen Sheridan tanks down Rue de Champs du Mars to the white two-story building next to the Normandie Bar and started wrestling gunmen, dumb and dumbstruck, to the ground, flex-cuffing the *malfaiteurs* and tossing them into trucks. Inside the building, the troops confiscated a disappointingly small arsenal of M-1s, Uzis, pistols, frag grenades, nail-studded clubs, gruesome trophy photographs of mutilated corpses, and— a future point of great contention between the United States and Aristide's Haiti, since we refused to give them back—a mother lode of documents. Something about state-sponsored terrorism loves paperwork— the self-serving illusion that dirty work is just like any other business and one must tally one's successes.

Amazingly, someone inside the headquarters had had the presence of mind to phone police headquarters for help once the soldiers started to pour through the doors, and they came roaring up like the Keystone Kops, a dozen of them piled onto a Toyota truck. Within seconds, the infantrymen had them disarmed too, facedown on the pavement, boots on their backs, and rifles at their foolish heads. The cops who didn't take it personally were merely handcuffed. The ones who started to squawk had gray duct tape wrapped all the way behind their heads and back across their lips five or six times. Then the policemen were tossed into the back of an army truck and returned to sender, stamped with the misery of their enormous humiliation. The moment provided chief of police Michel François with an epiphany, and by nightfall he'd be well on his way to the border, seeking asylum in the Dominican Republic, feathering his fall to disgrace by taking with him the police force's pension fund.

However temporarily, the *Fraphistes* were not so fortunate. Although Toto had not been taken into custody, nor had his second in command, Shelton proudly announced, "We have detained four of the most notorious, the primary thugs, and with their accomplices, the number we have detained is in double digits. We will dismantle this attaché system, this ninja system, if you will. We call them thugs." But not for long.

One thing Americans seem to be especially keen on is rehabilitation— or at least its appearance. Before the dust had even settled over the FRAPH bust, Toto Constant had begun to mutate from leprotic plague into a seemingly benign form of democratic influenza. A few hours after the destruction of his headquarters, he went on the radio to insist that any weapons found in the building "belong to some military who go there." His second revelation was a brilliantly transparent example of pandering to the new sheriff in town. "FRAPH is a political party," said Toto, "not a paramilitary group." What a funny guy! But he had given the Americans something to build on, and they decided to host a press conference for the FRAPH commander down in front of the palace the next day. "Here's your chance," Shelton told him. "Either you do it or we'll hunt you down like a dog."

The American embassy set it up; Meade provided the security. Behind a perimeter of U.S. troops and concertina wire, Haiti's new spokesman for the democratic dream stepped up to the microphones and, proclaiming that "violence no longer has a place in our society," announced his endorsement of Aristide and his intention to enter FRAPH into the legislative elections. Standing nearby, Stanley Schrager, whose assassination Constant had called for only two days earlier, curled his lips into a smirk. Two thousand disbelieving Haitians pressed against the security perimeter and screamed.

TALKING HEADS: SCHRAGER

BS: Why such support for FRAPH?
Stanley Schrager: Aw, that was always overblown. There was never any support for FRAPH unless it came from the CIA, and if it did, I was

PART FOUR

Operations Other Than War

We have good corporals and good sergeants
and some good lieutenants and captains,
and those are far more important than good generals.

—William Tecumseh Sherman

THE IMAGINARY COLONEL

However much spin the White House and the Pentagon put on it, however much they declared it was so, the U.S. military operation in Haiti was no more multinational than the Republican Party is multicultural, even though the U.S. Army had taken to calling itself the MNF. So I thought it curious, the day I returned to Limbé, that I wasn't the only outsider requesting Captain Barton's permission to move into the casern with the Special Forces. I arrived at the FADH's 53rd Northern District Headquarters about the same time as a French colonel, sweating under the weight of his rucksack. We both sat on a simple wooden bench along the wall and introduced ourselves. "Where'd you come from?" I asked.

"I'm not here," he said affably. "I don't exist."

"Oh. You're imaginary?" Flights of fancy were at an epidemic stage on the island.

"Well, no, it is not exactly like that," the colonel elaborated. "I am here in Haiti, but I am not *here,* with you. I am actually in Port-au-Prince."

He had a long aquiline nose, high cheekbones, silver-screen eyes, and a mischievous smile; very Belmondoish and endearing. The ranking officer of a French Army commando team sent to Haiti to protect his government's consulate and evacuate French nationals during the American invasion, the colonel quickly found himself afflicted with inactivity. After two weeks contemplating the unwarranted swagger of the U.S. high command and the clement challenge of their minimalist campaign, he made up his mind to disappear, north into the blue mountains, and attach himself to the Green Berets, the only soldiers really doing anything interesting on the island.

One of Mark Boyatt's staff officers, a Special Forces lieutenant colonel, was taking a chopper north to some of the ODAs; the French colonel had hitched a ride, hoping to get to Grande Rivière du-Nord, where he'd heard a young captain was making a name for himself, but the Chinook, low on fuel, was turning back to Gonaïves after the Limbé stopover, and one place was as good as another, as long as he didn't have to sit idle in the capital at the Joint Task Force headquarters.

Not long after the first lieutenant colonel left, there came another one, the battalion commander, Schroer, driving down from Cap Haïtien to inspect his A-teams. Judging from everyone's hardened demeanor, the colonel's inspection tour was unannounced, unwelcome, and gruffly prescriptive. Gone from the team members was any fraternal bonhomie, the effortless but surefooted professionalism, the cavalier disregard for the perils of schmoozing with journalists. Today, at least, the NCOs called me Sir, and I replied in kind, addressing them by rank, which was easy because they were all sergeants of one kind or another. All handpicked out of the regular army, elites, extroverts, they held themselves in high esteem and were outspoken to a fault, which made it disconcerting to find them walking on eggs, regulation-issue stone-faced grunts.

First, the lieutenant colonel dumped on the NCOs for having jungle sleeves—shirt cuffs rolled up above their wrists—an exceedingly petty dress code violation in a zone of conflict, especially in the tropics, but for older officers this obsession with uniforms was a legacy of Vietnam, the first sign of a breakdown in discipline; next thing you knew, they'd be slicing off *bouki* ears, stringing necklaces. Second, the lieutenant colonel fried Captain Barton's ass in a skillet: What in the fuckety-fuck was the captain doing—starting a nap clinic? Why wasn't he running patrols out to the other towns in his district? Why hadn't he told the people here to clean up their marketplace? It was a goddamned eyesore. Why hadn't he set an example by policing his own compound? It was a garbage pit. The detachments in Gonaïves and GR du-Nord were operating balls-out, while here in Limbé everybody was daydreaming. If the captain couldn't do his job, the lieutenant colonel snarled, he'd get somebody out here who would, quicker than you could say *I am a worthless dipshit, sir!*

Haiti was Captain Barton's first command in the field, and despite the callous set of his shoe-box jaw, he was stupefied by the lieutenant colonel's excoriations, which were fundamentally uninformed, unrealistic, and unjust. There were solid reasons for the captain's dilatory pace, more than even Barton himself was aware of. He couldn't know, for instance, that unlike the Special Forces in Gonaïves and Grande Rivière du-Nord, he was starting from scratch, in control of the only district headquarters outside Cap where the FADH had abandoned their post. Nor did Barton know that for a week the other units had been patrolling their outlying areas in Humvees, or FADH Toyotas, whereas Barton's two Humvees were airlifted into Limbé only yesterday (as soon as they were off the bird, he had loaded them up with men and sent them out on recon). And if you gave him the heavy equipment necessary to scrape up the high sierra of crap, the years of accumulated filth, in the marketplace, fine, but the job wasn't going to get done without a front loader and a dump truck, and even if you got it clean, you were never going to get the ugly out of it without rebuilding the market from the ground up. As for the mess in the casern, guilty as charged, but he needed authorization to hire laborers, because the team was otherwise occupied. Lieutenant colonels, however, approve results, not listen to captains whine about their problems, so this lieutenant colonel got back in his Humvee and left, after reiterating to Barton that this was the captain's last chance to pull himself together.

At ease and all alone on the island of his rank, Captain Barton glared into space, spit brown streaks of tobacco juice, cussed himself breathless. "Don't quote me," he said, looking my way. His own battalion commander was squared away but back in North Carolina, unable to protect him, and Barton was stuck with this asshole Schroer, in danger of being mickey-moused right out of his bars. "Shit, if I get reassigned, you can damn well quote me then."

Although he wasn't getting it from anybody, he deserved a measure of sympathy. He had grown up mostly in Kentucky, had graduated from Murray State and officer candidate school, then got a commission in the regular army before being ticketed to Fort Bragg, but no matter how much money taxpayers spent, you couldn't truly prepare an American soldier for a mission like Haiti, or a Kentucky boy for a place like Limbé. I kept thinking of the teenage MP whom Ed and Susan had bushwhacked the week before in Port-au-Prince. They'd been driving through a neighborhood and encountered a mob intent on beating a woman to death. She was a *loup-garou,* the mob howled as Ed and Susan rescued her; you've got to kill a *loup-garou* when you find one. They put her in the car and handed her over to the first American soldier they saw, this pimple-faced kid who would probably never be the same: *Here, take her, crowd's after her, she's a werewolf, she just ate two children,* you *deal with her, we've got a dinner date.*

The team's first night in the casern, an obese, smooth-skinned FADH deserter came to the gate seeking asylum for the night, a notorious bad guy by the name of Raymond Cadet. He made a lasting impression on ODA 311, not only because of his immense size but because he was wearing a dress. Miatke locked the guy up with the other detainees, wondering whether this was a case of self-delusion, disguisewise, or lifestyle, because he remembered reading intel about transvestites among police chief Michel François's top staff. Whatever, Cadet wore a dress in and, the next morning, a dress out. "Wasn't even an attractive dress," said Top Miatke. "You ever see a six-foot-three-inch, two-hundred-twenty-pound black guy in a dress who looks cute?"

But such incidents were hyperexoticisms, admittedly sensational yet not representative of the quotidian flow of Haitian life or the rectitude of the majority of Haitian people, and too many outsiders seized upon such anecdotal stingers to denigrate the singularity of Haitian culture, as if you could map the American way by profiling its Michael Jacksons. Nevertheless, Haiti loosened up the id, lubricated your imagination with the most startling evidence. "I don't think I'll ever be the same," Captain Barton would often say, "by the time I get back home."

Barton wasn't just any visitor, though. From the minute he walked into Limbé, he was, much to his distaste, the contemporary version of a Roman procurator, the sole authority over the lives of three hundred thousand people living under primitive conditions in a mountainous, isolated six-hundred-square-kilometer administrative district. This wasn't Pandora's box, it was her warehouse, chock-full of the urgent banalities and minutiae of civic dispute. The incessant blast of arguments started the first morning: two different guys showed up to claim ownership of a bicycle left behind in the casern—a classic Haitian dispute, Solomonic, deceptively trivial, and potentially lethal—and the variations on it hadn't stopped since, a twenty-four-hour-a-day yammer that was driving everyone, especially Top and Barton, nuts.

Anybody with a grudge against his neighbor denounced him as a macoute, sort of a local form of McCarthyism. The Special Forces had lost count of how many times the baroque rules of engagement had changed

in the past five days. And no matter what the army claimed about the lin-
guistic versatility of its Special Forces, the Limbé detachment's collective
knowledge of French (although it would steadily improve) was just about
at a level that would get them fed in a Parisian bistro. There were moments when you *knew* getting shot at was better than this—Hercules,
shoveling a century's worth of corruption out of the stalls.

How perverse symmetry was, with its sophomoric jokes, to be the source
of both beauty and irony. The casern I had moved into was built by the
Marines during the 1915 occupation, one of the outposts from which they
viciously stamped out the Caco Rebellion, routing the nationalist guerril-
las from the surrounding mountains and restoring power to the elite mulatto families, then training an army that eventually became the FADH.

The architecture was basic—a long shedlike structure facing the
marketplace, thick concrete walls, the front higher than the back so that
its tin roof sloped downward toward the rear of the compound. Among its
outbuildings was an austere mess hall; rubble-strewn, chicken-pecked
open ground clumped with banana trees was ringed by a high cinder-block
wall. You entered the casern at its center, and ten good steps would carry
you through to the exit. A jail cell and, behind that, an arsenal occupied
its right half. To the left of the entrance was a bull pen, where the communications specialist, Sergeant Jim Pledger, had set up his radios and
satellite link. Behind the bull pen was a small office, and in the remaining
third of the building, a small barracks crammed with four double-decker
metal bunks, rucksacks, MRE (Meals, Ready to Eat) cartons, and an
abandoned file cabinet. It was here, on the bare wire webbing of one of
the upper bunks, directly above Sergeant Pledger's own rumpled nest, that
I stowed my gear. Across the tiny, oven-hot room, the imaginary colonel
claimed the bunk above Captain Barton's.

"You don't mind if I move in above you, do you, Sergeant?" Pledger, sitting in the bull pen and fiddling with his radios, looked like a martial version of the *Wizard of Oz* scarecrow.

"Go ahead, brah. You don't mind if I fart, do you?" Pledger cackled,
then cut loose to preview our nights together. Flatulence equaled bond-
ing, it seemed, in the scatological clubhouse of Jim's uncouth mind, which
reserved its brilliance for all things electrical.

One of the engineering specialists, Sergeant Bob Fox, invited me back to the office, where he was conducting preliminary intel, sifting through the casern's files and a box of IDs—attaché cards issued by the FADH, FRAPH membership cards (two hands shaking in the background logo, a dove perched on each wrist over the words *La Reconciliation,* signed by Toto Constant and his cofounder, Chamblain)—gun permits for revolvers, and a score of drivers' licenses, two from Florida. A quick flip through the paperwork revealed an ominous tidbit of information: two weeks prior to the invasion, a Lieutenant Lumas had organized an anti-U.S. FRAPH demonstration attended by twenty-five hundred people in Plaisance, the second-biggest town in the district, a half hour's drive south through the mountains on Route Nationale One.

The Special Forces were still confused about FRAPH—were they here to take them down or protect them?—and I thought Fox might want to check up on this Lieutenant Lumas, considering FRAPH's psy ops campaign regarding the imminent death of American invaders. It's at least awkward, at worst disastrous, when journalists have better or, dare I say, more objective intel than the military, which should have known with some clear operational sense of the political landscape that the CIA had spent three years attempting to demonize Aristide and that the agency, as well as factions within the State Department, the Pentagon, Congress, and the National Security Agency, were working at apparent cross-purposes with the White House on Operation Uphold Democracy. From such cross-purposes come history's Vietnams.

Outside the office window stood a gigantic mahogany tree, and in its shade a peculiar row of five wooden chairs, nailed together along their backs, where Captain Barton and the imaginary colonel, who had already eased himself into the operational flow, were receiving visitors: delegations, complainants, claimants, job seekers, AWOLs, local dignitaries, scam artists, and lunatics. At the moment, they seemed to be holding an encounter therapy session with ten or so members of Haiti's own Generation X. Those guys, I was told, were the Committee of the Young, a local Lavalas student group. "They're trying to assert some level of authority," said Top Miatke, who obviously had no appreciation of the Haitian fondness for committees, "but they've been students all their lives, they're too good to hold a job because they're educated, and they're basically a pain in the ass, coming by all the time unannounced, wanting to be the big mugs in town."

I wandered back to the bull pen, where one of the sergeants was transmitting an encrypted report to the Forward Operating Base in Cap Haïtien on a miniature, olive-drab computer: *Dissident groups continue to lay low.* Outside the front windows, the marketplace was stuffed with vendors, creating the illusion of an active economy, a thousand capitalists hoping for someone to buy an orange, a sprig of basil, a bulb of garlic.

When the sun went down, the Special Forces cranked the diesel generator, the only electricity in town except at the Baptist hospital. In the open-sided mess hall, I quietly ate my first MRE—chicken à la king (warmed by a nifty little heating unit that emitted an odor like burned fertilizer when you added water). "Pretty good," I said with my mouth half full, when somebody asked, and the team looked at me as if I were some odd hillbilly child who would eat bologna and pretend it was steak. Slowly, I was accepted as designated audience, the dutiful listener, and team members began to include me in their sphere of conversation, direct wisecracks toward my end of the long concrete table—*long*, the length of three picnic tables set end to end.

JC Collins, 311's medic, told me about the previous week's meeting with Doctor Hodges, from the hospital. "Hodges thought we were just going to come in, screw things up, and leave. But we're not here for just a cosmetic screwup," the sergeant said wryly. "We're here for the long-term screwup, the whole system—we're going to get it all." At twenty-five, Collins was the detachment's youngster, and Sergeant Ernie Brown, at thirty-seven, was its senior citizen. Ernie was black (with Cherokee blood), had the presence of a big man although he was under six feet, and, by his own admission, was so classically good-looking that he couldn't let it pass without comment. "Mama," Ernie would say, examining himself in the side mirror on a Humvee, "how did you do it? *Damn!*" Tomorrow he would be in charge of the first resupply mission to Cap, shopping for sheets of tin, wood, and nails to begin repairing the collateral damage caused by the downwash from the choppers. The helicopters had blown over the walls at the soccer field; houses all over town had their roofs torn off and interiors rearranged by the blast from the rotor blades.

Ernie jotted down a list of materials. Someone reminded him to add chicken wire to stretch over the casement windows in the barracks. "Grenades," Ernie explained for my benefit. They could just as effectively close the shutters, but the room would be too hot. Later, when I climbed up over Pledger, onto my squeaky bunk, which was only a few inches below the sill of one of the open windows, I was just too tired to fret about grenades and took my behavioral cue from the fatalistic snores of my barrackmates. "If somebody really wants to do it," they'd told me, "it'd be the easiest thing in the world to punch our ticket and take us out. If you're unconventional forces, it comes with the turf." I was most worried by the scenario that most worried them—getting hit by sniper fire when we went out alone at night into the pitch-black compound to use the slit-trench latrine.

Throughout the night the radios fizzed; men coming off watch gently roused their replacements. Before too long the evening achieved a measure of serenity impossible to imagine in daylight, and I couldn't help but think that although the military, since the end of the draft and the subsequent fade-out of the war in Vietnam and its parallel universe of protests, had no more relevance to or impact on my daily life back home than Antarctica, it really wasn't so bad to be here among these people, these soldiers.

FIELD NOTES

04 OCT 94

Colonel Boyatt's field notes indicate that on October 4, he began simultaneously addressing all Special Forces teams throughout the island each evening at around ten on the SF commo network. These nightly updates were called Fireside Chats.

FIRESIDE CHAT

1. Force protection: The attempted attack on Les Cayes was fairly well planned: Grenade attack timed with power outage and shooters positioned outside. Lots of CS gas, which could be used to force people out of buildings into shooters. Watch the night attacks.
2. Critical to remove key leaders of FRAPH and Attachés identified as instigating violence. Pick them up as detainees.

◻   ◻   ◻

GR du-Nord: Cpt Griffin (FADH CDR from Cap Haïtien) showed up to-day unannounced and began talking with garrison. This is not good. . . . Cpt Griffin has been reported as having been one of the most brutal FADH commanders. He supposedly is a good friend of Cpt Jacques, the garrison commander, now in detention for threatening the Americans.

Missionary who runs a road construction mission (18 years in Haiti) has warned us to be extra careful because they are smart and devious. Info is that GR du-Nord was and is the center of gravity for resistance to U.S. They have a 2 phase plan.
Phase I. Resistance using Attachés.
Phase II. Use FADH soldiers. Info is that these people paid attention to Somalia and their plan to use ambushes to kill Americans and have home support in U.S. to pull us out.

THE LIMBÉ MUDDLE

He was destined for the stew pot, this rooster left behind in the casern, crowing imperiously well before sunrise. How shrewd of Lavalas to choose an ineradicable mascot, there every dark night and brightening morning, in every village, throughout the time and space of the regime, waking up the people, *zombis arise!*

By seven o'clock a crew of laborers was hard at work in the back of the compound, leveling the casern's private banana grove with machetes. One of the former detainees, medevaced to Port-au-Prince for treatment, had talked his way onto a helicopter headed back north. Now here he was at the gate, bawling to be let in—an impetuous homecoming for a man nearly beaten to death last week.

His name was Pierre Pasteur. He was short and burly, and his jaw remained grotesquely swollen, the white of one eye blood-red from getting socked. Pierre, from the moment he presented himself of his own volition to Captain Barton, had a huge advantage over almost every other Haitian in Limbé, despite the unresolved questions about his past: he spoke perfect English, carried a driver's license issued in Fort Pierce, Florida, and insisted he was an American citizen who needed the SF's help to get himself back to the States.

Are you FADH? I asked him. Attaché? Police? No, he said each time, quite disappointed I would think so. He did, however, have friends on the police force, he explained, and they would come to his house, where he lived with his two sisters, to socialize, and that's what got him into trouble, guilt by association. The crowd came roaring ahead to disarm him anyway but, finding no weapons, went ahead and beat him for the hell of it, beat him with sticks, rocks, fists, tore down the house and thrashed him to within a cat hair of his miserable life.

Somebody had said, *Let's kill him.* Somebody else had said, *No, let's take him to the Americans.* Now he pleaded with Barton to let him live in the casern, issue him a safe pass, and he wanted the captain to give him a job, preferably as, wouldn't you know, a policeman. Within minutes, Pierre had established himself as camp toady.

After breakfast, I found Captain Barton and the imaginary colonel out back under the powwow tree, their heads together in an already remarkable and unorthodox collaboration. The army hadn't the foresight to provide Barton with an interpreter, and seizing Limbé and the 53rd District was considerably more challenging, linguistically, then the language exams back at Fort Bragg, in which you could easily fake your way into the pass margin; so the imaginary colonel, who spoke flawless English, was heavensent. Although, as translators go, you couldn't say the French colonel was particularly conscientious. Not only did he seem especially receptive to Haitian circumlocution, but he loved to talk himself and often appeared to forget that the captain was sitting there beside him, "like a pig staring at a wristwatch"—Barton's words—without a clue.

"What'd he just say?" Barton would intermittently interrupt the imaginary colonel, who would plow ahead unconcerned. "What's he say?"

Ten or twenty minutes later, after intense and animated conversation, the colonel would come up for air, take magnanimous notice of his fidgety counterpart, and make a small effort to console him. "Oh, it was nothing. Zees man says he is very happy we are here."

Even if Barton had had ten times the men under his command, and a fleet of Humvees, his laundry list would have been ridiculously formidable: 1. Clean up the marketplace (to placate the lieutenant colonel: forget it). 2. Cooperate with the FADH (only there were no FADH now remaining in Limbé, except for a teenager, Private Joseph Paraison, who claimed he was exiled from Port-au-Prince for his Lavalasan views and had nowhere to run when the SF took over the town). 3. Rebuild a local security force (out of the general population, if he had to, said the lieutenant colonel, only Barton couldn't pay the recruits or arm them, so he would have to find trustworthy people he could persuade to risk their lives during this tumultuous transitional period for love of country alone, which, naturally, not many were eager to do). 4. Recon the scores of other towns, villages, hamlets, and outposts in the 53rd District, assess each one's security needs, and make contact with all the *chefs du section* (Haiti's infamous rural sheriffs, who had a medieval reputation, ruling their isolated parishes like private fiefdoms). 5. Whatever it took, no matter what the cost or who he had to kill to do it, first, last, and foremost get all his men home alive.

The military argot of the day separated the population of Haiti into two irreconcilable classes: the "goodies" and the "baddies." However murky the line between the two, certain assumptions and guidelines applied. For better or worse, and with the exception of homeboys urging the crowds to violence, Lavalas and its members and advocates were goodies. All elected and appointed officials were goodies, until proved otherwise. Because of the shootings at police headquarters in Cap, and their rampage through the streets of Port-au-Prince during the first days of the invasion, all Haitian cops were baddies (though in the northern districts this was a moot category, since all the police had flung away their uniforms and crawled into the bushes). At least in the 53rd District, all FADH deserters who persisted in their dereliction would be presumed baddies, but any who were willing to show Captain Barton an ID card and come back in would be treated conditionally as goodies. So-called attachés and so-called macoutes might or might not be baddies, depending on the available evidence, on who was denouncing them and why. The *chefs du section* the Special Forces weren't sure about, though they had some sense of their collective disreputability. As for the FRAPH, somebody up the chain of command was going to have to sort that out, but right now the SF were going after them.

It wasn't a very precise, subtle, comprehensive, or even knowledgeable reading of the forces at play in Haitian society, but it dared to clarify a mission that, from a soldier's perspective on the ground, was precariously vague. It also allowed the captain and the imaginary colonel to formulate, optimistically, a plan for the improvisation of a Haitian security force that, if they were all clever enough, would eventually render the American military presence superfluous, and everybody could go home. The gist of the plan was best expressed by a single French word, *ensemble,* and a single French gesture, a gathering sweep of the imaginary colonel's hand.

A mix of the old and the new, a balance of FADH retro-goodies and Lavalas proto-goodies. Barton and the colonel would select the FADH (if they ever found the nerve to return); meanwhile, they would prompt the notables in Limbé and Plaisance and wherever else a FADH casern existed within the district to convene town meetings, select candidates for a transitional police force, present the recruits to the population, and let people vote or somehow voice their opinion on their acceptability. *Voilà!* Democracy so raw you can almost smell its placental blood.

No sooner had Captain Barton and the imaginary colonel finished explaining the scheme to me than they were given the opportunity to float it before some likely participants, people whose fate rested on the success of this jury-rigged version of reconciliation. We rose from our chairs under the mahogany tree to shake the hands of the delegation from Plaisance: the huge, bald-headed, light-skinned mayor, a quintessential politician with a molasses smile, caressing us with flowery French phrases; the short, lean, dark-skinned FADH commander of the Plaisance casern, a quintessential martinet, sizing up the invaders through horn-rimmed eyeglasses. With him were two junior officers. All three soldiers were dressed—disguised—in civilian clothes, and how it must have disheartened them to be out of uniform. Everyone sat down, and the imaginary colonel outlined the proposal. The FADH officer—a lieutenant—bounced in his chair, waiting for a chance to respond.

"If you mix new Lavalas police with remnants of the old security forces," the lieutenant was finally able to say, his body language as animated as his voice was passionate, "we must sleep together in the casern, and there is so much hate, the Lavalas people will kill us as we sleep." Instead, the delegation requested daily U.S. patrols in Plaisance. Captain Barton could only sigh and explain he lacked the human resources for anything more than intermittent visits. In the meantime, Barton said, he wanted them back in uniform and back in their casern. Hearing this, one of the junior officers jumped to his feet—no need for the imaginary colonel to translate disgust.

"I don't think it will work your way," argued the lieutenant, "but if the situation stays this way, I will return to the casern. You should understand, however, that Haiti is not a civilized country." His other subordinate, a corporal, offered to present himself for duty at the Limbé casern if Captain Barton would give him a uniform. His own had been burned by a mob, he said, and "without a uniform, no one will respect me."

"If you come back and word hard first," Barton told him, "then we'll give you a uniform," but the corporal was old and stubborn and not ready to accept this condition. "No," the imaginary colonel interjected, admonishing the SF captain, "you have to tell them what to do. Instill it, not suggest it."

Turning aside, the colonel whispered to me, "The Americans don't know how to colonize a country—the French are the ones who know how to do it." The imaginary colonel had been born in Algeria, a blackfoot, scion of the elite colonial families, and had served throughout Africa, but we weren't going to talk about that right now. Before they left, the three FADH soldiers clicked their heels, offered salutes to the *blancs*—one fierce, one arrogant, one malleable. "What was that lieutenant's name?" I asked after they'd gone. It was Lumas, Lieutenant Lumas, who throws big parties for the FRAPH.

The petitioners were lined up, waiting for an audience under the leafy canopy of the enormous tree, which, during the tête-à-tête with Lumas, I discovered had a duck residing in a hollow niche at the base of its trunk. Next in line was the leader of the Youth Committee and a small, gentle-mannered young man who claimed he was the Aristide-appointed vice delegate to Limbé, back out into the daylight after all these years underground, and anxious to seize control of the town's affairs. Shortly after the coup, he said with a thin smile, the military had fired upon him in his house—"Thank God they were bad shots." Paul James, the bellicose Youth Committee leader, made his own bid for a piece of the action. Captain Barton snorted. "He wants money," summarized the imaginary colonel, "and he wants power, and tomorrow he maybe wants to kill people." Barton told the pair he had called a town council meeting for that afternoon, which they were welcome to attend. Inside the tree, the duck quacked.

◻   ◻   ◻

The town hall was in an advanced stage of disrepair, its ceiling and wood floor caving through in patches from both water damage and termites, yet someone had made an attempt to salvage its dignity with gray and yellow paint. The somber visages of former mayors hung on the walls, however crookedly, and its handmade chairs and benches were sturdy, arranged in a semicircle around a simple wooden table, where Barton and the colonel took the seats offered them. The mayoress, Madame Bruno, had the shape and disposition of a cannonball. The justice of the peace was a tall, frail, and elderly man with a missing leg. For forty-two years the head-mistress of one of the local schools, Madame Bazin was a paragon of bour-geois femininity, though her bun wig was slightly askew, her purse noticeably empty, and her position unclear. Unlike Madame Bruno, Madame Bazin easily succumbed to the flattery of the imaginary colonel, the smoky sensuality of his voice.

Most everybody else in the suffocating upstairs room seemed to be Lavalas, stalwarts or fair-weather upstarts, squeezed solemnly against the walls, and their schoolboyish presence threw Madame Bruno into a snit. She growled at the vice delegate when he attempted, insincerely, to give her a pro forma embrace. She wouldn't deign even to look at him, turning her face sideways and up toward an unkind god; nor would she sit until fi-nally the imaginary colonel seduced her with her own importance, and then she sat, but the chair inadequately contained her ample bottom and had to be exchanged for another, wider one.

"There is a security problem that we want you, the esteemed notables and elected officials of Limbé, to solve," the imaginary colonel began. Captain Barton clearly disliked his new role as military governor and sat impassively, M-16 propped against his chair, and let the Frenchman talk. It was spellbinding, his speech, his manner, the diplomatic charisma, his impassioned engagement with the moment, delicately but systematically milking the venom from the fangs of the serpent. Drop by drop, he drained the room of acrimony, until these bitter adversaries—the avari-cious past and the starved future, face-to-face as never before—were each mollified, and then he began to patch together a consensus out of the din of vigorous argument. Finally, everyone agreed—they would work in uni-son to build a new police force.

"We want fifty new police."

"That's too much," said the imaginary colonel. The notables worried about how much the recruits would be paid. "I don't know," said the colonel. "But they will be paid."

"No," said Barton, "they will not be paid, but whoever works well I'll recommend to be sent to the new training program." The notables asked how long the transition period would take. "I have no idea," the captain told them, adding that he didn't agree with command's position to make them work for free, but he couldn't do anything about it. The imaginary colonel, though, teased out their hope, telling them Captain Barton would request a clarification on this issue and solve the problem of who would pay them and when. Tomorrow among themselves they'd hash out some type of selection process, then meet with the captain and the colonel again on Wednesday.

"Now," said Madame Bruno, peering through the oversize frame of her designer eyeglasses, "we have beaucoup problems here in Limbé, Captain." She wanted a truck to haul town trash to the dump; the canals were malarial, so she wanted them dredged and cleaned; she wanted electricity; she wanted— Barton stopped her. Make a list, he said.

"Please, Captain," Madame Bazin interjected, pursing her withered lips. "No more helicopters over the marketplace."

When the meeting adjourned, Barton felt the impulse to sightsee, stroll around town; he'd been "too busy racking my brain back in the compound" to have seen much of it. Although he was concerned about putting untrained people on the streets as cops, he felt upbeat, relieved that there were no demonstrations at the town hall. He picked up a crusty old penny lying in the dirt and gave it to one of the small boys in our entourage, who laughed at its worthlessness. Despite the lush tropical backdrop, the desolation of the neighborhood we walked through reminded me of Aristide's bleakly realistic hope, the only goal he could afford: "We will move from misery to poverty with dignity."

Newly inspired by the American intervention, the citizens of Limbé were out sweeping the streets with palm fronds. "Bonsoir," Captain Barton called out. "Bonsoir." These people were "better than Africans," the imaginary colonel declared. We came to a domino game, one player's lower jaw bearded with pinching clothespins, the penalty for losing. "It hurts, it hurts," he lamented, slamming down a tile on the table.

"Bonsoir," said the captain.

Farther down the dirt road, a group of women sat on the stoop of their house, munching sugarcane, and Captain Barton asked if he could try a piece. *The American soldier eats with us!* The crowd of onlookers cheered in amazement, because the Haitian military, afraid of being poisoned, would never take any food the population offered. *Foo!* everybody exclaimed at once as an old woman bent down to tap Barton's foot. *Foo*— crazy. Madame Bazin, who had accompanied us, turned away and chupsed her tongue, as you might imagine she had every day of her life. She had the bearing of a wasted monarch; her black pumps were worn and dusty, and she carried a Kleenex in one hand, her empty purse in the other. "I wanted to be a nun," she proclaimed out of the blue, "but the nuns said I had too much character."

At the edge of town, the road dwindled to a footpath, and we went on, Pied Pipers, shadowed by a pack of adults and playful children; a jump-about Marxist, whom the imaginary colonel advised to stay quiet and calm until after the fifteenth; and a bare-breasted woman of Amazonian stature, her T-shirt and blouse folded in a bundle and carried on her head. At the town's abattoir—a mucky, shit-splashed clearing in the bush at the path's end—we turned around and saw a black bull with impressive horns tethered to a stake in a banana grove. Barton flashed on *Apocalypse Now*. "When you come back," the captain said to me, "I'll be up in the hills like Marlon Brando, taking matters into my own hands."

All along the street, people read their missionary Bibles, mouthing the words in Creole. As we walked on, a little boy slipped his hand securely into mine for a few blocks, then wordlessly slipped away. At the corner where we turned into the marketplace, a group of young men listened intently to a transistor radio and, as we came even with them, lifted their heads to tell us they were sorry: an American soldier had been shot in Les Cayes.

Back at the casern, the radio traffic reported that FRAPH was organizing. Colonel Boyatt wanted to know if the local FRAPH were extorting people in the market, as they were in the capital, and in response to the incident in Les Cayes, he placed everybody on a higher state of alert for the next three days and asked for a voice check-in from all SF detachments on a regular basis. They knew him, he was from their company, the trooper who took the hit in Les Cayes. Staff Sergeant Donald Holstead, shot in the back last night by a FADH officer while coming out of the latrine.

ODA 311 was still being reinforced by a second team, ODA 315, commanded by the reticent Captain Fritz Gottschalk. At dinner, one of Gottschalk's engineers, Sergeant Roger West, 315's security specialist, briefed the fourteen-man detachment: "If we're overrun by FRAPH, we get up on the walls and shoot down on them. If we're overrun by superior forces and have to get out of here in the middle of the night, nobody's going to find us, so we'd better decide on a save-our-ass LZ." He assigned each man a firing position within the compound and ordered them all to sleep with their weapons. Starting tonight, he was going to set trip wires in the rear of the compound, your basic early warning system—pebble-filled tin cans strung on a line.

For the first time since the street battle in Port-au-Prince, I felt myself getting queasy and stepped outside for some air. Two Haitian men crouched over a brazier, backlit by hellish orange light cast off from haystack mounds of burning garbage. The team was torching anything they didn't haul in with them, and during the afternoon several laborers had waded into the flames to reclaim the FADH's dented aluminum bowls.

A distraught, bare-breasted woman appeared at the front gate, her back plastered with bloody bandages, and troopers went to check it out. Her story was this: a vagabond tried to move into her house and make her his sex slave, she refused, he slashed her with a broken bottle, and now she wanted soldiers to drag the fellow out of her house. JC and Miatke put her in a Humvee and took off. Meanwhile, another cut-up woman came in, complaining that her son-in-law tried to kill her grandchild. The SF hated arbitrating domestic violence; if the FADH ever returned, they told her, they'd send them to investigate.

"Why help one woman and not the other?" I wondered out loud. "Hey," said Sergeant Pledger, "no second-guessing from the journalist, or we'll strap food on your back and shove you out the gate into the crowd." Miatke and JC came back. The woman had a credible story, but when they removed the vagabond from her house, she went in, walked back out with a club, "and fucking lambastes him." They locked the guy up, his skull bleeding, in the front room—the prison—of the casern. "Got your ass kicked, didn't you, son," said Top Miatke. "Got yourself a good old-fashioned Haitian ass whip."

"I just wish she kept them titties covered," said JC. "I've had pancakes thicker than that."

For some reason I didn't immediately understand, two pretty teenage girls were standing near the bull pen, their shirts yanked up and their pants pulled down. "They're showing me they haven't stolen anything," explained Top, rolling his eyes, a little embarrassed. "Man, girls have been coming in all day long." People were starting to assume free access to the compound, and he wanted it to stop.

In the bull pen, Commo Jim sweated over his array of radios. "It sucks," he said. Some problem with the system—the satellite alignment, interference, something. He couldn't transmit digitals, but he could talk. I pushed through the plywood half-door separating the bull pen from the bunks, stepping over Ernie Brown, who preferred to sleep in his clothes on a thin pad on the concrete floor, like a *restavék*, the children sold by their parents into indentured servitude. Lying atop my bedroll, I smoked a cigarette until the noise blurred—the generator, the radio, the snoring, the murmuring voices in the marketplace—and I fell asleep thinking maybe I should find an empty water bottle, in case I had to piss during the night.

The last words of Colonel Boyatt's transmission had been *Shoot first!* which had made the team very, very happy.

IN VITRO DEMOCRATIZATION

They were mightily concerned about being ambushed along the route, Captain Barton and the imaginary colonel, the next morning when they took the Hearts and Minds Show on the road. I hoisted myself into the open bed of the Humvee alongside them, taking a seat on the tail-busting wooden benches built into the sidewalls. A driver and a security backup rode in front, protected from the sun by an oilskin awning. Since I had traveled the length of Route Nationale One three times, the road was too familiar to warrant much thought, but the officers had never been out on it before, and they made me nervous, switching seats according to the contour of the terrain, scanning the ridgetops and bushy roadside for snipers.

At the hamlet called Camp Coq, halfway between Limbé and Plaisance, a large *manifestation* obstructed our passage, the crowd bouncing to the euphoric fever rhythms of homemade trumpets and drums, sort of the cultural antithesis of the Mormon Tabernacle Choir, singing in a thousand uplifting voices the "Cédras Go Eat Shit" song. Two more Humvees—the first American military traffic to take the road north from Gonaïves—arrived from the opposite direction, carrying Barton's superior and nemesis, Lieutenant Colonel Schroer, who vaulted out, to a flurry of salutes. "Aw fuck," I heard the captain say under his breath, and watched his face go blank.

A Lavalas marshal blew an admonitory note on a whistle, and the crowd settled down to let the *blancs* talk. The lieutenant colonel asked how the cleanup was going. Barton grimaced, but the big man had the gung ho disease, he was already holding forth, spilling out a blather of deluded advice. Hold a big mass meeting in the marketplace, he fantasized, "and tell the people we're not here to give you food, we're not here to give you money, we're here to help you reestablish your government, but if you're going to go crazy, we're not going to help." Set up a court and jail for criminals, but send the politically motivated troublemakers to Port-au-Prince. "You can pick out the bad guys," the lieutenant colonel revealed. "They wear fresh clean clothes, Ray-Bans, and a lot of gold jewelry. Everyone's anxious to get this ball rolling and get these places stabilized in the next six or seven days, because [Aristide's return] will be a very destabilizing thing."

Keep cranking, said the big man. Behind the officers, the demonstrators quietly held up a blackboard chalked with demands and pleas. The imaginary colonel gave a speech about the marvels of the nouveau Haiti, and as we left, he waved and blew kisses, reciprocating the crowd's adulation. Captain Barton looked glum.

"We're a sign of hope," the captain mused sourly, "but it's a lot of false hope for what these people really think Artiside and we can do."

Judging from the level of tension in the air when we motored into town, the population of Plaisance had not yet invested in such expectations. Lieutenant Lumas's casern had been *dechoukéd*, his fourteen soldiers had run away, but the old fox was in uniform anyway, out in front of his gutted headquarters, waiting for us. "There's beaucoup violence here," he reported, his mouth curled into a grim smile.

We went inside, targeted by the murderous looks of out-of-uniform soldiers from the casern in Cap Haïtien, standing across the plaza. When the mob spilled into the building, Lumas had tossed a CS grenade, and its residue lingered, stinging my eyes and nostrils. I toed an empty box of American Eagle 9mm Luger pistol cartridges on the floor, trying to envision the trouble that had swirled through these rooms. Lumas and a fidgety man in a black suit coat who claimed to be the local delegate joined us in the back of the Humvee, and we proceeded to the town hall. The Haitian officer, I noticed, unbuttoned his holster to cock his sidearm before stepping inside, alight with arrogance. The townspeople called Lumas "The Pastor," because he was a proselytizing windbag.

The town hall of Plaisance was insufferably hot, pungent with the smell of unwashed bodies, my own as well, and overfilled with humanity, the windows and doorways bricked with disembodied faces, even the road outside pooled with spectators. Again, the imaginary colonel's oratory soothed the many-voiced beast. The contending factions gradually came to terms on the process of composing a new police force: the first selection would be made by the population, the second by Captain Barton, the third by the United Nations at some future date.

As in Limbé, with the dispatch of the business at hand, the meeting quickly regressed to its more natural dynamic—passionate shouting, denunciations, and overwrought appeals. Like flash fire, the bloom of hatred consumed the room's oxygen. The imaginary colonel was thinking to himself that the poor people wanted a revolution immediately but didn't understand power. I found myself suddenly gasping, soaked through with foreboding. You didn't have to be clairvoyant to register the aura of death haloing some of the speakers, to see there were people here who wouldn't survive the days until Aristide's second coming, and I shuddered at the bravery of the young man who stepped forward to hand Captain Barton a list of armed attachés and FRAPH hoodlums he alleged were continuing a reign of terror in Plaisance. Lieutenant Lumas, whose sinecure was all but over, erupted into a diatribe against Lavalas, and then the de facto delegate sprang out of his chair, objecting that his name was included on the list. But the guy had a pistol on his hip; you could clearly see the jut of its stock concealed under his jacket.

Unable to breathe, I pushed my way out of the stifling heat of the room. On the street, a high-strung kid who looked as if he were being hunted asked for my confidence. "I've spent six days in the jungle, hiding," he said under his breath, his eyes darting as a crowd swelled magnetically around us. It was vital to him that I know "everyone would be killed" if Aristide failed to return, but there was nothing I could say to comfort him, short of *Come with me, I'm taking you out of the nightmare.* "FRAPH will kill me anyway for talking to a journalist," he said, his scarecrow body shaking, and he disappeared back into the anonymity of his horror.

Inside, the meeting adjourned. Lieutenant Lumas announced he would be unavailable until further notice, he was taking his family to Port-au-Prince. "He's been *unassed*," said Captain Barton, prematurely, because Lumas would still be holding on, his claws sunk into the decomposing carcass of power, when we returned in several days to swear in the new police force. Barton wanted to insert a permanent squad into Plaisance, ASAP, but he'd never have enough men for the job.

During lunch, one of Captain Gottschalk's guys made a postcard by cutting a square out of his MRE carton, then addressed it to President Clinton at the White House: *Dear Bill—Having fun in Haiti. Wish you were here. Just looking forward to Nov. elections. Love, Middle-Aged Republican.* It was no exaggeration that many of the troops weren't terribly fond of Clinton, but their disapprobation, for the most part, pivoted on a single issue—gays in the military (with an asterisk for gun control, and another for draft dodging, although the concept of conscription was foreign to the modern army and many of the Special Forces were still in kindergarten when the services went voluntary).

On the team, they bitched about missing deer season in North Carolina or holidays with their families, and they bitched incessantly about payroll and about the perceived ineptitudes of command. But the truth was, they generally weren't dissatisfied to be ordered, by any president, into a theater of operation. Except for a few snivelers, it didn't matter where or when, and without being indecorous, they were proud to perform, strut their stuff, to be doing what they'd been meticulously—and expensively—trained to do. (The price tag for Green Berets ran about $140,000 per man, enough to send every one of them to Harvard for four or five years.)

Here at the front end of Operation Uphold Democracy, at least, they knew why they were in Haiti, even if the folks back home didn't know. Without guile or quixotic naïveté, and with a growing if not yet full appreciation of the political and moral ambiguities impacted into the jaws of the mission, they weren't afraid to spell it out—the *De Oppresso Liber* riff, we're here to free the oppressed. And in Haiti, a nation not unlike, say, the state of Mississippi in 1866, the motto applied. Was Haiti worth one American soldier's life, that gut-check measurement appropriated by political partisans? Perhaps it would have been better to ask how strong an army can truly be, if the dread of casualties induces paralysis. In the vast space between isolationism and nuclear warfare, the soldiers had business to take care of, staying alive right there at the top of the task list, and they didn't bother to ask themselves such questions.

That afternoon, we were off the pavement, headed deep into the countryside on a torturous, kidney-jarring dirt road to "liberate" a string of mountain towns—De Gobert, Margot, Pilate—places abandoned by Port-au-Prince, invisible to the world, and long lost to another century, another continent. Throughout our slow hour-and-a-half drive to Pilate, the road was lined with peasants running from their huts and gardens to cheer and applaud, dancing spontaneous jigs, dashing after the Humvee to grasp our outstretched hands, whooping and waving their straw hats in the air, mile after mile, chanting, *Blanc! Blanc! Blanc! Oui! Oui! Oui!* (pronounced *Way! Way! Way!*) *Merci! Merci!*

"Now I can begin to imagine the joy of soldiers entering Normandy," said the imaginary colonel, and it was easy and beautiful to believe that sentiment, watching the seismic waves of exhilaration that rolled in our dusty wake.

We were all astounded, and upon our entering Pilate, something happened that would seal our astonishment in memory. As we came over a hill that dropped us, unexpectedly, into the center of the village, we realized that we were face-to-face with a funeral procession, the street filled with mourners, women shrieking with grief, pulling at their hair, old men with sorrow-filled expressions shuffling behind the pine coffin, carried in a style that was a legacy of tribal Africa, atop the heads of two muscular pallbearers. We stopped, they stopped. For a split second, the world stopped, its wires hopelessly crossed, the mourners walloped with a thousand miraculous volts of revelation. Then someone flipped a circuit breaker: the funeral-goers shook their heads clear of disbelief and instantly reinvented themselves in one great boom of divine elation and deliverance, twirling one another around like children on a playground, the old women hopping in the air, with their bony arms fluttering above their heads, frisky old men skipping in the dirt, and the pallbearers, their black faces sequined with light, danced onward to the cemetery, the coffin dipping and pitching above their heads like a rowboat on the open sea. This was freedom to the unfree, its first sip so intoxicating it transformed funerals into celebrations.

Passing through De Gobert the first time on our way up the road, we had halted at the *avant poste* to speak with the *chef du section,* who we had been told was armed and threatening people. The fellow wasn't around, but the imaginary colonel found his frightened wife and commanded her to have her husband report to his post and await our return. Now, reentering the village, I could hear the mob ahead, feel its quaking anger, before it actually came into view. There on the porch of the *avant-poste* stood the *chef,* not merely contrite but scared to death by the look of him, his rifle trembling in his hands, trapped by a crowd of hundreds.

Barton and the colonel elbowed through the uproar to the man's side. The two SF soldiers with us, Sergeants Cassius Williams and Tom Milam, the always smiling backup medic (both reinforcements from Gottschalk's team), clambered out of the Humvee with their M-16s leveled. Special Forces invariably reacted to impending chaos with supernatural composure. It wasn't something you were predisposed to believe, but the commandos were *nice.* They disdained helmets and body armor, made a real effort to chat with people, to act nonthreatening, yet whenever they stopped smiling, my fear reflex would skyrocket and I immediately took note of the nearest ditch, the nearest wall or tree.

In De Gobert, Williams and Milam stopped smiling. "Get those people to move back *now, goddammit!*" Captain Barton screamed from the porch, where it seemed the mob was about to snatch up the *chef du section* and lynch the bastard. Sergeant Williams was African-American and as such had to constantly adapt to a conceptual problem among the Haitian peasantry, who automatically assumed that anyone with dark skin was, and could only be, a *neg*, the Creole word for *man*, and *negs* could only be Haitian. Ergo, a black soldier was a Haitian soldier, a traditional figure of terror. Williams made a sudden prodding move with the barrel of his rifle, snapping at the crowd to move back, yet when the people directly in front of him recoiled with stark, pathetic fear, he lowered his M-16 and apologized profusely.

"I'm sorry, I'm sorry," he said, with heartbreaking regret. "Look, I'm not going to shoot you—just please calm down."

On the porch, the captain and the colonel discussed the pros and cons of disarming the *chef du section,* who seemed not unskilled in the dramaturgy of role reversal, pleading his innocence in slobbery tones, stumbling through a soliloquy in which he declared himself a good man whose only recourse was to leave De Gobert for a more secure environment or be unjustly *dechoukéd* by Lavalas.

"I know he's not a good man," the imaginary colonel leaned forward to confide in Barton. "And if we take his weapon he's a dead man." There was too much shouting, too much pushing; three years of silence coming uncapped in our faces, and the control began to fray. "They don't quite like him, do they?" said Barton, making his decision.

In the next instant, the *chef du section* was disarmed and lifted into the back of the Humvee, and we scrambled to our seats, Williams hollering, "Go for it, Tom!" and Smiley Milam floored the gas pedal, the tires spitting rocks into the air. The mob sprinted after us, howling. He was as skinny and unctuous-looking as his own mustache, the *chef du section,* with sadistic eyes that refused to meet your own. He wore a much-soiled bill cap, which read *Dr. Seltzer's Myrtle Beach.* In the crowd, people had grabbed my arm to recite to me the names of this man's roster of victims, so I was dumbfounded when, about a mile down the road, the imaginary colonel handed him back his battered M-1 and one of three clips of ammo—eight rounds. I made no pretense about objectivity, but now I was about to cross a far more serious line.

"What are you doing?" I asked.

"He's not a really good guy, but he's not a really bad guy," reasoned the imaginary colonel, looking at me as I supposed I was looking at him, as if there was something vital we had each failed to notice in the other.

"Maybe he'd be a really bad guy if you gave him an Uzi," I said. "It's not for me to say, but I think you're making a mistake."

We stopped. Captain Barton and the colonel exacted a promise from the miserable man not to return to De Gobert but to find his way to Plaisance or Cap Haïtien and behave himself. Despite my argument, they let him out with his rifle and eight rounds, and we quietly watched him creep away into the bush. Ad nauseam, the three of us discussed the right and wrong of the decision throughout the long ride back to Limbé. Several days later, we learned that the *chef du section* had returned to De Gobert to resume where he had left off, pursuing some very bad habits, and the two officers had to return to the vicinity to tramp through the jungle and root him out.

"He couldn't shoot me," the colonel said afterward with customary panache, the sparkle in his eyes that of a man thoroughly enjoying himself. "I am a ghost."

"Maybe so," I had to say. "But he could have shot eight other people."

"You?"

"Could happen."

"Don't worry about that," said one of the team members. "We'll probably shoot you ourselves before anybody else gets around to it. We missed you the first time."

Back in Limbé, the resupply helicopter had knocked down more walls, knocked down a tree, knocked down more houses, and injured a little girl, which started a fracas, and now the detachment would be resupplied by ground from Cap. Sergeant Ernie had been running around town, handing out money to the victims.

Walt Plaisted and Roger West, who were supervising the laborers, couldn't figure out how much to pay the laundry woman. Roger loved his workers, especially Michel, who had lived in the market, sleeping on the ground in all that filth, before the sergeant hired him. Fortified by his new job, Michel stopped wearing rags, rented a room, purchased a sleeping mat, a pan, a spoon, and a kerosene lamp, but the room was so small that his feet stuck out in the rain when he lay on his mat.

Intel reported that Lumas was hiding a mortar and two heavy guns. Captain Barton, still choking on the tension in Plaisance, wanted to put a four-man detachment there, but it just wasn't going to happen, and he would never locate The Pastor's weapons cache. Miatke had developed a tentative e&e plan—*head for the riverbed*. Kids were crawling all over the front wall, and Top was trying to figure out how to keep them off without creating a hazard or a threatening posture. A rumor making the rounds in the marketplace, that Barton was fixing the price of rice, had nearly caused a riot.

In hopes of better reception, Commo Jim had repositioned one of his radios on a windowsill in the bunkroom, more fizz and foot traffic to keep me awake at night, and I reclined in my bed, swabbed with insect repellent and grumbling to myself, until 10:00 P.M., when, across the room, someone woke Barton to listen to Colonel Boyatt's evening transmission, his Fireside Chat. In the dim glow of a flashlight, the drowsy captain leaned over the radio, taking notes, esoteric bulletins that nobody wanted me to hear, no matter that I found them barely interesting—SF mumbojumbo, freqs, and coordinates—but then I sat upright, alert, as Boyatt segued into a homily about the nature of democracy: *you guys out there know that democracies can't work without a loyal opposition, blah blah blah, for instance, when the Republicans are in power back in the States, the Democrats are the loyal opposition, et cetera et cetera, and in Haiti the loyal opposition is FRAPH.*

"Huh?" said Captain Barton.

FIELD NOTES

5 OCT 94

Thiote: People on the coast are pro-Cédras and did not give team a warm welcome. Check on reports of old 600-man Cuban training camp near Jacmel. Language is mostly Spanish. . . . The Catholic priest is in tight with the FADH and seems to control. . . . Baptists have hospital and people like them. People seem to feel threatened by religious strife and don't want to talk religion. . . . The people think we came to feed them and turn their power on.

Les Cayes: Werewolves is an organization of FADH officers dedicated to guerrilla warfare/terrorism.

06 OCT 94

Policies

Cannot detain [Haitian] National unless they are caught in the act of committing a criminal offense.

Everyone needs to build a list of "bad boys" in our AO. To be supported by records i.e. criminal activity. Submit ASAP.

Must keep records of all weapons taken from civilians/FRAPH.

Gonaïves: Gros Morne is a large town ½ way to Port-de-Paix. Large civil disturbance, crowd going after FADH. Calmed crowd by telling them that if the crowd did not disperse and remain calm, then U.S. would leave and turn town back over to FADH.

Fort Liberté: Don't send the 10th MTN to the town. Counterproductive. Calisxe, FRAPH chief, is the former Ambassador to UN.

UNSTABLE AND INSECURE

The swearing-in ceremony for Limbé's new volunteer police force was disrupted by a former airport detective in a blue-and-white-striped seersucker suit, who quickly rose from his chair to loudly claim that he, not the one-legged old man, was the duly appointed justice for the city, and as such he demanded to be included on the selection committee. Captain Barton looked briefly up at the ceiling for an escape hatch, then closed his eyes and shook his head. Everyone in the room seemed chagrined by this man, who was apparently *foo-foo*. The imaginary colonel ordered him to sit down and control himself, which worked for a moment, but then he sprang to his feet again, infuriated. "It's against the law, what you do," he brayed (and who could argue with that?). The imaginary colonel glared at him with true menace, told him to shut up, and recommenced the meeting.

A janitor from Cap nominated himself for the new police force and was told to go away. Someone from Lavalas stood up to denounce Pierre, the camp toady: *He's an attaché, he's a dangerous man, you can't predict what he'll do. If you let him go, we promise we won't hurt him.* Barton said Pierre stays put, and that was the end of it. The imaginary colonel summoned each of the new civil inductees to sign an oath of service, which the captain had previously composed on his laptop computer.

That everyone readily agreed to the voluntary terms of the contract impressed me. The air was tangy with sweat and sweetened by beautiful hymns that wafted down the street from the nearby cathedral, the melody punctuated by the hammering of a coffinmaker. Death's carpenters, they make beautiful coffins in Haiti. Even Madame Bruno was more congenial today, wearing a sailor-cut white dress with blue polka dots. Her community projects shopping list contained more than thirty items: a jeep, a truck, two new schools, a kids' library, a new abattoir, and so on.

After the two-hour meeting, Captain Barton, it seemed, was experiencing mission "itch," the converse of the much-discussed and politically feared mission "creep." Orders from command—to provide a safe and secure environment—were wide open for interpretation, and that irked Barton, who hungered for more, and better defined, guidance.

"I think what we're doing is a model," the imaginary colonel said to bolster him. That much was true—Limbé was the first locales in Haiti to try to form an entirely new security force. The population thought it was a fair and workable system, and there were no longer mass demonstrations in the market, no boiling crowds, Still, they both fretted that somewhere along the chain of command there'd be an HQ desk jockey who was going to undo what they had accomplished here today. They couldn't shake off the fatalism. The imaginary colonel's affection for the Haitian people was flowering, and it depressed him to entertain the notion that he might well be colluding in a double cross.

"The French Army," the colonel said, I supposed empathetically, "is very well known for betraying its word."

While American-enforced entropy continued to slowly unravel the regime, decentralization had its own more natural counterforce, and daily events in the countryside seemed to bunch together, shifting power, gaining momentum and weight, threatening critical mass. Certainly the team's concerns were justified, because the manner in which power was beginning to be redistributed on the ground, at the grassroots level, contradicted the big picture of American foreign policy regarding Haiti.

Washington didn't particularly want Lavalas invited to the kitchen of state; rather, the grand design of the policymakers was to manipulate a stasis between opposing forces, into which they'd insert Aristide and their own will and then hand off to the United Nations.

And except for letting the army's engineers tinker with the existing electrical and water infrastructure, there were not going to be any community projects in Haiti assigned to the military. No nation building, brah—an order direct from the White House. Instead, the idea was for the troops to hand the ball off to the NGOs and the PVOs, and the tree-huggers would dig the place back out of the grave. But by the end of the first week in October, the Special Forces started looking around and grumbling—the NGOs and PVOs, vaunted and saintly, were no-shows.

At night, Top Miatke sat on the cool front steps of the casern, holding class—English-Creole lessons and instructive stories from American history—with ten high-spirited but attentive town kids, schoolboys in search of a school. I put on a pair of NODs (Night Observation Devices) to watch the fruitcakes and evangelists who stumbled around the market-place after dark. Clumsy ghosts, the technology made them appear washed in luminous phosphorescence as they flailed blindly about the stalls. A woman squatted to urinate, and the piss came out from between her legs like a ribbon of green fire.

"What's the meaning of life?" one of the precocious boys on the steps questioned me in Spanish. "Which is the truth?"

They asked us about the space race, which they called the War of the Stars. When I lay down on my bunk for my nightly exercise in sleep deprivation, no one would believe me, but a bat landed on my pillow. Methaquin nightmares, said JC; it's almost better to have malaria than to take that stuff. Commo Jim's two radios were going all the time, making a noise like aerosol cans sprayed in irregular bursts, but it was an aural mask, easy to nod in and out of. Getting chicken wire for the windows, I heard, had become a priority. I could not, or would not, imagine it—a grenade sailing into the room, painting the walls with our blood.

Every sunrise brought a file of people straggling in from the bush with tales of treachery, apostasy, and disaster. A group of peasants demanded the arrest of a bourgeois woman who they said had defecated in somebody's front yard, though this actually turned out to be a dispute over water rights. A patrol was sent to investigate the Great Goat Murder, the Two Pigs Caper, and so on.

Pierre, the toady, was running a collateral damage scam out of the casern, coaching his pals on the other side of the wall how to file false claims with the military. Top Miatke wanted to boot him out on his ass but Captain Barton had allowed himself to imagine Pierre was useful, simply because the rogue spoke English and was ostensibly servile.

A carton of crisp, wonderful, palate-cooling apples arrived with the re-supply from Cap. Also a new crapper, a wooden box containing a five-gallon bucket, a great improvement over the wide-open slit trench. There was an unconfirmed report of a grenade attack on Special Forces holding a town in the central plateau. Barton heard an American was killed, but command, he thought, wasn't keeping the team well informed.

Six FADH soldiers had cast their fate with the gentlemen of 311 and were now back in uniform, living inside the compound. One of the district's forty-eight *chefs du section* trudged in from the bush, begging Captain Barton to let him keep his job. "When you catch a thief, do you beat him up?" the imaginary colonel asked him. "No, not too much," the fellow replied. Meanwhile, the lieutenant colonel continued dithering about the nasty marketplace and had to be persuaded by Captain Barton not to shut it down.

Sergeant Plaisted routinely practiced knife fighting out in back of the headquarters. "That's not something you really want to do, is it?" I asked him one evening as he held an instruction booklet in one had, a K-bar in the other. "Nope," Walt said, "but I don't want to be caught short." Though Walt, whose favorite poet was Donald Hall, had a degree in American literature from SUNY, the only book I had so far noticed around the compound was *Marine Sniper: 93 Confirmed Kills.*

All day long, a mountain of charred trash smoldered in the rear of the compound, and in the evening the heap flickered volcanically, its tendrils of pale, sour smoke mixed with greasy black fumes, now that we were soaking our waste bucket with diesel fuel and burning it. Forget chicken wire; the team now shuttered the casern windows at night, turning the barracks into a sauna. Ernie had the right idea, curled up on the cool floor like a foundling, the headphones of his Walkman clamped over his ears, nodding off to Lionel Richie, and I remembered him out in the countryside earlier in the day as the patrol searched a FRAPH chieftain's house for weapons, his eyes dangerously hard as we were engulfed by a mob intent on vengeance, crazed people pushing the limit, and JC saying, *Yo, brah, does your 40mm know who are the good people and who are the bad people?*

The tension was so bad I felt myself seizing up with fright. We were out on an alluvial plain with nowhere to take cover, and of the differences, not so many, between myself and these soldiers, this was the most fundamental, the one big lesson, pitiful but true: in the worst situations, whenever it seemed as if we'd be overrun, all I could think was, *Shoot those motherfuckers.* True or not, that was the hard, hard knowledge I walked away with each time—if the rifle had been in my hand, not theirs, I would have vomited out my panic in bullets, I would have opened fire. The line between us wasn't decency or courage, but training, discipline. They knew what they were doing and I didn't, and there were times when it was depressingly clear that I'd be willing to let others pay the price of my fear and inexperience.

"Look," the captain had said, "we shouldn't be afraid of the crowds. They're either going to cap us or they're not."

"*No, sir,*" Ernie contradicted him emphatically. "They're not."

I finally had to tell the toady Pierre, who we'd learned was a drug dealer, to stop saluting me; it was getting on my nerves.

Throughout the night, as team members rustled through the barracks, going on watch or coming off, radio traffic kept assuring the ODAs that FRAPH, FADH remnants, and attachés were most definitely organizing attacks against Americans, especially after nightfall. *The fun never stops on Radio SF, your voice for the Haitian Vacation. And here's a heads-up for all you hooch bitches in Limbé: Boastful Bobby Lecord, released by our zookeepers in PAP, is putting together a drive-by shooting for 311. Remember to return fire, fellas. Sleep tight, don't let the werewolves bite.*

Early the next morning, a subdued Lieutenant Lumas wandered in, dressed in civvies and a peasant's straw hat, wanting to move into the casern with us. Captain Barton told him to forget it, get back to Plaisance, get back in uniform, and be ready for a town meeting by noon. At an outdoor nightclub in Plaisance, thirty-one candidates were to be presented to the population, who would approve eight for the new police force.

The club was nothing more than a *ramada* over a concrete dance floor inside a high-walled enclosure. A table was carried in from the street, then a tablecloth, and then chairs for the captain and the imaginary colonel. "You see," said Francky, a local photographer and unemployed journalist, "we are civilized." An uproar ensued when the candidates learned belatedly that there was no money involved. Lumas jumped to his feet to say he wanted discipline here at the meeting, but the crafty mayor—as tall as Madame Bruno was round—placated the young men by implying the American captain would instead give them food, perhaps some clothes and shoes, although Barton had never discussed such a goodwill arrangement.

"No money," Francky shouted over the noise. "If they knew there was no money, they wouldn't have volunteered."

The townspeople poured into the compound, and a Lavalas functionary asked for the proceedings to be translated into Creole, so that the population would understand. A candidate stepped forward to be grilled by the audience, who asked him if he'd ever been in jail for committing a "dirty trick."

"My document is virgin," he answered.

Okay, the crowd said. *You're in.*

Most of the candidates, like the next youth to step forward, were either students, teachers, or both. "I just finished all my studies in philosophy," said the second man, "and now I teach at the sisters' school." *Accepted,* said the crowd. Francky's brother, who couldn't have been more than eighteen years old, also made the cut. The seventh to be interviewed declared with vigor that he wanted only to serve his country, regardless of compensation, and for this example of selflessness he was soundly applauded. "Cheer for that!" people cried out around the circle of spectators. The ninth candidate couldn't seem to explain himself sufficiently when someone identified him as FRAPH. In the clamor that greeted this revelation, the youth was muscled out of the meeting, the town's scapegoat, everyone shrieking, "He's fallen down."

"This is democracy in progress," said the ever enthusiastic imaginary colonel, who each day seemed increasingly exuberant, Santa Claus in gray fatigues. "Big smiles," he would often remind the team. "I know it's very tiring, but try. In Africa it's the same. You have to wave and smile all the time, but if you don't, it's the beginning of the gap."

The roster was completed, and Lieutenant Lumas took center stage to deliver a petulant sermon, grousing that he doubted the new recruits would respect military discipline. One of the Green Berets left out front to guard the Humvee took a grenade off a kid in the crowd. We ate lunch, and children skirmished over our MRE trash. I shared my ham slice and crackers with the suave mayor and the local interpreter, a schoolteacher, who hadn't so much as touched a banknote for more than a year.

"Who knows where this thing will go?" Captain Barton mused out loud. "It could all backfire on us, couldn't it?"

PREPARATIONS FOR THE SECOND COMING

Because they wanted to make the country clean and pretty again for their savior, smoke was now a constant in Limbé, lending a dreamlike texture to the air as the townspeople grew serious about cleaning up the streets for Aristide's return. With machetes, they also hacked down most of the trees along the roadside and debranched the ones left standing—this as a result of command's order that Captain Barton clear the defunct power lines to facilitate the restoration of electricity to the area. When Doctor Hodges's youngest son, Paul, stopped by the casern to accuse the Special Forces of destroying the environment, Sergeant Miatke readily admitted that the team was partially to blame.

"We were told to get the power lines cleared," Top explained. "We're just following orders."

"That's the Eichmann defense!" accused the doctor's son.

The Hodges were a for-profit operation. They had built themselves an enclave of estates, a little Pétionville, on the road to Bas Limbé, and didn't look kindly upon destitute customers or unscheduled charity. Miatke's face reddened, and Hodges backpedaled toward his pickup truck. *Be mature, man,* Top told himself. You came all this way to invade some raggedy-ass country, and the first person you really felt the desire to kill was another American—a missionary fraud who spent the past three years managing an airport for narcotraffickers.

Each morning, obeying Barton's orders, the Haitian soldiers raised their country's flag on its pole up front and planted themselves in the guard kiosk at the gate. The police recruits fell into haphazard formation to be drilled by the FADH sergeant, Jerome, a lugubrious man who seemed to stoop under the weight of congenital indolence. *Can't do,* his sluggish body language said. Barton gave the FADH back their M-1s and made them accompany the team on patrols, but the SF held on to the ammunition.

Captain Gottschalk and three of his men were being pulled back to Cap to sit on the B-team at Alpha Company's Forward Operating Base— answer phones, route the intel, play with computers, haggle with support units. In the mess hall were three fresh faces—chogee boys, FNGs (fucking new guys)—come to shore up the team.

The team grumbled constantly about Pierre, who had struck it rich here at Chez SF, but Barton was unwilling to cut him loose. "We have one hundred percent identified ourselves with Aristide," said the captain, who was quickly losing patience with Lavalas hotheads, "and behaving like everybody who isn't pro-Aristide is a bad guy, but I don't believe that."

The moral, legal, and practical ramifications of disarmament greatly perplexed the detachment, a confusion compounded by command's vague and varying instructions on the issue. Since the intervention and the populist *dechouké*ing of the northern caserns, there had been a not inconsiderable redistribution of weapons throughout Haitian society, and no one at Command and Control in Port-au-Prince seemed to know just what to do about it. "I don't think we should be complacent," Top Miatke argued at the team meeting after dinner, "because I've talked to a lot of people who've said, 'Come the fifteenth, everything's going to change around here.' "

Hollis Peery, one of Gottschalk's leftovers, wasn't worried about that. "After the first few rounds are fired, it's over with," he said.

"Well, there's nothing we can do about a guy with a forty-five who pops up, goes *pow pow,* and ducks down into the crowd," said Top. "But I think we have an awesome chance of surviving a frontal assault. Get those forty-millimeters cranking, throw frag grenades, take out the front thousand, and the four thousand behind them are going to think twice."

Listening to Top, Sergeant Roger West diagrammed plans for fortifying the front gate, which was highly vulnerable to a drive-by incident, so wide open the FADH guards couldn't even stop stray dogs from coming in. The mess hall had been constructed in the shade of a breadfruit tree, and the tree constantly dropped rotten grenades on the tin roof. *Blam!* Roger paused; the smile on his face turned momentarily brittle. It was always loud and nerve-racking, a conversation stopper. The first night the chogee boys were here, one of them took cover under the table, gaping at the team's almost inhuman display of sangfroid, when a breadfruit bomb detonated on the roof during chow. For myself, it was an ugly, heart-pounding rehearsal: If anything was going to happen, this was how it could happen—out of nowhere, *blam!*

Roger seemed lost in thought, staring at his clasped hands, his expression distant. He was an Oklahoma boy with gleaming black hair, a Potawatomi orphan who had been adopted by Choctaw parents and raised to be a devout Christian. "How does this story end?" he asked. He looked down the table at me and then answered his own question. *We go home.*

There was something transcendent in his voice, a casting away of deadly trifles. Words that made you suddenly calm. The tone of Roger's voice lodged in my memory and held alive the sense of everything in the years ahead—the monthslong burst of action, the receding, soon-to-beforgotten events. Three words had never sounded more poignant and meaningful, or contained such a matter-of-fact expression of immutable faith. *We go home.*

Schools had reopened; the road was filled with mothers pedaling bicycles, children balanced on the crossbars. Farmers to the field, women to market, scavengers to the newest source of wealth in Haiti, the army's trash dumps. Lieutenant Colonel Michel François, we heard, joined the irregularly scheduled Macoute 100-Mile Dash for the Dom Rep border, perhaps booking himself into what Herbert Gold called "the Crying Suite for Deposed Haitian Presidents" at the Santo Domingo Hilton.

Captain Barton was up and ready at dawn and sitting in a Humvee on the edge of town by 7:00 A.M., for a scheduled rendezvous with a company of Tenth Mountain infantrymen. They were coming from Cap for a show of force in Limbé and then Plaisance, and the captain wanted to calm them down before they sprang it on the populace. He was going to recommend to their commander that they not even go to Plaisance unless they just wanted to recon, drive around, glare, frown, because if they didn't stay cool, the exercise would prove to be woefully deconstructive. The conventional guys didn't have to relate to people and consequently weren't any good at it. All the Tenth Mountain knew how to do was dig in, run in place, or freak out, and in only a minute they could undo all the delicate work that Barton and the imaginary colonel had accomplished.

Two gunships circled overhead—a Cobra and a Kiowa—and Captain Barton looked at his watch, thinking, *Anytime now,* but no one came. Finally, the captain gave up on it and went back to the casern. One of the Hodges boys had stopped by to say he'd seen a sixteen-vehicle convoy steam past town at 6:30 A.M., headed south on the highway as if en route to the Battle of the Bulge. But Barton was already on overload, frazzled by the crowd at the gate, and he grabbed Pierre, lingering behind the guardhouse, to serve as a go-between, which only inflamed the throng. A Lavalas demagogue, Jean Moulin, aka Bossman, was there acting out, screaming, "We are poor people and this man has robbed from us."

"Look, he's translating for me," the captain said, getting himself into a shouting match, and then, fuming, he turned his back on everybody and returned inside the casern, growling out loud to himself that the team had to arrest Bossman, whom I had no fondness for myself, because he had been one of the leaders of the rock throwers the day I'd been trapped inside the building with Susan and Ed. Still, it was an immoderate move— I hated to see it and had to walk away—this toady Pierre tolerated simply because he spoke English, masquerading as an American citizen, protected, fed, visited by his family, and causing a rift between Barton and his men.

Along the compound's back wall, Sergeant West and his industrious crew of laborers were stringing a barbed-wire half-apron, like a mean game of cat's cradle, to foil a rear assault. A letter arrived from Port Margot, saying the FADH deserters from the Cap Haïtien garrison were organizing in the vicinity, *please captain come protect us because a lot of weapons are in town. Thank you and God bless you.* Mistaking the SF for a taxi service, two schoolteachers came to the casern to ask for transportation. A man stubbornly refused to be turned away until he saw Captain Barton, because someone had killed his pigs.

The justice of the peace had finally returned to work, writing a flurry of mandates—orders for arrest—although plenty of the townspeople of

Limbé considered incarceration cruel and unusual punishment and preferred a quick beating to a jail sentence. In the lockup, a woman detainee sat cross-legged on a mat, bare breasted, fanning herself with her shirt, jailed for an indeterminate length for thrashing a woman and a boy with a stick. A fourteen-year-old girl presented herself at the gate, confessing to the woman's crime, which just confused everybody. Should they put the kid in the slammer, should they let the other woman go? It was like passing out migraine headaches, asking a soldier to be a civilian policeman.

The FADH contingent had expanded to twelve, one of them brought in with his ass hacked off, and the logistics of feeding the Haitian soldiers had become an issue. Ernie Brown suggested the team buy from the local economy, rather than use the military bulk as they'd been doing. The nouvelle police had drawn up a list of demands—they wanted food, a salary, uniforms, respect; they wanted breakfast at 8:00 A.M. Barton's aggravation was starting to grind on the team, and I was relieved when he finally blew his cork.

"Everybody wants some fucking thing I can't give!" He stamped around like Ahab on deck, yelling. "Everyone wants a soldier to be stationed at their goddamn house!" He had only thirteen men to baby-sit hundreds of thousands of people spread all over the map. The new police force was a joke. Orders through the chain of command were conflicting. C&C— Command and Control—made terrific data sausage but served forth lousy support, and Colonel Boyatt and his battalion commanders, the men felt, were like old ladies at a bad art show, infatuated with pretty pictures. It was the entire postmodern new world order peacemaking conundrum, amplified by unconventional training and doctrine, the rules and roles no longer clearly laid out. "I can't keep this shit straight," the captain raged, then retired to his bunk to steal a little sleep from his twenty-hour days.

Madame Bruno, the mayoress, had amended her litany of wishes to include a teen club and electric outlets for her office. "Is midnight basketball on that list?" Sergeant Fox asked dryly. The town of Bas Limbé requested an immediate response to their earlier request to be rescued from a plague of attachés. "We'll go over there and give them the democracy speech, the Aristide speech, the peace and reconciliation speech, buy off a few days and come back," Captain Barton decided.

After dinner and the team meeting, the second medic, Tom Milam, got a poker game going, high stakes, million-dollar pots. "What if you use up all your luck tonight, sir?" Smiley Tom needled the captain, whose face was created by God to play five-card draw. Captain Barton was preoccupied by Jean Moulin, the Bossman, who some people alleged was the head of all the thieves in the area; others disagreed, arguing that the hyperkinetic Bossman was a patriot, a brave leader of the local resistance to the regime. To the captain, he was only a hothead, a shitbag. "We're going to have to bring him in," Barton said, "and read him the riot act." Tom, a million-dollar winner, dealt another hand, and I listened to him explain to me that when he went along with us on patrols into the countryside, he'd pack two separate medic kits—a trauma bag and a snivel bag.

Out in the marketplace, someone had turned up the volume on a boom box, and the cardplayers paused, their chins cocked and raised like hounds sniffing the air, trying to determine why the music seemed familiar yet weird, then everybody recognized the bluesy guitar notes at the same moment, "House of the Rising Sun," sung in Creole. Strange, I thought, like hearing a friend's voice coming out of somebody else's mouth.

"You know, if I got to leave Haiti on October 16, 1994," said JC Collins, squinting at his cards through black-framed paratrooper eyeglasses—that killer-nerd look, "you'd see me dancing buck-ass naked, dick a-swinging, out there in the marketplace, though I'd like to keep my boots on."

The three chogee boys, teamless victims of command's mix-and-match-the-battalions approach to Operation Uphold Democracy, were each sort of off center: One seemed perpetually homicidal, one had an effeminate lisp and mannerisms, and one was about as squirrelly as a guy could get, and it was this one, the squirrel, who now walked into the mess hall with a strained smile, bleeding from his hand. He had cut himself deeply with his buck knife, peeling sugarcane out in the market, where he liked to wander alone, "meeting neat people."

"Oh, God," yelped the lisping chogee. "I go down at the sight of blood."

The two medics, Tom and JC, sat their patient on the bench and went to work, made him hold his hand over a bucket to catch the blood, then began squirting Xylocaine onto the wound. The squirrelly chogee turned pale.

"Don't you have a smaller needle?" he begged. "I told you all I was a wimp."

JC spit tobacco juice into the blood bucket. "Man, I haven't even punctured you yet."

"Next time you see him with another stick of sugarcane," said Tom, opening up a package of suturing thread, "disarm him."

"This is training for me. I got to get down there and look at it," exclaimed the lisper, bending over to inspect the wound. "Oh, my gut's churning. I have a great sympathetic reaction to things like this."

Hollis Peery walked in, assessed the injury, and jeered at the fuss. "Put a fucking Snoopy Band-Aid on it, man, and get out of here."

"Ow! Ow! Ow!" the team mocked, hooting with laughter, while JC and Tom stitched up the chogee.

"I'm gonna have bad nightmares now, man," whimpered Hollis cruelly.

I slipped away to the front barracks, stripped off my boots and jeans, and, careful not to step on Commo Jim, hoisted myself up into my bunk. A few feet away across the cramped room, the imaginary colonel lay in his running shorts and sleeveless T-shirt, making notes in his journal. I lit a cigarette and closed my eyes, then opened them again when I realized the colonel was talking to me. "I made a mistake, maybe," he said, and I knew what he was talking about: letting the *chef du section* in De Gobert keep his rifle. "But what's done is done."

FIELD NOTES

07 OCT 94

FIRESIDE CHAT

1. *FRAPH:* we know that FRAPH is inciting volence against Americans. However, we cannot attack the FRAPH as an institution. We can detain FRAPH members who are verified as threatening U.S. security, caching weapons or conducting violence against the civilian populace. We cannot close FRAPH facilities or organizations. We must support the democratic principle of a nonviolent loyal opposition. . . .

5. Don't forget our relationship with FADH. We are not here to disarm them. We are here to work with them. . . . Give FADH a chance to address the bad elements.

08 OCT 94

Detainees: Only detain for 24 hours unless in possession of sufficient legal statements or caught in the act. Must keep records of all detainees. Can't be accused of taking down a legitimate political party.
FRAPH is the opposition party.

09 OCT 94

FRAPH: Fairly disorganized but still talking about killing Americans. They have picked tomorrow as a date to kill a high-ranking U.S. officer.

10 OCT 94

1. Cédras has resigned. . . . We are rapidly approaching 15 OCT. Be ready for anything. Violence will occur. Do your best to control it. Do your best to CO-OPT the people to help you control the violence. But remember you won't be able to stop it all. Watch the LAVALAS. In some areas they are as bad as the FRAPH.
2. There will not be a 100 most wanted list. This apparently is not legal. We will provide a list of personnel considered to be dangerous.
3. We do have some FADH we want to keep safe. Primary on the list is the LTC Cazeau in Hinche. ODA 371 be sure nothing happens to him.

LE BORGNE

Sometime during the week, hell night had descended on Le Borgne, three hours from Limbé on a virtually impassable road. Its garrison was overrun and five macoutes murdered, their families and friends nowhere to be found. Runners arrived daily at the Limbé casern with reports that the people of Le Borgne were at war, and it was past time for the Special Forces to get up there.

Barton and the imaginary colonel also wanted to make contact with the legendary Marc Lamour, who had not been seen or interviewed throughout the life span of the regime, though in April Susan Benesch had nearly gotten herself killed trying. Now she and Ed Barnes and the interpreter Gary rushed up from Port-au-Prince to join the expedition.

Le Borgne and its surrounding peaks, dense and timbered, were a mythical source of hope for the nation throughout the three years of the de factos—the hideout of Haiti's one and only guerrilla leader, Marc Lamour, and the center, everyone believed, of Lamour's armed resistance. In April 1994, the Haitian army mounted the largest military operation of the de facto government to hunt down and capture Lamour, whom they accused of stockpiling weapons with Cuban assistance and training rebel fighters. Under cover of darkness, several companies of heavily armed FADH, led by Lieutenant Colonel Josephat, marched up the roadless valley beyond Le Borgne into Lamour's sanctuary, burning entire villages to the ground, hundreds of houses, razing schools and crops, but they never caught Lamour, who with his followers retreated deeper into the impenetrable mountains.

"Whoever says Marc Lamour says Aristide," the Haitian peasants would boast, but they weren't sure anymore if he still existed, their own humble version of Robin Hood. During the American occupation, Lamour would even manage to elude the Green Berets, his official but unnatural allies, who regarded him as something like Haiti's Che Guevara, a well-armed revolutionary with connections to Castro, rampaging through the countryside with a band of anything but merry men.

The Humvee plunged deep into a green river, the water swirling over the driver's boots, and lurched onto the opposite bank, making a clanking sound, one of the fan blades busted off the engine's cooling system. The muddy ruts beyond were steep-sided and uneven, tilting us from side to side at severe angles, until the skin on my forearms was chafed raw from clinging to the Humvee's wooden side rails. An hour out from Le Borgne, we arrived at a coastline Polynesian in its splendor, tranquil turquoise bays cupped by mountainous headlands and, strangely, not a fishing pirogue in sight.

We crossed a bridge over a transparent channel that separated a vast virgin mangrove swamp from a sandy lagoon. A little farther on, we found ourselves bumper-to-bumper with a Land Rover filled with *blancs,* coming from Le Borgne, and out jumped a short, pink-faced pumpkin of a man, a few strands of white hair plastered to his sweaty skull, an expensive camera around his neck, and his pants soaked to mid-thigh.

"Where have you been?" he complained, in heavily accented English, peering at us through wire-rimmed eyeglasses. "Captain, we've been waiting all day. You were supposed to be here hours ago."

"Now, who the fuck is this guy?" Barton said under his breath, "and how does he know where we're supposed to be or not be?"

Susan recognized him instantly. Father Jean-Yves Urfie was the editor of the five-year-old weekly *Journal Libeté,* Haiti's only Creole-language newspaper, printed clandestinely throughout most of the regime. Urfie's Creole nickname translated as Skin Inside-Out, meaning, from a Haitian point of view, that he was one of them—black. He was arrogant, self-important, and a genuine hero, one of the tyrants' most hated gadflies, and he rightfully viewed the foreign press with great suspicion, especially since he had been betrayed by *Rolling Stone*'s geopolitical mugger, P. J. O'Rourke, in the summer of 1994. "Please, I'll give you background information, but I cannot as such give you an interview and be identified," Urfie had told O'Rourke, who later described him in print as "a leftist French priest wearing a Chicago Bulls t-shirt." In Port-au-Prince, there were five French priests, four of them right-wing and only one a Bulls fan. Fortunately, your average macoute didn't read *Rolling Stone,* but *Libeté* had lost most of its correspondents through exile or murder during the coup d'état, and the children who sold it on the street corners kept getting disappeared.

"Did you find him?" Susan asked, and the priest patted his camera, smiling as though it were his stomach and he had just eaten something wonderful. Urfie was Marc Lamour's mythmaker, one of the very few men in Port-au-Prince whom Lamour trusted. Word of our impending expedition to Le Borgne had flashed on the grapevine—Radio 32 (the number of teeth you're supposed to have in your mouth). Father Urfie had collared a CBS film crew and rocketed north for a scoop, figuring foreign media plus U.S. military equaled security in the hazardous lost world of Le Borgne, and when we had failed to materialize as expected, the priest and the film crew had forged ahead without us, into the jungle, to beat us to the story.

"You won't find him now," Father Urfie was telling Susan, but loud enough to be overheard by the soldiers. I thought it incongruous, hearing a high pitch of glee in his voice, that the priest had a petty streak of competitiveness, but he was after all a journalist. "It's too late in the day to go walking in the mountains, and anyway, he won't see you without me."

Susan climbed back into the Humvee; Urfie and the CBS crew made a U-turn and raced ahead of us into Le Borgne to film the town's "liberation." Once upon a time, Le Borgne had claimed a place in the larger world, its value prized on the board game of colonial intrigues. The town sat on a bight of land between two exquisite bays pressed like pillowy fat blue breasts against the coastline. On its western flank, an emerald river emptied into the sea, and on a knuckle of rock rising out of the water, where Le Borgne's now deserted casern was situated, once stood a Spanish, and then a French, fortification, judging from the cannon strewn at the base of the casern's walls and half buried in the street below.

On the off chance that we might find a few scared FADH holdouts, we mounted the escarpment to search the garrison, but our boots echoed through empty rooms—even the garbage had been swept up, which was not the protocol for your typical *dechoukaj*. From the casern's rooftop patio, you could look out across the channel to the eastern half of Île de la Tortue—Tortuga, as it was called in the seventeenth century, the Caribbean's most famous haven for buccaneers and the historical source for that gastronomic mainstay of suburban American life, barbecuing.

Down the hill we jogged, into a warren of salt-rusted shanties, decomposing nineteenth-century mercantiles, and abandoned warehouses, to a unique reception organized in the town plaza, where a frighteningly disciplined crowd applauded us on command from several rigid and dour-looking Lavalas marshals. The NCOs formed a security perimeter, while Captain Barton, the imaginary colonel, and the journalists met with a welcoming committee—all so young, so stiffly courteous—who had assumed control of the town. Their American-educated leader, who seemed incapable of speaking in a voice louder than a pained whisper, introduced himself. You could see the lights come on in Susan's dark eyes, and we all leaned closer to hear the half-conspiratorial, half-obsequious susurrations of the lone black sheep in the notorious Bennett family.

Edgar Bennett had the gaunt face, wispy body, and pronounced cheekbones that somehow added up to an image of glamour when housed in his famous cousin, Michelle, the man-eating Vampirella who had married Baby Doc and maneuvered her father into a position of control over several state-owned enterprises. Her uncle—Edgar's father, Lionel—was Haiti's supreme coffee baron and, as such, considered the entire population of northern Haiti his private work force; he paid the coffee growers and harvesters subsistence wages for their lifelong labor. Lionel's list of archenemies had one name on it, written in blood, a rural agricultural activist by the name of Marc Lamour.

Edgar himself was in a tight spot, a semirespectable English-speaker with blood ties to a family of beasts, pushed out in front by the local Lavalas warlords to handle public relations—not to be fully trusted, not to be readily dismissed. Nervously, he began to explain to Captain Barton that he was in possession of a weapons cache, which he wanted the Americans to confiscate and take away. "Where did the weapons come from?" asked the imaginary colonel. The casern. "What happened to the soldiers there?" asked the captain. A shrug. Hard to say; the town was in chaos. "Their families?" Maybe they ran away. Everything about Bennett's mannerisms, especially his haunted eyes, so swiftly averted, personified guilt, and I could only surmise that the curiously well-behaved population of Le Borgne had folded itself in around a dark secret, perhaps many secrets, since the Americans had come ashore.

The arms cache was piled into the bed of the Humvee. The palaver turned to Lamour. Was he in town? Could we meet him?

"No," whispered Bennett, his head hung low. "It is not possible to see Marc Lamour today." He was up at his camp in the mountains; he had been here earlier, but he had left. If the captain wanted to see him tomorrow, it could be arranged. Arrange it, said Barton, squinting into the late-afternoon sun, and we headed back.

A few miles down the road, where the track paralleled a crescent of beach that glowed invitingly in the bronze twilight, the captain ordered the driver, Walt, to stop and then vaulted over the tailgate to scramble down the strand to the water's edge. "I've got to at least touch the ocean," he called back to us. A gentle wave lapped over his boots as, stooping, he tested the water with his hands, the only time I ever saw Barton do something frivolous and young. Susan seized the moment to crack open her laptop and key in a few notes for the story she would have to file tomorrow. When the captain sat back down next to her, leaning forward to see the screen, she scooched closer to him and scrolled the stories she had written throughout the past week, and for the next twenty minutes Captain Barton indulged in his own personalized wire service. Susan, I suppose I should mention, was a good-looking woman, darkly attractive, petite and shapely, her brown eyes sensual behind her studious glasses; she was blithe and easygoing in the midst of the gladiatorial soldiers, and you could hear their testosterone hum like power lines whenever she was around.

The road was even worse than I remembered. The ruts tossed us together into crashing embraces, Gary slamming into me slamming into the French colonel; Barton bracing himself against Susan's tiny shoulder, Susan steadying herself against the captain's knee. We planted our feet wide against the mound of FADH rifles to keep from being catapulted from our crude seats. Loose bullets popped into the air between us, and halfway back to Limbé, when we stopped for a leak and Roger, riding shotgun, asked if anyone wanted to switch places, I took him up on the offer. After hundreds of miles in a Humvee, I still hadn't ridden up front, and I couldn't have chosen a better time to do it.

Within minutes, we came around the flank of the mountain straight on into a fierce squall, the cold windblown sheets of rain soaking everybody in the back before they had a chance to break out ponchos. I urged Susan to come up front with me, under the awning, or at least to hand me her computer to keep dry. She was the only one I was going to share the single seat with anyway, and she scurried forward to sit in my lap the rest of the way, neither of us dreaming that Barton's perfectly unobjectionable conduct toward her that day would be presented as evidence against his fitness to command.

Back inside the casern, the team seemed delighted that Ed, Gary, and Susan would be spending the night. After showers and dinner, we remained at the long table in the mess hall to eavesdrop on the team's nightly meeting. Lavalas had threatened Top Miatke with a violent demonstration if macoutes weren't disarmed and jailed. A swearing-in ceremony for the nouvelle police, scheduled for tomorrow, had been canceled; the brass in Cap Haïtien had decided the concept was too good to inaugurate in Limbé and were stealing it for themselves.

As the soldiers' meeting wound down, the journalists' team meeting ignited, and I found myself in the uncomfortable role of arbitrator between

Ed and Susan, who had begun their discussion about tomorrow's itinerary in amiable enough fashion but were soon hissing at each other, and now the negotiation had developed into a hushed but nasty argument. "Man," said Ernie, "it's a good thing they don't give journalists guns."

The two sides seemed irreconcilable. Ed couldn't see beyond Marc Lamour. Susan, however, couldn't afford the luxury of wasting another day tromping around the countryside in search of a phantom. Back and forth it went, the team fascinated by our bad behavior—*Jesus Christ,* somebody remarked, *the press is just as fucked up as we are*—and after ten minutes of this, I wandered up front to the casern and sat outside the door with Hollis Peery, who was on guard duty, his eye on a broken-down tap-tap out in the eerie marketplace, a group of men with their shoulders bent toward the vehicle's rear end trying to jump-start it.

"Haitian push-by shooting," said Hollis.

His expression was a constant, a wide-eyed half sneer buffered by stubborn patience that wanted you to know that he knew that everything going on around him was unreal, and unworthy of his time.

Susan had loaned Ernie her bar of green apple-scented soap, and he wandered out of the shower stall with a towel wrapped around his waist, talking about the soap like it was some fine new kind of drug.

GUERRILLAS IN THE MYTHS

Susan had won the evening's quarrel and persevered in her retreat to Cap Haïtien with Gary and the vehicle. After breakfast, the two of them drove off, and Ed and I climbed into the Humvee for what Susan had correctly predicted would be a wild-goose chase. To date, Captain Barton and the imaginary colonel had managed to recon only fifteen of the district's forty-eight sections, and on the road to the coast the people seemed to be anticipating us. Village after village, we passed incipient *manifestations,* the crowds shouting for us to stop, the imaginary colonel cupping his hands around his mouth to shout that we'd come back later. "It's difficult," he said, "when you have a prime minister's schedule."

Finally, though, on the outskirts of the hamlet of Bayeaux, we were stopped by a heart-wrenching tableau—a son pleading for his father's life.

An elderly soldier stood crestfallen at the center of a mob, looking as if he had been born into his undersize steel helmet, while the valiant son, himself a member of Lavalas, spoke touchingly in the old man's defense. "I don't approve of the job of my father," he said, with tears in his eyes, "but I don't want the people to say he is a brute, or a bad man, because he was a good man. A good man who worked for a corrupt regime."

"Fine," said the mob, but he represented what they didn't want, and he would have to step down.

"Please," the son begged Captain Barton, "tell the people not to throw rocks at my father or hurt my family."

"He would arrest us for no reason," said the mob. "We'd have to sell our animals and land to get out of jail. We don't want to compromise or negotiate anymore with the old macoutes."

All were yelling at the top of their lungs, and the colonel shouted himself hoarse, striving for the middle ground. This sort of recriminatory vignette, repeated often throughout Haiti, threw the Special Forces for a moral loop. The imaginary colonel retired the old *militaire* on the spot, confiscating his rifle, and the crowd seemed mollified, at least temporarily, and we drove on.

An hour beyond Le Borgne, on a rocky four-wheel-drive track, the road ended at the frontier town of Bassin Caiman, on the banks of a magnificent jade-green river tumbling out of the rugged mountains, a Haiti out of time and place. Not long after we had left Le Borgne and entered the jungle, we had begun to smell the char, and minutes later we passed by the remains of a house, burned to the foundation in an arsonist's duel. "Macoute," said our guide, Marc Lamour's brother-in-law, who had been supplied by the whispering Edgar Bennett. "Where is he?" asked the captain. *Dead.* "Who killed him?" *The people.*

We passed by a waterfall, a pair of giggling girls bathing in its pool, and then the rare ruins of an old plantation, with an antique iron molasses boiler, the size and shape of a satellite dish. In Bassin Caiman, the secretary of a saturnine welcoming committee, a slight, bookish-looking youth named Nicodeme, answered evasively when the imaginary colonel asked for Marc Lamour. Begging our patience, he sent a runner up the valley across the river. In the meantime, we were invited to sit in the blistering sun and wait. An hour passed, then another. "It's complicated," said the contrite Nicodeme, attempting to explain the delay.

"Aw, bullshit!" said Captain Barton. When he headed for the Humvee,

Ed and I pulled Lamour's brother-in-law aside, quickly arranging to return the next day without the soldiers.

That Lamour had refused to come out of the mountains, to descend from the olympian summit of his *maronnage* to meet Barton and the imaginary colonel, was a disappointment but no surprise. He had no faith in armies, Haitian or American, and who could blame him. Lamour was the symbolic descendant of Charlemagne Peralt, the leader of the Cacos, peasants who rebelled against the first American occupation, earlier in the century. Peralt, lured to a meeting with Marines bearing a flag of truce, was betrayed, murdered, and subsequently crucified on a door and put on public display in Cap Haïtien by those same Marines. The current occupation could hardly have looked more hospitable, or the Americans more trustworthy, to Lamour.

When we returned to the village of Bayeaux late in the afternoon, its mob was back in business. The people had beaten and trussed up two macoute brothers, one a former member of the presidential guard, who wore a Dallas Cowboys T-shirt and owned a private stock of fragmentation grenades, which were handed up to us by the crowd like some poisonous form of local fruit.

That night at the Hotel Christophe, Ed and I—glad for a time-out from the U.S. Army's boozaphobia—got happily crocked with an eclectic mix of UN observers, whose business it was to watch the Americans watching the Haitians, while the press corps watched everybody, an expanding telescope of voyeurism. We had not seen much of Susan, who spent most of the evening in her room, chained to her computer. At breakfast, the smoldering tension between Susan and Ed flared up again while Gary and I poked at our omelettes, but in this latest installment of the feud, Ed held the high ground. He had already acquiesced once, and, not to put too fine a point on it, the banged-up Mitsubishi was his. He'd hire her a taxi, he said, and another interpreter, but Gary was going with us today, back into the mountains. Refusing to acknowledge Ed's strong-arming, Susan fiddled with her shortwave radio, her face abstracted, scanning the dial for news from Port-au-Prince.

Red-faced and inarticulate and stuttering, Ed appealed to me to intervene. "Come on," he said, the three of us were a team; tell her to stop being so pigheaded. Susan aimed her forbidding gaze at Ed, then at me. "Stop being such a wimp. *You decide,*" she said, and she endured my protests for only a moment before she began to cluck her tongue, and I said, "Fine, get in the car and let's go."

Lamour's brother-in-law met us in the forsaken village of Bassin Caiman, and with the inevitable entourage—a pack of young boys, a man walking a pig, a man with a stool on his head, a little girl in a powder-blue dress and black baseball cap, who held my hand firmly the entire way— we hiked up the most paradisaical valley I'd seen anywhere in the tropics. Within minutes, we had passed through the envelope, out of the common-place Haiti that too frequently offered up visions of hell on earth, walking for an hour and a half among the round, skull-white stones of the river's alluvial plain, fording the channel seven times, splashing thigh-deep into refreshing blue pools, and it was as if we had passed through a veil, led onward to where the land uplifted and suggested the virgin splendor of pre-Columbian Ayiti, a vestigial Eden tucked away and shielded from the ruination of five hundred years of genocide and greed.

Finally, we began to ascend the densely timbered slopes where Lamour and his people had lived for so long like runaway slaves, and came to the burned-out clearing in the jungle where one night in December 1991 the FADH set fire to Lamour's house. Maximum hinterlands. One by one, peasants in tattered clothes, internal exiles, began to emerge from behind the curtain of flora, marveling at our presence, our perfect *otherness,* until once more we were at the center of a rambunctious crowd, everything saturated with the otherworldly color of tropic melodrama, like a Susan Meiselas photograph.

Haiti very much remained a country where people died violently every day, and I realized, in the damp silence that preceded our acceptance in the historical haven of the maroons, that my sense of security had become overdependent on the Green Berets. But another Haiti existed, a lost Haiti, in the towering misty mountains of the north, and sitting down on the crude wooden stools offered by these people chased by fire and hatred into the depths of the forest, I found it impossible, as they began to tell their stories, to feel anything less than welcome—or, at least, at peace.

Throughout their long ordeal, all of them had been forced to huddle in caves, eating wild breadfruit and foraging for roots, one man with his thirteen children. "Oh, God," he cried, whipping off his cap and falling theatrically to the ground to stare up at the sky, "I had so many problems." For our benefit he made a joke of his suffering, and we laughed, everybody laughed. A woman said she was pregnant when she fled into hiding and had given birth to her child in the jungle.

A hunchbacked dwarf pushed aside the legs of the crowd to come forward and tell me that when they escaped in the night, and each time they continued their circling exodus throughout the years of the de factos, he couldn't run as fast as the others and so his friends had taken turns carrying him on their backs. "When I go to sleep at night," he said, "I am no longer praying to God, I am praying to Aristide, because he is the only one who can save me." No one could tell us how many people had been killed, because so many just disappeared, and it wasn't possible to say what had become of them.

We began to hear a *manifestation* coming up the river valley, its call-and-response singing resonating gloriously out here in the wild. Strong male voices traded off the call, the crowd answering as one, their voices welded together joyfully, and before long a *ra-ra* band burst into the clearing, playing hollowed-out sticks and drums, a real trumpet, a piece of PVC pipe that, blown into, made an *oompah* sound. The dwarf took my hand to come dance with him. Another dancer had wrapped himself in love vine, which resembled bright-orange spaghetti. "We love you," someone said in English. The man was Haiti personified, the archetypal peasant, tall and bearded and barefoot, wearing a floppy straw hat, and over his shoulder hung a straw haversack—called a *macoute* in Creole, the etymological source of *Ton Ton Macoute,* Uncle Macoute, the bogeyman of Haitian fairy tales, who would abscond with wayward children in his bag.

We'd been waiting over an hour for an audience with the community's prince, and now a grim-faced emissary appeared out of nowhere to report that Lamour would not receive us. He looked at Ed and me, his eyes piercing and steady. The fete came to a rude stop. Ed and I erupted in unison, diving toward Gary to translate our twin streams of objections and insults—three days of chasing after this fellow were enough.

Ten minutes later, the crowd suddenly hushed and there was the forty-six-year-old Lamour, walking down the path that disappeared into the surrounding jungle, a lean, bearded man in black canvas shoes, white T-shirt, olive-green suit pants with a faint stripe, and the ubiquitous straw hat of the farmer, soft-spoken as he apologized for his guarded behavior. His charisma was apparent from the moment he entered the clearing, pulling over a rough-hewn bench to converse with us as his disciples pressed in around our nucleus.

Born into coffee, the son of peasant cultivators, Lamour years ago became a synonym for trouble when coffee shoved him into politics and he began organizing agricultural co-ops, an activity that made him the mortal enemy of the status quo. Lionel Bennett had Baby Doc arrest him in 1984; for six months, he was severely beaten and mistreated in his jail cell. Aristide had appointed him the delegate from Le Borgne, but then the coup sent him back into the mountains, one of the handful of high-profile supporters of Titid in the provinces who remained in Haiti and survived. And then, so rumor had it, somehow he started receiving weapons from God knows where and passing them out to peasants in the mountains.

"I still don't know what's going on in the country," he said, pausing often to measure his words as he tried to explain why he had given the American soldiers the runaround. "The [Haitian] military are still attacking the people." It was all very confusing—so much bluff from the U.S. and the UN and the OAS, so many games. "The international community made the election," said Lamour. "Why did they talk so long with the people who made the coup? I still have my doubts about the current situation, because the international community could have solved the problem long ago if they wanted to. And now I don't have a clear understanding of why the Americans are here. Why wasn't there another solution?"

The gravity of his shyness bowed his head forward, his elbows resting on his knees, as he answered our questions, and I wondered what it would take to make him smile more than his natural reserve seemed to allow, or to make him laugh heartily and long. He was muscular despite his slightness, and even if, in his iconoclastic life, he had never committed an act of true greatness, he nevertheless seemed a great man, and certainly the people hovering over us thought so, fixated by his every word and gesture. We asked Lamour if his grand reputation as a resistance fighter was justified.

He began his reply as he often did, *First of all, I want to be clear with you,* and paused for Gary to interpret. "Yes," he answered, both carefully and ambiguously, "I'm a fighter because I've been fighting against the macoute regime," but he had only one gun, he said, an old .45 pistol he toted for his own protection.

They had nothing, Lamour said, and nobody to help them but themselves. "I dream of Haiti becoming a noble country, where there is not fighting all the time," he told us quietly, gazing up at his ragged followers, his manner absent of the didacticism one might expect from a rebel leader with vaguely Marxist visions of history and class struggle. "I have convictions," he said, "but not from books." In an impassioned voice, he swore it was reconciliation he most wanted, not revenge. Reconciliation, the great geopolitical panacea for the end of the millennium—the lion would lie down with the lamb, the rapist with your daughter.

"For me, the only way Haiti can be saved is for the Haitian people to have a national conscience. I want each Haitian to say, I will not do *this* because it will hurt the country. I want everybody to forget himself in order to *see* the country." The international community could help, he believed, but not that much.

He stood up to signal an end to the interview. Whoever Marc Lamour was, he was no less a mystery to me now than before. Already the dark, wet vegetation seemed to be reclaiming Lamour, taking away the flesh and leaving behind the mystique.

On the twilight walk back through this idyllic valley, steamed with the fragrance of wild jasmine and wood smoke, thunder bowled through the green peaks and a spectacular rain squall drenched the mountains. As I splashed through the river, I wondered how much it mattered what Lamour had said to us, the discreet language, the pretty and inspirational words, because in the end, the man and the land itself, the unexpected and magical beauty of the guerrilla's besieged sanctuary, shared an identical point of view, the only available point of view.

Maronnage. Survival. The faded memory of Haiti's soul, the hope for a dignified future, both obscured by an endless cascade of blood and oppression and waste.

FIELD NOTES

11 OCT 94

10. *The FRAPH:* Anti-Aristide and anti-U.S. radical elements are still active. Start increasing your force protection measures. They hope to disrupt things by killing Americans.

12 OCT 94

3. *Cédras:* Panama has accepted Cédras. His date of departure is unknown by me but should be soon. . . .
10. *Aristide's Return:* Major media and personalities event.

13 OCT 94

1. Aristide arrives 1200 hrs on Saturday. Next 72 hours are critical for Haiti. Expect celebrations and/or violence to start Friday. Work the local community, the streets, priests, community leaders, and especially the Lavalas leaders. No bunker mentality. Be out-presence. Use common sense. Be careful. Force protection to maximum level.

14 OCT 94

3. *ODB 360:* Dessalines Barracks. We estimate that up to 2,000 weapons from the order of battle are missing from the palace and/or Dessalines Barracks. . . . ODB 360 is to intensely search, look for subbasements. You have two days. . . .
8. Shooting at Belladere: Our guys are all OK. One FADH wounded. Situation well under control.

LIFE WITH COMMANDOS: YOU'RE LUCKY I DON'T SHOOT YOU

Top Miatke was simmering about what was going on in Cap Haïtien. People were coming by the casern, saying, *Give us food; in Cap the American army gives free food,* and he still raged over the fact that Limbé had been denied the opportunity to inaugurate the new volunteer police force. No one in command could get beyond the mentality that innovations had to start in a major city and work their way out to the 'burbs. This morning, the new police were learning how to take apart, clean, and reassemble their M-1 rifles. A young local entrepreneur, Michael, had volunteered as an interpreter, even though the battalion had sent the team two sad-sack translators from Gonaïves. They were sitting in the back of the compound, dressed in rumpled suits and ties, reading their Bibles.

Susan, Ed, and Gary had left for Port-au-Prince to cover Aristide's scheduled return, now only three days away. Captain Barton, the imaginary colonel, and a couple of the NCOs weren't around either, and I asked Top where they'd gone.

"Up to Le Borgne," said Miatke, "to see Marc Lamour. It was all arranged yesterday.

How? I asked.

Can't tell you, said Miatke. "They're wasting their time," I said. "Lamour has no confidence in American soldiers. He doesn't know what their mission is in Haiti."

"Hey," said Smiley Tom Milam, "as soon as we figure out what our mission is, we'll let him know."

A piece of cardboard was now taped over the barred window in the door of the detention cell. You could hear something like wild-animal noises coming from inside the room. "Whaddya got in there?" I asked. "A fucking lunatic," said Top, "and if he doesn't settle down, I'm going to beat his brains out. He took a shit on the floor and started throwing it out the window at us. You want to see him?"

No, thanks, I said. I wanted to hear the story.

"Ah, the story," said Top.

◻   ◻   ◻

Patrol went out yesterday morning to check on the gravel pits near the river, because everybody in Limbé has decided the gravel is theirs, so they've been stealing it by the truckload. Patrol comes to the bridge and they can't believe what they see. Here's the guy in the middle of the road, all tied up with a rope. His hands are tied in front of him, his elbows trussed to his sides, his knees are tied, his ankles are tied, and he's trucking along, taking little baby steps. Patrol stops. Why are you tied up? they ask, and the guy says, I don't know, so they start to cut him free. Someone walking by says, Hey, better not cut that guy free, he's a madman; his own family tied him up and it wasn't so easy, because he's foo-foo, he tried to kill his family, and he eats his own shit. But by this time the patrol has got the guy untied, and he gets frisky, swinging and kicking; patrol can't calm him down, can't get him to make sense. It's clear he's a motherfucking menace to decent people, so there was nothing they could do but wrestle him to the ground, slap a pair of cuffs on him, throw him in the Humvee, and when they brought him into the casern he started to go for me, I had to draw my pistol on the son of a bitch. We found his family, but all they said was, Hey, you got him, he's yours.

Captain Barton and the imaginary colonel didn't roll back in until nightfall. They'd had a long day of it, hiking up the valley beyond Bassin Caiman for their "arranged" rendezvous with Marc Lamour. After sitting around waiting at the ruins of Lamour's house, they got disgusted and left, headed south to Plaisance, then up into the mountains again to De Gobert, where they'd run a half hour into the bush, chasing down the *chef du section* and finally disarming the scoundrel.

Someone told Barton about the new translators, who were still out in the middle of the compound, looking tired and abandoned, as if we were holding them hostage, and he walked over to check them out.

"Are you both staying here?" the captain asked.

"I am from Gonaïves," managed one of the fellows.

Oh, Christ! the captain said under his breath, and turned to the other interpreter. "How much English do you speak?"

"Yes."

"Yes?"

"Yes."

Barton walked away, utterly nonplussed. The folks at battalion were out of their frigging minds and he was going to lose the imaginary colonel on Sunday and then what? The captain headed to the bunkroom to shed his BDUs for running shorts and a T-shirt, and an hour later he wandered into the the mess hall, where I was drinking a cup of coffee and writing in my notebook, which I automatically closed when he sat down next to me at the uncustomarily empty table.

"So what were you just writing?" he asked casually. "Notes. Impressions, basically. Things like that."

"Do you mind if I take a look?" he said.

At first I didn't know what to say, although I was fully cognizant of the fact that any self-respecting correspondent would reply, *Sorry, sir, but that's off limits, I'm sure you understand.* Just as plenty of media-chary climb-the-ladder team leaders in Haiti, confronted by my request to move right in with their detachments and make myself at home, would have politely closed the door in my face.

I was feeding off the Special Forces, they knew it, and if there was going to be a problem with what I wrote, I wanted it settled now.

Anyway, I rationalized to myself, there was little chance Barton would open the notebook to a touchy or impolitic passage, or maintain his interest in my scribbling long enough to get me in hot water. I slid the book across the table to him and watched him open it, holding my breath, then groaning with chagrined capitulation. He jerked backward, his face ashen, as if a snake had just made a strike at his nose. "What the hell is this?" he exclaimed, and began to read out loud: *Captain Barton is in over his head.*

"What's that supposed to mean?"

"Come on, Ed," I said, the first time I addressed him as anything other than captain. I was out on a limb. Soldiers and correspondents hadn't been randomly tossed together on such intimate terms since Vietnam, where the mutual respect that had reached its zenith during World War II had come crashing down; few people believed it could ever be the same again.

"You started at the front of the notebook, and you said yourself, back during those first town council meetings, that you felt like 'a pig staring at a wristwatch.' If you keep reading on"—I reached over to flip the pages forward—"to the more current entries, you'll find I've written, 'Barton seems to be growing into his role,' which is the truth and you know it. You got off to a rough start."

"You're lucky I don't shoot you."

Maybe it will come to that, I thought, but as the captain read on, finally snickering at team antics there on the page, I let myself breathe again, and we left it like that, neither of us quite sure of the other.

Back on the front steps of the casern, the enrollment in Top Miatke's nightly chautauqua had grown to fifteen. The kids had asked Top to get them a bucket loader to clean up the head-high banks of festering garbage in front of their homes around the marketplace. We'll do it ourselves, vowed the kids, if the adults won't.

A disheveled, dreadlocked troubadour stood out at the gate, singing to us: *I am your friend, I'm hungry, give me something.*

"No, go away," the mean-eyed chogee snarled at him.

"You could be more tactful," said Top.

Unlike many provincial towns throughout Haiti, Limbé by now had a functioning city council, an interactive police force, and a justice of the peace. Not since the fire-breathing Lieutenant Colonel Schroer, however, had any of the muck-a-mucks come to check up on Barton and his team. In fact, the Third Group commander, Colonel Mark Boyatt, was avoiding Limbé since his two visits the first week of the infil, when he had looked Captain Barton in the eye and decided that the team leader was "clearly sub-par." The headshop in Cap scoffed at ODA 311's self-proclaimed accomplishments, unwilling to believe the team was that far ahead of the curve. Given Command and Control's trend of undoing the work of the ODAs, before too long the team wasn't even going to be able to venture outside of the casern, their credibility worth nothing in an increasingly hostile environment. The Joint Task Force wasn't just putting out disinformation *through* the teams; they were putting it out *to* the teams. Cap was simply releasing all the detainees the teams shipped to it; the international community sniveled that the U.S. military was running concentration camps in Haiti, and orders had come down through the chain of command, forbidding the SF to arrest any suspect without first gathering three sworn statements and ample physical evidence and then filing a mountain of paperwork. The U.S. embassy and Meade kept changing the rules, and the Green Berets were trapped in the muddle, turned once again into political pawns.

By the end of the month, the Tenth Mountain was redeploying five thousand MPs back to the States, regardless of the fact that the Haitian Police Academy wasn't scheduled to be on line until the end of December, at the earliest. Everything the team had been told in Gitmo about the terrific prospects for civic action on the ground in Haiti had fallen by the wayside. Clinton had categorically said no to all civil affairs projects except electricity, and all the engineers, all the dump trucks, all the food distribution schemes, were confined to Cap and PAP.

"The way it sounds to me," said Top Miatke, who'd been talking on the radio to the commanders of various units, "our mission here is over. We're to stay in the casern and combine with the police work. The picture they painted for me is we're not going to progress beyond what we've already done."

Regression, though, was a real possibility. The team was without logistical support—"It doesn't exist," said Top. And the mercurial, nonsensical rules of engagement were giving the Green Berets nightmares. You could shoot somebody before you could pop a canister of CS gas on them, unless you had previously secured written permission at the colonel level, predicting when and where the gas would be used. You were better off putting a round in somebody—at least you wouldn't face court-martial for using gas without authorization. And as for the ever present friction between the conventional and unconventional forces, General Lay-low Meade would shit papayas if he knew the snake eaters were out patrolling the countryside with only one Humvee, four soldiers, and unreliable radio contact. Three times Barton had requested a squad of Tenth Mountain adolescents to come help him out at the casern for the next three days, but the mothers running the division weren't letting any of their boys outside the gates of Cap unless they traveled in a reinforced platoon—about forty guys, with mortars and armored vehicles—and were accompanied by either a battalion commander or an executive officer. That being the case, the captain's request was ignored.

"Oh, well," said the glum Captain Barton. "We can't let up, I guess."

On a patrol to Bas Limbé, the captain stopped at the primitive *avante poste* on the village green to help build, by the team's very presence, respect for the young volunteers—boys, really—who now composed the town's police force. To demonstrate he had nothing to give them except moral support, the imaginary colonel turned out his empty pockets, but the cadre wasn't about to waste the opportunity of a visit from the soldiers. Only a short walk into the bush, their leader explained, lived a *chef du section* who continued to molest innocent people. The new civil police wanted him disarmed but were too timid to try it themselves. Off we went on foot, splashing across a pair of rivers, jogging through the miasmic steam bath of the coastal plain, and after thirty minutes of this comedy, whatever element of surprise we had started out with was as wet as our clothes. Finally, fifty yards ahead in a grove of banana and mango trees was the *chef*'s swaybacked clapboard house, and here the Haitians' bravery ended and the entourage of villagers held back. The imaginary colonel and Barton proceeded, the NCOs unshouldered their M-16s. The *chef* answered the pounding on the door and, shaking with fear, invited the officers inside. Dried corn hung from the ceiling, old newspapers had been glued to all the walls, and everything—the bedroom doors, the pantry, desks, wardrobes—was strangely padlocked, the ultimate in domestic distrust.

"I have no revolver," the *chef* protested weakly, but the soldiers followed his terrified wife from room to room, her dirty dress a cobweb of rags, an iron ring of keys in her trembling hand, while they searched in the fetid darkness for weapons. The imaginary colonel busted off a lock on a cabinet when the wife failed to produce a key. Inside were FADH identity cards, epaulets unstitched from a uniform, a few corroded bullets, and an empty holster. Outside, we now had drummers and a hootenanny. *Desarmé macoute!* everybody sang.

Unperturbed, the guide trotted us onward to a second house, where another alleged macoute, smiling modestly and surrounded by his wife and children, held his ground, refusing to be intimidated. "Yes," said the man, "I have a pistol," and he produced a rusting .38 from his belt. "No, I don't shoot people, I don't molest people, I keep the gun to protect myself and my family."

The interrogation began and ended amiably, and we trekked back to the village, Barton and the colonel exasperated by how easily they'd been duped, but it wasn't over yet. On the road back to Limbé there lived a macoute with a big weapons cache, one of the junior lawmen said, and he would take us there. By the time we arrived at the house it was closed up and empty; the soldiers scoured the grounds and garden for any sign of recent digging, then the imaginary colonel broke the padlock off the front door, but the subsequent search produced nothing more ominous than a single shotgun shell. The crowd outside wasn't at all happy that we had broken into the house, and finally it dawned on the soldiers that they were being jackasses, snared in an intervillage rivalry.

Back on the main road, there were vigilante checkpoints, schoolboy guards wearing stolen helmet liners, waving rifles made from lumber. One callow warrior held a child's plastic machine gun. The casern was beginning to resemble Fort Apache, barbed wire everywhere, concertina wire looping through the air out front, sandbagged firing positions on the roof, at the door, at the gate. Even the team's vehicles were parked for tactical advantage, to provide cover in case of an attack. The good folks at Cap had sent the Special Forces ten body bags, which they assumed the team would need on Saturday, when Aristide returned.

"Did you ask for them?" the imaginary colonel wondered. Captain Barton said no, that if he had asked, the Tenth Mountain wouldn't have given them to us.

THE CHICKEN TAKES BACK THE EGG

Friday morning, October 14, the Aristide countdown began. The world predicted wholesale bloodshed, and the military's script called for twenty-four hours of massive payback. Bandits were reported operating along the entire length of Route Nationale One, from Port-au-Prince to Cap. We made a run to Plaisance, where the fence-jumping mayor handed over more confiscated firearms and requested an around-the-clock Special Forces squad to keep the lid on things, but again, Captain Barton couldn't spare the men.

Everywhere, people pruned and swept the roads, groomed their dirt yards. They whitewashed pebbles and stones and composed slogans and greetings and symbolic designs along the paths and thoroughfares, poor men's billboards. They constructed *ramadas* from palm fronds and banana leaves, festooned with red and blue flags and paper garlands, turning the landscape lively and gay, the countryside that was the true parlor of their lives readied to receive its messiah. "We will stay awake all night," the people called out to us as we passed, easygoing people perhaps on the brink of mayhem. "We are too excited to sleep."

Around midafternoon, pandemonium was preceded by wild cheering in the Limbé marketplace, a ball-game noise that snapped you to your feet, heart fluttering, those days in Haiti. It was a sound you'd run to, a sound everybody would run to at once, even though you really wanted to run away. Here came the Lavalas rads through the crowd, the irascible Bossman in the lead, driving before them a stumbling, panicked woman, middle class and middle-aged, the moment's pitiful scapegoat.

"Kill her!" people screamed as the mob chased the woman through the gate of the casern and she came up the steps panting and terrified, like someone trying to pull herself free of a lethal undertow, an ocean of rage sucking at her legs. Top Miatke and several of the sergeants stepped forward to halt the crowd. The woman slipped between them and collapsed on the bench inside the door, her chest heaving; the look on her face would be familiar to anyone who has ever pulled somebody out of a car wreck in which everyone else has died. When her breath returned, she mumbled her innocence over and over. The Bossman and Top, on the threshold, confronted each other and the mob below chanted its accusations: macoute, traitor. A woman who betrayed Lavalas loyalists to the FADH.

Nonsense, said the imaginary colonel, but who knows? A pair of Chinooks appeared overhead, circling low above the marketplace, adding to the havoc. "Now you must live in the casern!" the crowd, pleased by the sweet irony of it, shouted at the woman. The most hated and dangerous place in town was today its only sanctuary, with the only ecumenical policy, blind to all association with its past.

To prevent a riot, Barton stuck her in jail with the lunatic and fetched the Aristide-appointed delegate to assuage the crowd, but it had become clear to the population that the authority of the Special Forces was unexpectedly finite, that their presence was to a great extent a facade, and that the Americans had precious few resources with which to intervene in the tumultuous affairs of the district. What, if anything, would make the big dog bite?

The delegate threaded through the mob, mounted the casern's steps, and made a lackluster attempt to calm everyone, but his own comrades— the Committee of the Young—threatened him as well. Bossman and his sidekick, Paul James, wanted everything to be "pure," whatever that meant, and James taunted Sergeant Miatke. By Sunday, he proclaimed, Lavalas would be partying inside the casern.

"No you won't," said Top.

"Yes we will."

"No."

"Yes."

"What *is* tomorrow?" Top jeered. "Take Advantage Day for every ass-hole in Haiti? National Punk Day?"

Miatke inched forward, the committee inched backward. A few minutes more and the mob had receded back through the gate into the marketplace, which by late afternoon had come to resemble the lower reaches of hell, an unsaved world on fire. I sat out front atop a row of sandbags, watching the disruption with Mike, the volunteer interpreter, who ran a small woodworking business on the outskirts of town. "If the dark opens," Mike said, "we all die."

But the dark was always opening and closing on Haiti like the jaws of Jonah's whale. The insanity itself was darkly fascinating, veiled with tri-umph, and I sat and wondered how many soldiers, how many *blancs*, how much aid, how many dollars, how much time, it would take to neutralize or leaven so much hate.

Captain Barton said he was sick and fucking tired of being in the fuck-ing police biz, and was just about ready to let the Haitian soldiers loose and beat the shit out of everybody like they used to do.

Team members wandered into the mess hall to sit down and eat, and by the time the entire ODA—except for the guards out front—was present, the gravity in the room had changed, as if each man carried with him twin slivers of anxiety and bitterness, and only when they were all joined to-gether did they accumulate into something that deserved to be called dread—businesslike, and qualitatively different than fear, which most often required action to trip its switch—and the dread formed like a thin layer of ice over everybody's words, over everything, until you didn't much care about what might happen, or you cared too much, and it thirsted for movement, event, even blood, which seemed to be the only things that could push the dread away.

After dinner, it took only a few minutes for the team meeting to turn contentious, with abrupt and elliptical arguments about how to deal with the inevitable violence to come. The medics asked everyone to start carrying rubber gloves in their pockets. The NCOs wanted more lucid and specific guidance, but there were no further orders from command, only silence, do what you need to do. "We can't beat them up," said Top. "We can't shoot them. We don't have the authority to bring them in and lock them up. Their man's going to be in the palace, so maybe the best thing is to befriend them. But if we rough them up, then they're going to say let's fuck the Americans, but that won't work because we'll just shoot them. There's no correct answer. And if the casern turns into a refugee camp, it also turns into a target."

Back and forth it went, back and forth: What are we supposed to do if the shit goes down? "If we get out of here with all my guys alive," said Barton, "and nobody gets killed in Limbé, then the mission will have been a success, and whether we put barbed wire on the walls, or whether we used Pierre inappropriately, all that will be meaningless."

"I want guidance, sir." The not so latently homicidal chogee, always having a bad day, challenged Miatke and Barton, his snitty tone shockingly insubordinate, although nobody seemed terribly surprised by his aggressiveness except me. "What am I supposed to do if I see someone getting whacked out in the middle of a demonstration?"

"All right," Captain Barton finally barked back. "All right, damn it. If you see arson, rape, murder, *stop it.*"

Sergeant Fox asked me if I knew how to use a gun.

Curse or cleansing, the rainy season had blown back upon the land. Before midnight it started coming down and coming down, and even despite the deluge, out in the streaming, flowing, mud-clogged darkness we heard the *manifestations* begin in earnest in the early hours of October 15, the noise made submarine and cataclysmic by the weather, like some Western drama on a distant television, snatches of the sound track—Indian war party—filtering through the roar of the squall, the whooping and hollering of braves in the flash flood of victory. Behind the walls of the fort, the team discussed points of defense in hushed voices—"I hope it rains all damn night on those *manifestations*"—and by sunrise, the island of Haiti had exhausted itself, spending its animus in a spree of gratitude, dementia, and exultation, the people too worn out to do anything but stand dazed, steaming in the carnival sheds they had erected along every roadside, and listen to the radio to finally hear what everyone was waiting for, the easy little lie that the generations-old nightmare was over.

At 6:00 A.M., any soldier lucky enough to nod off was annoyed out of sleep by the last demo's last hurrah, the crowd's jerky metabolism burning through the dregs of its reserves. In the front cell, the lunatic paced like a filthy emaciated animal, a feral creature that had outrun its own soul. *Fucker's gotta go*, announced Top, not happy to be managing a guesthouse for Haiti's chronic unwanted and newly dispossessed.

In the office at the back of the casern, to which Captain Barton had removed her out of propriety, the macoute woman sat, ungainly as a newborn, on her mat bedding, composing herself for one of those days. Out front on the steps, relatives waited with her breakfast and the soldiers waited for the only thing in Limbé worthy of their trust, which was for the killing to start. But we were wrong—the government, the American military, the UN observers, the media, Barton, all the soothsayers and omen readers and jabbering prophets with their dark and sexy fantasies of doom.

I thought they might have to rope the lunatic to haul him out of his cell, but the poor devil came out like a bull into the ring. A trio of sergeants tried to channel him toward the back door and the interior of the compound, but the crazy man spun in their hands and flailed. Miatke, who was short and hated being teased about it, went Napoleonic; the lunatic's behavior was a personal affront, and he wrestled him to the ground. The permanent crowd in front of the gate cheered, believing the American had decided to get serious with some bad-ass macoute. With his knees, Top pinned the lunatic on his stomach. The other NCOs wrenched his arms behind his back and pinched together the sticks of his legs; out came the flex cuffs, and then Top dragged and kicked the miserable man through the back door and pitched him onto the rear of a Humvee. Haitian rodeo.

When Sergeant Ernie Brown slid behind the wheel of the Humvee and the captain filled the passenger seat with his baby-faced sullenness, I figured what the hell, time to tour, so I mounted the bed of the Humvee and sat down as far away from the frothing hog-tied lunatic as the limited space would allow, pretending I was in no way part of the lunatic's troubles, though of course I was. Pretending I was invisible: the ultimate delusion for a white man in Haiti.

We weren't even out of town before Ernie started pressing Captain Barton to make a decision about the lunatic. *Come on, sir, you're the officer—what are we going to do with this bag of shit?* Barton prevaricated: if we dropped him anywhere close to Limbé, maybe he'd have his parents strangled by lunchtime. Worse, maybe he'd beeline back to the casern and tempt Miatke to do great harm. Only kings could make the mental space to afford a maniac mascot. More than anybody I'd ever been around, soldiers seemed to need the one thing they could least expect: rational people, enemies whose sole virtue was an adherence to logic, however cold-blooded. About the only thing you could count on was that wherever we deposited the lunatic, he'd become an instant pain in the neck for somebody.

Barton twisted around in his seat to air the options. "Maybe we should take him to the hospital in Cap?"

"What hospital in Cap?" I said. I knew of no hospital in all of Haiti that was equipped to handle a patient like this one, though every hospital in Haiti mimicked the ambience of a psycho ward. "Most of the world, you know, lets them wander around. You ever been in a lunatic asylum in the third world? Remember when American planes mistakenly bombed the nuthouse in Grenada? Some people wanted to call that an act of mercy."

"That's cold." Ernie laughed, a high-pitched giggle like a whinny, some small part of him amused but the rest right there, locked on the captain in a void of sympathy.

"Yeah right. Listen to you. Mother Teresa."

"I just don't feel right about this," said the captain. "There should be someplace we can take this asshole," but the lunatic was already in the only place he was ever going to be, and the captain had become a man driving around with his own gunnysack of private sins, looking for a message, for the handoff, for any brand of grace at all to assuage his conscience, the lunatic rampaging through the china shop of the captain's moral universe: Did he deserve compassion, or was he walking insensible waste to be flushed out of sight? The right and righteous answer was unavailable.

We were halfway now between Limbé and Cap. "Sir," Ernie pressed on, his voice turned derisive. "Make up your mind, sir."

Both soldiers stared straight ahead through the windshield, their jaws set, and we rode another klick or two in silence, sliding out of the mountains and into the bucolic magnificence of the coastal plain.

"Sir?" said Ernie, one syllable of unmistakable contempt.

"It doesn't seem right," said the captain.

I suggested we take him to Cap and insert him into the stream of foot traffic. Something about the urban ecology seemed better suited to the meanderings of the insane.

"Sir?" said Ernie. "Sir?" Barton wouldn't answer him. "Sir, we're running out of miles, sir. What do you want to do? Tell me—what—to do—*sir.*"

"All right, goddammit!" Barton's beefy face went pale, then flushed with anger. "Pull over here, stop right here. Goddammit!"

We eased to a stop on the side of the road, the air fresh and occasionally sweetened by a breeze carrying the nauseating perfume of organic rot, the landscape cane fields and pastureland, palm and mango groves, stretching for miles—the sort of terrain that made colonials drool, murderous with greed—until the land heaved up into a wall of blue-green mountains, capped by Henri Christophe's Citadel, the largest mountaintop fortress in the New World, on the eastern horizon. I vaulted out the back of the Humvee and walked forward, out of the way. Ernie and the captain came around from the front, the tailgate clanging down as they unlatched it, rousing the lunatic, whose head bobbed down between his splayed knees, to a fierce-eyed state of alertness.

"End of the road pal," said Barton and, to my dismay, hopped into the bed of the Humvee, unsheathed his K-bar, and cut the prisoner free of the plastic cuffs that bound him. The captain back-stepped off the rear of the vehicle to the ground and stood there with his hands on his hips, but the lunatic wouldn't move. Chin up, trying hard to concentrate, to keep his eyes from roaming, he wanted no part of whatever he sniffed in the air.

"Come on, get the fuck out of there," growled the captain, but the fellow wouldn't budge, and the three of us stood there watching the madman draw his own inscrutable line in the sand. Like a mustang coming off a tranquilizer, the befuddled terror in his eyes sharpening to outrage, he bared his surprisingly good teeth, strange language bubbling in his throat.

"Get the fuck out of there now!" the captain commanded, to no avail, and I watched the meanness flow into his face. Ernie stood to the side, cradling his M-16, trying not to look amused. "Get out!" screamed Barton. "Get out right now, or I'm going to climb back up there and kick your ass!"

The lunatic started edging backward, crablike, on his palms and heels, keeping his eye on Barton as the captain grabbed the wooden side railing to hoist himself into the Humvee and I thought, *Oh, shit,* because Barton had left his rifle propped against the front seat, its black barrel sticking invitingly into the air. If the lunatic lurched for it, I'd be the one who'd have to stop him. Who knew if any thought so lucid and cunning had illuminated the lunatic's mind, or if the lunatic knew what I didn't, how to lock and load, clear the 16's safety and actually shoot the thing, but I preferred the possibility to be strictly academic.

By now Barton loomed over the fellow, shouting, while the lunatic cowered and cringed theatrically, his forearms raised in front of his face like a thespian's to ward off evil, flinching from blows that were only imaginary, an indisputably pathetic life form, sputtering nonsensical curses like an antichrist, his electrocuted buckwheat hair littered with bits of straw and twigs and grit, his torn, unbuttoned shirt as filthy as a mechanic's rag, his cutoff shorts like woven mud, held up by rope.

Barton gave the sky a look, like *What's it going to take?* "Get up, goddammit, you piece of shit, get up or I'll beat the living crap out of you." He bent to grab the lunatic by the shoulders and pitch him from the Humvee, but with an amazing burst of energy the fellow slapped at Barton's hands and scuttled out of reach. The captain started side-kicking him with the flat of his boot, tried to work him into a half nelson, anything to not hurt him but make him move. With furious desperation, the lunatic tried to weld himself to the bench slats, but Barton pried him loose, the guy writhing, swatting back aimlessly and kicking willy-nilly, until the circus act had gone on far too long. The captain grabbed a fistful of the lunatic's roped waistband and hauled him up by his middle. For the briefest moment they clambered together like dancing bears, but then the rotting cloth of the man's shorts tore away in Barton's hands as he flung the lunatic out the back of the Humvee, his pants slipping down around his knees, his coal-black penis floured by dust as he sprawled on the roadside, defeated. He slowly came to his feet, gathering the remnants of his shorts, trying to cover himself, clearly shamed, his lean chest heaving, bursts of broken language spilling off his tongue, and I had to think that even his illness had not delivered so terrible a blow to his vestigial dignity as this. The road had been eerily empty, but now several laughing children appeared out of nowhere, took one look at the situation, and said *Foo!*

"I don't want to see you back in Limbé, you understand me?" Captain Barton bellowed at the lunatic, who only sputtered on like a crazed child, his eyes already darting beyond the reality that had swooped down on him like a hawk and deposited him here, wherever, this other part of a madman's unendingly mysterious and ever boiling adventure.

We got back into the Humvee. "Can you believe that son of a bitch?" said the captain, and we continued on without another word between us on the matter.

As we drove through the streets of Cap, under a lattice of crepe streamers and handmade banners, Haitian and U.S. flags wherever you looked, it was embarrassingly clear to us that there wasn't going to be any violence on this day of hangovers and resurrection. Block by block, the population clustered into scrap-and-frond party hooches, listening to radios, entire disco-size sound systems installed in cramped stalls, waiting for empty television screens to fizz to life with images of Air Force Two—stuffed with celebs, media elites, congressmen, exiles, lawyers, State Department security commandos, and Class A suit-wearing, highly lethal rent-a-cops, landing in Port-au-Prince—cooking lunch on charcoal braziers while they started to sober up or started to drink again, but generally gliding happily on the cool, fresh thought of peace.

We headed out toward the Tenth Mountain's bivouac at the airport. "The Tenth has a lot of trouble with what they say is our superior attitude," said Ernie, strapping on his helmet and unrolling his sleeves. We parked in front of the Special Forces FOB, across from the Tenth's mobile chow unit. The three of us ducked under a canvas flap to break the boredom for ODA 312—Captain Fritz Gottschalk, Sergeant Cassius Williams, all the others, cross-eyed from staring into computer screens. After a while, I went back outside and started taking photographs of the cooks over at the stoves: Hey, how about some of these T-rations for the snake eaters out in the bush? Sealed aluminum trays of roast turkey, chops, pork and beans, cases of apples and juice and pop. Ernie and Roger West hated doing this, begging the Tenth Mountain, begging even their own quartermaster, for what should have been theirs without asking.

As I loaded contraband into the Humvee, the FOB's S-2 intel officer, a tall, straw-haired captain, came out to shoot the shit. The S-2 had been tasked with a superhuman aggravation, one of the Mission's Big Jokes: to build a database of baddies, only—here was the punch line—he had no one to give it to. We weren't in the criminal justice biz, so what was the point? No one in command wanted to touch it. A database like that was only another type of tar baby, and if no one up the chain had to make a decision about who was on the list and who was off, then no one would have to take the blame. The only problem was the A-teams had to make a dozen decisions every day about who's hot, who's not.

The S-2 was a good guy, a connoisseur of the more egregious ironies, the only soldier out of Fort Bragg I ever heard cut Clinton some slack, not that that had anything to do with anything. The captain was one of those sensitive, troubled idealists throughout the government and the military who willingly manifest themselves as inside sources, and so I asked him how Marc Lamour ended up in his database as an attaché and murderer. I could see by the captain's reaction that this was not a great question.

"How'd you hear about that? This stuff's way classified."

I told him the truth, that I had inadvertently seen something I wasn't supposed to; nobody was to blame—or everybody was.

"That was a mistake," he said. "Marc Lamour is not an attaché."

"Murderer?"

The S-2 said he wasn't sure. Maybe, maybe not. His contacts had some rather incriminating things to say about the resistance leader.

"Who are your sources? Lionel Bennett? Third cousins of Lionel Bennett? Peasants paid off by Lionel Bennett?"

The captain sighed painfully. "You know I can't tell you that."

As we spoke, Aristide was on the ground, addressing the dancing multitudes outside the national palace, urging calm, punctuating his message of reconciliation by releasing a white dove into the air. After the coup d'état, the tyrants had told the population to forget about Titid, that the little priest had less chance of ever setting foot again on Haitian soil than an egg had of flying back up a chicken's tail feathers. Yet now the egg had returned to the chicken, and the chicken was tethered to the table leg of Washington politics. The miracle had a low ceiling, and even the Americans couldn't reverse all the centuries of history, the hate and pain and misery, and stuff it back into the dumb but tenacious bird that was Haiti's draconian past.

Before the sun went down, there was a moment that couldn't have happened yesterday and, tomorrow, would be impossible to re-create. About an hour before twilight, the woman who had been accused of being a macoute asked the Special Forces to help her go into hiding, to take her to a friend's house far into the countryside, where she could seek refuge. Top Miatke thought it was a good idea to get rid of her and agreed to spirit her out of the casern. Two NCOs joined us in the Humvee, as well as the adolescent FADH private, Paraison, and precocious Kevin, Top's favorite camp kid.

The weight lifted free of the woman's shoulders once we'd passed the city limits and were rumbling through the fragrant countryside, down roads we'd never been on before, jammed with rummed-up revelers who, when they saw us, embraced the air and each other, shouting themselves hoarse. *Thank you, Thank you, Thank you,* they cried out; they had learned to say it in English, to be certain we understood.

"I'm not a macoute," the woman tried to explain to us. Her husband was a supporter of Marc Bazin, the former presidential candidate who had lost out to Aristide, and that's why, she believed, all the trouble started. In one of the crowds on the road, Paraison recognized a FADH comrade, a deserter from the casern, and talked him into joining us in the Humvee.

We were deep in the jungle, deep into what many people in the United States would without hesitation call the heart of darkness, feeling perhaps the slightest flutter of dread, something the size of a monkey's paw tightening in their chest. The light was glowing, golden, the road for miles so dense with ecstasy that we crawled along, barely moving. Suddenly the bravest of the Lavalas horde started clambering aboard, five, six, seven, twelve, twenty, twenty-one, everybody in Haiti was in this Humvee, and we rolled along through the forest and fields, dancing and singing—a magic, illusory bubble of reconciliation.

"I have worked for the glory of the Americans," the imaginary colonel said, hamming it up, his eyes lit with irony, the next day as we boarded the Chinook that would take the two of us down to Port-au-Prince. I remembered the last village I had ridden into with the pair of officers, Barton and the French colonel. The captain had stood in the back of the Humvee with his arms spread wide and told the suddenly quiet crowd, as he would later tell the lunatic clutching at his nakedness on the side of the road, "Now you are free."

PART FIVE

Baby-sitting Ogoun Feraille

Every free breath poisons the tyrants' atmosphere.

—William Gass

FIELD NOTES

16 OCT 94

1. Yesterday was a watershed. Attaboy to all. . . .
12. *Uniforms:* Keep hats on if outside. This is a focus of attention.

17 OCT 94

7. Fuel for electricity. After tomorrow's delivery to Hinche and maybe Jacmel, there will be no more fuel provided by U.S. gov't to any location. Tell your town mayors and city councils that this is now a gov't of Haiti responsibility. The electricity will probably go off again for a while.

18 OCT 94

5. *Operation Light Switch:* We may be back in business. We have convinced TF 190 that we cannot allow the lights to go out.

21 OCT 94

1. Congratulations. . . . You are on a roll, doing miracles with almost nothing. You continue to astound the world. You are making history. Don't let up now. Keep aggressive, keep pushing.

22 OCT 94

4. *Babies:* You have now delivered a total of four new babies by my count. The latest was a candlelight caesarean operation that saved the lives of both mother and daughter in Belladere.

5. *Democracy and Justice:* Indication from some of you is that the people have their own understanding of democracy and justice. They think democracy means they can do anything they want. They think justice means revenge. You must clarify these points.

SOLDIERS (NEW AND USED)

I went to find Gary, the first thing I would do each trip to Haiti, asking around for him on the streets of the slums behind the national palace in downtown Port-au-Prince, where he lived with his senile grandmother. I was unhappy going anywhere without him, partly because of my dependence on his trilingual skills, but more because I craved his easy companionship and abiding decency, the ever thoughtful insights he offered into race and revolution, his gentle humor and quick laugh and general unwillingness to despair even though, like most Haitians, he had nothing, and no visible prospects for the future.

In 1963, when Gary was three years old, his father, a FADH sergeant, was murdered by François Duvalier. His mother fled without him to Miami, and five years later his hapless grandmother sent him off to an orphanage in Port-au-Prince run by Pentecostal missionaries from Maryland, an experience he refused to discuss. The missionaries had taught him both English and scarring humiliation, and white evangelists had given him his first and only job before the invasion, translating sermons for preachers on the fire-and-brimstone circuit, zealots who chastised him for diluting the impact of their message by his refusal to mimic their spirited delivery. Then along came Operation Uphold Democracy, the soldiers, the journalists, the dollars, and Gary's life got a lot better, though it would be wrong to say it had changed.

Together Gary and I had been stoned, shot at; together we had pushed our way forward into the raving lunacy of riots, stumbled through scenes of devastation and resurrection, fed and protected each other, shared the same bed when no other lodgings were available, got silly drunk, talking about love and lovers, music, politics, soldiers and macoutes, the sins of white men, black men, and God, about the distances that separated us, seemingly forever.

Usually I would come with Susan to track down Gary in the slums, but Susan, burned out by the beat, had left the *Herald,* and taken a sabbatical from journalism. Ed Barnes was in Bosnia, Yves Colon and Peter Slevin were back at their desks in Miami. Two months after Aristide's return, the story and the mission were no longer of import to the American public. At the hotels, it was out with the media, in with the aid bureaucrats and entrepreneurs, and here I was on my own, standing on a street corner filled by people with nothing to do, asking a pair of young women, *Kiko tay Gary Metellus?* A while later, Gary appeared from within the dense hive of shanties and shops, and the mood on the street brightened, because Gary's paychecks helped finance life in the neighborhood. Within minutes, he had packed an overnight bag, which was all he ever packed, and we headed north.

It was the old FADH who welcomed us back to the casern, our first "friends" in Limbé since the day Bossman and Paul James and all the young warlords and the town itself had stormed the headquarters of Haiti's 53rd District, pelting us with rocks, and the snake eaters of ODA 311 had dropped from heaven and we all imagined we were dead. They were all there, along with a few new faces, sixteen ex-*militaires* and sixteen guns, the whole crew of semi-rehabilitated baddies, faintly pleading, faintly murderous, commanded now by the mercurial Lieutenant Lumas from Plaisance.

A bright-eyed surge of recognition—*Oh, it's you!*—and joking reproaches: *Where have you been? You abandoned us.* The need for me to be someone who could help them rose and fell in their eyes and turned into sad smiles, a resigned sweep of Sergeant Jerome's hand. "We consider ourselves prisoners. We don't really have an attraction with the American soldiers. Look what they have done to us."

What the team had done was box them in, board up the two back entrances leading from the casern into the compound, nail plywood over the rear windows, and lay down rolls of concertina wire from the corners of the building to the outer wall, denying access to the grounds and out-buildings that composed three-fourths of the garrison, where the Green Berets had now established themselves with a vengeance, planting the old FADH like a windbreak between themselves and the people.

It was in the American command's prospectus to vet the FADH, cull the officers and enlisted men they considered fit for service, then set the Special Forces to work fulfilling a mandate specific to their doctrine—the training and professionalization of foreign troops—until (another wave of the magic wand) Haiti could claim possession of a modern army, obedient to civilians, committed to the preservation of civilian rights, sworn to up-hold democratic principles and in love with their own integrity.

Aristide, however, was being a bit queer on the issue: Not willing to trust the Yanks, he thought it prudent to vet the FADH himself, only he equivocated and parried with his handlers, dragged his heels doing it, and then, early in December, in defiance of American exhortations, he gave the masses the Christmas present they had always dreamed of and began to disband the army altogether, shut it down, abolish its presence in Hai-tian society. The macoutes and the elites could barely contain their out-rage, the Americans clucked like disappointed parents, and the masses were once again bewildered as legions of ex-FADH were mustered into what was now known as the IPSF—the Interim Police Security Force—macoutes no matter what you called them, window dressing for the American military, who would enforce Haiti's tenuous law and order until they could eventually be replaced by an all-new professional police force, which the U.S. Justice Department and the CIA were still figuring out how to create.

The plywood wall opposite the bull pen was stapled top to bottom with a hundred crayon drawings by local schoolchildren: insect-like helicopters spitting fire, stick soldiers shooting stick macoutes, Humvees, tanks, *We love America.*

"Now you guys are cops, eh?" I said to Sergeant Jerome, who was dressed in his new uniform—white shirt, blue pants, black ball cap—which had been issued only the day before. The old FADH looked embarrassed, pained, amused, and finally disgusted by my suggestion. One day, a helicopter had come and whisked them away to Port-au-Prince, where they were taught how to arrest people, how to fill out warrants, how to behave. But how could you be a cop if you weren't allowed to carry a gun? if the people wouldn't listen to you? if you couldn't beat *malfaiteurs*? if the judge wouldn't come to court? if the court ignored the law? if no one paid you for your trouble? if the acronym IPSF didn't make sense in your own language?

"Not cops," muttered the old FADH with muted rage; every glance between them was complicated.

"We're laborers for the American soldiers."

"They treat us like criminals."

"Well, what the hell," I said. "At least everything seems very peaceful."

"No!" they carped in unison, in both English and Creole. "No peace, no peace." They were angry and resigned to their position and afraid, men calcified by powerlessness and fear, men with useless secrets. A portly corporal, sitting hunched into himself on a rusty folding chair, tipped his head back and let his eyes burn through me with malice. "Haitian people are like jungle people," he snarled, "so there can never be peace in the country."

"But you're a Haitian yourself," I said as he looked away in revulsion, unwilling to discuss his complicity in a process that made all abomination self-reflective.

While it was not possible to like them, neither was it possible to hate these men, these old soldiers, as the people did without reprieve and with unrelenting fury, as the government did, as the Green Berets did. And it was true, they were prisoners, condemned men. You could feel them cowering inside themselves, not good enough men for anyone to want to save, yet not bad enough to have to run for their lives, or even brave enough to seize their own fate and disappear into the mountains, into the slums of Port-au-Prince.

"What we are told to do we have to do," said the mopey Sergeant Jerome. "I'm just following the process, but I am a pessimist. I'm getting tired of people telling me bad words, treating us like jokes."

The sergeant and I stepped back out onto the front steps, and he shouted across the wire, telling the team I'd returned. Gary and I went into the marketplace, down the wall to the solid iron gates that opened into the compound, and waited for someone—a tall, skinny black guy I'd never seen before, dressed in fatigues—to let us in. This was Wesh, the team's new interpreter, a Haitian-American petty officer on loan from the navy, with a grandmother down south in Jérémie, and we followed him toward the mess hall, which had been converted into the team's operational center.

Here were the radios, the maps, the computers, the arsenal, and, with Christmas only ten days off, a Christmas "tree" made from a tripod of confiscated rifles strung with Styrofoam peanuts, 30.06 ammo, colored lights sent by someone's parents, and capped by a miniature plastic evergreen mailed to JC Collins from his wife. Red stockings hung from the barrels of old M-1s stacked along the wall, and on the food-prep table lay a bonanza of gift-wrapped presents, already opened: mom's cookies, snacks, letters from schoolchildren, a Frisbee, cassette tapes, pictures of toys the wives had bought for their kids.

The tempo of the mission had flattened and staled, turned purgatorial. Jim Pledger and JC sat opposite each other at the long concrete table playing cards, their brown T-shirts sweaty, their biceps muscular and tan. Commo Jim looked sideways at me, trying for my benefit to maintain his boredom, then looked back at his hand and discarded. "Where you been?" he said. "Whadja bring me?"

JC guffawed, and from the back of the hall I heard a soft, circumspect chuckle. I hadn't noticed him before, a soldier sitting at a desk, writing in a journal. The medic introduced us, and after I had shaken his hand, he went back to his work, in a chaste and temperate world of his own.

The comparison couldn't be avoided—the new captain looked like an altar boy, like an introverted, overly serious Radar from television's *M*A*S*H*. A recent graduate of Notre Dame, Captain Mike Stefanchik was short and very young—in the month he'd been in Haiti he'd turned twenty-seven—and although he spoke in a hushed voice I had to lean into, the syllables squirted out from between his thin lips with the speed of liturgy, or anxious confession. He was also trigger-happy.

"Captain's squared away," JC said as I sat back down. "We told him about you," he added cryptically, and whatever the NCOs had said would hold for another month, guaranteeing my access to the team, until Captain Mike's commanding officers started telling him about me, and my presence would turn negotiable.

"Where is everybody?" I asked Commo Jim and JC, who exchanged glances, hearing the question behind the question. Since the story had dropped far off the front page, I was a type of tourist, an object of ambiguity, if not by now suspicion—*What are you writing there, brah?*—but I had also become sort of a mascot for the team, a foil, comic relief, a way to measure the nonmilitary world, a curiosity and a break in the routine.

"You know, right after you and that French colonel left, Colonel Schroer showed up and took Barton away," said JC innocently. "He's been relieved of his command."

Because they didn't seem to be particularly broken up by Captain Barton's departure, perhaps they expected no one else would be, and they registered my lack of shock or surprise without comment. Yet I was shocked. A few days earlier, back in the States, I had phoned Barton's wife and heard the news but not the story. "What happened down there?" she begged me to tell her, trying without success to keep from crying. Something had gone wrong with the team, but Ed wouldn't tell her what. "Ed and Bill Miatke were such good friends before they left for Haiti. I don't understand what could have happened." All her husband had told her was that he was being reassigned to Les Cayes and not to worry about it. "Tell him his son isn't a baby anymore, tell him . . ." Well, more tears.

Candor has never been considered a military virtue, and however much I probed them, all Jim and JC would say was that Lieutenant Colonel Schroer had taken away Barton without any explanation; it just sort of happened, a natural event, a common mystery. Their uncomfortable and defensive body language was less than convincing. JC's eyes shifted away from contact, while Jim's locked on, taunting and hard, daring me to pursue the topic. It was clear the new captain wasn't going to get involved with this, but I could sense the acuity of his attention, and so I let it drop for the time being, the three of us knowing full well that Captain Barton's dismissal had been red-zoned, that we could never really put it aside but would return to it again and again.

FIELD NOTES

24 OCT 94

5. *Optempo:* We must maintain a sense of urgency. We seem to have lost the bubble on intel. We do not have a clean view of what is happening with the FADH and FRAPH that have gone to ground. In Somalia, there was a very apparent lull just before 3 OCT ambush.

30 OCT 94

3. *Captured Bad Guy:* Today in St Marc the team captured CPT Ravix. Wanted for shooting at Aristide in 1990. Killing a child in St Marc. Running drugs. Ordering other assassinations. Good job. . . .

5. *Terminology:* Be clear in your selection of words in sitreps. Maybe weapons search is better than weapons raid to accurately describe an activity. Higher HQ gets very interested in terminology, and we are required to clarify.

01 NOV 94

1. *Uniforms:* Stay in uniform outside, no matter where you are. One of the soldiers from an outlying area was visiting, sitting in a vehicle with his hat off. He was seen by MG Meade, who personally escorted the soldier into the JSOTF HQ for correction. Let's be smart.

04 NOV 94

4. *Mission:* I understand some of you are concerned we are doing things we were not trained for and are not defined in our missions. Maybe I can help clarify. You are doing unconventional operations. You are doing nation building from the grass roots. You are doing our motto "De Oppresso Liber" in the truest sense. You are accomplishing this thru, with, and by relationships with indigenous elements. In fact, you are doing this thru, with, and by two basically opposing elements to help them meet in some middle ground. You are providing the example of a professional army, a free citizen, of a democratic nation. You are providing both sides with liv-

ing proof of what they can do for themselves and you are providing the stability to give them a chance to try. The reason they come to you first for everything is their nature. Whoever owns an area is the authority for everything. You own the area in their eyes. By de facto, you are the ultimate authority. They have little concept of anything else except as you teach them. . . .

9. *De Oppresso Liber!* Hit hard, hit fast, shoot first!

CRIMES OF THE CENTURY

The detachment had been whittled back to its original six A-team members—Top Miatke, Ernie Brown, Bob Fox, Walt Plaisted, JC Collins, Jim Pledger—plus the new captain and Wesh, and its area of operation, already vast, had been expanded by a third. The chogees had been farmed out to new AOs in the hinterlands; Hollis Peery and Smiley Tom Milam were put behind desks with Captain Gottschalk and the rest of their team at the Forward Operating Base in Cap Haïtien; and Roger West had been rotated back to Bragg for schooling. In September they'd been told they'd be home by Christmas; now they hoped to get home by March 11—179 days on the temporary-duty payroll.

I had brought two dozen cans of snuff, yesterday's newspapers, an eclectic assortment of magazines. JC grabbed *Penthouse,* flipping right to the centerfold with hungry eyes. Commo Jim's wife sent the big lunk her back issues of *Cosmo* and *Women's World:* too odd for words. Something a bit kinky about that, I figured. To stir him up, I had specifically brought the dittohead his own game of Crossfire—the most recent issues of *The Nation* and *American Spectator*—but Jim, who dreamed of being a pilot, became riveted by a copy of *Military Aviation.* Gary, who at first made polite conversation with Wesh in Creole but then had sat down near us like an expressionless statue, gratefully pulled a book of political cartoons in front of him and stared at the drawings, trying to crack the code on the alien humor of *blanc* culture.

The team respected Gary and treated him as a friend, yet whenever we were inside the compound I noticed his general unease, his desire to be invisible. Here in the compound he was treading water, separated from his active role and anxious to be outside the walls, where we would once again be on our own, mates and accomplices. He held the American soldiers in esteem, recognized their sacrifice and marveled at their ethics, the inexplicable decency of their patience, but however much he had come to like them, he knew the absolute truth about them, that they were dangerous. Not necessarily to him; just dangerous.

Ignoring the torpidity, I kept prodding the team for news. Ernie and Bob Fox were on a supply run, Top and Walt out on patrol. The anecdotes dribbled out as the two sergeants turned the glossy pages. Chow had improved; the team had purchased a charcoal brazier, so they were able to slaughter (the medic's job) and barbecue a pig for Thanksgiving. Bob Fox and Walt, the team's senior and junior engineers, had taken to running laps inside the compound—like squirrels on a wheel—getting in shape for a ten-K Christmas race being hosted by the Tenth Mountain down in Port-au-Prince. The lack of organized PT was a hole in their collective lives, so they'd built a workout station in the shade of a tree next to the quarters where the team now slept—a dip bar, a bench press; barbells made out of tin cans filled with cement and plugged onto each end of galvanized pipe.

The two engineers had also built what they thought of as a dream latrine. It had arms and a bench for reading material, paint, even a light, but when Walt installed the switch, the city power—the most unpredictable of entities here in the kingdom of unpredictability—came on and knocked him on his ass. Electricity ebbed and flowed, a windfall of opportunity. No matter the time, day or night, when the power came on in Limbé or Cap Haïtien, lights would pulse, radios would blare, welders would pop awake and set to work, women would iron clothes, and, at three in the morning, bleary-eyed kids would open schoolbooks.

The town was the same as before—running feuds in all directions. More and more, the real enemy in the SF's mind was General Meade, who had apparently gone off his rocker, driving around the countryside in a froth, disemboweling Third Group's officers and enlisted men for uniform violations. The word went out among the Green Berets: Make believe the Tenth Mountain is a *foreign army* and work with them accordingly.

Under this gray cloud of convention, the team had tried to conduct its business. They'd humiliated Paul James for his Lavalasan antics—

spray-painting graffiti on the gate: DEMOCRACY, YES. RECONCILIATION WITH THE MACOUTE ARMY, NO! "He who sins dies," James had stupidly threatened the new captain. "Don't ever talk about death around me again," said Stefanchik, his finger in the guy's face. James had to scrub off the paint and offer a public apology, and ever since, he walked around like a beaten dog. He resigned from the Youth Committee of his own volition, taking a megaphone into the marketplace to preach brotherly love. A Notre Dame conversion.

ODA 311 had also, finally, got the FADH pulling twenty-four-hour guard duty around the first of November, but it hadn't been easy. Ougousse, the medic, had refused. Walt Plaisted, the sergeant who could talk lovingly about the prose of Wendell Berry, locked him in the casern's jail, woke him at dawn, gave him a shovel and made him dig holes until sundown, then made him stand watch midnight until 6:00 A.M., gave him back the shovel and made him start digging again, but tubercular Ougousse had started spitting up blood—"Man," said Walt, "I never seen anybody break so fast"—and now the FADH/IPSF had nicknamed Walt "The Punisher."

But no matter how hard the team tried to motivate, or intimidate, the FADH into action, they mostly lay around in the back of the compound, bitching, and now, even after they'd exchanged quarters and reversed roles, the old FADH/new IPSF sat around in the casern all day, still bitching, and everybody knew that if they went out to town to enforce regulations or make arrests, they weren't going to come back alive, which is why when a woman in Bas Limbé hired a man to kill her husband, the team had to go there themselves and arrest the murderer. They were tired of arresting murderers, but who else was going to do it? They arrested the woman too, put her in the small cell in Bas Limbé's *avant poste,* as primitive as a frontier lockup, and that same night a crowd broke into the jail and beat her to death.

The crime of the century, though, in the team's mind, had happened the night before my arrival back in Limbé. Around twilight, Sergeant Jerome came dragging his sorry ass over from the IPSF casern to inform the team that he had apprehended a "very bad man" and wanted to be told what to do with him. Captain Stefanchik told Jerome to imprison him or take him to court. Two of Jerome's men walked him down to the courthouse but returned a while later to say they couldn't bring the man back.

What do you mean, you can't bring him back? said the captain. We can't bring him back, they said, and we need more rifles.

Captain Mike issued them four more rifles, and now six IPSF went down to the courthouse. Those six soon came back. We can't get him out, they said; we need the truck. Okay, said the captain, take the truck. So the six IPSF took the pickup truck and drove down past the far side of the marketplace to the courthouse, but they were back honking at the compound's gates within five minutes: We can't get him out. What kind of bullshit is this? thought Stefanchik, and he said, Walt, let's go, so he and Walt walked down there, the dark night suddenly filled with noise, quarreling knots of people, voices yelling as they approached the courthouse. Walt noticed Bossman Jean Moulin's red ball cap bobbing as always in the middle of the ruckus, a looming nuisance.

They pushed their way through the crowd and went inside, where the judge told the new captain that the "very bad man" happened to be an attaché, but Stefanchik was too green to understand the full implication of what *attaché* meant to the mob in the street. The captain tried to talk to the crowd outside, telling them they had to let justice take care of this: We're going to take him back to the prison, and meanwhile you should talk to the judge, let him take your statements. Stefanchik spoke in French, but not many people in the provinces understood French, the language of the ruling class, the language of power. The captain went back inside. The attaché was short, like the captain himself, so Stefanchik wrapped his left arm across the back of the man's shoulders, holding his M-16 in his other hand. The six IPSF with their M-1s formed a cordon around the pair, and with Walt covering the rear, they went through the door, wedged into the crowd, and started moving, making the turn onto the main street.

People started flying out of the darkness through the cordon, coming in at all angles to kick and punch the attaché, walloping him on the head. The captain still had his arm around the man, and the blows were glancing off him as well. They had just gotten to the block between the park and the marketplace, when Stefanchik said, *Screw this*, spun around, flicked his rifle on semiautomatic, and fired off two or three rounds. *Whoosh!* The street cleared, except for a few punks, and when the captain turned around, there was Walt back at the corner, wrapped up with the Bossman.

Stefanchik pushed the attaché into the arms of the IPSF and told them to get him to the casern, then he ran back to help Walt. The downward pressure toward something evil was suffocating. "Let's get out of here," he yelled, but Walt had his blood up, grappling with the wiry Jean Moulin. "He grabbed me," Walt roared; you could hear in his voice that his whole being was committed to the struggle and he didn't want to release his grip on Bossman. "Okay, Walt, move forward!" the captain ordered, and when Walt finally let go, Stefanchik grabbed Jean Moulin by the arm and pushed him toward the casern, prodding him along with the barrel of his rifle.

The new captain had never seen the Bossman before and didn't know who he was; it startled him when the fellow started yelling in English. "Don't push me, don't push me, man!" They were halfway across the marketplace and the crowd had begun to regather, when Stefanchik for no reason he could explain, let Bossman go, telling him he'd better come to the casern tomorrow, or something dumb like that.

The Humvee screamed up, with Top and the boys. They had heard the shots and were ready to rock, but the incident, at least for the moment, was over. Back in the light of the compound, everyone could now see that the side of Walt's head was coated with blood. After that, of course, Jean Moulin disappeared, and the team, its killer instincts aroused, became obsessed with hunting him down. *That's the one thing you don't do, brah: you put one finger on one of us, and we'll come deliver the bill*—a fair and rather modest rule number one, I thought, for an occupying army.

Inside the mess hall, Commo Jim had rigged up a low-wattage radio station, and for two hours every night and for the first time in history, Limbé had a groove in the air that was all its own, the script carefully composed by Captain Mike in printed block letters, the sounds and the vibes brought down and around and back at you by Wolfman Wesh: *This is a special dedication for Jean Moulin the Bossman. Yesterday he got ahold of an American soldier. That was a very bad thing to do. You don't know how bad but you will, I promise you that, remember my promise.* Wesh's liquid voice segued into an audio wave of musical aggression, something nasty from the sound track of a martial-arts flick. Clearly, in the six weeks I'd been away from Limbé, the town had developed a serious attitude problem toward the Special Forces, and ODA 311, I was beginning to see, had all but exhausted its supply of charitable impulses.

On our way to spend the night in Cap, Gary and I detoured to Grande Rivière du-Nord to see how the crackerjacks on Trent Suko's team were handling the muddle. Suko had gotten a tip about a weapons cache in GR du-Nord's Masons' lodge. I don't think so, Captain Suko told his sources—he had an image of Masons being an upright bunch with a long tradition of community leadership—but the town's patriots persisted. Oh, yes, they said, the Masons' lodge was a FRAPH clubhouse; the Masons hid weapons there because they felt the soldiers wouldn't go in.

The team took the mayor and several ex-FADH with them on the raid. Breaking the lock off the door and stepping inside, they glanced brusquely around at what seemed to be an austere meeting hall, then one of them opened a closet and froze. *Jesus!* The space was stacked top to bottom with human skulls. They pried up the floorboards, and underneath were skeletons draped in chains.

Suko ordered the FADH sergeant to see what was behind the door at the bottom of a stairwell, but the man was pop-eyed, sweating bullets, and wouldn't budge. *Get in there,* Suko commanded, but the team had to kick down the door themselves. The light beamed below into the sour, gamy darkness, and the first men stepped cautiously into the subterranean chill and down lower into an earthen pit, seeing an altar covered with lumps of candle wax and human bones. That was weird enough but not as spooky as the paintings on the wall, anatomical graphics—a liver, a brain, a heart, blobs of other organs, illustrated directions on how to dissect a human being, the Haiti of nightmares and myths and bad movies and the wet dreams of racists.

Suko, however, took it all in stride; he had anthropologists' blood in his veins. He picked up a ceremonial spear, then some of the ritual fetishes—this place was actually sort of cool. When the team didn't find any weapons, the captain made them replace the floorboards and put everything back where they'd found it, then they relocked the lodge and left, saying, *Right on with your bad voodoo selves.*

Wanting to know more about what he had just seen, Suko went to the town's rectory and knocked on the door. The sanguine priest explained: "Well, they're not robbing graves or killing people, if that's what you're worried about. A lot of people they die, they arrange to have their bodies interred in the Masons' lodge. Perhaps you know already, *vodou's* ingrained in the Haitian culture. I don't think it's good, but it's not really bad here. It's not evil but rather base superstition. It's even in the Catholic Church, and whether I like it or not, you're not going to get rid of it."

Suko found the priest's opinions levelheaded and faintly soothing, and he thought to himself, Hey, what about Westminster Abbey—everybody's buried in the floor there too. Hey, if you want to see bones, go to Rome.

Things had come a long way since Gitmo, where the rules of engagement, especially for Captain Craig Marks and his team, were annotated to allow for unusual provisions. Marks's A-team had been deployed into Port-de-Paix, on the northwestern coast, an area where, if you could trust the intel hysterics, wild-haired witch doctors in loincloths and Ray-Bans worked day and night over boiling cauldrons, cooking up an invasion-sized batch of poison extracts to repel the Americans.

The Pentagon had no way of knowing how serious the Haitians were about using the highly lethal "voodoo" powder. The chemicals weren't effective anyway unless they got into a victim's bloodstream, customarily through a skin abrasion, though the eyes, nose, and mouth were portals of last resort. The chain of command wasn't going to take a chance on its happening, so Marks's ROE had been amended to permit his men, if approached by Haitians with *clenched hands*, to shoot to kill, the idea being that kamikaze voodoo priests, to protect their evil kingdom, intended to throw the breath-stopping white dust into the faces of the soldiers.

But it never happened. Chemical warfare, whether primitive or refined, elicited the most uncompromising reaction from one's enemies, and could be employed successfully only against weakness. It was true that during Haiti's slave insurrections poison had been used as an agent of mass destruction, but as a modern weapon of war, the vaunted powders merely provided the FADH and its allies with yet another option, should they so choose, for committing physical and cultural suicide in the face of American firepower.

Earlier in the century, the Marines had done their Christian best to eradicate *vodou*, to criminalize even its most innocent manifestations, but by the time the Special Forces arrived in Haiti, the world had evolved enough for the American soldiers to assume a radically different posture toward the practice. In a very short time, they went from regarding *vodou* as a potential threat to welcoming it as an avenue for a few laughs. They saw no need to repudiate or denounce what to them was a religion manqué but instead were content to mock the men—mostly but not exclusively macoutes—who exploited the power of *vodou*'s image and imagery. It was a strange wrap of incongruities: Third Group's right-wing political passions muted by the cultural relativism of the most politically correct army ever fielded.

The spirits switched allegiance, and Captain Marks and his men—all the Green Berets in Haiti—became the Supreme Practitioners, the guys with the most jacked mojo in town. All over the island, the Special Forces were vanquishing werewolves with silver bullets. Night patrols transformed themselves into the living dead by flipping their night observation goggles front to back, which turned the eyeholes into twin cones of ghoulish green light, burning crab-stalk eyes in the darkness. Throughout the countryside, villagers believed that after sundown the SF transformed themselves into hobgoblins wandering the curfewed streets, sparring with recalcitrant *loas*.

When Captain Marks started opening up his AO, he and his men walked into mountain hamlets and presented themselves as the macoute-cleaning service. "We're into pest control," announced the captain, running a hand over his shaved skull. By now Marks was known far and wide in Haiti as the notorious Tet Caylé—Captain Bonehead. "How can we help you God-fearing folks up here? What's your greatest problem? Is it education? Is it macoutes stealing around at night?"

"Oh, we have very big problems," the village elders invariably told the soldiers. Vampires were coming into their houses at night and stealing their babies' souls. Stealing babies' souls was the number one reason for discontent in the hinterlands.

Ah, well. Let's look in the manual for this one. Captain Marks instructed his men to start carrying four chem lights in their pouches, different colors to ward off different evil spirits. They tried to keep the exorcisms color-coded: Green chem lights were for werewolves; for general hauntings, yellow; blue ones for problems with more esoteric trickster spirits; red ones for vampires stealing babies' souls. You shook up the light stick, sliced off the plastic top. Mothers would queue up with their swaddled infants. A commando made the sign of the cross on the child's forehead, and when the sun went down, the crucifixional smudges would begin to glow with heavenly protection. If it was a big family and they had a lot of problems, the Green Berets did the Moses treatment, passing the chem light over the door of their house. And that was the end of vampire abductions in the northwest mountains.

Marks told himself it was just a Haitian cultural thing: *We like to be scared.*

VOLUNTEERS AND
GRANOLA MUNCHERS

In the fruity morning sweetness of air and light, there was Sergeant Miatke sizing me up with his pale, small eyes, bemused and wry, a look deliberately prosecutorial that said wherever I'd been I had it easy. Our lives had been and always would be different, radically so, regardless of the intimacy of shared risk and brothering midnights that were now between us, and I knew that Top, the most volatile and yet most tender man on the team, was always going to greet me this way.

Rivalry between teams was not to be discounted, and it irritated Top Miatke to hear I'd been over in Grande Rivière du-Nord, visiting Captain Suko's House of Wonders, probably sucking up and gaping at these heroes. "All the big shots ignore Limbé," said Top with a slight sniff, not fully content to be anticool.

Nevertheless, everything was on hold this morning, because the boss had promised a visit—Colonel Mark Boyatt, the army's foremost unconventional-warfare advocate and enthusiast, cheerleader, cross-pollinater of ideas and solutions among the lads. A commando-scholar, he had even ducked out of Haiti in November to lecture at Tufts University on the many beauties, from the UW perspective, of the Special Forces' mission on the island. The beast was *his* operation, this was the tiger destiny had chosen him to ride, and he wasn't shy about promoting it as the greatest opportunity since Vietnam for the men who wore the green berets. However much the future of war could be foreseen by the laser beam and the microchip, the future of peacemaking and peacekeeping would depend on the resilient human skills that were the essence of SF doctrine, and Boyatt owned that future, at least for the time being, lugging it around with him like the Ark of the Covenant to dazzle nonbelievers.

Miatke was occupied with dull homework, sitting at the mess hall table hunched over like a weary man, his nose in a notebook binder, the briefing book command finally issued as a splendid afterthought. The sergeant tried to make conceptual sense of the administrative structures of town and district, like studying the blueprint for a pile of rubble that was once a building. I knew Top well enough by now to know he was biting his tongue, swollen with suppressed and apparently bitter words, like *Barton* and *Meade*, and that he meant to erupt and spew those words on me, the willing, bottomless ear, but that I should back off until he was good and ready. Making myself a nest atop a cot in the far corner of the mess hall, I fixed a cup of instant coffee and, hearing the radio crackle with pilot noise and the new captain crank a Humvee, invited myself along to fetch Colonel Boyatt from the LZ at the soccer field.

The Black Hawk eased out of the sky, rolling clouds of dust over a ragtag pack of children, who listened skeptically to the fantastic tales of kids decapitated, squashed, blown into the trees by rotor wash, shouted at them by Petty Officer Wesh. *It's ten thousand machetes! Run for your lives!* (The schoolteachers solved the problem of children jumping up from their seats to see the helicopters by handing out extra math homework.) Then the bird was dying with a banshee screech, and Boyatt and his aide-de-camp were hatched onto the field. Back during the rock-and-roll days of the invasion, even as his men took over the island, the colonel was so low profile it took the media several weeks to figure out that Boyatt was the Elvis of Operation Uphold Democracy. My day would come with Boyatt, but this one wasn't it, I soon realized, as the colonel's eyes passed over me, giving up a half smile to another faceless media flea crawling through the luxuriant fur of The Story. Inside the compound, with apologetic politeness Captain Mike blocked me from entering the mess hall, off limits during Boyatt's visit, he said in his racing whisper.

Out front in the yard of the casern, like sparrows huddled on a branch, were the volunteer police that Captain Barton, the imaginary colonel, and the town had labored with such diligence to muster. I was a familiar and not unfriendly face who had attended the miracle of their brave birth and had saluted their promise. Now here they were, third-string nobodies living on a plank bench underneath a tree, doomed to flat-eyed observance of the useless but anointed IPSF, clinging to the slowly rotting apple of hope given to them by the American soldiers, waiting to be roll-called into a meaningful life.

They leapt toward me like starved and neglected phantoms, invisible to all eyes but my own. Clean and pure and able-bodied (if a bit slight), they were being eaten alive by their innocence. They'd never been rewarded with so much as a nickel for their time, yet they held steadfast to the assumption that *Bar-tone* and the imaginary colonel would return to rescue them, promote them forward into the interim training program, and although I already knew they had no chance of being recruited, I didn't have the heart to tell them.

Looping back out through the marketplace and into the SF compound, I arrived just in time to float a question past Boyatt as he prepared to leave: "Sir, what's going to happen to the civilian police?"

"Who?" said the colonel, flashing the courtly smile of a great and busy man; you could see such smiles every day on Capitol Hill, disappearing into limousines, but his prefect's eyes were already beyond me, beyond Limbé.

"The civil police force stood up by Captain Barton and the French colonel," I said.

"Ah," said Boyatt as he stepped toward the Humvee, "the volunteers in the community watch program." The colonel said casually that they were making a contribution, or doing a fine job, or some faint praise equally damning, but the truth was, the creation of the ineffective civil police was an act of desperation, another of democracy's placebos, the best the Special Forces could do, given no resources or help from Meade. The colonel and I would discuss the subject again, but by that time its proportions would have grown twisted and diseased, multiplied to tragic.

Admiral Miller, as he was not reluctant to say, had his act together. He had a fine appreciation for the fact that much of what the White House got the country embroiled in overseas required more manpower than just the Department of Defense. A wide spectrum of interagency response had to be dovetailed into the Haiti mission for it to be productive, but by the time Miller found himself looking squarely into the eye of his own video cam, telling the commander in chief that "We see the assistance network, the humanitarian effort, the multinational contribution, coming together quickly, as we have planned," the admiral had to know he was bluffing.

Despite Miller's efforts, the early lack of interagency support became a major shortcoming for Operation Uphold Democracy. For months, the NGOs (nongovernmental organizations) and PVOs (private voluntary organizations) were virtual no-shows, skeletal crews dryly composing further studies, evaluating earlier evaluations, assessing Haiti's needs ad infinitum. If everybody who had pledged to be there on the ground had been there, the admiral believed, the mission would have been spared the fog of ambiguity that became its trademark, it wouldn't have taken thirty days to remove Aristide from the plush hell of D.C. and blast him back into the palace, and the tar baby could be passed forthrightly off to the UN, where it would be gummed and paperworked to death.

You might think that when a magnificent army invades and, with nary a shot fired, conquers, they would then at least *imagine* themselves in control of the society they now occupied, but that wasn't the case here. The American willingness to assert their de facto status as the last word on Haitian law and order came and went in a tumultuous, bewildering flux, measured in nanoseconds. They were there but could barely find their voice; they were good at making themselves look busy, but the central operational question that remained unanswered was, *Now what?* "Haiti's Vietnam without the bullets," Tony Schwalm, one of the Special Forces majors, had said to me, "all the way down to 'What are we doing here?'" Haiti was "a rucksack march with no pick-up zone. 'Are we there yet?' *Keep going.*" (The admiral held up his hand for me to stop: "But don't lay that at the military's doorstep. Who said we had to set up sessions with Cédras?")

The admiral's mission was to get ashore and establish a stable and secure environment *for the troops*. Whatever the President had told the Almighty Voter on television on September 15 had rapidly attenuated down to force protection under the auspices of General Meade. That attenuation made the mission absurd: U.S. soldiers had invaded Haiti for the primary purpose of protecting themselves. Stopping the brutality wasn't in the mission. The Haitian military was supposed to police itself while the agencies and departments and Aristide himself sorted everything out, but nobody came to sort it out. The Department of Justice had promised a series of international police monitors to provide a bridge between the U.S. military and the Haitian police forces, but where were they? Miller wanted Haitians working Haitian problems, he wanted Cédras immediately out and Aristide immediately in, he wanted to vet the FADH and make them anew, but there were all these little turf wars breaking out among bureaucrats, diplomats, and the military.

"It was sloppy, right?" said Admiral Miller.

The vacuum held, and the Special Forces A-teams hurled themselves into the lawless muddle without a road map, "burdened," as Miller would say, "with assessing the situation as they found it . . . until the overall umbrella could be established." Now it was December; after three straight months of miserable downpour, not an umbrella in sight. ODA 311 had assessed the situation, all right, and it was getting on their nerves in a bad way.

The international police monitors who had started to arrive in-country wouldn't come out of their hotels, the Argentinians were keeping the pimps happy in Cap Haïtien, the Guatemalan team wasn't doing anything because the Tenth Mountain didn't trust them, and the Tenth Mountain wasn't doing anything but guarding itself. "Fuck all these infantrymen," said Top Miatke. "Every dollar spent on them could have been spent more constructively on engineering units, medical units, MP units, who at least have the skills to make this country better."

Finally, in the diffusing contrails of the invasion, the humanitarians had begun to appear, isolated sightings and then a great fluttering on the horizon, like a migration of monarch butterflies. At the compound (I was beginning to think of it as 311's hideout), it was goodbye to the testosterone—Boyatt and company—hello to the pheromones: Ann and Carol, two facilitators from the International Organization for Migration, a Geneva-based NGO contracted to serve as USAID's handmaiden in Haiti. Carol had been living in the Hotel Christophe since September, determining the needs of Cap Haïtien and various municipalities throughout the Plaine du Nord. Ann—a former foreign-aid adviser to the Republican Party (like being a sin consultant to the Vatican)—had just arrived and was busy reassessing Carol's assessments. Together they had come to Limbé to meet with Captain Mike and the mayoress, Madame Bruno, whom they expected to identify potential civil affairs (CA) projects for the town, for which the IOM would then provide funding.

When the women walked in, for a second the men looked wrung out. Inevitably, women broke the monotony by eroticizing it. Lechery brightened in the soldiers' eyes, lust was on the telepathic currents. They'd gone three months without touching female flesh and were due for three more of blue-balled abstinence. Madame Bruno rumbled in, dour-faced and hugely bothered. She touched the women's extended hands as if they were last week's fish, looking over and beyond the new captain's head as she greeted him with an utter lack of enthusiasm, not quite able to believe, it seemed to me, that this sprat, this puny white child in uniform, could exert influence over her small but only world.

Beyond the introductions, the episode was short on etiquette, toffee-skinned Carol translating into Creole and the captain piping up intermittently in surprisingly passable French. For the most part, though, the three of us sat back out of the line of fire and watched these two battle-axes of the same alpha species, the dark-haired Waspy American in blue jeans and man's oxford shirt, the Haitian in her Sunday dress and saucer eye-glasses, measure each other's formidability and then go at it.

Until now, there had been a preposterous twenty-dollar ceiling for A-team CA projects, under which 311 had managed to clean out a reservoir and roof a school. The money had inflated to a realistic thousand, but for Ann, today's magic number had stuck on twenty-five. She interrogated the mayoress about Limbé's budget, and Madame Bruno answered with supercilious harumphs. Funds were always irregular; the town would ship off tax revenues to the central government in Port-au-Prince, and for at least the past ten months not a gourde came back. Madame counted off the community's priorities, and Ann latched onto the pestilential market-place, the first horror, overt but superficial, endured by any visitor to the casern.

Did the mayor's office employ street cleaners? Yes. Tools? Six wheel-barrows, but only two in working condition; the other four were "dead." Ann pressed forward with the hitch: an integral part of IOM's philosophy of development was to seduce a community into contributing the labor, mostly volunteer, for a project, and the IOM would supply the tools and expertise. On this basis, Ann announced happily, the IOM was prepared to grant the municipality of Limbé twenty-five bucks to repair its wheelbarrows.

"Now," said Ann, "when can we start? I'd like to get the marketplace cleaned up before New Year's."

Madame Bruno, however, was not touched by this charity and countered that her schedule was too filled up to do anything before January. Captain Mike and I looked away from each other, trying not to be smirking know-it-alls.

"Perhaps you have a deputy or a scheduler who can help us?" Ann proposed. She argued for speed, and Madame Bruno scoffed at her impertinence, the niggling altruism of the *femme blanc,* the mayoress as unmovable as her great size implied. Ann jumped aboard another subject, dogged in her resolution to solve problems she had not yet begun to fathom. Maybe this was the right way to do her job, her style of cold efficiency dictated by the fluorescence of faraway offices, but it was not the way to get anything done—though maybe not getting anything done *was* her job.

"What about electricity?" Ann asked. "How much do people pay, how much would they conceivably pay, for electricity?" Madame Bruno responded with a withering roll of the eyes and never bothered to reply.

The captain remained poker-faced. The second wave had commenced.

"Tree huggers!" said Commo Jim, cackling like a maniac. "Our prayers have been answered, brah."

FIELD NOTES

19 NOV 94

7. *Our Mission:* Don't get discouraged with what you are doing. . . . It is normal in UW to be faced with a confusing, seemingly disjointed and non-supportive political environment. . . . What an opportunity, your own UW world.

22 NOV 94

6. *Redeployment:* You have become too important to U.S. policy to go home just yet. Apparently, the administration wants to ensure a policy success in Haiti and believes your continued presence is absolutely essential. Supposedly, President Clinton himself, at a briefing today, approved the decision for all SOF to stay in Haiti at least until sometime in JAN 95, at which time the situation will be reassessed. In reality, this is a very big honor.

05 DEC 94

1. *Jacmel:* Captured killer of the two U.S. embassy Haiti employees. I understand he was seeing a voodoo priest to get a potion to make him invisible so he could escape. Not. Good job, guys. Everything is cool.

2. *Werewolves:* . . . The guys at Magasin killed a werewolf several weeks ago with silver bullets.

06 DEC 94

6. *Attitude:* I need each of you to listen and think about what I am going to say. There is a perception that we have an attitude problem. That we think we are being picked on. That we have a chip on our shoulders. You are the finest professionals I have ever worked with. So I know. But if we are giving this perception we are doing something wrong. . . . I ask you to help me turn this perception around. Appearance is the first step—no one is watching, but I expect you to enforce uniform standards always. Military courtesy: Salutes, demeanor, snappy, smart, crisp. Haircuts and mustaches—strictly regulation. The perception is not what we are, so we must work to change that perception.

BITCHFEST

They were on security alert that night. There was to be a *manifestation* to grab a hostage, something like that, something to do with Bossman, perhaps, or something to do with the IPSF. It wasn't clear, but the threat deepened the quiet within the compound and got mixed up with the suggestion of Christmas and made the darkness seem cooler and mysteriously comforting. The voices in the marketplace never really rose above a rich murmur, like traders camped outside the gates of a medieval city, and in the distance an under-the-skin pulse of drums.

A Humvee patrol was mounted, a fuck-with-Bossman's-mind posse. Walt and Bob Fox and Commo Jim and Captain Mike and Wesh strapped on load-bearing vests and armed themselves. Out the gate we went, slowly into the night, no headlights as we edged through dark, empty streets, the engine a soft chutter telegraphing our presence rolling by. You could feel people freeze behind their curtains as we cruised past Bossman's mother's shuttered house, turned around at the end of the lane, and came back— *You can run, but you can't hide, Bossman*—then worked a grid of blocks and alleys up toward the far end of town. Jim wore night-vision goggles so he could look in the windows at women in various stages of undress. Occasionally I could see people in the candled shadows of their homes eating from tin dishes, splashing water into their faces from plastic basins, playing cards at a rickety table, children curled asleep on floor mats, as we slipped almost noiselessly through the blackness, a consummate foreignness prowling on the edge of the town's dreams. Caretakers, monsters.

The houses ended. We were in a place I'd never been, a dirt clearing and, beyond, a canebrake scratched with light as the captain flicked on the headlights to illuminate a half-burned makeshift *vodou* offering or shrine or fetish, hard to tell. I hopped out the rear of the Humvee to squat over the objects—a smudged *vévé*, sticks arranged in some cryptic but uninteresting fashion, a charred calabash bowl, strips of scarlet cloth. Nothing more than colorful trash to everybody but Wesh, who wasn't afraid of any man but was afraid of *vodou*.

This was where the drums had heated up, where the night-blooming *manifestation* had prudently contained itself. The team talked derisively about something I had never heard mentioned in Limbé—gangs. They'd divided the town into sections called Iraq, America (which started at the market and went three streets deep; this was Bossman's neighborhood), and Israel, and the disputed territory between all three neighborhoods was called Kuwait. The Red Army was supposedly Bossman Jean Moulin's gang; the Iraqi Army was led by a professional criminal named Thoby Frasier—aka Saddam Hussein; and the punks who lived behind the Baptist church had formed the Israeli Army. The SF thought it was nothing more than vandals' fantasy, but they weren't sure.

We piled back into the Humvee—Captain Mike squashed the fetish under the tires as he turned around—and we motored without any further pretense of stealth back to the compound. I parked myself at the table while the detachment rotated through their shifts, one man on security, one man with me on radio watch, trying to get someone to talk about Captain Barton, but they didn't particularly care for the subject. The soldiers took deep breaths as if readying themselves to answer my questions, a little animosity would leak out when they exhaled, but that was it—until later, when Top came on for a post-midnight eruption. With the throaty cough of the generator in the background, we conversed in low voices, batting around the minutiae of our lives, trading opinions like baseball cards, an everlasting bitchfest in the middle of the night.

◻   ◻   ◻

Top Miatke had officers on his mind. Their weight pressed down on him from above and made him sore and cantankerous. Haiti wasn't worth losing your ass for, losing your career, few things were, and the threats he had to listen to were stressing him out: *If the general sees you and your uniform ain't right, you're gone.* He kept thinking about Command Sergeant Major Bone, probably the most feared man in the Special Forces. Command Sergeant Major Bone was a Book Man, Mister Walk-and-Talk AR 670-1—the uniform regulation—a parrot for the conventional army's viewpoint: *You're not special!* Bone liked formation at six-thirty in the morning, organized physical training, nine o'clock formation with an inspection of haircuts, mustaches, and uniforms. Be here at this time, that time. You go, you come back, another formation, another inspection, fuck your grades, fuck what you learn in school and what you're able to do.

When Bone visited Haiti, his only concern as far as Top could tell was you better have on cotton-web black belts, you better have perfect uniforms, you better have haircuts, and you better look like soldiers. Bone thought all SF were rogues, and what he focused on had nothing to do with the mission and nothing to do with what made the Special Forces excel in Haiti. All this in-house bullshit, yet back in Washington, Top had heard, in order to be able to speak intelligently these days, you had to know terms like ODA, ODB, FOB—you had to be able to talk SF.

The SF hierarchy was afraid of the conventional forces, Top truly believed; they'd go out of their way to please the General Meades and General Closes, trying to prove that, hey, we're in the army too. "The hell with it," Top said. Either this country needed a special operations capability or it didn't, and you don't chop control of Special Operations Forces to a division commander like Meade. It didn't matter that the son of a bitch was fifty-four years old and a two-star general. He wasn't mature enough. Instead of saying, This is who the Special Forces are, this is what they can do for me, and turning them loose, Meade fouls them up, puts them under his SOPs, and then harangues Boyatt and Potter and every Green Beret who crosses his path because they look different, because he thinks they're punkish, faddish, because they want to wear high-tech boots and gloves without fingers in them.

As for Boyatt, Top felt the colonel was caught up in a strange romance with Haiti, disconcerting his troops with some of the doctrinal scenarios he saw in the mission: *You have to deal with competing guerrilla factions* (*i.e., the people and the FADH*) *and get them together against a common enemy, anarchy,* said Boyatt on his fireside show. *You have to organize and arrange for education of the guerrilla force children,* but the late-night messages got garbled, and more than one team thought Boyatt was telling them they might organize a medical service for the FADH, start schools for FADH children. It was Boyatt's opportunity of a lifetime, said Top, and yet the colonel couldn't understand why his team leaders weren't crawling all over him to kiss his ass.

The mission was whitewash, politically motivated junk. No matter how hard he looked at it, Top couldn't find a trace of U.S. national interest anywhere. The embargo never should have happened; Americans could have effected change in Haiti without bringing in the military—Boyatt's plan for training a refugee mujahideen force was the ticket. Coming in here soft was only going to prolong the struggle. The fricking Haitian army no longer even existed, and yet the people were still convinced the U.S. was in bed with the FADH. But how, Top wondered, could you ever be in bed with such worthless creatures?

When Top kicked the Haitians out of the compound and into the front headquarters on Thanksgiving, they all freaked out, and Top told them, Too bad; you guys made your bed, now sleep in it. The people will kill us, they whined. Did you think about that before you beat people for the last three years? Top said. It's time to pay the piper. Sergeant Jerome thought Marc Lamour had issued a standing order that Jerome was to be captured and brought up to Le Borgne to be executed; now he was afraid to sleep in his own house. When Top ordered him to go make his first arrest by himself in his new role as IPSF, Jerome begged for the use of a helicopter. Get a rope and drag the guy in, said Top. I don't have a rope, said Jerome. And although Meade thought that IPSF shouldn't be deployed in an area without international police monitors, the team was never going to get IPM help in Limbé, because there were no three-star hotels, no restaurants, no bars, and no nightlife. After the team begged and begged, the IPMs drove down once from Cap Haïtien, looked aghast at the civilian police, said, "Well, you've got a crude system here," and left.

Top thought sometimes that he was living among Frenjies from *Deep Space Nine*. Out in the marketplace, a woman had built a cage to house her psychotic mother. A nephew chopped his sleeping uncle's head into three pieces while the victim's five sons stood by. It was justice, the sons said; our father killed somebody long ago. With pit bull ferocity, an eleven-year-old girl was bitten to shreds by her eighteen-year-old sister, who, after their parents died, had wanted the two-room house for herself. The vice delegate wouldn't trust the one-legged judge with a key to the courthouse. David Hodges was livid that the SF had arrested a FRAPH leader and his wife in Fort Liberté. "He's one of the finest men I know," sputtered Hodges (the couple were dispatched to Port-au-Prince but released within twenty-four hours—by order of the White House, or so the SF rumor went).

At the tiny wattle jail in Petit Bourg de Port Margot, two prisoners escaped by pissing on the wall and scraping a hole through the mud daub. In the Limbé jail, Top had a banana thief, a pig thief, and a jewel thief. The three were so happy in their detention they sang at night; they'd been there so long now that they had begun to boss around new prisoners. The one-legged judge told the banana thief, All you have to do is tell me you took the bananas and you're free, but the banana thief wouldn't admit to his crime because he was gaining weight in jail. Throughout all this madness drifted Top's old friend the lunatic, still tied up, waving at the SF as though they were birds of a feather.

It was late, almost four o'clock in the morning; you could hear the rustle of *marchands* arriving in the marketplace from the countryside when I finally asked Top Miatke about Captain Barton and we had the first of several conversations, spread out over the year and a half ahead, until what amounted to the captain's court-martial.

When you and the imaginary colonel left, Top said, Barton fell to pieces, he quit. The French colonel wasn't there to do his talking and his work for him anymore, so he stopped making trips into the countryside, he started sleeping in, he thought he'd been run ragged, he started sleeping during the day, he wouldn't stay awake for Boyatt's fireside chat, he stopped shaving, he started sleeping with no clothes on at night, he started leaving his food lying around, he started arguing about he's not going to pull security at night, he fell asleep on guard and then denied it, he gave money to Paul James and then denied that too, he wasn't doing shit but arguing with people who came in with problems, screaming at them in English.

"He fell the hell apart, I mean just totally," said Top, so they relieved his ass just like Boyatt wanted from the get-go and brought in Shore, a temporary captain, and then the team got Captain Mike. "Shore and Stefanchik were one hundred and eighty degrees different than that man," said Top. "They fit in from day one with the team. They were planning their time over weeks-long periods. Barton was trying to do everything minute by minute and never had a fricking plan. Both of the new captains were like, *Top, give me a time to pull guard. I don't give a damn what time it is, and if somebody has to pull an extra shift, I want it to be me.* Barton's attitude was [Top mimicking a simpy whine], *I gotta pull guard!? But I'm a captain, I'm an officer.*"

Top went off duty and Ernie Brown sat down, rubbing his puffy eyes. Ernie had never been called anything so much in his life as *blanc. Blanc, blanc, blanc.* "Who's a *blanc?*" he'd say. *Je suis noir,* but the Haitians would only stand there looking at him, screaming *blanc.* His skin was the same color as theirs, but they weren't seeing it. He and Bob Fox went down to Plaisance to fix the water main, and this guy looked straight at Ernie and said, White! *in English.* Nah, said Ernie, un-unh, no, N-O. It was almost too much for someone born black in Alabama in 1956. In Haiti, black was the color of man—*neg*—and white—*blanc*—was unfortunately the color of both abandonment and salvation.

A white American soldier told him that Haitians didn't respect black American soldiers, which wasn't true but it pissed him off, and he told the guy, "I really don't give a shit about them respecting me, so long as they do what I say to do." There was racism in the military, sure; anybody would be a fool to say there wasn't. People are going to be people: "Remember where I grew up—Birmingham in the sixties." He'd seen it in the service, but how much of it there was or how bad it was he couldn't say, because it was such an easy thing to hide. He could honestly say, though, that in uniform he'd never been discriminated against. *Knowingly.* The environment was ripe for it, but he never heard any racial comments in Haiti, not from the team anyway. It was just more or less *Those People.* When he first arrived he was touchy about that; they would say *Those People,* and Ernie would tense up.

That was before he started turning bitter himself about the Haitians.

When he'd first arrived on the island, he couldn't bear to eat if hungry people were watching, and hungry people were always watching. It took him a long time, too, before he could look people in the face, because he knew they wanted something and he knew he couldn't give it to them. One day, there was a guy on the road who had this cow, hard to tell who was walking who. It was hot and this man looked miserable, but when he looked up Ernie waved, and the man's face just lit up, like it meant something to him, somebody knew he was somebody worthy. Ernie began to go out of his way to send that message. There were times when God in heaven knew he didn't want to be there, he didn't feel like being nice, but he would always wave, always try to connect. When you saw a little kid working his ass off for recognition, jumping up and down, how were you not going to wave at him?

But one day a few weeks from now, Ernie would come back from patrol and the news would be on the field radio that his friend Greg Cardott had been killed in Gonaïves, shot through the heart going after a FADH officer who had refused to pay a five-gourde toll at the entrance to town. That same day, Ernie would quit waving. From the time Sergeant Cardott was shot until the time Ernie left, he maybe waved at three or four people, but that was out of sheer habit, his hand automatically going up. He'd smile, but it wouldn't last. *I just didn't want to be nice to them anymore.*

SANTA CLAUS ABSOLVED

Saturday morning, Gary arrived late and disoriented, looking as though he'd spent the night in a Cap Haïtien disco, and we prepared to head out for a day trip along the northeast coast. As I threw my gear into the back of the car, someone called to me from behind the imposing cat's cradle of barbed wire that now divided the compound into separate camps. It was one of the IPSF transfers, a former FADH corporal from the garrison in Cap Haïtien, who, after Colonel Josephat abdicated, had gone into hiding himself and contacted Haitian army headquarters in Port-au-Prince, which assigned him to the large casern in Ounaminthe.

"Is it true you are going to Ounaminthe?" he asked, wanting a ride, and we picked him up outside the wall, where he waited for us at the sandbagged entrance, reluctant to step out into the marketplace. A quick-change artist, he had shed his uniform and was dressed in civilian clothes, gray trousers and a white guayabera. His name was Corporal Alphonse Ostel, and in Ounaminthe he'd eventually been shipped off to IPSF training and reassigned to Limbé. "I had to be posted where people don't know me," he said. But he was still on the payroll in Ounaminthe. If he wanted his November salary, he had to go pick it up himself, and he was much obliged for the lift.

I didn't make a habit of catering to the FADH—occasionally you'd encounter someone in FADH khaki whose bloodshot eyes burned into you like embers, whose rotten breath seemed like an exhalation of evil. But many seemed like ordinary and unimaginative men, genuinely unaware of the role they played in their nation's long descent from grace, and the corporal seemed to be such a man. He was trying very hard to understand, he said, leaning forward between the seats as we motored past the rich but empty pasturelands of the northeast littoral, why the people were justified in their disrespect for the army, the servant of law and order. Everybody knew, he opined, that Haiti was a difficult country to govern and the abuses were exaggerated.

The road was reasonably well paved and straight, and we sped along across open, endless savanna, passing cargo trucks loaded with fruit and empty bottles, headed for the border crossing at the Massacre River, which separated Haiti from the Dom Rep. It was often exhilarating to move through the Haitian countryside, absorbing what is or used to be its beauty, but my pleasure in driving was mitigated by my dread of arrival. Journeys simply terminated, the road dropping you into squalor, the architecture of backwater and clutter, an uninspired grid of battered buildings, streets empty of comfort, maimed communities. Places, like Ounaminthe, I could never imagine as true destinations.

The Ounaminthe garrison had a small IPSF contingent, but I was taken aback by the omnipresence of FADH who remained in uniform, even running armed patrols into the town. Here at his former post, the corporal became visibly younger, less formal and docile. A gleam of vitality spread across his face as together we mounted the steps. He was back among comrades in a place where he did not have to daily anticipate denigration, where he did not feel the dark tug of the future. The release from these anxieties made him stand taller, and in the restored self of his tallness I thought I glimpsed the hubris of the man he once, not so very long ago, had been.

Winter came to the tropics. By midafternoon, a long shelf of dark clouds had edged out the brilliant sky overhead, gilding the mountainous horizon behind us, the interior dramatically illuminated like a divine sanctuary, shiny peaks a magnetic north for the spirit. We entered the seemingly deserted port town of Fort Liberté, hoping to find something to eat, and crossed paths with Fort Liberté's SF detachment, its captain, Tony Risi, a charismatic, handsome Italian-American. The team had their own house, reminiscent of a surfers' bungalow, which the captain appeared ready to turn into a hostel for us for the night, but I declined the offer. Our gear was back in Cap, at the Hotel Christophe, and I wanted to leave early in the morning for the south.

"Ah, the south!" said this talkative, likable captain. He had just been reassigned to the northeast from the southern claw, where General Meade had busted him for driving without a seat belt, never mind that his Humvee wasn't equipped with seat belts. For his own protection, JSOC had tucked the captain away in Fort Liberté.

"When you were down there," I asked him, "did you run into a guy named Barton?"

"Sure," said the captain, "the new XO for Charlie Company. He's doing a good job. He's well liked in Les Cayes."

We returned with darkness to Cap Haïtien, joyous humanity weaving through soft yellow breaths of light cast by hundreds of candles and tiny oil lamps along the broken margins of the broken road. The people had taken back the night, said Gary. For once the city was beautiful, a city of flickering doorways and tongues of illumination, its decay absorbed by the darkness that swelled only two steps beyond the brave lights. When we stopped at a candlelit bar to buy a bottle of rum, Corporal Alphonse slid from the car to melt away into nervous anonymity. We went on to the Christophe, where, because UN and IMP personnel were flooding into town, the competition for rooms was stiff enough to inspire Henri to raise the rates. A plastic Santa Claus sat atop the registration desk, another white man with a sack of promises thrown over his shoulder.

In the half-light of dawn, I was awakened, as I was any morning I bedded at the Christophe, by the screeching, whistling oratory of plump raven-size birds the Haitians called *kwacks*. Gary, however, child of the slums, could sleep through any racket. I'd often give up trying to rouse him and would go down to breakfast alone. This morning, though, he had chosen to be prompt, coming groggily to the table to stir half the sugar bowl into his coffee.

"This trip to Jacmel—we'll make it in two days, right?"

"No," I said. "We should reach by nightfall."

Gary was disbelieving; he had never heard of such a feat, driving from the top of the country to the bottom in one day. "It can't be done," he warned. "I think only an American would think to do this."

However pressed for time, I had no intention of leaving the north without wishing ODA 311 a peaceful Christmas, a safe if not especially happy New Year. For whatever reason, Gary chose to stay by the car while I ducked inside the mess hall to say goodbye and be reassured I would find that the door remained open on my return at the end of January. When I went back out into the sunlight, Gary said that the civilian police had asked to speak with me. God almighty, I thought, look at them there on their bench, as they always were on a Sunday morning, under the tree across the impassable wire, unswerving in their dedication to an inspired lie.

We drove out of the compound, up a hundred feet to the public entrance of the casern, and walked in. The police rose like obedient, affection-starved sons for an audience with their patriarch, grasping my hand with ingratiating fervor, and I asked them please to sit back down, and sat with them and listened as they unburdened themselves, sick with the irony that for them a white man who simply deigned to listen to them was a straw of hope to cling to in a sea of indifference, unwilling to admit that the very fact of my listening was also the signature of my powerlessness.

They were, collectively, slender and young, dressed cleanly in pressed blue jeans and white shirts, immaculately bleached and ironed, and in my eyes, perhaps in my eyes alone, they were supremely virtuous. One would speak, passionately or bashfully, and then another.

"We've been working here for three months, but still we haven't even been given a meal, we haven't been given uniforms."

"We left our houses, our wives, and our children for twenty-four hours a day, to guard the casern and keep order when the ex-*militaires* went for training."

"We would not be talking to you now if we did not have a heart for the country."

"We have nothing, not even rice to feed our babies."

I told them what I knew, that the American soldiers could do little besides recommend them for the new national police force now being organized but still many months away from existence. I promised I would advertise their plight wherever I went, whenever I spoke to Haitian officials, and asked that they write their names in my notebook as I passed it around: *Laurent, Philippe, Israel, Jean, Fritz, St. Vil, St. Amour, Gedeon.* It was Christmas, and my heart went out to them, these lost angels and forgotten saints, the idealistic youth of a society where the social contract had been forever unsigned. It would only cause problems for the team, handing out money, and I knew it, but there was nothing else to do. I surreptitiously folded a fifty-dollar bill into a tiny square and pressed it into the hand of the group's leader, to be shared among them for food. Their gratitude bubbled up, and I hated it as much as the poor quickly learn to hate charity.

I would never see these eight young men again. In less than two months, they'd be gone from Limbé, vanished like frightened birds, each a fugitive and wanted for murder.

FIELD NOTES

14 DEC 94

8. *Taxes:* Encourage all to work with mayors and city councils/municipal assemblies to develop system to keep large part of taxes for local use. No U.S. personnel should touch any tax money. Tax money could fund sanitation, water projects, electric projects, road work, pay public workers and schoolteachers, pay for prisoners' food, justice of the peace and judges. Ensure strict accountability of funds and audit. First step should be to develop a budget.

17 DEC 94

4. *Taxes:* This seems to be causing some consternation.

HOW TO COOK A CAPTAIN

We were in Gonaïves, stopped at a roadside camp where women squatted next to coal braziers, stirring fire-blackened cauldrons of goat stew, beans, and rice. A few yards ahead, an SF soldier was driving sixteen penny nails clear through the length of a two-by-four. "What's going on?" I asked, getting out of the car to talk to the sergeant, my eyes glancing over the name patch on his chest, which, in a few weeks, would be torn by the bullet of a defiant FADH major: *Cardott*. Oh, he said amicably, we're just trying to help out the folks here. Too many vehicles had been ignoring the tollbooth; maybe these spiked boards would make them think twice about speeding past the collectors. The spin was, this was the townspeople's idea, but highway tolls were a foreign concept to Haitians. Boyatt was always on the radio at night soft-selling team-inspired decentralization. "There's a fine line between what we do and revolution," I'd hear an SF lieutenant colonel say one day, and even if that wasn't true most of the time, it was almost true in Haiti.

The Gonaïves tollbooth was part of that campaign, and Boyatt and Lieutenant Colonel Schroer loved the scheme: make the people who used the city's thoroughfare pay for its repair. That the ultimate cost of the toll would be the life of Gregory Cardott troubled no one but the Special Forces themselves. Inevitably, everybody else—the media, the Pentagon, the White House—would interpret the young Green Beret's death as irrefutable evidence of Operation Uphold Democracy's extraordinary success: more than twenty thousand combat-ready American troops in Haiti, and only a single KIA. Before long even Sergeant Cardott's name had receded behind the undeniably good news of the triumphant statistic and its message for a body-counting public.

Haiti would not be Somalia . . . of course.

Traveling after dark was to be avoided—the nighttime roads were far too hazardous—but three hours of daylight remained, and I was sure we could make it from Port-au-Prince to Jacmel. Traffic in Carrefours, the capital's southern slumburb, usually resembled a slow-motion rugby scrum, but this Sunday afternoon it had mellowed to the level of, say, rush hour in the South Bronx. We lurched through the stream of tap-taps and the ant-flow of people in good time, rounding the coastline westward along the Bay of

Gonâve, past the occasional sleazy tryst resorts and FADH bordellos, then cutting due south at Léogane and twisting up into the saddest mountain range on the planet, the first mountains I had ever seen that made me want to vomit, a line of ravaged peaks like a ward of cancer patients, a hardwood tropical forest from horizon to horizon reduced to little more than rain-crumbled rock.

The month before, a hurricane had passed here, carpet-bombing the cordillera with water that the bare mountainsides could not hold or slow, and the valleys channeled the torrent toward Jacmel. In the ensuing flood, more than eight hundred people drowned, more than five hundred houses lay crushed to flotsam, more than a thousand people were left homeless, and Jacmel's quaint streets filled with mud and orphans. Major Tony Schwalm and his FOB were the heroes of that heartless nightmare, throwing themselves into the black flood to rescue dozens.

The sun was up but low and balled by the time we reached the pass to begin our descent to the coast, the darkness pooling far below in ravines and folds, the air chilly enough to force us to stop and put on jackets. The blackening slopes fell toward a sea of ridged pewter, ringed by the tiny tasseled silhouettes of palms.

The granular light drifted up off the land like smoke. We were in trees again, tunneling through pockets of encircling darkness, and I failed to recognize the signs—a slender leafy branch stuck in a small hole in the pavement, a woman on the roadside stepping away from her cook fire to wave, and I wondered over her shadow in the rearview mirror. If Gary hadn't shouted *Stop*, in another few feet we would have jumped a fault in the pavement, landing on what remained of a hurricane-mangled bridge or plunging twenty feet down into a river. To enter Jacmel you must cross three bridges, but all three had been swept away by the punishing downpour of the storm.

We backed up to a bulldozed track that led down the bankside to the water, and Gary tested its depth, my spirit sinking as I watched him go in over his knees. But exhaustion had made us bold and reckless. On the far bank, a pair of headlights fell down the chute leading to the water, and a small pickup truck splashed intrepidly into the river. Spellbound by the map of its white wake sliding downstream, I triangulated a course, and as the truck gunned its way out I accelerated in, feeling the steering relax midway and the tires skip sideways with the force of the seaward current, but then we were skidding up the opposite bank, and on to another fording.

Now it was pitch black, and we found ourselves weaving slowly through a nightscape of immense upheaval and waste, bogs of rank mud in all directions, the gray trunks of uprooted trees scattered like the bones of dinosaurs. This was a floodplain, and its strange desolation seemed to stretch forever. Finally, we rounded a pile of debris, and in front of us was an obsidian slice of the river. The hurricane had splintered it from its channel like a hammer smashing down on a stream of mercury. The river was everywhere, but in threads, and now so were people, scores of shapes gliding through the darkness, some cupping the fragile flames of candles, voices calling to each other in soft questioning, confirming tones. I cut the beams, and the whisper of discovery went up. *Mon Dieu*, here's a *blanc* for Jacmel!

I peered into the darkness at this migration of the powerless and unrequited through a water-scarred starlit wasteland, the people known to me more by the liquid noise of their feet than by the immaterial density of their shape, trying to develop some rudimentary sense of direction through the black wet heaps of land beyond to a distant tree line etched in charcoal. For a moment, the unruly world seemed caught in a deep, peaceful lull between plague and recovery, between one battle and the next, the spirit of man and the spirit of earth consecrated, it seemed, by the ongoing primal struggle, and in this moment of respite, both were surpassingly beautiful.

A hand reached out to rest on my forearm, propped in the open window. The darkness had been given a face, and I looked into the white-toothed smile of a teenage boy. *Blanc,* come, follow me, he said. It seemed counterintuitive to understand that, against the odds, Haiti's children were well raised. He would shepherd us through the hazardous channel, and we rolled in the river behind him as he waded ahead through the glint of water lapping around us, the night's other travelers like herons in the shallows, pausing to mark our passage, their voices bodiless. *Bon soir, blanc. Bon chance, blanc. Bon Nwel*, Merry Christmas. The soldiers saved our lives, *blanc*. When we were at last safely on the other side of the fractured river, the boy turned back the way he had come, to resume his homeless journey on the opposite shore. This, too, was Haiti, the Haiti of young Samaritans and unsolicited blessings.

◻   ◻   ◻

In the morning, we headed west along the scalloped, angular beauty of the southern coast, past fishermen hauling their communal nets, palm trees canted over deserted beaches. We were going to Les Cayes, where I expected to find Captain Barton, though beyond the finding itself I had no expectations, having never before been privy to the disgrace, if that was indeed what the captain now endured, of a military officer. By noon, we had arrived in the bustling port and began asking for directions to the American soldiers. On a back street in a quiet middle-class neighborhood, I thumped the iron gates of Charlie Company's walled headquarters, digging for my press credentials to appease the suspicious glare of the SF sergeant who opened the gates a crack to question me.

Wait, he commanded, and a few minutes later, down came Barton from the ops room, a vacant waxy expression on his boy's face turning radiant once he spotted me, and I realized with some embarrassment that the captain saw in me the reflection of his own redemption. My presence here was proof that he was a good soldier, a worthy human being, and although I agreed with the imaginary colonel that Captain Barton had conducted himself in Limbé with physical and moral courage, I remained uncertain of his more quotidian virtues, and despite my recent late-night conversations with Top Miatke and the team, I didn't understand how the captain had fallen to this position, or the forces that had brought him down.

Spry and jocular, he led me to an interior courtyard, pulled two bottles of Coke from a gurgling refrigerator; we sat at a small table in the shade of a stairway. With pleasure, he accepted the dozen cans of mentholated snuff I'd brought him from the States. "My wife thinks I quit," he said. "Your wife's pretty broken up about all this," I told him. "She asked me to find out what happened." Among all the myriad pressures bearing down on him, the captain had no room to accommodate his spouse's. "She's a military wife," he said. "She's going to have to stop all the goddamn crying and deal with it."

"So," I said, "you've been promoted."

"Yeah," said Captain Barton. After he was pulled from Limbé, he became a sort of houseboy at the FOB in Cap Haïtien, doing odd jobs, fetching sodas for the desk jockeys. Mostly he sat around in a deep funk for two weeks, his brain on a loop day and night. *What was wrong? My standards were low? Uniform? Hygiene? Spirit? Well, kiss my ass, my standards have never been low.* In fact, Barton's standards were not recognizably different from those of any other ODA I had visited for more than a few minutes. Then Charlie Company mentioned to Colonel Boyatt that they could use an XO, Executive Officer, a drudgework job nobody really aspired to in the SF—logistics, personnel, administrative tidying. A weird form of banishment that, on the surface, resembled advancement. "I guess they figured I couldn't do any harm here," the captain reflected, the sarcasm in his voice arching out toward cynicism.

"Ed," I said, "I've just come from Limbé, spent a few days with the team."

"What'd they tell you?" he asked, and I watched his jaw harden.

He thought things were going fine in Guantánamo. There was no tension or anything like that with the planning for the infil; he just wanted to make sure it was straight, clear in his own mind. They ran through this one rehearsal three, four times, with the team behaving like a bunch of little kids. *God, there he goes again, making us do it over!* They imagined they were crossing the main road into Limbé: Okay, Bill, what do we do? *Uh . . . uh . . . we're going to take the second left and go down.* No, we're not, the captain would chide. We're taking the first left and going down. Okay, great, let's do it again. Well, Barton told me, we could half-ass it out in training and do a onetime and not get killed, but I'd seen how the team functioned—*You can't tell us what to do, you're making us feel so little*—and I said this time I don't care what they think, I'm going to make sure I know it and they know it.

"Falling apart?" Barton scoffed. He and Bill Miatke had a good understanding, at least that's what he thought. He might have been a little wired, a residual tension because of how things were going previously back at Bragg as he tried to whip the team into shape and here they were counting off the hours that would drop them into a combat situation. He told Miatke, I'm going to keep things tight—things come from me. Almost a one-man show. Going into Limbé, he didn't want, *No, let's do this, let's do that.* In a way it was funny, he told himself. Normal enlisted-man stuff. Maybe he had a sarcastic tone to his comments, but the truth was, they didn't know the route for entering Limbé, and if you don't know it, and you claim to know it, then the only person who ought to feel small is *you*, not him for making you feel small. *Oh, God,* they said, *you don't trust us.*

"You know, if everybody went through the rehearsals clicking, clicking," Barton said, "I wouldn't have said anything but *Great job!* Okay? This is the army."

And on it went, from Gitmo to Port-au-Prince, from Cap into Limbé, the team nipping at Barton's holier-than-thou authority or, just as readily, decrying his lack of assertion, swinging moodily from attitude to attitude but always in the team's mind resisting his leadership, until one day the higher-ups invited the team to mutiny, pound testimonial nails into an officer's coffin, and they did. For almost a month, Colonel Boyatt had been firing heat rounds at the captain, sighting in on a career he could only perceive as anathema to the image and substance of the Special Forces, and finally, bull's-eye, the rounds hit their mark. Barton had but one true nemesis, and that was Colonel Boyatt, who had visited ODA 311 twice during the detachment's first week in Limbé, and both occasions had proved disastrous for the captain.

The first visit, forty-eight hours into the anarchy of the infil, the captain had trudged across town to the LZ at the soccer field to say good morning to the Third Group commander. Boyatt gave him the once-over, looking into his eyes, and at that moment realized that here was a Kentucky boy who "could not cut it." ("He was defeated within the first three days in Limbé," Boyatt would later try to convince me. The colonel had looked into the captain's eyes and read washout.) Boyatt noted with extreme distaste that his captain had not shaved and his BDUs were rumpled and ratty. He asked Barton for a briefing and received what was to his ear a basinet full of complaints. Without another word, the colonel walked back to his helicopter and left.

Several days later, a chopper appeared over the compound, circling. Without success, Commo Jim tried to raise it on the radio; he's on the right frequency, but nobody's answering. The bird veered off to the LZ, and on board was Boyatt, bilious and fuming because the ODA failed to make radio contact, because no one's there at the soccer field to meet him, because he must again be sorely entertained by the inadequacies of this sniveling, slobbish Barton, who would suggest that the colonel might want to double-check his own frequency before accusing the team's commo man of screwing up. After that, Colonel Boyatt intentionally stayed away from Limbé, because he knew if he saw Barton again, the captain would be leaving with him on the helicopter.

But in a few more days—the day, in fact, that I moved in with the team—Boyatt would resolve to send a gardener to Limbé, a Lieutenant Colonel Rendall from his own staff in Port-au-Prince, to pull this weed Barton from the team, a blight marring the colonel's pure vision of the perfect mission.

"Colonel Rendall came," said Barton. "I picked him up at the airfield, and he had the French colonel and my replacement with him." Barton saw the other captain and thought, What's that mean? Something ain't right here; he's got his bags. Rendall said, I'm here to take you away for a couple of weeks. Barton, said, No, you're here to relieve me. Rendall said, Well, however you want to put it. But when Barton asked why, the lieutenant colonel didn't seem to know. He said he was just sent up there to take 311's captain back to Port-au-Prince. "And," admitted Barton, "I got fairly upset."

"What do you mean, 'fairly upset'?" I felt I had to ask. Barton's father had been a lifer in the army; the captain had a brother in the national guard, a brother in the Marines, a brother in the reserves. The military was his oxygen; his brain cells were saturated with the history of warfare. Everywhere he stepped in Haiti, he made visual and institutional analogies to *Apocalypse Now*. Death could fairly blow the lights out on such a universe; death was a fair player. But no training or experience had prepared the captain to accept a demise so unnatural as this, the dishonorable x-ing out of his existence by casual fiat. A bullet he understood. You're an officer, and the flag on your casket is mud in the face of those who would say you were puny and feeble and undeserving of your bars. In a voice seared with contempt, Sergeant Miatke had confided to me that the captain sat out back in the compound under the powwow tree, "bawling like a baby," when Rendall came to relieve him. However perverse it was to press the issue, Barton had never lied to me when I asked him a question he could legally answer, and I needed to know if Top was selling him short.

"Just tears started coming out of my eyes," he said, tilting his head back at the horrible memory. "I just couldn't believe it. What did I do or say that was so terribly wrong?" And then he calmed down and gathered himself and went back and Rendall said, Well, tell me what's going on. Barton told him the same things he told anybody else who came there, sitrep-speak, just like with Schroer and Boyatt—the entry, the patrols, the meetings. You tell them that, and it's like, *We don't want to hear that. What are you doing about your problems? We want solutions.* But this was a time when there wasn't a solution to every problem.

Rendall said, Well, I don't know what the big problem is. If there was a weak team leader, that still shouldn't matter, because the team itself would pick up the slack. But what kind of slack was he not pulling? Captain Barton wanted to know. Rendall jotted down a note and gave it to Barton's replacement to give to Colonel Schroer, who was due in for an inspection tour that afternoon. Leaving both Captain Barton and the captain he had brought with him in Limbé, Rendall went back to Port-au-Prince, handing off the problem to Schroer.

Captain Barton sat under the tree in the back of Limbé's casern probably an hour, in a daze of self-pity and shame and bewilderment. Then Lieutenant Colonel Schroer drove into town from Cap, and Barton remembered Miatke there in front of him, saying the colonel wanted to see him. He got to his feet and steeled himself and went into the casern. There was Schroer, and the captain said, *Hi, sir my name is . . .* and extended his hand, but all the colonel did was brand him with a censuring look and turn away. Schroer would later say his initial impression of Barton was that the captain was out of uniform, that he was not wearing his top, his BDU blouse, but instead had met him in a T-shirt full of holes, and again Captain Barton was mystified, because not only was he dressed out in a full set of BDUs, but the colonel dinged him because he'd had his sleeves in a jungle roll.

Barton retreated to his bench under the tree and waited while Schroer read Rendall's note and questioned the team. Eventually the colonel came out and sat with him and glanced around the rubbish-strewn compound with a mightily offended look on his fleshy, bureaucrat's face. Before I begin, he said, let me just point out some things. A couple of guys were in T-shirts. A couple of guys loading a Humvee were wearing round, floppy boonie caps—the army issued them to the troops, but now Barton guessed maybe they weren't supposed to wear them. Is that the standard here? Schroer scolded. Is that the standard, Captain?

Well, said the lieutenant colonel, softening a bit, tell me what's going on. Barton repeated the same briefing he had given Rendall, but he was still shaky, punch-drunk, and found it difficult to push his words out into the clear stream of confidence that was music to a superior officer's ears. Schroer said, Well, what are you going to do? Barton said, Sir, I told you what I'm going to do and what we're doing. The mayor had been threatened and was in hiding, the elderly delegate had been beaten and now refused to assert his authority, the lame justice of the peace cravenly denied his position. Here was the political infrastructure of the town and its immediate environs, the anchor of legality for the lives of thirty, forty thousand people, and the rope had been cut in the midst of a tempest. Schroer said, Well, *you're* the authority, you're Wyatt Earp. You need a justice of the peace, make someone the justice of the peace. You need a mayor, then hire a mayor. Barton said, Sir, we're working to get them on line, but we have to work out some protection for these people.

But it was all bullshit, it was unimportant. The mayor came back only to showcase her worthlessness, the delegate abdicated to the vice delegate, who did whatever he wanted, the justice of the peace issued warrants that weren't worth the paper they were written on—but first the method behind the madness needed to be looked at carefully by the team and understood. Jesus Christ, thought Barton, we can't even plan something at Fort Bragg without it taking a week, two weeks, but in a matter of four days I'm supposed to reconstruct intact the governmental mechanisms of a couple hundred thousand people?

But whatever he said to the lieutenant colonel went in one ear and out the other, and Schroer wanted to talk about Patton, Patton was the man, Patton in Bavaria in the immediate aftermath of the war, Patton *blah blah blah*, look to Patton for the answers, but the colonel didn't know that Barton's German-born mother was a survivor of that war and that her son had been nursed on its campaigns. Barton looked at his boots, fighting the impulse to shout out, Bavaria! Germans! Sir, that's a stupid-ass analogy. How in the fuck can you compare Haiti with Bavarian Germany?

The captain looked at the lieutenant colonel, and all he could see was a two-hundred-pound knee programmed to jerk: Do things fast, don't give me excuses, Captain. Just make it happen so that I know something's happening, and why isn't that goddamned marketplace cleaned up? There it was, the bedrock philosophy on which to build an army: *If you look good, you are good.*

Schroer said, Well, what do you want to do? I want to stay here, Barton answered. Okay, said Schroer. He was going to give the captain a break and be back to check up on things in a few days. Then he rounded up the replacement captain and left, but of course that wasn't the end of it.

Eager for me to stay and hear him out, Barton offered me another Coke, but I told him I couldn't. Gary was waiting for me in the car, and we wanted to get back to Port-au-Prince before nightfall.

"You know," he said, "no one could answer where this magical point was where the team's mission wasn't going well."

"I think the team would say it happened when I left with the imaginary colonel," I told him. I could see he hated to hear this charge repeated. It knocked the energy out of him and drove an appeal into his dejected eyes for me to take him at his word.

"I can admit my mistakes," he said, "but it was just three, four days, and nothing changed whatsoever. Monday we went up to Le Borgne, Tuesday we had meetings scheduled in different towns, Wednesday it was the same, then Schroer came to yank me on Thursday morning, and now they want to assign all the good things the team accomplished over to the French colonel, simply because he spoke French. It gave the illusion he was in charge."

As Barton walked me to the gate, his eyes welling as he recalled the excruciating sleepless weeks he spent, an outcast in Cap Haïtien, his thoughts turned again to the team, especially the deterioration of his relationship with Top—Miatke's walk-away, fuck-you attitude; his reluctance to get out into the countryside, his curt voice.

"You know, Captain, you also have a curt voice." I said this because I held both of these men in esteem and therefore was divided in my loyalty. Barton seemed to accept this mildest of criticism without resentment. He let it go and he let me go, but not before throwing a grenade.

He followed me over to the car and turned to grasp my hand, shaking it goodbye, remembering to tell me that the Alpha Company commander, Major Fox, had asked each member of the team to sit down and record their grievances against their captain. Barton, walking around like a zombi at the FOB in Cap, had inadvertently seen these reports lying on a desk and had scanned them, one would assume, with furtive intensity, looking over his shoulder. Miatke, said Barton, had complained that the captain had lent too much credence to "the reporter" and was unduly influenced by what "the reporter" said. "And listen to this," said Barton. The team members who went with us on the first trip to Le Borgne had accused him of sexually harassing the correspondent from the *Miami Herald,* Susan Benesch.

Colonel Boyatt identifying FRAPH as the loyal opposition; military intel labeling Marc Lamour an attaché and murderer: these I had wanted to believe were guileless confusions, honest mistakes. At the very worst, systemic blunders, which would organically self-correct. For the first time in Haiti, I felt the American military operated a shadow economy of verisimilitude, a black market in lies. Once made personal, the political no longer enjoyed the benefit of doubt.

PORTAPRENS

Up the mountainside, on the sunny, unapologetically civilized patio of the Hotel Montana, one of Haiti's few progressive business leaders was telling a trio of journalists that in preparation for the forthcoming season of elections, he had just bought an apartment in Miami. You had to wonder what had taken him so long. The capital's cosmopolitans were measuring the progress of the American intervention by the city's skyrocketing crime rate, which had the elites appalled, but they seemed to accept the change with jaded humor. "We're becoming just like you," said the smiling business leader. "Like Atlanta, Miami, Houston, New York. Haitians aren't used to so much crime, the way you Americans are."

It was true; the entire metropolis of Port-au-Prince seemed to be experimenting with democracy as a form of felonious catharsis. MREs caught in traffic were being yanked from their Mercedeses at gunpoint. Downtown, the kids who changed my dollars into gourdes were regularly shot in the head and relieved of their bankrolls. There had been a payroll

heist at the American embassy, which ended in murder. Gangs were forming in the slums, the richest families were hiring private armies, vigilantes
lynched thieves from lampposts, mobs hacked to death macoutes who
were suddenly recognized on the streets. Somebody would occasionally
heave a grenade at one of the radio stations, and a deadly game of payback, with carefully selected victims, was being played between hit
squads that one could only assume were devoted to either the new or the
ancien régime, a call-and-response chorus of unsolvable assassinations
that crescendoed, in the days leading up to the fourth anniversary of Aristide's inauguration, the first week of February 1995, with the machine-
gunning of Mireille Durocher-Bertin, Stanley Schrager's on-air nemesis.

The pretty young mulatto Durocher-Bertin—an American-educated
lawyer and mother, who around the time of the Governors Island negotiations had become Cédras's preferred network apologist—marketed the
tyrants to international audiences with more than a little success: the generals were struggling to uphold democratic principles, the army was noble
and misunderstood, the poor people were killing themselves to make us
look bad, Aristide was a communist and was criminally insane. Durocher-
Bertin's lawyer, who allegedly claimed several prominent narcotraffickers
as clients, died with her in a splatter of bullets. The murders were a palace
hit, a drug hit, a turf hit, a double-agent hit, a right-wing shut-her-up hit,
or an attempt by the CIA to destabilize Aristide's fragile presidency, depending of course on whom you listened to. The FBI sent a team of investigators, who failed to crack the case, they claimed, because Aristide
refused to cooperate.

Portaprens was a city balanced in midair, and like a patient revived from
a coma, it had begun to remember bits and pieces of its former life. Without electricity, the population eased into a self-imposed curfew beginning
at sundown, except for hundreds of schoolchildren, who gathered each
evening outside the national palace to study under the mobile security
lights of the U.S. Army. Nights at the Oloffson, I trained myself to deaf-
ness, gradually learning to sleep undisturbed by the echoing shotgun
booms, the pop of small-arms fire, that skipped about the surrounding
neighborhoods—often, but not always, night watchmen blasting away at
the drunken rustle and stealthy footsteps of their own fear, the terrifying
wind.

At the Oloffson, everyone pondered who had Micah's head and why.

Some guys had broken into Micah's place in Carrefours, whacked him, decapitated the corpse. Now some heavy-duty lout was probably walking around with the fixer's head in a crocus sack, or was using it as a center-piece for a bedroom altar, or kicking it up and down the alleys of Cité Lib-erté in a game of macoute football—who knows?

I was sitting at the Oloffson's bar, after hours, with Richard Morse and Daniel Salcedo, a scientist/activist/consultant from Washington, D.C., who was in Haiti to lobby the Aristide government to establish a human rights abuse database and begin the legal and exploratory work that must precede the arrival of a team of forensic anthropologists Salcedo had summoned from Central America and Argentina. The team would exhume mass graves, with the hope of supplying the gruesome evidence of atroc-ity, the indelible horrors that resisted even death and decomposition, to the newly appointed truth commission.

We expanded our analysis of *the situation*. Where did communism go? we wondered, recalling the tyrants' prophecy of an Aristide-seduced Haiti infested with Marxist-Leninists. If it could vanish in one day, was it ever here to begin with? Meanwhile, Cédras had successfully promoted the idea of mob rebellion to the U.S. military—the mouth biting the hand that feeds. Who in their right mind in the White House or the Pentagon would advocate embroilment in the geopolitics of ingratitude? And yet, for rea-sons on which we shared no consensus, it happened. "I don't know if the American military know what they did," said Richard, "but they saved an entire race of people down here."

The soldiers out in the countryside seem to understand that, I offered. Daniel thought that might be so because the U.S. military was a vertical hierarchy, one of the rare institutions in our society where class analysis was alive and well—thus, a priori, the armed forces empathized with the lower classes. That's true to a point, I said, though it preferred the rabble to be uniformed. The military admired its own capacity to make small lives big, but if you weren't careful and industrious and loyal, if you didn't hug the program tight, it made those lives small again.

Higher up the mountain, at Camp d'Application, we were allowed to preview democracy's embryonic future, or rather the very callow young men on whom that future would largely depend. The standards for the freshman class of recruits entering Haiti's first police academy had been set high: out of twenty-five thousand applicants, seven thousand were tested and five hundred selected for training, a seven percent pass rate. You had to be literate, healthy, ostensibly sane; high blood pressure or unsteady eyes could disqualify you.

The lucky five hundred—nonthreateningly attired in blue pants, white short-sleeved shirts, and HNP (Haitian National Police) bill caps—were marched by their handlers onto the parade ground, to stand in fine formation for an hour, roasting in the sun while important foreigners murmured their approval. Very impressive from a neocolonial point of view, history begging to repeat itself, but what was Haiti to do?

Class had started on Monday, five days earlier, for the trainees, whose education was now the shared responsibility of the U.S. Justice Department and the Royal Canadian Mounted Police, with France and, of all places, El Salvador—not exactly a model for principled modern law enforcement—helping out. (Journalists who had worked the Latin American beat throughout the eighties were personally outraged by the inclusion of Guatemalan, Salvadoran, and Argentinian police officers in Operation Restore Democracy, since many of those same correspondents, like Larry Rohter of the *New York Times*, had been treated roughly by each force while investigating their manifold records of abuse, violation, and murder. When Rohter asked someone in the State Department what Guatemalan police could possibly teach Haitians about the self-restraints of democracy, the official asked him to consider the bigger picture: *Think of Haiti as a carrot,* he suggested to the journalist. *Look at the splendid benefits that accrue—respectability, community, money—when you play ball.*)

Aristide appeared on the reviewing stand, elegant in the blue business suit and power tie of his presidency—no Gorbachev, no Mandela; his potential for greatness limited perhaps by the fact that he was born to Haiti, insignificant to the larger world. Half the recruits at attention saluted, half didn't, a discrepancy in protocol the drill sergeants would likely address in next week's lesson. Speeches followed: *You are the rock upon which we will build the new Haiti.*

Aristide: "What have we done with our freedom since 1804? Who has protected our freedom since 1804? In the past, the army only wanted to think about itself. This is a cultural problem, because in a house, every kid wants to be chief. In the past, with the army for role models, every kid wants to be the big man. I hope the new police will be role models like doctors, people who take care of others."

Lofty, stirring words, their inspiration resonating across the parade ground. I scanned the ranks, fully expecting to recognize one or more faces from up north, Barton's and the imaginary colonel's volunteer police ascended to their rightful place in the realignment of the constellation of civil power, their youthful earnestness illuminated with pride, but I saw no one I knew.

"I don't want this to be a black day," Aristide told his police recruits at Camp d'Application, dreading a future that would return like a battering husband to Haiti, cruelly intent on remarrying its past, "but to be the day of light for democracy."

MISSION SAG

I had gotten into a bad mental habit, thinking of ODA 311 as *my* team, a writerly conceit that took loose account of reality, and the reception I received when I returned to Limbé at the end of January was not what I had come to expect. Vendors blocked my route into the market square, requiring me to park on the cemetery road and slog in through an ankle-deep goulash of muddy filth, created in part by a layer of sandy topsoil brought in by a dump truck and spread thinly atop the crud, with little effect. Vegetable and charcoal sellers had also established themselves directly in front of the compound's iron gates, and when I saw them squatting there on a patch of dryness, confident they were in nobody's way, I thought to myself, Well, it's over. Armies come and go through history, but when soldiers exit a campaign, they take their stories with them. I walked farther along the wall to the casern's entrance—the building had been repainted white and sea blue—and ducked in for a look, relieved to see Humvees in their customary space back beside the mess hall.

It was the medic, JC, in no hurry, who came to get me, shaking my hand with a carefully measured transfer of warmth, saying I was back just in time. The team would be leaving Limbé by the fifteenth of February, to bivouac in Cap until March 1, then home to Bragg. "What the hell were you doing up there in the States?" he asked as we walked to the hall, his tone alerting me to the news, not entirely unanticipated, that I had caused trouble and that my mischief had amused him, if not others. "You're a regular celebrity in these parts—That Bob Guy." JC snickered, bouncing his head and thrusting back his shoulders, JC's homeboy shuck and jive.

Inside the mess hall, the best welcome I could get from Top Miatke and Captain Mike was lukewarm hellos, their dispassionate eyes intent on reevaluating who I had been, who I was, who I might yet be, now that they had a better understanding of the consequence of our relationship, no longer potential but fact. They were soldiers, I was a correspondent. The eventual impact of our association was tacit—never concealed, only delayed by the seemingly casual pace, the deceptive ops tempo, of my work. It was clear they were not particularly pleased to see me, and I said so. Top didn't want to talk about it, and then he did.

Even now, he said, the chain of command would frequently end their transmissions with the query Has That Bob Guy been around? "What the fuck did you do?"

My reportage had begun to surface. Admiral Miller had tracked me down to bitch about a magazine cover story, and in January I had published an op-ed piece, "Our Two Armies in Haiti," in the Sunday *New York Times*, which by the following morning had been reprinted in the *Early Bird*, a Department of Defense clip sheet, and placed on every desk in the Pentagon, something for generals to read with that first cup of coffee. The truth of the argument that the U.S. Army was a blunt tool, incapable of scalpel-like precision and versatility, depended on which U.S. Army you were looking at, the piece suggested. In Haiti, I wrote, the conventional army with its twenty thousand infantrymen seemed misplaced and misled, superfluous and perhaps even counterproductive to what had rapidly become a peacekeeping mission tailor-made for the army's unconventional forces—specifically, Special Forces A-teams, whose sophisticated training and multidimensional skills were redefining military success on the ground in an ambiguous, low-intensity conflict that helped clarify the post–cold war tactical environment in the third world. The conventional army had a binary brain, hit/don't hit, and it was past time for the infantry to pack up and go home. On the other hand, the piece cajoled, whoever was doing cost/benefit analysis for the Pentagon's shrinking budget might want to pump more resources—and confidence—in the direction of the Green Berets.

The page editor at the *Times* balked; the piece was too laudatory. "The Special Forces aren't perfect, are they?" she argued. Oh, right, I conceded. I had overlooked a significant flaw, and I willingly added a caveat to my final draft, voicing concern about the confusion surrounding the SF's perception of, and conduct toward, good guys and bad guys, and pointing out that their commander, Colonel Boyatt, was playing a dangerous game with FRAPH by repeatedly encouraging his troops to regard the terrorist group as "the loyal opposition."

Throughout January 1995, the media had nudged the SF into the furnace of controversy. Shortly after my piece appeared, Larry Rohter reported on his visit to the ODA in Jérémie, which took place on the same afternoon Sergeant Cardott was shot and killed in Gonaïves. The team, ravaged by dengue fever, had enraged Jérémie's population by detaining, at the behest of local FRAPH warlords, a popular priest and Lavalas hero. To make matters worse, the team sergeant had met the correspondent from the *New York Times* with his pistol drawn, ordering Rohter to "State your business." A most troublesome posture, and the tension ballooned during Rohter's interview with the team's captain, who broke off from the conversation, snapping, "Are you grilling me? This sounds like you're grilling me!"

Other journalists were drawing attention to similar lapses in SF neutrality in the Artibonite, where some Green Berets had taken a shine to local *Fraphistes,* and in Hinche on the central plateau, where the ODA had been harassing Chavanne Baptiste, a well-known peasant organizer and Aristide confidant, and compiling a list of friendlies and unfriendlies, the unfriendly column loaded up with Lavalas. Apparently someone with a bigger paycheck than Boyatt's had told him to knock it off, and by the time I returned to Limbé, the colonel had already reversed himself on the question of FRAPH's political status and, officially, the loyal opposition had been demoted back to the ranks of thuggery.

Whatever we say, the guy writes everything down. Though they downplayed it verbally, the team's uneasy behavior spoke volumes, and it was difficult to tell what sort of hot water they'd been in because of me. It was in their eyes: they didn't know what to do with me. But it was Top's call, and Top struggled with it. That the process was symbiotic seemed to be a secret we shared. He was the king of monosyllabic courtesies during the day, but when we sat down together at night he blew out gusts of language, and wasn't it ironic that for years no one would really pay attention to what you had to say, and then along comes someone who does, and every time you open your mouth there's the queasy feeling that you're digging your own grave.

At lunchtime, the team had grilled a big pot of steaks, and when Top told me to sit down and help myself, I wasn't hungry, but seized the invitation, fixed a meat-slab sandwich, and sat down. The palaver started, and the mood turned toward a better, more familiar rhythm.

Ernie Brown had shipped out two days earlier, and a quiet, skinny, red-haired Alabama kid named Jay had arrived to replace him. Wesh was gone too, the happy victim of a paperwork snafu, and the team had been reinforced by Phil, the new Haitian-American interpreter, and two psy ops pranksters, who'd been away for a few days, broken down somewhere in the bush. Walt Plaisted and Jim Pledger came in as we spoke, pouring sweat from a hike into the hills. Jim was twenty-eight pounds lighter from the heat, PT, and an alcohol-free diet. Ross Perot, at the request of Colonel Boyatt's wife, Nancy, had given every ODA barbells for Christmas, plus a TV, then two weeks later VCRs, after somebody told Perot the televisions were useless outside Cap and Port-au-Prince.

"Everything's really quiet," said Top. Disaffected, he just wanted to go home, collect his TDY pay ($3.50 a day for 179 days) and his imminent-danger bonus (150 bucks a month), and perhaps the time was nearing for that. Command was organizing a schedule for the team's move to Cap, the start of the weaning process. Profile reduction—"A lot of the kids in town think we're gone," said Captain Mike. There had been no more *manifestations*, no overt political skirmishing. There were signs of optimism, hope, an economy trying to rise from the dead, and generally, said Top, the population seemed to have told itself, *Let's just get on with our lives.*

When it came time for me to move on to Cap Haïtien, I asked if I could return the next day, a Sunday, and remain overnight. Captain Stefanchik and Top exchanged questioning looks. All right, they said reluctantly, as if they had no choice, but Top walked me to the gates to find out what time I planned on showing up. "Around breakfast," I said—the wrong answer.

"Well . . ." The master sergeant hemmed and hawed. "Lieutenant Colonel Schroer's coming in the morning."

"Oh," I said. "Would you like me to steer clear until he's gone?"

"Well, for the captain's sake, it might be best."

"Why hesitate to tell me?"

"Well," said Top, "I didn't want to offend you."

Somehow we had become awkward co-conspirators. A quasi-illicit, vaguely seditious element had slipped into our relationship, and our self-interests had proliferated into a tangle. Back in the casern, Captain Mike was on the radio to the FOB in Cap, passing the word up the chain of command that I was back in town. By Monday, the Public Affairs Officers at the Pentagon and the Joint Special Operations Command in Fort Bragg would be phoning my home in Florida with generous offers of assistance.

Sunday noon, and the lieutenant colonel hadn't come and probably wouldn't, said the captain; probably because of me, he said. Schroer was a straight army guy and took objection to the fact I was ODF—*Out Dere Flappin'*. So I could stay, said Captain Mike, but I'd have to hide or clear out for an hour in the morning—General Scott and Boyatt were passing through.

The sag in the mission had turned palpable. The IPSF were exploring the depths of lethargy, awaiting a new commander from Ounaminthe, since their leader, Lieutenant Lumas, had bugged out once again to Port-au-Prince, focused on securing his pension.

Commo Jim, mad hillbilly scientist, had wired together a grapefruit and an orange and discovered that the two fruits generated enough current between them—1.4 volts—to set off a claymore mine. Bob Fox, Walt, and Top were in the mess hall, watching a Star Trek movie on Ross Perot's VCR. "We came all the way over here to watch this movie," said Bob, who at the age of thirteen had begun writing recruiters, begging to join up and become the only thing he ever wanted to be, an engineer in the army. Captain Mike sat at his work station, reading Zola's letters on the Dreyfus affair in French. He seemed to be constructed of cubes—square-headed, square-shouldered, square-hipped. One day in the near future, he'd show up on the *CBS Evening News,* and command, after viewing the clip, would grouse about how he had appeared too low-key. That's probably what kept him out of West Point, Stefanchik would joke—no media presence.

Bored myself, I jumped at the chance to ride out to the countryside with the captain and Walt to check up on a fellow named Reubens, the new IPSF *chef du section* in Petit Bourg de Port Margot. Reubens this, Reubens that, said the captain admiringly, and I soon understood that all he hoped for in the "new" Haiti was personified by the *chef*. Every Sunday afternoon, the small, good-natured Reubens walked from hamlet to hamlet in his area, preaching human rights and reconciliation. We found him at the village's *avant poste*, attending to his lone prisoner. The captain's conversational French had become excellent, as had his body language, the cultural connect of animation, gestures, and earthy humor that was the essence of Haitian expression. I'll help you in any way I can, the young captain told Reubens. Stefanchik would even try to get him a visa if he wanted, but the *chef du section* said he was determined to stay and help rebuild his country and would become an electrician if he wasn't selected for the police academy.

The police academy was a subject that troubled the young captain's good heart. Since I had last seen Stefanchik in December, he had followed Barton's and the imaginary colonel's lead by organizing civilian police teams in Acul-du-Nord and Plaine du Nord, towns encompassed by the team's expanded ODA. Radio traffic during the first week of January began alerting teams that the academy selection process was about to commence, but nobody was prepared, nobody had the proper forms; yet the Haitian government went ahead and started broadcasting an application date with only two days' notice.

Captain Mike hopped in a Humvee, went to Cap, found the regional delegate, and told him, Hey, I've got dozens of patriots down in my AO, working hard since October. The delegate gave him forty application forms—not enough but better than nothing. He made twenty extra photocopies, then drove around handing them out. Four days later, the captain collected all sixty application packets and delivered them to the delegate's house. Forty-five were kicked back for incompletion, but seven of the eight volunteer civilian police in Limbé, three in Plaisance, and two from Plaine du Nord were accepted for the entrance examination.

The captain wrote a letter of recommendation for each of them, but you needed to be telepathically wired to the system to know what came next. Regulations were announced out of the blue, photo IDs were issued surreptitiously, the testing schedule was never published, and the multi-choice questions on the test itself were a cultural obstacle to the candidates. Ray Kelly, a former police chief from New York City, was running the operation, being micromanaged by the State Department, and the chain of command was always screwed up in a multinational operation. The captain rounded up all the candidates and drove them to Cap to take their test, but there was no test.

In the end, Stefanchik couldn't help any of the volunteer police. Their applications to the academy would be turned away; the volunteers in Plaisance, who'd been working for so long without any support whatsoever, would abandon their casern. Reubens, in whom the captain had placed so much faith, the one Haitian he believed was selfless, would disappear—maybe he just had to go and find his own future, the captain thought—and the civilian cops in Limbé would soon find themselves fugitives from the wrath of their original benefactors, relentlessly hunted and pursued by the Green Berets.

JC concocted a tomato-beef noodle soup from a variety of sources, scraped a gallon tub of margarine off hundreds of individual pats, and set out rye bread from the quartermaster in Cap. Night patrols were now a rare event, and instead of an après-dinner team meeting, everyone sat dull-eyed at the table, watching a movie on the VCR. Top reminded Walt to clear the stroke books out of the latrine before the general's visit in the morning. Then he remembered one of Captain Barton's mortal sins.

The Monday after the imaginary colonel and I had left, General Potter had scheduled a visit to Limbé; the team learned about it the night before on the fireside chat. Everyone was still in the good graces of Schroer, who was receiving heat from Boyatt for not relieving Barton. Now, said Top, you've got to remember that Potter is the Joint Special Operations Task Force commander. Barton, however, had made other plans, to meet with a Tenth Mountain captain in Cap Haïtien to discuss the future of the team working with the infantry, not any specific mission. Potter was running late, and finally Barton, said, *Fuck this. Tell the general I couldn't wait.*

Bad.

Three days later, Captain Barton was relieved, and the company commander, Major Fox, came down from Cap and said, What the hell happened here? Why didn't I know about this? And Top told him, Well, you know, I didn't think it was going to lead to this. We had some problems, said Top, but we were working through them. Major Fox wanted written statements from everybody, so Top got the team together and said, "Listen, everybody here has come to me and complained about one thing or another, and I'm telling you right now, you guys better put it in your statement, 'cause if it ain't in your statement, it ain't going to be in my statement."

"I was trying to put the monkey on their backs," Top said. The movie was long over; one by one, soldiers had slipped out of the mess hall for their bunks once the conversation turned to Barton. "They were the ones who complained to me, and yeah, I'm the one who had to talk to Barton about it, I'm the one who had to get into arguments with him over it. But I said, 'It's part of what led to his relief—you better be man enough to write it in your statements.' "

I asked if he'd written in his own statement that the captain had sexually harassed Susan Benesch, and Top said yeah, it was one of those things. He'd never made that ride to Le Borgne himself, but the three guys who did go came back complaining that Ed had made an ass out of himself in front of Susan, hanging all over her, and so Top had to confront him about it.

"This is ridiculous." After first hearing of the charge, I told him, I had spoken to Susan herself, who was willing to address any proceeding in defense of Captain Barton. "It's wrong."

"I don't know," Top said.

But I did know, and as troubled as I was by the accusation, Susan was more so. No rational woman wanted false charges of this nature brought against a man, because too often any woman had to face real sexual abuse, and it was vital, legally and morally, to preserve your credibility. "There's no fucking way it happened," I told Top. "It was a bumpy road, we were all knocking into each other. We hit a downpour, and I said, 'Susan, climb up front with me and get out of the rain.' And then there's this complaint that Barton had hit on her and she was so offended that she had to escape him by coming up front. It's bullshit, Bill."

I wasn't and had never been a soldier, and my perception of Barton was necessarily circumscribed by my life outside the military. Nor was I prepared to call Captain Barton an outstanding leader of men or marvel at his intellectual capacity, but I had firsthand knowledge of what other teams in the north were doing at the same time Barton was in Limbé. I knew what kind of support they had, what kind of resources, and I had a sense of how and when Barton wasn't supported or resourced in an equal fashion, so I couldn't fault Barton for the hand he was dealt, because it was a tough hand to play.

But I would never understand exactly how the captain supposedly avoided work by patrolling the countryside. When he was out there, he was humping, even though his capacity to achieve anything was umbilically tied to the imaginary colonel; but if not the colonel, then who? Without the colonel, Barton's making hand signals to people, because he can't communicate. It's always going to bug me, I told Top, that Captain Barton wasn't provided with an interpreter from day one. Guns spoke every language, violence was multilingual, and if you're infilling to kill enemy troops, your bullets speak for themselves; but if you're deploying to do business, make peace, have town council meetings, and toast your brains with complex administrative proceedings, where are the interpreters?

"You're right," said Top. "That's the army's bureaucracy. Every team going in should have had at least two interpreters."

Still, Top wasn't about to let Barton off the hook, and I listened quietly as he laid out a litany of final grievances.

"His integrity was shot with me," said Top. "Barton should never have been in SF. He wasn't a good enough leader to be in SF. How he ever got through selection, I don't know. But when you're around him, if you have a compassionate bone in your body, he can bullshit you into forgiving him, letting him slide."

Haiti made days long, but never so long as Top and I could make them, once we got together for our midnight sessions. Barton had been shipped back to the States in January, and it was time for us to drop it. Weary and divided, I pulled off my boots, told Top good night, and spread out my sheet on a cot. By the time I woke up, the team was worried that General Scott's impending visit had been expanded from fifteen to forty minutes; maybe that meant they were already in trouble. With everybody focused on housecleaning, I brushed my teeth and headed for the latrine, where the porn mags had been replaced with Garfield the Cat cartoon books. The chopper made a pass overhead just as I cleared out of the casern.

¤   ¤   ¤

"The mentality has not changed in Haiti," Henri said, unlocking the safe in his office at the Christophe to exchange my dollars for a grungy stack of gourdes. "They know the white is coming and he is leaving. All they have to do is wait. What the people are saying now, the U.S. came in 1915 and realized they could not do the dirty job, so they created an army. That's what will happen again."

Or maybe not. The UN—a third-world employment agency, Top Miatke called it—had been enlisted to keep the lid on Haiti for two years, until the end of 1996, a time frame nobody on the ground at the moment thought sufficient. The U.S. was leaving the Special Forces on board, plus several thousand grunts from the Twenty-fifth Infantry: logistics, quick reaction, a lot of support units, and a substantial command headquarters run by a U.S. general by the name of Kinzer. But because Meade, and now General Fisher, had failed to demilitarize the operation at the appropriate time—the higher-ups were afraid to train infantry to become peacekeepers, because then you had to retrain them to kill—the U.S. wasn't handing over a going concern to the United Nations, which was good at taking over existing structures but short on development and improvisation.

"You will have a two-tiered UN operation," an Irish military observer told me under his breath, "basically based on race, and if a Haitian shoots a UN soldier, they'll shoot a Bangi, because nobody will care."

FIELD NOTES

21 DEC 94

2. *Bosnia:* Hear today that President Carter negotiated another truce in Bosnia. Guess we know where we'll go next.

07 JAN 95

1. *Search and Sezure* [sic]: I do not want anyone conducting any searches or seizures during 1800HRS–0600HRS. This is in the Haitian constitution. Hot pursuit of an incident during the night is OK. If you feel you

need exceptions, then ARSOTF is the approval authority, on a case by case basis.

14 JAN 95

1. *Cinc Mtg:* I was in a meeting [censored]. . . . Amb. Swing stated that the FRAPH was not a political party. That the FRAPH was a bunch of thugs who maintained power thru terror and intimidation. We can tolerate them as long as they work toward nonviolent participation, but do not give appearance of being close to them.

15 JAN 95

1. *School Supplies:* If you were king for a day, how much school supplies would you need for your area? Let me know. . . .

3. *Haitian Positives:* Need you to report each week at least three projects or things that the Haitians are doing to help themselves. So far all press seems to be what someone else is doing for them. Progress is showing what they do for themselves. . . .

6. *UNMIH:* You can slowly start preparing the populace for the fact that the UN is taking over at the end of March. They do not have reason to worry. The UN will also work to maintain a stable and secure environment. [Weapons policy censored.]

20 JAN 95

4. *Macoute Leaflets GRDN* [Grande Rivière du-Nord]: Text of leaflets found in GRDN, 19 JAN. For us 18 months is like 18 days. The Lavalas speak of reconciliation, but we have our weapons ready. We have magic and mystical weapons to take care of your chemical weapons. We also have death powder and water horses testicles and machetes.

25 JAN 95

1. 25th ID confiscated 18 crew served weapons at Bowen airfield. There are still weapons out there that the FADH has not told us about.

28 JAN 95

4. *Realignment*: Around 15 FEB we will move out of six locations: Aquin, Ft. Liberté, Mt. Organise, Gros Morne, Thiote, Limbé.

01 FEB 95

5. *Tomorrow*: Tomorrow is Ground Hog Day. If you see your shadow, we will be here six (6) more months.

06 FEB 95

6. *Local Police/Neighborhood Watch:* In areas where you have insufficient IPSF, try to encourage the local community to take action themselves.

ANSANM, ANSANM, NOU SE LAVALAS (TOGETHER, TOGETHER, WE ARE THE FLOOD)

Gary and I were finishing breakfast on the veranda at the Oloffson, about to head north into the mountains as soon as I settled the bill, when an American woman who worked in the palace for Aristide asked if we had heard about what happened in Limbé. There was some sort of catastrophe, she said. Six interim police were murdered, and Dany Toussaint, Aristide's new security chief, had confided to her that disgruntled ex-FADH had staged an attack on the casern.

"Where were the Special Forces?" I asked, incredulous, and dreading the answer, whatever it was. They weren't there, she said. Today was Monday, and the assault on the casern had happened late Saturday night, the second weekend in February, but that was all she knew.

By early afternoon, we were in Plaisance. As if he had been waiting all day for our appearance, my friend Francky jumped into the road to wave us down. "I want to leave this place, this terrible place," he said, so terrorized, so frantic. "I want to leave and go anywhere and forget I was ever here."

"Is it true about Limbé?" I asked.

"Yes, yes," said Francky. *Le hing-hang*—disorder—and five dead.

At least the body count was going down. "Who did it?" I asked. Francky shrugged, bug-eyed; his fear was contagious. "Where were the American soldiers?"

"They left, they went to Cap," said Francky, and his voice tapered off and succumbed again to his despair. "This is a bad place, bad things are happening."

You had to love Haiti not for what it was but for what it wanted to be, but in between this and that, you still had to survive. Francky took my hand in both of his to say farewell. He was closing his photography shop and going into hiding. He seemed to be falling apart, and his demeanor had an awful effect on our nerves. We drove ahead slowly, in a silence full of misgiving. "You know what Haitians say?" Gary finally remarked to me, looking down at his knees. "Haitians say sooner or later the Americans will leave earth and go somewhere else to live."

Two platoons of Twenty-fifth Infantry riflemen, body-armored and combat ready, were patrolling Limbé when we arrived. A psy ops team was driving around town in an armor-plated Humvee wired for sound, lecturing the population in the voice of Papa God:

People of Limbé. There is among you a group of savages.

Around the first of February, a new IPSF lieutenant, Lieutenant Antoine, arrived at the casern in Limbé from Ounaminthe to replace the forever absent Lieutenant Lumas. He carried with him a glowing letter of recommendation from Captain Metz, the team leader of the Special Forces in Ounaminthe, attesting to his professionalism, fair-mindedness, and sense of duty. Immediately, this new lieutenant set to work and, guided by ODA 311, resolved difficult problems in Pilate and Bas Limbé, serving warrants issued by the judge, doing what he was supposed to do, without complaint or problems. Anyway, he made Top Miatke and the boys happy, and that by itself was a miracle.

Also during the first week in February, the justice of the peace had come to the compound to pay Top a visit and eventually got around to the topic of Jean Moulin—the Bossman: why was the team going after him? Because our chain of command believes this man is a danger to

Americans, Top responded, and the judge said that Jean Moulin had asked him to come talk to the soldiers and ask Captain Stefanchik for a pardon. Can't do it, said the captain. The best way for Bossman to stay alive and out of trouble would be to lie low for a year. End of conversation.

"We knew we had to leave," said Top, welcoming us to his nightmare du jour. "I knew something might occur, but nothing like this." Inside the gates, the compound was filled with unfamiliar faces—psy ops guys, Caricom IPMs, intel officers, SF reinforcements. Miatke and the captain had decided the team would leave Limbé the previous Friday, under cover of darkness, so no one in the town would have time to organize a *manifestation;* Limbé would simply wake up Saturday morning to the reality of itself and go on from there.

After receiving orders to pull back to Cap, for three days the team moved nonessential gear up to the FOB. Then, late Friday, they piled the remainder into the Humvees, and after the last Radio Limbé broadcast from inside the mess hall, Commo Jim packed up the transmitters, while the other guys walked over to the rear of the casern and, to the astonishment of the IPSF, pried the sheet of plywood off the back door. Okay, here's what's happening, they told the ex-FADH. We're leaving. We'll be back every so often to check up on things, and in the meantime we don't want you running all over the place back here.

An hour later, they were billeted at Base Camp One at the airport in Cap Haïtien, organizing mounds of gear, getting ready to go home, thinking the mission was over and relieved to be able to sit back without posting a guard, without somebody waking them up in the middle of the night to report a stolen goat, relieved to be able to grab a plate of hot chow from a real kitchen, make phone calls home whenever they pleased, do PT without running in rat circles. Life of Riley, but it lasted less than twenty-four hours. They planned to return to Limbé the following night, just to keep people on their toes, and make sporadic visits throughout the week. Top had expected somebody would create a minor disturbance, the disorder-as-entertainment syndrome, but he had never imagined how quickly the town would be consumed by violence. Since yesterday, they had recovered four bodies, two in Limbé and two in Petit Bourg, and at least five more IPSF were missing and unaccounted for.

"The evidence points to the volunteer police," said Top, rocking me backward on my heels, "and Bossman was in on it too."

Captain Mike had called a meeting of the town officials, which had just commenced, and I dashed out of the compound, with Gary in tow, across the marketplace to the *mairie,* where Stefanchik, his Haitian-American interpreter, and West Indian International Police Monitors were grilling the Limbé notables—Mayoress Bruno, the judge, the new delegate and vice delegate—their mugs as inexpressive as suspects in a police lineup. Master Sergeant Phil, the interpreter, speaking for the young American captain as the imaginary colonel once spoke for Barton, insisted they come clean. People in Limbé had told the Special Forces that the attackers were thieves who came here from some other part of Haiti, but that possibility was ludicrous, and everyone in the room knew it. The notables, a chorus of denial, kept repeating the same lie, that they had no idea who was responsible for the atrocity.

"The same people who caused this problem are the same people who chose the volunteers," one of the IPMs—a muscular black man, large as an NFL lineman—said with supreme disgust, each word like a punch coming out of his mouth.

"Even though these guys were chosen by the people doesn't mean the people were involved in the crime," replied the delegate, and I understood now that Limbé itself stood accused of murder.

The Special Forces were looking for the civilian police to get to the truth of the matter, but the civilian police had disappeared. "They are considered guilty until they show themselves," said Captain Stefanchik. "If they're innocent, why are they hiding?"

The people in Limbé were sympathetic to the volunteers, said the IPM officer, unsympathetically. The West Indian, leaning forward in his chair for emphasis, was flanked by serious backup—guys in sunglasses from the Windward Islands, undercover head-knockers, IPSF investigators from Cap—standing against the wall, their gigantic arms folded across their chests. "The lieutenant," he chupsed, "was taken from the casern through a neighborhood, and still nobody knows anything."

"There were a lot of people in front of the casern," said Captain Stefanchik, relentless in his enmity toward the notables, "but we can't find even a single witness."

"You should know the system of the Caribbean people," argued the delegate. "Maybe somebody saw but is afraid to tell. What can we do if he doesn't want to talk? When the American soldiers left the casern, if they communicated with the civil leaders, we would have told you not to leave the town, or to leave four or five soldiers behind."

"We told the police, the IPSF," said Stefanchik, and I was drawn by his frosty disdain, his abrasiveness; how much bigger and butch the quiet, thoughtful captain had made himself this afternoon. No bookworm squirt from Notre Dame with wire-rimmed specs and ashes on his forehead, the boy had morphed into a scalding inquisitor. "You know what I think? That if I did tell you we were leaving, it would have happened earlier, the same night we left."

A flurry of banging and hammering resounded through the room from across the street, where the coffinmakers were once again busy. The captain and the IPM investigators exchanged grim looks, and the meeting was over. The entire town, it seemed, had been placed under house arrest.

The intel so far was sketchy, but the U.S. Army was depending on its aviary of sources. It had happened like this, maybe: The team slipped out of Limbé at 2200 Friday evening. On Saturday, Mondesire, one of the first FADH soldiers to return to the garrison after the infil in September, was corporal of the guard throughout the day. During his morning shift, five or maybe as many as eight volunteer police came poking around the casern, asking if the Special Forces were coming back. Another source reported that the civil police met at midafternoon at the Catholic parish hall for a three-hour-long planning session, with the priest and the three neighborhood gangs, including Bossman, in attendance. This sounded strangely fastidious, this forum for undigested democracy, given that the ultimate plan was to go berserk.

At 1800, Mondesire went off duty, and Corporal Alphonse Ostel, whom earlier in the month I had given a lift to Ounaminthe, came on. Sergeant Jerome and Lieutenant Antoine were in the casern, along with nine other IPSF. Several of the civilian police returned, played cards for a while with a few of the ex-*militaires*, and left, as did Mondesire, who went looking for something to eat. He was on his way back when someone engaged him in conversation, which, coincidentally, prevented him from returning to the casern. At the same time, for some reason Sergeant Jerome said he had to leave the building for a few minutes to go home. With twilight fading into darkness, and while the lieutenant went into the back of the compound to start the generator, the remainder of the IPSF contingent, except for Corporal Alphonse, took off, just as a crowd began to form outside the gates. In the crowd was at least one volunteer policeman, who claimed he had taken a criminal into custody and wanted to bring him ahead into the casern's jail.

But the volunteer lost his nerve and retreated, just as the crowd overflowed and snagged Corporal Alphonse, who refused to crumple under the blows of a spectacular beating. Alphonse broke free and lurched into the marketplace, where another group waited in ambush, overwhelming the corporal, battering him with sticks and tire irons. His weapon was ripped out of his hands and fired, but somehow Alphonse broke loose again and made his way to the hospital before collapsing. What happened after that the Americans weren't yet clear on, but one thing was certain. The crowd fell upon Lieutenant Antoine and dragged him into the marketplace to thrash him, then tossed him onto a ricksha cart and wheeled his gravely injured body back behind the town toward the river, to finish him off.

Not long after that, Top and a couple other NCOs rumbled into town, like game wardens checking on the wildlife. All the sensory information was wrong, creepy. Saturday night, and the streets were all but empty, a smell of burned rubbish in the air, and when they reached the deserted marketplace they began to brace for trouble. Directly in front of the casern, the *marchands'* stalls were smashed, flimsy tables were overturned, fresh blood pooled on the ground. The gates to the compound were thrown open, and inside the casern the generator was running, the lights were on, but no one was around. The M-1 rifles and ammunition had been carried off, the building was trashed, and the IPSF pickup truck was nowhere in sight. Adrenaline cocktail.

They radioed back to the base at Cap Haïtien. The infantry took their time discussing everything and then finally moved out to Limbé with a couple of platoons and the rest of 311, which had gathered up its gear, the team members figuring they were back on the guest list at Chez Limbé. At 0200 Sunday morning, the convoy arrived at the rock quarry on the north side of town, where they hooked up with Top, who remained behind with Bob Fox and the Twenty-fifth Infantry riflemen while the rest of the team walked in on a back road, hoping to surprise *malfaiteurs*, lasso strays. When they reached the compound, the captain radioed the troops back at the quarry to come ahead and the team bedded down until first light, when they resumed their presence patrols, seriously angry men. Gone were the rules that kept the world in balance.

A few witless or otherwise brave Haitians began popping up at the casern, like Jerome's son, who said his father had come home, they both had heard an awful noise outside the house, and so they fled, and Jerome was now in hiding in Cap. Someone else came by to report he'd seen three armed civil police go to Jerome's house and search it, and Mondesire walked up and said he'd seen Alphonse get beaten and the corporal was now in the hospital.

Some of the guys went to have a look. The corporal had taken devastating blows to the head, and as he spoke to the soldiers the stitches burst open and blood ran down the man's swollen face. Hips to shoulders, his back had been lashed with iron rebar, splitting the skin in some places, in others leaving behind the ringed pattern of the metal. His neck was inflated like an inner tube from jawline to collarbone from being choked. Back at the casern, the team had begun hearing rumors about two dead IPSF—the lieutenant and another ex-FAHD, named Nikola, plus the lieutenant's girlfriend, whom he'd brought with him from Ounaminthe.

One of the rumors was about a body buried somewhere along the river. Commandos mounted up for a Humvee cruise out to the edge of town. Crossing the bridge before the gravel quarry, Walt glanced upriver and noticed four guys on the bank, too well dressed to be peasants, carrying plastic garbage bags. The Green Berets gave chase but lost them in the bush, then they called in reinforcements, which swept the riverbank to no avail. But the team, not realizing it, had passed within rock-throwing range of Lieutenant Antoine's body.

Later that afternoon, the mayoress came to the casern and told the team that the civil police were mixed up in all of this, and the captain stared at her pin-eyed, demanding, "What are you going to do about it?" Madame Bruno waxed philosophical, rambling on about the need for education. Lieutenant Colonel Schroer came up from Gonaïves to show the command flag; VIPs were shuttling in and out, and it began to seem that the only thing missing from the circus was a striped tent.

Night ticked slowly by and the drama flattened out, no problems except ODA 311 had been returned to go, and Top bedded down thinking he never saw it coming, he should have seen it but he glazed. What was happening now he understood was of the utmost consequence, and he didn't want his time in Haiti wasted, but here were all those months just unraveling, breaking apart. Once the town decided to kill the lieutenant, there was nothing to look forward to and nothing to look back at, as if Bob Fox had spoken the only truth available in the world when he'd said, "You can do something good one day, and it doesn't seem to mean shit the next."

Major Fox came down from Cap; while Captain Mike and Top were briefing him, someone came to the gate to say a body had been found in the river. The team investigated and found a dead man where the previous night they'd seen dozens of candles flickering bewitchingly from the bridge. A cow thief, people alleged. The vigilantes had broken his arms and legs. One thing's for sure, said the captain. Limbé is a shit magnet.

The Twenty-fifth pulled back into town in the afternoon, intensifying the severe level of animosity already there on the streets. The West Indian IPMs from Cap thundered into town like the FBI on steroids; they had a list of suspects, a list of sources, and a tip to look for the lieutenant's body in a certain area down by the river. The Caricom cops said they'd just have a walk around on their own, and JC Collins tagged along with his trauma kit.

They strolled the riverbank, sniffing the fetid air, eyes out for a fresh grave on the sand and gravel bars. One of the West Indians paused, listening. Over the soft sound of the water he heard the high-pitched buzz of flies and followed their whine to a disturbed patch of ground; bending over, he saw an eight-inch circle of human flesh, the uncovered back of Lieutenant Antoine, who had been hurriedly buried facedown. JC found a stick and began to dig him up.

Antoine's shirt was missing, his pants and underpants were pulled down around his ankles, his balls inflated to the size of goose eggs. He had been stoned and stabbed, his jaw and nose were broken, his skull was crushed, he'd been hacked on with a machete, he'd been shot, and he'd been torched from the knees up. The ineffable pain and horror on his face suggested that he hadn't been dead when his torturers flamed him. His hands clutched the soil—the lieutenant had been alive when they shoved him in the hole.

A platoon from the Twenty-fifth secured the area. Someone brought a body bag, and JC let the grunts take over. He had already inhaled enough of the corpse, and the young infantrymen were eager. The same source had told the IPMs where to find the lieutenant's mistress's body; they scoured the area thoroughly, gagging at the stink of something dead, but never found it.

The next morning, Tuesday, a volunteer policeman from Petit Bourg came to the casern hollering that the beloved Reubens was in trouble again; he was out in the street in Petit Bourg, his rifle in his hand, holding off a big crowd, which had tied up a house with rope so the thieves inside couldn't escape. The mob had already killed one thief, and Reubens had locked the other one in the *avant poste,* but now he needed backup. When the posse arrived, they took the live thief into custody and found the dead one in a field, lying on his back, his arms tied together, yams stuffed into his mouth.

"He stole his last meal," said the people standing around. The man had suffered deep puncture wounds in his abdomen, machete slashes to his head and legs, and his heels had been hacked off. Top noticed that, as with the lieutenant, the dead thief's pants had been pulled down around his ankles. He asked the bystanders if there was any significance in this; maybe sexual torture was part of the local homicide drill.

"*Bon,*" said a man in the crowd. "Before they kill a person, they pull down his pants and beat his ass with a stick."

"Oh," said Top, "so that's what that means."

Yes! Yes! Everybody began to laugh. It was what the FADH used to do, beat their asses, but democracy had universalized the pleasure, democracy had given them this satisfaction. It was the tyrants' ace in the hole when they had labored to justify themselves to Washington. Mob justice. Anarchy. The unrestrained masses.

FICTIONS

Stay safe, be careful, De Oppresso Liber, rasped a chipper Colonel Boyatt, signing off on the evening's fireside chat. Ranger body armor had been issued to 311 that afternoon, and "U.S. government officials" were headed our way tomorrow—spooks or black ops raiders; Captain Mike wouldn't say who they were. My permission to stick around would be reevaluated in the morning, when I expected to be told to pack my bags, because something fast and hard was going down.

The lights in the mess hall were running off a small portable generator brought in to allow the team to hear better at night—that meant no movies on the VCR too—and as the foot patrols deployed at regular intervals into the streets, you could follow their progress through town by listening to the dogs, which would shut right up with a fire blast of pepper spray. The patrols were constant, the town was being woefully harassed by the Special Forces, and no one was better at it than the psy ops team, low on the food chain except in their own minds, although you did well to remember that the first request at the Paris peace talks was for the U.S. to cease all psychological operations in Vietnam. In Limbé, the mind game squad was run by an SF reservist, a pharmacist from Texas, who was making life psychedelically miserable for the population. Besides their daylight harangues, the psy ops merlins were going out at 11:30 P.M., three in the morning, and sunrise.

A round-the-clock party, spring break in hell. As soon as they were beyond the gates, the pharmacist would goose the siren on the armored Humvee, then blast Pink Floyd at rock-concert volume. Phil the interpreter would start the doom-and-death rap, freshly penned by the unforgiving Captain Mike:

People of Limbé, rise up! The cowards responsible for the murder Saturday eleventh of February are afraid. They are afraid of you—the good people of Limbé. They are afraid of your love for justice and for what is true and right in God's eyes . . . and so on.

"If I can't sleep at night," said Sergeant Jon the pharmacist, "they can't sleep at night." Or any of us, he might as well have added.

The lights are suddenly doused. Everybody scrambles for his guns, because there's some kind of disturbance outside the casern walls, but whatever it is, it's nothing.

A half hour before midnight, out rolled the mind fuckers in their Humvee, the world's biggest boom box blasting warped white-boy heavy-metal blitzkrieg music—Peter Gabriel and *The Dark Side of the Moon,* a lack of imagination there but to the Haitian ear the melodic equivalent of the spirit of Ogoun, erupting with insanity. Then the tinny voice of Papa God, alias Phil, screeching into the town's dreams—dreams of possession, dreams of things to buy, to eat, to drive, to destroy—echoing off the mountains: *People of Limbé, rise up!* which they undoubtedly did, shuddering awake from their thin pillows and woven mats and sad, sweaty mattresses to comfort the children in the *blanc*-haunted darkness.

Top, Commo Jim, JC, and Fox began gearing up for a midnight foot patrol, *prêt-à-mortir* fashion plates, strapping on their LBE vests, double-checking handguns, rifles, and clips, looking around for their night-vision goggles. Near the food-prep table, Jim had taken a Magic Marker to a large ammo crate I'd never noticed before and written on its lid, *Pandora's Box.* The patrol vanished out the gate, and I began to understand what Stefanchik had going for himself: the pattern, the ruse. Earlier in the evening, it had been the same routine: first, psy ops cranked the volume; a half hour later, foot patrols. The suspects remained in town and the idea was to keep them off balance.

The 311's mission had been jeopardized by the IPSF killings, and the team took it personally, intimately—this was all a lot more personal than modern conventional war could ever be. "No matter who did this or how it turns out," said the young captain, "they're going down." The Special Forces wanted the IPSF back in Limbé to reestablish order and maintain a presence; they wanted the IPSF to conduct their own investigation with help from the IPMs; they wanted the Haitian judicial system to locate and indict the people responsible for the attack on the casern. The team had so far resisted being handed the lead role—if Americans tried to do it, they were going to be the bad guys. So far, the IPM investigation had turned up all but two of the twelve IPSF who had been in the casern on Saturday, and they were spilling accusations and hearsay like gutter spouts in a squall.

"If Jerome had balls this big," JC said, his fingers making a marble-size circle, "he would have warned the lieutenant and the corporal before he slunk off, and they could have been sitting there with their M-1s, waiting for those yucklefucks."

From what the team's own sources in town—including the Hodgeses at the hospital—were telling the Green Berets, every indication was that Jean Moulin was in on the plot, the civilian police were in on it, the gangs and the criminal element were in on it, the mayor, judge, and vice delegate seemed to know it was going to happen, and there were people in town who were convinced that knowledge of the attack went all the way up to the highest levels of the Haitian government, and whether those officials helped plan it or not, the sources insisted, they condoned the killings.

The patrols slogged back in. "I saw two dogs take a kid down," said Top, a non sequitur, a punch line with no joke behind it. He and Fox had picked up a xeroxed leaflet conveniently left in their path by someone posing as the Haitian National Military Resistance, a counterpunch in the psy ops brawl, and we gathered at the table to puzzle through the Creole:

After the drumbeat, here we are, members of the Resistance Militaire Nationale d'Haiti. We are surprised to see how some sold-out Haitian soldiers are turning into domestic servants being made by the Americans to pick up trash, throw out shit, dig holes in the casern for a latrine. (We all looked accusingly at Walt the Punisher.) *Therefore, we, the members of RMNH, we can't stay cross-armed in front of a situation like that. We'd rather die standing than die on our knees.* ("Don't matter to me either way," said Commo Jim.) *What happened Saturday 11 Feb. in the Limbé casern is a lesson we give all sell-out soldiers who already forgot the crimes the assassin American military did to us on Saturday 24 Sept. at OKAP police station. . . .*

"I hope somebody does something," said JC, though nobody paid any attention to what he was saying. "I just want to shoot somebody."

Top Miatke and Captain Stefanchik had reached the point where they couldn't breathe in without smelling the odor of the volunteers. The propaganda sheet from the so-called RMNH seemed but one more example of their treachery, an embellishment of their original betrayal. All the civil police had failed their entrance exams to the police academy: they'd lacked confidence, they'd counted on being selected the old way—who you knew, not what you knew—and they'd convinced themselves that Captain Barton would magically reappear and swing open the door. "We went way out of our way to help them," said Captain Mike, "and that makes this worse."

Those policemen, said Top, after they failed their chance to get into the police academy, were upset, but he never thought they were so upset that they would commit murder. They were upset, but they were still coming in, hanging out, working, yet the wind had been knocked out of their sails and the team thought, Well, they'll just throw up their hands and say to hell with it, we got screwed again, we've been screwed our whole lives, and they'd go on to something else. Then the next thing you know, they're collaborating with Bossman, and the bloodshed commences.

It would be some time before the Americans knew it, but what had happened that Saturday evening in February when Limbé was free to shape its own future or reembrace its past, was not quite what the soldiers imagined.

Thursday morning, a photographer I'd been working with came down from Cap to see what was going on. Get some chow, the team told him, and he rummaged through the mound of cartons on the prep table. "Are there breakfast MREs?" he asked. "Yeah," said Sergeant Fox. "Those are the ones you eat before lunch."

Brushing my teeth out in the yard, I watched Commo Jim jogging on the rodent track inside the compound, eleven laps to the mile. He was down to 197 pounds from 230, at least half of them from the reduced swelling in his liver. The air pumped rhythmically overhead, and I looked up and saw a Black Hawk circling, circling, locked onto a recon, the S-2 intel captain from the FOB up there with a video cam, filming the layout of the streets. Back inside the ops center, Captain Mike was over at his desk, composing the day's Intimidation 101 lecture:

People of Limbé, the Time is Now!

The savage dogs who killed on 11 February seek a return to the old ways. The ways of murder and torture. Justice and order are poison to them. They want blood. They believe you are weak—but you are not. You have the choice. Stand up now against them. If you do not, soon you will be their victims and they will be "beating your ass."

There was too much frustration in the room, too much energy in town, gone from jittery to jagged. There was Bob Fox in the corner, holding a match to what I assumed were the night's assault plans.

"I think you and the photographer are going to have to pull back to Cap today," said the captain, who looked paler by the day, a kid who stayed in his room all summer long. "Boyatt will be here within the hour."

"I probably want to stick around," I said, offering to send away the photographer, who wanted to leave anyway, as a fake compromise. "Come on," I pressed, appealing to my one advantage—my history with the team that predated him. "Talk to Top." Top, I had begun to believe, wanted me everywhere, wanted me to see everything, as if he had decided to hell with the limits, we're an open book, brah.

"I don't know," said Captain Mike, wavering, and we left it at that.

I fixed myself a paper cup of coffee and sat down with the fun-loving pharmacist, who was making a list of Deception Options:

2. *Convoy noises: Drive trucks round compound for five minutes. Record.*

3. *Dogs barking: Go out and get 2 dogs, tie them together. Record.*

The pranksters mounted up again to go Noriega the town with brain-splitting rock and roll; you could almost hear the population's neurological wiring crackle and almost smell the smoldering hatred. Unless you punctured your eardrums, there was no way to filter out the awful din, and they were being driven to the edge, but not of confession, which was the ostensible point of the exercise. About twenty minutes later, the metallic-voiced Papa God boomed right outside the compound's wall in the marketplace. *Honey, I'm home.* The photographer, who had joined them on this last circuit, climbed out of the armored Humvee, looking as if he had just dropped acid.

A team of Caricom IPMs arrived shortly thereafter, returning the casern's missing pickup truck, which the gone-underground IPSF had been using to run a tap-tap service in Cap Haïtien. Another SF team from Cap pulled in, extremely cool, as if they were in the casual habit of dropping by and making themselves at home, which made me suddenly realize the obvious, that reinforcements had been quietly slipping into the compound throughout the morning.

The team seemed to take a deep breath, trying to steady the tension. JC started working a crossword puzzle in *People* magazine, the cardplayers laid out games of solitaire, and then the lull of normalcy dissolved with the *chup-chup-chup* of a Black Hawk performing tight 360s above the casern— Colonel Boyatt, still stuck on the wrong frequency. The captain's anxiety level soared as he sent a Humvee racing to the landing zone and told the photographer and me we'd have to leave the building. ("You haven't seen That Bob Guy around, have you?" Boyatt asked the NCOs who came to pick him up on the LZ. "As a matter of fact, sir. . . ," said Sergeant Fox, grinning.)

We backed off about twenty paces, resting on the team's workout bench, still negotiating with Stefanchik. The gates opened, the gates closed. The affable Boyatt and his official friends were in hardy good spirits—"Oh, this, this is just a little thing," said the colonel in his minty Tennessee drawl—and the entourage breezed into the ops center.

After a while, some NCOs wandered out of the meeting, troopers I didn't recognize. The photographer, being a photographer, got itchy and audacious, wondering if it would be all right if he clicked off some pictures, and we sidled up to the doorway. "Ah, the fiction writer," said Boyatt, showering me with optimism. "The glass is half full." To accommodate the camera, the colonel dropped his boot off the bench where he had propped his foot, correcting his bearing.

The fiction writer.

These were the first words Colonel Mark Boyatt said to *me* rather than to the nameless correspondent I had been to him, one of the tail-wagging pack who had followed his trail for months, trying to determine if the spoor we inhaled had been laid down by a hero.

His acknowledgment was a dismissive double entendre, however good-natured the delivery, a many-layered joke to let me know I was on his radar screen, to test my own mettle, perhaps, and I had to bend laughingly to the colonel's sense of gamesmanship, his easy half smile and sly charm. Except for the spark of steel in his eyes, Boyatt looked like a soft-spoken Jesuit curate, a pious and professional man given to ascetic disciplines.

Sure, I told Boyatt, I am the fiction writer. And perhaps if I'd had the presence of mind, I would in turn have acknowledged the colonel's own considerable talent for creating fictions—mysteries, intrigues, secret and elusive victories, missions good and bad, holy and unholy—imaginary worlds meant to reinvent the blighted human landscape of places like Haiti. A few weeks earlier, when I and other correspondents had published reports accusing Colonel Boyatt and his men of aiding and abetting terrorists, I could not foresee that a year later, long after he had left Haiti and returned to Fort Bragg, the charge would still be there, resurfacing in the national and international media, hanging over the colonel and the Special Forces and the job they did in Haiti. A year later, I would still be trying to exonerate Boyatt and his soldiers from my own allegation.

I made a successful pitch over the captain's head, soliciting the field commander's permission to stick with the team overnight. Then Boyatt and his coterie left, and I sent the photographer back to Cap and went to find Top Miatke, whose face was masked in what I had become accustomed to thinking of as the master sergeant's death stare.

"So what'd Boyatt say?"

"Take the town back," said Top, his blue eyes glinting.

OGOUN FERAILLE, THE GOD OF WAR

Each time I turned around, more Green Berets strolled into the compound, until the afternoon had become a reunion of old buddies comparing gripes. Someone in the marketplace tossed an anonymous letter over the gate, a folded sheet of paper, inscribed on top with the helpful instructions, *You can read. It will help us.* It was most enlightening, more than anyone in the compound was ready to admit at the time, after so many months of not knowing whom to believe about anything:

Hello white Americans. You can read its the truth.

People who live in Limbé are in danger due to thugs who aren't afraid to do anything and they won't learn a trade in order to survive. The assassins profited to steal and among them they have Israel Belizaire. He's in a place called Chabote, a little up the way of Gran Ravine. Then go to Anro Leve where the pump is and ask for a man there who sells property, his name is Sadame. Is a club (gang) and they all have weapons. . . . If you all leave we are going to die at the hands of thugs. Please arrest them. We have hope in you Americans. Now they have put the word out. We are afraid to come and tell you because they are all in the streets. The day you pack up and leave Limbé will be upside with thugs, who have weapons in their hands. And arrest the guys that live in Anro Leve. That's where they took the person they killed Saturday night. And they claim to be Lavalas.

Thank you.

Hello black Haitians, I said to myself, composing an imaginary response to the letter's nameless citizen. You have infuriated the warriors, and the names on the arrest warrants issued by the judge in Cap Haïtien are not Israel Belizaire and not Sadame—but Bossman and the volunteers, whom tonight you are going to feed to Ogoun Feraille to propitiate the *loa* and his servitor, the white American soldier, and win mercy, and you must understand that in the white American soldier's eyes, there is no Lavalas, there are only macoutes and liars. That, too, is the truth, and I can tell you nobody in here has forgiveness in his heart, nobody in here can even say what this whole thing is really about anymore.

Video technology had come to the trenches, Ross Perot's VCR now an instrument of tactical support. Soldiers huddled around the TV screen, studying the aerial recon footage shot from the Black Hawk earlier that morning, three raiding parties watching a celluloid loop of Limbé's streets played and replayed until everybody committed the layout to memory, then each leader rehearsed each step that would bring his team to the target, then each man rehearsed the position he would take up outside one of the houses that were going down, then everyone coordinated the nasty dance that would bring them busting through the doors. The SF had never been in any houses in Limbé, never once opened a door, and they expected people to be more than a little surprised. Any threatening behavior, Boyatt had told them in answer to their questions about ROE, would be "fair game." No warning shots. According to the rules, fire your weapons only to kill.

"When you're on the B-team," said a nervous black interpreter who'd been brought down from the forward operating base at Cap, "this sort of stuff is like culture shock."

They were busy, happy, focused as surgeons; the anticipation of action was like a miracle cure that had suddenly made them healthy after months of chronic maladies. "We had to become politicians, and I can't be a politician," said JC, repacking his trauma kit. "I'm too opinionated, I know the difference between right and wrong."

At twilight, the town was treated with another dose of psy ops, communal radiation therapy, and as the pressure mounted, the Green Berets grew more serene, natural and lucid and free of bravado. What was there to brag about? They had every conceivable advantage. Even the wise guys transcended their shoulder-rolling, pelvis-cocking, hip-hop smart-assery and connected with total concentration to the business at hand, which, despite the soldiers' expertise, was fraught with peril. Two Humvees arrived with more reinforcements, and an intensive review of the raids began. Challenges and passwords were established. If any IPMs or IPSF got shot inside a house, the Twenty-fifth's quick reaction force would come in and cordon off the entire neighborhood, then the snake eaters would go in and clear the building room by room with capstun grenades. Chances were, two or three houses would resist, said Top. "Get your grenades out, your chemlights out, your flex cuffs out, the parachute flares." The IPM/IPSF crew were due to arrive from Cap Haïtien in three hours, and Bob Fox made necklaces out of red chemlights for the cops, so the SF wouldn't shoot them by mistake if a firefight broke out.

I was awed by the exactitude of the preparations, the competence and ease of the men readying themselves for violence, and it had become self-evident that the psy ops served a double purpose—not only to frazzle the town's nerves into a confessional mode but, more important at this point, to overlay the town's unsweet dreams with a pattern of crazy noise to disguise the raiding parties' movements. Which meant that H hour would coincide with the next scheduled psy ops patrol, at 3:00 A.M.

The true pressurized weight of what was about to happen struck me as I stood back and watched the soldiers dress for battle. In all the time I'd been in Haiti, I had never seen, no matter how dire and threatening the circumstances, what I was seeing now—Special Forces outfitted in full combat gear, strapping into high-tech body armor, buckling the chin straps on Kevlar helmets. Even in the worst of times, the team's posture had remained *soft,* wearing forage caps, forgoing bulletproof vests, gambling their personal safety on the sartorial message that they had come to Haiti to help, to build rapport. But hearts had curdled, minds had been poisoned.

"What happens next?" I asked Captain Mike, who had joined me and Top under the stars. His uniform and helmet seemed a size too large and had the funny effect of making him seem twelve years old.

"We wait for a go," he said.

As we were speaking, in Cap Haïtien Major Fox and the sardonic S-2 captain were rousing the justice commissar out of bed to have him sign the arrest warrants, a technicality that had to wait until the last minute for fear the judge or his cronies would tip off the town. Any minute now, the major and the intel officer were due in at the casern. Then the teams would lock and load, psy ops would roll, a chopper would position itself overhead, a medevac unit would go on alert, and Limbé, slumbering uneasily, would snap wide awake.

My throat parched, I went to the storeroom for a cold drink and was stunned to find the ex-FADH, ex-IPSF Sergeant Jerome there, the embodiment of woe, in his own mind Haiti's number one victim. Poor Jerome, a dog under the feet of so many unkind masters—you wanted to give the guy Prozac and kick him out the door. The soldiers, he said forlornly, had made him come back to the casern, but only for tonight, and then he was free to go into hiding again in Le Cap.

"What happened here last Saturday?" I asked.

"It was very bad, very bad, very bad." Jerome's jeremiad.

"But you escaped."

"Yes, thank God."

"Why didn't the lieutenant and the corporal escape as well?"

"We ran for our lives." Jerome shrugged. "What could we do?"

"So the volunteer police attacked the casern?"

"Yes, the civil police."

"But you ran away, you didn't see them kill the lieutenant?"

"Yes, but I know."

In the mess hall/ops center, the energy had turned sharp, contradictory; guys were cheery as scouts at a jamboree, excited and raw with anger, flirting with meanness. This was why they joined the army. "The lieutenant the volunteers killed was a good guy, he really was," said Commo Jim. "He was an innocent person. We came in here and we schmoozed and we schmoozed, we tried to be friends with them, and that's what got us in trouble, because we schmoozed too much," and now it was time to get real, go out into the dead of night and do dangerous work. Then Major Fox and the intel captain came in out of the darkness to address the soldiers, and it was painful to hear the humbled cadence of their words—the raid was on hold until daylight.

"We're not going to get anybody," Stefanchik said. "We're going to look like fools."

The plan had crashed head-on into a perfumed zombi, the post-Duvalier Haitian constitution, which in order to curb abuses by the FADH or the FADH's more overt variations, disallowed the arrest of suspects between six in the evening until six in the morning, sundown to sunrise, so that even the most undeserving of citizens might enjoy a peaceful night's rest. The American military was intent on going to absurd lengths to be a law-abiding occupier of a nation other than its own, and probably it was true that only American soldiers would obey a law like this.

The teams were good to go, their adrenaline had been revved for a green light, but they worked for the army, and the army had a genius for jacking them around. Each of them had developed an on/off switch, and so they set down their rifles, stripped off their armor, spread sleeping pads on the ground, and simmered into unconsciousness, to click awake three hours later, cocks crowing on the far edge of night, as two truckloads of West Indian and Haitian cops motored quietly into the compound. Then they quietly brushed their teeth, resuited in armor, cradled their weapons, folded the appropriate warrants into their vests, and launched the raids.

"You coming with us?" said Top.

"I'm not," I said. I'd spent so much time in Haiti looking for trouble, and now I felt that I'd found enough of it, but it was more than that. Something had begun to make me feel despairing and confused. Even as I believed in these men, if not always in their judgment, my faith in the mission was dissolving. I had seen the muddle and the drama, the misery and the death, to the point of oversaturation, and I knew I didn't want to see it anymore. And the team knew that even when you hauled yourself out here, nothing was ever clear. One minute you extended your sympathies in earnest, and the next minute you rescinded those sympathies with a vengeance.

"We can still win," I heard the S-2 say, suiting up to join a team that was short a man. Nobody asked, *Win what?*

The heavens brightened as the *marchands* began to gather in the market-place. The exquisite lavender of dawn lasted only a moment, the color draining as low clouds of fog with charcoal undersides drifted over the sil-houettes of treetops, and tendrils of mist curled in the decreasingly empty streets, tempting the breeze that would arrive with sunrise. For all its ug-liness, Limbé, like any tropic backwater, was beautiful at dawn and dusk, its light most sensual, its fragrances of cook smoke and flora most seduc-tive, but then the blinding sun would lift into the perfect sky and start slow-cooking the rot. The psy ops wagon went round and round and round, making Limbé quake with surreal music, electric-guitar riffs that cut through the atmosphere like a hog being slaughtered on the world's biggest sound system. A chopper hovered about a hundred feet over one of the neighborhoods.

Now more air support was in the white sky, a second chopper fishtailing over houses. The radio crackled, teams reported themselves in position. But everything was fucked. The town was awake, they'd been awake, everybody knew what was happening by now, anybody with a guilty conscience had bolted, and anybody who wanted to be a hero had a frag grenade in his hand. Someone on the radio said there was a problem with the one-legged judge, who appeared terrified and didn't want to go along with the soldiers, but they needed to be able to point at his authority and dragged him along despite his protests. The sky became rose and mauve with sunrise, but it didn't much matter that it was a lovely morning.

The radio crackled again: A suspect was running for the river, into the inhospitable arms of the Twenty-fifth Infantry. Another crackle: Captain Troutman's team had begun to transfer prisoners to the casern.

As it turned out, Haiti's pantheon of resistance wouldn't be inducting any heroes on this unpleasant morning. The volunteer police and gang leaders had vanished into the bush; everyone but Bossman had the sense to step out of the path of the charging bull. Sergeants Walt Plaisted and Bob Fox approached the house of Jean Moulin's mother and took up their positions, while she stood on the threshold, yammering instructions back into the house, telling her son everything the soldiers were doing. Walt moved forward, telling the old woman in French to pipe down, but she kept spurting out language, and he unclipped the canister of pepper spray from his vest. He only meant to get a little splash in the air to discourage her, but the cans the military issued had a faulty push button—when you started spraying, sometimes they wouldn't stop—and from where Bob Fox was standing, it looked like The Punisher was hosing her down. A minute later, the can was still emitting a blistering cloud, everybody was gagging and crying, and the commandos waved at the IPM and IPSF to get inside and bring out anyone in the house.

Although the yard remained in shadows, by now the western wall of the casern's compound was painted with warming sunlight. Psy ops switched the channel to thunderous rock and roll; out in the marketplace, a crazy lady danced butt naked to the whipsaw beat, skipping through the stalls like a flower girl, holding her shirt wide open. The first load of prisoners pulled through the gates, packed into the bed of an IPM pickup truck. There were several young men who, because of their age, appeared to fit the bad-news profile, but the remainder of the handcuffed detainees, more than a dozen—grandfathers, mothers, young women, boys—seemed as if they'd been apprehended in a schoolyard or church. They were led to the rear of the casern for processing, then made to stand, debased, disconsolate, petrified, back outside against the building's whitewashed wall. The IPM brought in an unconscious teenage boy and laid him out on the ground. A medic hurried over to cut his handcuffs, check his vital signs, and place a pad under his head. Maybe a case of shock, he thought. Five minutes later, the kid was hit by an invisible lightning bolt and began to sob hysterically, his body jerking, seemingly on the verge of a seizure. The medic returned to calm him down. I don't know, he said, this guy's just terrified, I guess, or maybe he's faking.

In the marketplace, the fiasco was beginning to draw a crowd; schoolboys in yellow shirts and green pants lined up to watch the show. Another truckload rolled into the compound—more frightened handcuffed boys, more distraught women. The sweaty S-2 was back among us, saying, "A lot of these fish we have to throw back. They don't make the limit."

But this time at least the team had one of the prizes they dearly wanted. There was Bossman, to be sure, shirtless and shoeless, dressed in a pair of cutoff jeans, his arms pinioned behind him, and he was mouthing off like nobody's business. Major Fox yelled for the West Indian IPMs to keep him quiet. From inside the casern, the cops led Bossman back into the yard and set him down on the steps leading to the shower room, off to the side from the rest of the prisoners, and I walked over.

"Bossman, you know who I am, right?" I said, coming to stand before him. With his shoulders thrown back, his chest looked exceptionally muscular, his stomach a washboard, his knees scraped and dusty from however much he had struggled against his capture. His hair was shaved close to his skull, he had a mustache, he was raffishly handsome, a Haitian everyman, and his eyes flamed when they met my own, their heat lessening as he searched between rage and humiliation for his voice. I thought he nodded, but then I realized that wasn't right; he was trembling, quaking.

"You're the journalist, man." I knew he spoke English, had been in and out of Miami doing who knows what, but still it seemed unnatural to hear it. I asked if he wanted a cigarette, but no, he didn't smoke. "Look," he pleaded, the voice of a man grievously wronged, twisting his torso around for me to see how the plastic cuffs pressed into the flesh of his wrists. "Man, tell the soldiers come cut the handcuffs off me."

"They won't do it. They hate you."

"It's bullshit, man," he said, his demeanor, once so full of wiles, now contorted and reduced by the agony of whatever injustice had finally chased him down. Victim, victimizer. He looked like a child about to cry, and I found myself feeling sorry for the bastard, his rage once so uncontainable it had rendered him indifferent to his own safety, or mine. "I did nothing, man. It's bullshit, man. Man, why am I being treated so bad by your people?"

"Tell me why the soldiers arrested you."

"I don't know. It's bullshit, man. They just come into my house. Look, they even take my mother. What she do? What I do? I did nothing. She did nothing."

"The soldiers say you killed the lieutenant."

"*That's bullshit!*" Bossman howled, his voice broken with falsetto squeaks and cracks. "I didn't do a fucking thing, I am fucking innocent, man. I have never done a thing like that in my fucking life."

The soldiers hated him was all he knew; maybe they hated poor Haitians. He began quivering again and clamped his mouth tight when Top and Walt strolled over, waving ridiculous cans of a soft drink called Dr. Perky, to bone up on their mockery skills. *Jean Moulin, the Big Man, the Gros Neg, you're not so big without a mob behind you.* Top sneered, virulent and implacable; Walt laughed and snickered. But it was too easy a game.

"I didn't kill nobody," Jean Moulin implored, and went off on the innocent riff. "I got no problem. I got no fucking problem. I brought you sixteen M-16s. *You* got a problem. I gave him [Miatke] nineteen guns. *You* got a problem. The guys who killed are still free. I'm not crazy. The guys who do that shit are crazy, but I'm not crazy. The people who do that shit

is nasty, man. That shit's not fair. I see my people got some trouble, I try
to help. Since Captain Barton leave, nobody is my friend. I brought him
grenades, .38s, M-1s. Why would I take a gun and shoot someone? Any
gun I take I give it to you, because I don't want it. I'm not crazy.

"I want democracy. I want the President Aristide back and everything
cool and people get jobs. The Haitian police beat me after the coup,
knocked out my teeth. Look in my mouth, man.

"Something happened. I tried to hit an attaché man. I don't touch the
soldier"—Jean Moulin averted his eyes from Walt—"I touched the attaché man.

"Listen to me," croaked Jean Moulin. "The same day Barton leave the
post, Bill get mad at me. Bill doesn't like me, man. He treat me just like a
motherfucker."

"Why don't you shut the fuck up," snarled Miatke. "Piece of shit," and
after a minute he and Walt let the Bossman be.

Watching the commandos walk away, Bossman looked spurned yet still
defiant, and by the time he faced around to speak to me, the fierceness
had drained out of his expression and he was trembling again, three-
fourths naked and the sun not yet high enough to bring him out of the
shadows. The raiding party had taken Bossman first, before he'd had time
to fully dress, hustling him into one of the vehicles. His mother had
thrown his shirt and shoes in with him, and now he wanted me to help. I
found the IPM commander and told him Jean Moulin was cold and could
I bring him his clothes. The cop uncuffed him, and Bossman put on his
T-shirt, slipped sandals onto his feet. He thanked me, his dignity momentarily restored, saying this was the first act of kindness an American had
shown him in Haiti. Perhaps he had somehow failed to see this one small
gesture's precedents.

A UN observer from Bangladesh approached us, asking Jean Moulin
why the American soldiers had brought him here.

"I don't know."

"You don't know anything, eh?" the observer sneered, and I knew the
rest of the day would not go well for the Bossman.

The third raiding party returned with its haul of prisoners; the Twenty-
fifth came in from across the river with a pair of raggedy-ass guys who

looked like farmers. The badly shaken judge appeared at the gates, pan-
icking because the townspeople were holding him responsible for the
raids and threatening to burn his house. Also, he had come to meekly
protest the arrest of one of his assistants; there was no warrant for the
young man, who happened to be inside a targeted house. Too bad, said a
West Indian cop. "We brought him in and we'll interview him, and because you're the judge, you shouldn't get too involved in it."

A red-shirted old man who actually was a farmer had been mistakenly
arrested as he walked by one of the hits on his way to the fields. "We've
got to do the old thing," said the S-2. "Give him a Dr. Perky, a pat on the
head, and sincerest apologies from Bill Clinton."

The optimum snag had been projected to be around eight or nine suspects, but it was becoming clear that the final tally would be three or four
out of a total of twenty-two detainees, plus the gang leader Saddam Hussein's picture, black-tip armor-piercing M-1 rounds, some IDs, and a stack
of illegal voter registration cards. The suspects were mostly guys who had
gone into hiding during Aristide's exile; now they were being hunted by
the Americans, and the town was outside the gates, shouting, *It's the same
situation again!* The operation had been a bust, a failure, a self-parody,
much ado about something—the death of the FADH lieutenant—that
didn't matter to the population, and Limbé was again ratcheting up its already frazzled emotions. I could hear pockets of noise outside the walls
from many directions, bubbles of rage bursting through the surface of the
morning. The detainees' friends and relatives were clamoring at the gates,
and a furious *manifestation* had begun to form in the marketplace.

It was different, though, inside the walls. The soldiers had removed
their body armor and the atmosphere was jazzed, guys strutting about on
the shiny aftereffects of adrenaline. No one had been shot, no one had to
bring in the dead, the fearless West Indian IPMs had been outstanding,
and the IPSF from the Cap Haïtien casern hadn't tucked their tails between their legs, earning themselves a fraction of respect from the Green
Berets, a status that nevertheless did not include use of the SF latrine. At
the back of the compound, I saw a Haitian policeman helping a handcuffed
man urinate, unzipping the prisoner's fly and holding the fellow's penis.

"That's when you should be earning the big bucks," said one of the
NCOs, grimacing at the sight. "You have to aim it, shake it."

"He needs peepee tongs," said the S-2.

◻   ◻   ◻

I had spent a sleepless night and, needing coffee, walked back across the crowded yard, the air thick with the distress and gloom of the prisoners. One of the SF asked me why I had taken Jean Moulin his shirt. "He was cold."

"Then why didn't you throw a bucket of water on the dirtbag," said the soldier, which made me stop and look at him but I had nothing to say, because what was there to say? I couldn't fault the soldiers for hating the futility of their mission or for their growing animus, which was for the most part rhetoric and bluster. They had worked without rest or pleasure for almost six months and it didn't seem to matter, they had wanted a righteous and illustrious fight but couldn't have it, they wanted and even deserved glory but had to settle for the quotidian honor of doing their job, whatever that was. Now that the compound was populated with frightened detainees, the whole affair depressed me. Outside the gates, the demonstrators had started singing: *Children, do not be too wise to your friends, in case they become your enemies.*

I heard one of the spooks, another intel officer, say, "The mayor's as much to blame as anyone else for this. She has blood on her hands for selecting the civilian police," and I wanted to tell him, *That's wrong!* But I didn't know if it was wrong or not. All I knew was that I didn't belong here anymore. Or perhaps I belonged more than ever but in a way I could not handle, a way that made me feel complicitous in a grudge match.

Forgetting about the coffee, I stopped to watch a dreamlike tableau, detainees marched forward one by one, flanked by a pair of IPMs or IPSF police holding on to each prisoner's elbows. They were stood in front of the storeroom door, which had been draped with several layers of opaque olive-green mosquito netting, concealing an invisible authority. I watched as an old man in suspenders and a fellow who looked like a middle-aged businessman, dressed in dark pants and a white shirt, were brought forth, placed in front of the draped doorway, and then released. The process didn't make sense to me until one of the young blue-jeaned suspects was dragged up and stood glaring straight ahead; a second later, the edge of the netting jiggled, as if a lizard had scurried up it. The youth was whisked away and lifted into the back of an IPM truck, its benches already occupied by several of his comrades. Top Miatke was walking past, and I asked him to come over.

"Who's behind the curtain?"

"A source," said Top. "Someone who knows who was involved in the lieutenant's murder."

"Jerome." Who else but Jerome.

The FADH sergeant sat in the storeroom on a wooden chair, scared out of his wits but making himself useful by fingering every teenage male in Limbé. "Come on," I said, "Jerome ran away. How does he know what happened that night? There's nothing he won't do to save his own skin."

What would happen to these kids? I asked, and Top said they'd be interrogated by the IPMs, then taken to Cap Haïtien to be jailed until trial. The truck was filling up with the accused; the women and older men and adolescent boys were being set free. Eventually Bossman was brought forward to the doorway of judgment. Antichrist meets anti-Judas—the Marassa of persecution, the Gemini of the *vodou* deities, opposing twins attached by an eternal cord of conflict. The curtain tugged, and off went Jean Moulin, in the custody of the International Police Monitors from Barbados, to account for himself amid the ruins of Haitian justice.

The S-2 captain watched the IPMs take Bossman over to the outbuilding housing the generator, thinking, Uh-oh, Barbadians, they got a guy, they think he's a rat, they're going to make him talk. Even with the generator running, the S-2 heard Bossman holler like a stuck pig and went running over. The Barbadians were doing something—the captain didn't know what it was—something that didn't leave any marks. The S-2 dragged the IPM sergeant out of there. "Hey, listen," he said. "I don't know what you're doing in there, but you gotta stop it—there's a reporter here." He knew he couldn't say, Don't do it because we don't do those sorts of things where I come from. It had to be, Hey, we've got the world press here. Just cool it.

These were the last minutes I would spend in Limbé with ODA 311, though my unhappy relationship with the town would continue to unfold for another year. This, too, was the last I'd ever see of the rebellious Bossman, the most reckless and inscrutable of patriots, because the next time I came looking for him, he was dead.

EXFILTRATION

Everything continued to disassemble for 311. Nobody arrested during the raid was jailed except for Jean Moulin. *Manifestations* became a daily occurrence, growing bigger and louder throughout the week, the leaders threatening to close the market, close the road, close the schools. Then the schools did shut down, and the agitators tried to barricade Route Nationale One with rocks, but the team pulled up in a Humvee, threw the rocks into the bed, drove to the bridge, and dropped them into the river. *Hey, those are our rocks!* the crowd protested, infuriated but no less impotent than the soldiers.

Finally, a temporary truce was called and another town meeting held, Captain Stefanchik and Colonel Speer, the Twenty-fifth's brigade commander in Cap Haïtien, sitting down with a group essentially composed of Jean Moulin's gang. No one wanted to discuss the murder; they wanted to denounce American transgressions. A kid stepped forward to say the raid was something he would have expected from the Duvalier regime. The colonel very calmly answered, "I resent that you said that. This is nothing like the Duvalier regime, or you wouldn't be talking to me right now." Another youth jumped to his feet, pulled up his shirt, and announced that he'd been kicked and beaten by the Americans. He had a note from a doctor, saying not that an examination had revealed contusions, bruises, or other injuries, but that the guy was "suffering from kicks given by an American." Man, Captain Mike said to himself, you've got a good doctor. Then someone brought in a shirt with a torn shoulder, offered as further evidence attesting to the brutality of the raid. But not one plaintiff wanted to talk about the fact that the lieutenant had been murdered. Instead, it was: the Americans are no different than the ancien régime.

None of the original IPSF ever returned to the casern. Finally, Aristide sent his chief of security, Dany Toussaint, to Limbé to install a new contingent of interim police in the 53rd District, but the team viewed the entire affair as one more travesty forced down their throats. Toussaint brought with him a five-foot-tall, two-hundred-fifty-pound policeman from Pétion-ville, in his Pétionville uniform, to take over the casern and a squad of Haitian ex-*militaires,* wearing everything from fatigues with helmet liners to FADH khakis; Toussaint himself was in his FADH khakis. Within minutes, the marketplace was boiling with a *manifestation,* and Major

Toussaint addressed the crowd: *My name is Dany Toussaint; you probably heard me on the radio or saw me on television.* What fricking planet did you come from, Top wondered, and where do you think these people are? Maybe in Port-au-Prince Toussaint was the president's right hand, but what the people of Limbé saw was an officer in the FADH army, in khaki uniform, so forget it. The major tried again: *I'm Dany Toussaint.* Nobody responded. *I'm Dany Toussaint.* Nothing.

Then the *manifestation* heated back up; the Americans and Toussaint decided to retreat to the town hall and convene a meeting. They sat down with the mayoress and other notables and two young representatives from Limbé's newly formed Crisis Committee, self-chartered to complain about the Special Forces raids and psy ops bombardment. Toussaint, well spoken and well versed in the function of police in a democratic society, talked for almost an hour, but he didn't connect until he revealed he'd been part of Aristide's security detail in exile. Suddenly the major was Limbé's favorite son. The boys on the Crisis Committee were saying, *Hey, you're the head of the police, you can get Jean Moulin freed.*

"Well, that's not the way it works," explained Dany Toussaint. "As police, we can't arrest people or free people on our own," and he went back outside to address the crowd, which now cheered him, and the whole thing turned into a "Free Jean Moulin" demonstration.

On the last Sunday in February, command thought it prudent to stack another team into the compound, home decorators from Fifth Group. "I don't know how you guys lived like this," one of the Fivers nagged at Walt. "You could have done better."

"Up yours, man."

The Fifth Group chogee boys walked on eggshells and strung lights everywhere; they had a big thing about lights. They said, "Why didn't you put screens on the windows?" and Walt explained that the doors were always open, what's the point, all you'd do was trap mosquitoes.

Change for change's sake. Appearances! Appearances! They didn't blow into town under war conditions, either, but came carrying little red ice coolers and duffels crammed with personal gear. They drove Top Miatke crazy, running around behind the scenes talking to their side of the chain of command, which didn't yet have enough in-country experience to make the decisions they were making, saying things were screwed up, saying 311 was afraid to patrol, when they themselves wouldn't move down the street without a buddy pack of five or six guys. The only thing the reinforcements seemed to accomplish during the ten days they were slotted into Limbé was teach the market kids to sing "Old MacDonald." Everywhere you went, it was *E-I-E-I-O.*

"Free Jean Moulin" *manifestations* kept the town stirred up. His mother and sister would come to the gates and screech like harpies, but nobody in town knew that Bossman remained jailed only because he had gone one-on-one with Walt the Punisher. Meanwhile, the SF were trying to figure out if Jean Moulin had anything to do with the killing, and Captain Stefanchik kept thinking about another Jean Moulin, the heroic resistance fighter in Paris during World War II, imagining what would happen if the people of Limbé knew the legacy of Bossman's name.

Walt and the captain went to Jean Moulin's first court appearance, the entire area blocked off and secured by a company of Caricom soldiers, Bossman's supporters mau-mauing outside the perimeter. The SF wanted to keep Jean Moulin locked up until Major Fox's S-2 got whatever he could out of him about the murders, so Walt pressed the issue, even though by now he had cooled off and was loath to enter the unclean waters of the Haitian judiciary just because Bossman had wrastled with him. Given the chance, Walt might have pushed him around a little bit and forgot about it, but the guys on the team were dogging him. JC was mad, appealing to Walt to follow through with the case, but then the intelligence officer decided there was no way Jean Moulin was involved in the murders. Maybe he'd been trying to plan the assault on the casern, but nobody would listen to him, he'd been ignored, it wasn't his show, and although he knew who the perpetrators were, knew where the body was and all that, Bossman wasn't actually part of the conspiracy, which was why he'd been caught when nobody else was.

So Walt stood before the court and recounted his confrontation with Jean Moulin, who didn't deny connecting with one of the American soldiers; he just didn't remember its being Walt. He admitted he'd incited the riot; he'd wanted to get the macoute, he said. Then he went on a poor-me tirade about Top Miatke, how Top persecuted him, how every time he turned around, Top was gunning for him, how he couldn't lead a normal life because Top was making life miserable for him. This is beyond me, declared the judge, and passed the case on to the next level.

Walt and the captain returned to court the next day, and a prosecutor asked questions. "Why didn't you react?" Walt said he did, he pushed Bossman against a wall and prevented him from trying to kill the attaché. Walt got the impression that the court wanted to know why he didn't just go ahead and shoot Jean Moulin. The judge and the prosecutor nodded sagely when Walt said he hadn't come to Haiti to kill people or maim people or anything like that; he had come to help the Haitians install democracy. Well, they said, this is beyond us, and they passed the case to the next level, with a court date set five days later. First, however, there was a bail hearing, attended by the new delegate and vice delegate. The vice delegate argued so lividly for Jean Moulin's freedom that the judge and the delegate together decided, Okay, we'll release him into the custody of the vice delegate, on the condition that the vice delegate goes to jail in Jean Moulin's place if the defendant fails to show up for trial. Whoa, forget it! The self-righteous vice delegate retracted his offer, but it was too late, and Bossman was set free. Stefanchik just got more and more philosophical about it all, thinking that maybe snatching people and putting them into the legal system and letting them back out was the price the army had to pay for not becoming more involved.

A few days later, General Hill flew to Cap from his command post in Port-au-Prince, and after his second visit to Limbé, Captain Mike suddenly found himself in jeopardy. The trouble started on the Humvee ride from the LZ. Recent rain, the road a strip of puddles, and the general, who had a case of the ass that morning, started badgering the introspective young captain. *Slow down, you're driving too fast and splashing pedestrians.* The captain was going twenty miles an hour on a paved road lined with unyielding foot traffic—Stefanchik himself used to yell at the team when they splashed people, but with puddles and potholes everywhere, it was unavoidable. When they arrived at the compound, the captain took the general into the mess hall to brief him, but it was bad timing; with the doubled-up teams, there were ten guys just sitting around. Hill wanted to know what the hell the captain and his men were doing *right now* to bring the Limbé situation under control.

Captain Stefanchik always thought for a moment before answering questions, and the apoplectic general had no patience for him—murders had not been solved, murderers had not been brought to justice. Then on the ride back to the LZ, a Haitian flagged down the Humvee, holding out a dead chicken and claiming the captain had run over it on the trip in. By now the general had seen enough. He had the same grand ideas 311 had back in September, he was going to fix the place on his watch, but not, as far as he was concerned, if he had to depend on the Special Forces and officers like Stefanchik. Well, gosh, Mike felt bad about hitting the guy's scrawny-ass chicken—on the way back, he stopped and paid an extravagant compensation—but there was no way to appease a general on the rag. Boyatt came on the radio that night, saying, *I don't know which of you guys is out there splashing people and driving too fast, but if I find out who you are, you're through.* You could almost feel the gun pressed against the colonel's temple.

Five days after Jean Moulin had been released, Stefanchik, Walt, and the S-2 captain rendezvoused in Cap to attend Bossman's trial. The case had ascended to the top of the pyramid, which meant the judge wore a robe and a buffoonish Napoleonic hat. The court had ordered Walt to bring eyewitnesses with him, but the two IPSF/ex-FADH who were nearby in the marketplace the night of the incident had lost interest in the world outside their ratholes and wouldn't come. Jean Moulin, dressed in jacket and tie, sauntered into court twenty-two minutes late (Walt timed it). The room was filled with Bossman's rebel cheerleaders, Haitian journalists, a female observer from the UN, who was there to make sure everything was on the up-and-up; and a crowd outside was holding an anti-American rally.

Walt turned to the S-2 and asked for direction. "I've got what I want," said the intelligence officer, "but go for it if that's what you want." The S-2 added that he thought it would be better for Limbé if Jean Moulin did not go to jail. Walt went out to the street, where the captain was baby-sitting the Humvee, to seek his counsel. Captain Stefanchik seemed distracted, and it wasn't like him to worry about the vehicle. Something was going on, but it wasn't time to get into it. "What should I do, Captain Mike?" Walt asked. The captain was slumped in the driver's seat, struggling with a profound sense of emptiness. When they arrived in Cap earlier that morning, someone had taken him aside to tell him General Hill was calling for his head. General Hill wanted the kid from Notre Dame relieved of his command.

Stefanchik finally summoned the energy to answer Walt. "Whatever you want to do," he said quietly. Walt said, "I'll let it go. I really don't care." "Okay," said the captain. "Take the wind out of their sails."

The case was dismissed, and after a few minutes Walt came back out with the JAG lawyer, and then the captain drove to the FOB and parked, telling Walt they were probably going to be there for a while, so he might want to go sit in the chow tent, but Walt stayed with the Humvee for the next hour, wondering what was going on. Eventually Major Fox came out and asked him what he thought of Captain Mike. "Quite frankly," Walt told him, "I think he's the best captain I ever had." "Geez," said the major, "that's what Jim Pledger said." He told Walt what had happened and said they were going to try to stop this, they were going to try to protect the captain from General Hill. The major had already been out to Limbé to pick up Stefanchik's gear, and Lieutenant Colonel Jones, the SF battalion commander, was on his way to collect the captain and take him to Camp d'Application, outside Port-au-Prince. Walt felt himself, his heart, freeze solid. The Fifth Group team's warrant officer had clashed with the captain, and Walt was convinced the WO had played a part in his own team leader's downfall.

The captain was in shock, struck dumb by the thunderbolt of a general's caprice. He'd never imagined this would be how he'd leave Haiti— ordered to pack his bags and hit the road, his career in free fall. Colonel Jones finally pulled in and took him off to a corner and said, "We're going to put you on ice for a while." The next thing he knew, he was down in Port-au-Prince, buying junk food at the PX and enjoying a hot shower. By the time Walt got back to the casern, he was Godzilla's understudy. "This is all fucked up!" he kept yelling at the alien team, and JC, incensed that Bossman had walked, added more bad blood to the cauldron, comparing the courtroom farce to the Rodney King spin-off trial, cops being convicted to preempt riots.

It was a Thursday night, and ODA 311 wasn't scheduled to exfil until Monday, but Top Miatke got on the radio and connected with Major Fox up at the FOB. We're having a lot of personal problems with the Fifth Group guys, he told the major. We're done.

This was Limbé, the supply and demand of truth brokered by criminals, decent citizens tragically obedient to their fears. This was Limbé, and this was Haiti, a place that confounded the American soldiers, and against their will and desire, most of them learned to hate it.

Back in Fort Bragg, the team members reinserted themselves into the lives of their families and friends and lovers and quickly spent the TDY bonus they had earned during their six months on the island. Six hundred twenty-nine dollars for Commo Jim, which he used to buy a beat-up Bayliner bass-fishing motorboat. Ernie Brown made a down payment on a new car, JC Collins bought an old pickup truck for four hundred bucks, Captain Stefanchik bought a kayak, which he strapped to the top of his Saab 900. Walt was looking for a bigger house, now that his wife was about to give birth to their second child, and Top Miatke spent the money on a Dalmatian pup.

On March 31, the United States handed over Operation Restore Democracy to the United Nations, which made Top shake his head, thinking, Here we are, U.S. soldiers raised in the U.S. military, the most sophisticated military on the face of the earth, with the best educational system in the world, and the highest standards of any existing armed forces, and if we can't do it, what the hell's a Bangladeshi soldier going to do?

Later, I asked Top if he was glad he went to Haiti, and he looked into the sky for a moment and said, "Tough question. No carpenter likes to build a house and see it crooked and leaning and ready to fall down the day he leaves. But if he builds a nice house, he's happy about it, it's something he'll be proud of the rest of his life."

"You don't think you have anything to be proud of?"

"No."

"That's sad," I said.

"It is," Top said. "It is."

I told him what the Haitians in Limbé were saying about the United States. *Lave men ou, siye li a te.*

It looks like you wash your hands and dry them in dirt.

PART SIX

Beyond the Mountain

Beyond the mountain, more mountains.

—Haitian proverb

GE: Some of these guys in command are so out of touch. I heard one of the colonels say to an IG, "My boys love it down here in Haiti," and I'm like, "Who the fuck are you talking about?"

BS: Boyatt used to tell me that.

GE: You talk to any SF guy and that's a bunch of bullshit. I mean, if you would let us—

FN: —take care of the bad guys, like we were supposed to be doing, we'd have been happy. They send us down there, though, and then tell you the bad guy's your friend. Well, we're not stupid. We know a bad guy when we see him. But why are you making us hold hands with him now? Because now what you've done is you've just burned all the bridges that we were trying to build with the population.

GE: And not only that, Frank. There were teams that said, Oh, this sounds good to us—

FN: Yeah.

BS: —and started harassing and arresting respectable citizens because FRAPH was telling the teams these are the real bad guys.

FN: Yeah, exactly.

BS: And that's what stuck in the press, the lasting impression of SF's role in Haiti. Cozying up to the FRAPH.

FN: Exactly. And it all began with this wishy-washy policy we had going in there. I'm not even saying we had a policy when we went in. It went back and forth, it was just made up. So what happened as a result of that, you had these teams out there that were making independent decisions because there was no strategic guidance. So whatever the personality of that team happened to be, whether they were good old boys from Louisiana or they were somebody from Michigan, they made a decision based on what they felt. And a lot of times these guys are not that articulate. Soldiers are very simple guys—it's either black or white. You give soldiers a gray area, and that's where they're going to get into trouble. And you've got people out there who are all of a sudden making geopolitical decisions in their little area of operations. Should they be given that much latitude? Yes, but only if you give them clear, defined goals in which they're supposed to be accountable. This crap—*FADH is your friend, FADH is your enemy; FRAPH is your friend, FRAPH is your enemy*—what exactly is that?

BS: Moral confusion?

FN: Exactly. And some of these people are not that sophisticated to deal with that.

BS: And would you agree that some of the teams liked FRAPH much more than they liked Lavalas?

FN: Because they demonstrated force, they demonstrated discipline, and it was easy for them to go and associate with that versus what they saw was an unruly populace. So I thought, in that particular case, some of the teams out there were failing, I believe, because they were making, in my personal opinion, the wrong moral and ethical decisions. But who really failed was the command, for not providing all those teams out in the field clear and concise policy and guidance on what they should be doing.

BS: I'm going to defend command on this point, because it wasn't their policy, was it?

FN: Right. Command can't make any decisions in the political arena. That guidance is coming to them from those within that geopolitical spectrum. *Okay, General, this is what the policy is today.* The general goes, *Will you fucking idiots make up your minds!*

HOPE

Soldiers, as soldiers themselves frequently reminded me, don't make policy; politicians do. And because I was determined to find out who had ordered Colonel Boyatt to tell his Green Berets to regard a terrorist group as the loyal opposition, I was evolving, involuntarily, from garden-variety scribe to investigative reporter—something I wasn't and didn't care to be. From February throughout most of the spring, I spent much of my time canvassing the assembled characters—Boyatt in Port-au-Prince; the embassy crew; human rights lawyers; palace insiders; and other correspondents, Haitian, French, and American.

When Operation Restore Democracy ended, replaced by United Nations forces on March 31, 1995, I caught back up with ODA 311 at Fort Bragg and spent a morning with Boyatt in his office at Third Group headquarters. What did the colonel say? More than he could have, less than I hoped for, and in a manner that was not readily useful. At the United States Special Operations Command Headquarters in Fort Bragg, I was assigned a watchdog, a major in the Public Affairs Office, who escorted me to Third Group headquarters and, ignoring my request to talk to the group commander in private, sat down next to me in the colonel's office.

"'Major," said Boyatt, smiling wanly, "I'm sure you have something better to do," and when the handler left, the colonel got up from behind his desk, told his staff to steer clear for the next several hours, and closed the door.

You turn on your tape recorder. You say, Here's the on/off button, and then you start. Sometimes, rarely, it's like pulling teeth. I asked Boyatt what I had asked him in Haiti, what I had been asking everybody: Who told him to order his men to regard FRAPH as a sort of ersatz branch of the GOP?

"It came through the chain of command."

"Who?"

Boyatt, the intrepid colonel one readily imagined on a fast track to a general's star, shrugged. "Chain of command."

Not good enough. I suggested he and his men were taking heat that would be more fairly directed elsewhere. Boyatt sprang from his chair and pushed the off button, elaborating, but not for the record. After that meeting, Boyatt stonewalled for another year, protecting a system that ultimately would not protect the colonel himself.

I returned to Haiti in April after a six-week hiatus, tracked down Gary, and took him to dinner on the veranda of the Oloffson, which now seemed perpetually supervised by the angst-filled Jolicoeur, Graham Greene's jester, who had begun to practice what was for him a most unlikely form of patriotism, refusing to sleep with white women as a protest against the continued presence of American armed forces on the island. His personal sacrifice for the tattered flag of Haitian soverignty.

As we sipped rum sours and waited for our plates of stewed conch to be served, I asked Gary for a weather report, and his by now customary answer became, for me, a refrain for the American intervention.

"The people," he said, "are suffering with hope."

That truth made me think of another, an axiom that many Haitian children were actually taught in school: *Misery can't kill Haitians.*

Hope seemed less one thing, one solid and independent unit of the spirit, than a fluid composite, a grouping of a nation's dreams. But when it wasn't working right, hope, it also seemed, could feel the same as guilt.

Like most Haitians, Gary worshiped Jean-Bertrand Aristide, despite the little priest's administrative shortcomings. Haiti, Graham Greene once wrote, deserved to be ruled by its heroes, but what manner of political movement could you make out of eighteenth-century ghosts and myths, refugees and dead children, illiterate peasants and student activists who had never run a gas station, let alone a government?

Last month, Gary said, a gunman for the old regime who lived in his neighborhood had told him, "In 1997, the macoutes will be back in power."

"Fine," Gary had answered. "As long as it happens democratically."

Fine, I thought, but don't count on it; nearly everyone flunked democracy's curriculum the first time around. "What's the definition of a democracy?" I listened to Colonel Boyatt ask during one of our conversations. "Just because people hold elections is not a measure of democracy to me."

"One of the difficulties in a transitional society," Ambassador Swing had told me, "given the state of the economy and the mistrust on which some of these societies have been built over the years, is that you have everyone a little bit uncomfortable, because the majority who never participated in the formal sector or in governments rightfully have aspirations, and they're afraid that they're going to get the vote but their lives really won't change very much. In other words, that change will not really mean change."

And hope, as one of the several Special Forces field commanders who replaced Boyatt in Haiti often instructed his men, is not an operational term, nor was it an operational imperative during the SF's eighteen-month peacekeeping mission in Haiti. Meaning that to make a real difference for people, you had to have a plan—something more tangible than hope and more visionary than a grudging willingness to react at the eleventh hour.

"You know, I guess I don't understand," General Potter once told me. "I mean, we, with a quote unquote small amount of money, we could have had a tremendous impact on that country. Tremendous impact on that country. And we wouldn't have had to do grandiose programs."

Ou ban mwen espoua pou anyin, said Gary—that's what people on the street were saying. *You give me hope for no reason.*

The following day, I hooked up with someone in the embassy, who confided that the CIA mission chief had told him that the agency's perception of the United States government's attitude toward Haiti was to just "put as much distance as we can between March 31"—the day the United States handed off the mission—"and the day this thing falls apart."

"You have to have macoutes," an American missionary once told me, an evangelist running a dental clinic up north, "to make the country run."

311 REDUX—WILDEBEESTS

We strapped ourselves into the seat harnesses of the resupply chopper, and the door gunner handed out yellow foam plugs to screw into our ears. The pilot throttled up the engines and the machine scream of the turbine became nightmarish, like a sustained shriek of terror from a child, amplified a hundred times. The hammering whip of the rotor blades reached the critical revolutions per minute for liftoff; the thin aluminum fuselage of the CH-47 shuddered and bucked until you thought it might fly apart. But then the magic of vertical flight took over, the eerie out-of-body deathbed sensation of suddenly floating away from the world at high speed, like a movie where the camera zooms backward into the sky and a field expands into a continent. Bottomlessness in reverse, and Haiti swelling outward in magnificent crests.

By the summer of 1995, I had unexpectedly achieved quasi-VIP status among the Special Forces, which translated into unlimited (albeit pre-arranged) access to A-teams and the much-appreciated convenience of bumming rides on helicopters. ODA 311 had been given a little time at home and then turned around, plumbing their capacity for disgust, rotated in June for another six-month deployment to Belladere, in the barely accessible mountains on the Haitian–Dom Rep border, and I was headed up that way with a colleague, the writer Bruce Duffy.

A half hour later, we dropped to two hundred feet and began circling a pasture, scattering goats. There were Stefanchik and Jim Pledger and the lanky redheaded weapons specialist, Jay, watching us emerge from the rotor wash in a running crouch.

"Hey," said Captain Mike, as if we had spoken only the day before. "We were expecting you."

"How is it?" I said, shaking hands with the lot. JC Collins, Walt the Punisher, and Bob Fox were in Africa, teaching teenagers in Chad how to defuse land mines; Ernie Brown was on his honeymoon but would arrive any day; and Top Miatke was in Bosnia on Mission Impossible.

"Biggest worry we have here is a cow on the LZ," said Commo Jim.

ODA 311's new compound was a former agricultural station, painstakingly sandbagged and trimmed with concertina wire, as if it had been landscaped by people whose only goal in life was to be left alone. We slung our gear onto the porch of a concrete blockhouse, where each of us was given his own room, his own bed, his own shower—no slumming in this AO, no Limbé Hilton.

The compound itself, with its suburban cluster of houses, was divided ground, the elite Green Berets trying not very hard to coexist with a quartet of reservists, a civil affairs detachment, and a psy ops team (renamed TDT—Tactical Dissemination Team—to better comply with the sanitized jargon of UN peacekeeping). The reservists were billeted in houses near-est the gate, the SF in houses nearest the LZ, farthest from the road and its foot traffic, and it was rare to find the careerists and the weekenders sharing the same space if it could be avoided.

It was more of the same in the mountainous heights of Belladere: stew-ing idleness and busywork, the worthless weapons buyback program, se-curity patrols for the upcoming elections, mini-*manifestations*, a bean war with the Dominican Republic, and altruistic shadow play like that from the psy ops reservist Mike, who was in the habit of winging bonbons at children as we drove down the roads. Some kids get a candy, most don't, some have the candy ripped from their hands by bigger kids, and every-body learns a lesson about the randomness of charity. The mission was tantamount to standing by a paraplegic's bedside, telling the poor bastard he was going to walk again. The SF couldn't stomach the fact that their objectives had been shrink-wrapped again down to "presence"—*I'm there for you, brah*—and they were nothing more noble or useful than bored commandos who sat around the captain's hooch every night playing inter-minable games of spades, someone occasionally going outside with a flashlight to watch tarantulas crawl from the rocks as the evening cooled, someone occasionally taking potshots with his 9mm at pariah dogs snatch-ing food from the larder. Out on the perimeter every once in a while, a hapless goat would stumble into a trip wire, and a flare would streak into the sky.

In those days of the deliberately dwindling mission, when the pages of the SF playbook revealed nothing more than fuzzy doodles or were increas-ingly blank, we headed out in two Humvees toward Lascahobas, a cross-roads town where the mountains humpbacked off the plateau halfway to Mirebalais, to experience firsthand the conditions on Haiti's worst road. If anything, its reputation for inhuman wretchedness had been understated.

Less than a mile out of Belladere, we came to a washed-out bridge, forded a rain-swollen river, and then the extraordinary mud started, mud worthy of trench warfare in the Ardennes, army-stopping mud, though the Haitians slogged through it in a determined trance. Wherever the road-bed dipped below the high ground, if there was any drainage at all we'd slide into a chute of ruts, the wheel-sculpted earth walls as high as the

Humvee's rooftop. Without drainage, however, every low gradient on the road became a hellish soup bowl, filled to the brim with a stagnant ooze, varying from Olympic-size pool to pool only in its viscosity, which could turn deadly for the incautious pilgrim. The small paso fino horses of the peasants sank in this horrific substance to their underbellies. We passed a trio of young women in muck-coated dresses pulling on ropes to free an exhausted beast from the mud's fatal grip.

"Can we help?"

"*Non, Papa. Pas pwobwem.*"

Then, farther along in the filthy porridge, stuck here and there like ghastly mileposts, were the carcasses of dead horses and donkeys, sheathed completely from their floundering in chalky drying mud, like legless baked terra-cotta statues from a Chinese emperor's tomb.

After an hour of this nightmare, the slopping splashes no longer mattered; we came to a halt behind a hopelessly mired tap-tap blocking our way, and I waded through the mud to help attach a tow cable to its undercarriage. The whimsically painted cargo truck, with fifty or sixty passengers riding atop its mound of gunnysacks, headed for market, reminded me of a Hindu elephant in a bog. Unable to budge it from its pit, we cut a hair-raising detour through a farmer's sweet potato fields, Stefanchik walking down to the cultivator's wattle hut to pay him for damages to his crop.

"You gave him too much for our right of passage," I told the captain, not at all disapprovingly, as we climbed back up the slope to the road. Eighty bucks—a season's wages.

"It was his lucky day."

"He only had to wait fifty years to see it." (Sergeant Tom Milam had a fantasy: he was keeping a count on beggars, planning to grab beggar number 1,000 and pull him into the Humvee and say, *Friend, today's your lucky day, you're king of Haiti,* give him an MRE, give him a dollar, and take him wherever he wanted to go.)

We slogged on to Lascahobas, where the UN CIVPOL—Australian and Filipino cops—had requested an SF show of force. Lascahobas was a creepy town, a self-proclaimed FRAPH stronghold and unapologetically "antichange," as advertised by the Creole graffiti sprayed on its walls. *Aba blan*—Down with the foreigner; or, if you were racially sensitive, Down with the white.

We left Captain Mike and his NCOs with the Lascahobas gangsters and continued on with the CA team leader, Staff Sergeant Tom Hood, another reservist from Minnesota and a Vietnam vet, to Mirebalais. Captain Dave Troutman's team was in high spirits, having taken up residence in what was perhaps the swankest compound in all of central Haiti, there being a sudden availability of swank rental properties across the island now that Aristide was back in business. Chez Troutman—high walls, beautifully landscaped grounds, a two-story manor house, a swimming pool—also came with its own discotheque, now stacked with weight-lifting equipment. I thought the captain was pulling my leg when he told me the name of his landlord, the most legendary of the Duvalier-era vampires still alive—Papa Doc's Baroness of the Graveyard, Madame Max Adolphe, former warden of Fort Dimanche, Haiti's own little death factory. Madame Max had fled to Brazil during the *dechoukaj,* but like most genocidal criminals in the Americas who suddenly fall upon hard times, she now made her home in the United States—Miami and Brooklyn—and the Special Forces sent her a rent check the first of every month. This business arrangement was the military's basement of fair and square, and it dumbfounded one's overworked sense of irony.

Well, it wasn't Troutman's call, and we sat down to relax with cold cans of soda, just as the Royal Canadian Mounted Police came marching up the palm-lined drive in their bathing suits to arrest the team's swimming pool. "The sun is the enemy," declared the captain. Fayettenam was more dangerous, Mirebalais was a snooze. The new mayor had asked for the Green Berets' assistance enforcing civic laws that had been on the books forever and were forever disregarded. Traffic and parking violations, illegal tapping into the electric and water systems, illegal dumping.

"What's this ODA's speciality?" I asked out of curiosity.

"SOT Team 366. Close-quarter fighting."

Pity the fellow the commandos found double-parked in front of the town hall.

It was midafternoon by the time we left for what should have been a four-hour mud bath back to Belladere. Then the showers started, long, dark columns of rain marauding across the purple-and-green countryside. About twenty klicks out of town, we were flagged over by a guy on a motorbike. I tried to decipher the note he carried, my Creole insufficient to glean the specifics. Something about an accident; somebody killed something. I could only tell him to continue on to the SF camp in Mirebalais.

A few minutes farther along, we topped a small mountain and watched a veil of rain being dragged up the nearby slopes, and then we descended a misty gorge into a lush hollow, where the mystery became apparent, if no less unclear. At the bottom, where the road flattened and straightened, a crowd stood at the edge of a steep embankment, looking down into a rain-polished banana grove. Coming to a stop, we could easily read the group's aura, their collective sense of moribundity, and they stood grimly mesmerized in their wet clothes, nobody talking, their arms hanging uselessly at their sides.

Sergeant Hood grabbed his M-16, the crowd parted silently in the middle, and we walked ahead, our eyes following the raw, red lines of tire-scarred earth that ended abruptly when the massive tap-tap had become airborne and somehow landed upright below, catapulting its freight—animal, vegetable, human—in all directions. Tap-taps possessed an zoomorphic quality for me, and this one gave the impression of a large dangerous beast that had broken out of its pen and stopped here to graze, its nostrils flaring. Typically, the driver had run off, fearing his passengers, scores of them—miraculously, it first appeared, uninjured—might lynch him for his recklessness.

It was inconceivable that no one had been hurt, but when I asked if everyone was okay, my question provoked a spew of unintelligible answers, everybody talking at once, everybody wailing. A man stepped forward and beckoned us down through the slippery grass to a clump of trash, debris from the wreckage—squashed cardboard boxes and broken palm fronds. How unreal and melancholic it was to stand there on this small plot of cultivated jungle, the cloud-wreathed peaks above us and the air as dark and solemn as a cathedral's, and watch this man, his inchoate eyes upturned toward ours, watch this powerless man lean down and ever so delicately lift the wet dirty cardboard like the edge of a blanket covering his sleeping daughter.

In this bier of trash lay a young woman staring calmly into eternity, not at all surprised by its suddenness. Painted toenails, wavy black hair, a sky-blue pullover, a comfortable skirt for traveling. She was neither broken nor visibly crushed nor in any way mauled by death. We weren't even sure she was dead until Sergeant Hood bent over her to feel for a pulse, tenderly replacing the vulgar patchwork of her shroud and stepping away with a heavy sigh. She was beautiful, and for a brief moment death had made her utterly meaningless and intolerable beauty a powerful force on the planet, a phenomenon powerful enough to cow even a shutterbug like Duffy. No matter that he was on assignment, he tucked his camera back into his shoulder bag and never took a photograph of what he saw—"Ophelia floating down a river of debris surrounded by a hundred dusty, rain-spotted black feet," the greatest picture, he said, that he had ever not taken.

Amid thunderclaps and lightning, drizzle sifted down upon us, and a woman, the dead woman's friend, pleaded with me. Evidently there was another problem, a big problem still unresolved, but nobody could explain it in a manner I could understand. The motorcyclist had delivered his message and Troutman arrived with his NCOs, a medic, a translator, UN CIVPOL, yet still no one could root out the *thing,* the greater mystery surrounding the accident from the moment we knew of it. In the confusion, several men finally pulled Duffy and me aside, and we followed them down the road another kilometer to a small barn or schoolhouse, its bare wooden floor strewn with a dozen critically injured people.

Sergeant Hood and a Canadian policeman arrived, but the medic was back up the road at a second house, where the SF had discovered another roomful of mangled people. Hood pulled off his rain poncho and tucked it around a shivering youth racked by convulsions, the two halves of his chest sickeningly misaligned. There were people with compound fractures, broken legs, internal traumas, a woman with a crushed pelvis. The room had filled with gawkers, people everywhere, standing around. "God-dammit," the sergeant yelled at the translator, "you tell these people I want a full accounting of their injured."

The medic bolted into the room, and soon we were in the middle of full-scale triage. An IV bag in each hand, I squeezed fluids into the convulsing boy as fast as I could, one bag after another, to stabilize the effects of shock, then the medic pillowed him with morphine and we moved to the next victim. Back in Mirebalais, I had thought this medic was a scowling shit, but there were no clowns or idle malcontents here in the field, and I had trouble imagining there were better men in the world, certainly not in America, than Hood and Troutman and this medic and the other troopers, and I almost felt sorry for them. Unlike me, they had spent their adult lives training to help people in crisis, even if it meant killing others, but politicians were just as likely to risk these men's lives shoring up the guilty as rescuing the innocent, and the government did not want them here, nor did the Pentagon or the public. Nobody really wanted them except these broken people clinging to the world, a world no bigger or smaller than any other where you prayed for mercy, and sometimes even a lifetime of training made no difference whatsoever.

"It would be nice," an SF sergeant major told me one day in Cap Haïtien, "to be part of something that actually worked."

Sergeant Ernie Brown was back with the team. Freshly married, he was in dubious health, chronic sinus and stomach problems contracted during the Limbé deployment. He wasn't eating much, just drinking red vinegar and losing weight like a refugee. Yesterday's resupply bird had dropped him off, and today we were lazing around the hooch, all patrols suspended thanks to heavy rains.

Duffy in particular felt wasted by the previous day's events. You could see him try mentally to spit out the residues of futility and incomprehension. It wasn't so much seeing people hurt that depressed him, he ventured; it was the collective trance in response to tragedy. How the Haitians seemed to accept fucked-upness as an essential condition.

We were sitting at the table with Ernie, our new housemate, sorting it out. Ernie intrigued Duffy. He thought the Green Beret looked a bit like Little Richard, and he was drawn to Ernie's easygoing familiarity, the fluty multipitched range of his voice, slipping and sliding between technical discourse, philosophical rumination, and jive. That Ernie was also black was of the highest significance to Duffy, because, well, Haitians were black, so maybe Ernie saw something in all of this that he was overlooking.

"It's weird," Duffy admitted. "If I was in America, it would have been a lot more upsetting. But here . . . well, somehow it wasn't so strange. Really, I wonder why I don't feel worse about it."

Ernie straightened up in his chair, squaring his thick shoulders, and cocked his head quizzically, sizing up this white man. Perhaps some other black American soldier might have misconstrued the statement and seized on the apparent racism of Duffy's confession, I don't know. But what Duffy actually meant connected with something Ernie had been thinking about for a long time.

"Now, Bruce, ask yourself—Was *they* upset? The Haitians, I mean?"

"Well, no," said Duffy, "now that you mention it."

"Course they wasn't upset—*humph!* It's what I call the story of the lion and the wildebeests," said Ernie, his hands clasped in front of him like a judge. "Like in all them African movies. You got the whole plain filled with wildebeests, man, they all down there grazing, happy, when whoa! here comes Mr. Lion, and oh, God, he done drug off another wildebeest, tore his head clean off, and the wildebeests, they go, *Damn! Did you see that shit, man? Man, that was awful . . . but oh, well, it wasn't me, nuh-unh-unh, it wasn't me,* and they put their heads back down and go on grazing. The moral of the story is, it don't make no difference to them. None! Neighbor? Who's that? Ain't no neighbors here. Man, all they care about is, *Well, shit, it wasn't me.*"

THE POET OF SAVANETTE

Up high on the border at the edge of the world, in a pastoral valley boxed by timbered ridges, lived one of Ernie's lions, the FRAPH regional commander, Montero Norbert—poet, essayist, and, said the people in these remote mountains around Savanette, alleged pederast and murderer.

Down here in the trenches of a foreign occupation with elite troops well versed in the clandestine, you began to stumble upon chinks in the great steel wall that was the institutionalized secrecy of the American government—that other monster created with the bomb in World War II. People were human, people were careless—you put your eye to the chinks of the mission and saw sometimes disfigured creatures casting the shadows of respectability, men dutifully, patriotically, at work in their offices at the Pentagon, the State Department, the CIA, the National Security Council, the White House.

On one of the desks in the team house, someone had left out a document, a psy ops area assessment. The document evaluated the performance of the valley's IPSF contingent and, no surprise, the gang was *selling justice.* The assessment concluded with a précis on FRAPH, offering the reader a remarkably frank insight into the Special Forces' ongoing passive-aggressive and often promiscuous relationship with the terrorist organization in the Haitian countryside, and it named perpetrators in the Savanette area:

> *Cardeaun Soisette: Extortionist, accused of vampirism and murder. FRAPH member.*
>
> *Inerias Auguste: Accused of extortion, torture and other crimes. Reportedly owns an M-60, an M-14, handguns and other munitions. Current IPSF officer. FRAPH member.*
>
> *Montero Norbert: Allegedly committed torture and other crimes on 1/30/88, 1/16/91, 5/26/92, and 10/30/93. Former Commander of FRAPH.*

The list went on, cataloguing atrocities. Here, it seemed, was a sizable, well-placed, well-known, well-armed assemblage of rogues who had enjoyed, and still enjoyed, dominion over Savanette's population. One would be hard-pressed to say that the Special Forces deployed throughout the hinterlands were under any illusion about FRAPH's ubiquitous presence in their communities: who these men were, what sort of weapons they had, the crimes they'd committed, the crimes they remained capable of doing. Yet the assessment softballed Montero Norbert, failing to mention his alleged role in more than twenty murders, or his apparent predilection for having sex with children. Instead, the SF teams assigned to Belladere had, at best, ignored him with a watchful eye; or they pronounced him a rehabilitated patriot and treated him with the respect accorded to good ol' boys.

By now Captain Stefanchik had been in Belladere for several months and had not yet made it his business to meet with the FRAPH commander. He would not explain to me his reluctance for such an encounter, and I found that reluctance to be particularly mystifying. I waited anxiously for fair weather, so that we might pay him a visit, and when the roads were once again passable, we spent a fine morning journeying up through the border highlands into valleys nearly as magnificent as Marc Lamour's.

At the Savanette casern, the commandos engaged in ritual macho posturing with the surly IPSF. Duffy and I went wandering through town with a psy ops reservist from Pittsburgh and André the interpreter, gluing posters about the forthcoming elections and the still stupid weapons buy-back program on all available surfaces. It was Pittsburgh's trip, ostensibly, and he seemed to be making the most of it, drawing out the simple task into an ordeal. Given the captain's eagerness to return from his visit before dark, I split off from the psy ops adventure when I began to realize there was little chance I'd be able to borrow André's services that day, and went looking for Montero Norbert myself.

His house was neither modest nor grand but typical of a provincial *gros neg,* stuccoed concrete blocks with tan whitewash and a zinc roof, but its windows and doors were barred and shuttered, as if its people had moved away. I rapped loudly on the bolted front door, able to hear a radio playing in the back of the house, the sound of tableware being placed in a basin, but no one answered my knock, and when I called out, there was still no answer. The captain was down at the end of the street and I went to fetch him, but again his hesitation surfaced, and I had to coax him back up to the house. This time we tried knocking on a side gate in a wall—the entrance to Norbert's petty-bourgeois enterprise, a video theater, where he charged a few gourdes to watch bootleg movies on his VCR. Finally, a caretaker came to the gate, the captain spoke to him in French, and the man disappeared into the house to find Monsieur Montero.

He entered the side yard cautiously, eyes affected with self-pity, neither hubristic nor ingratiating but with the faint querying, contrite expression of a proud dog that's snatched a chicken from the henhouse. He was a large, bald man with sensual lips, whose muscles and stomach had turned fleshy, rounded by age and lack of exercise, yet you could see he had been a powerhouse in his prime, and even now you wouldn't want him to grab hold of you.

Dressed in sandals and a shirt-jac and trousers the color of his house, the color of the dirt road in front of his house, as if he had emerged right out of the Haitian soil, Montero Norbert was a type, like many of the *gros negs*—the Big Men—I had met and worked with throughout the Caribbean: a patriarch, a man who enjoyed the good fortune of having been born above the masses, a man who had been educated overseas, and nevertheless a man who remained *of the land,* living without ostentation among the people, yet more likely to cause their misery than to share it.

The captain explained what I wanted, a few minutes of the FRAPH commander's time. Hearing me ask Stefanchik if he would stay and trans-

late, Monsieur Montero haltingly admitted he spoke a little English—
more than a little, actually—and wondered if I myself spoke Spanish—"A
few words," I said—and with this rickety bridge established, the captain
announced I was on my own, that time was running out. We sat side by
side at a long table, our bodies turned to face one another. As I took out
my notebook, Norbert settled into his chair with an aggrieved sigh and
then addressed the issue head-on.

"What do you want to know about FRAPH?"

"The American soldiers have called FRAPH a political party," I said.

"FRAPH was never a political party," Montero Norbert replied peev-
ishly. "It was a security force. Some of those fools in the capital wanted to
call it a political party, but I disagreed with them. FRAPH was never
meant to be anything but a security force, and when they called it a political party, they lied."

"A security force against whom?"

"Against Lavalas, of course," he said. "I do not share Lavalas's ideology,
but I have a brother in Lavalas who's friends with Aristide. So we made
FRAPH for security against Lavalas and against the FADH."

"Against the FADH?" I repeated, dismayed.

Somehow he had managed to get himself into a pissing contest with
the FADH and had been locked up until he conceded that FRAPH was
an auxiliary to the military regime, and not the other way around. No
stranger to the perpetual Haitian scrum for power, Montero had spent
twenty-three years in exile for annoying the Duvaliers. His book of poetry,
Chants du Exile, had been written to memorialize those years. He went
into the house to bring me a copy as a gift, and copies of his most recent
essays, meditations on FRAPH and the current political debacle. Like
most successful bad guys, Montero Norbert was not an unthinking man,
and he saw himself as a scholar.

Regardless of how tactfully or how cleverly you pose the question, asking an accused murderer if he's guilty is a waste of time; I simply asked
why the villagers kept saying he was responsible for the many killings in
Savanette and its environs during the three years of the de factos. Monsieur Montero could easily have answered that he didn't know, but it wasn't
what he said. Rather, he brought history forward as his most reliable character witness. For generations, he explained, his family and his family
alone had owned the valley of Savanette, two thousand hectares, but then

the peasants had come to squat on every inch of the land. He had tried to remove them, but legally; he believed absolutely in using the justice system to solve his problems.

"What justice system? There is no justice system."

"Not now," he said with regret, "but there used to be."

"But it was corrupt," I said. Montero Norbert knew as well as I did that murdering squatters after paying off a judge was considered righteous sport among military officers and the ruling class.

"Yes," he agreed, and gave an unsure smile, "it was corrupt," but now perhaps Aristide would rebuild it and he could clean the squatters off his property. "I have a picture of him on my living room wall."

The captain came to complain I was taking too long. "Why don't you talk with him?" I asked Stefanchik once more as we walked down the road to the vehicles. Because, said the captain, the teams that had been up here earlier in the mission had been excessively "social" with the FRAPH commander. "It left the wrong impression," said Captain Mike, who wanted only to get back to his isolated quarters in Belladere, have some chow, and spend the evening reading a Maupassant novel.

The following afternoon, Duffy and I caught a lift out on the resupply chopper to Port-au-Prince, where we hoped to find Gary and head north to Limbé.

TET CAYLÉ

"Welcome to the last bastion of freethinkers."

Captain Craig Marks, the heir to all that ODA 311 had wrought, stood barefoot on the concrete threshold of ODA 362's small two-story house atop the last peak north on the outskirts of Limbé. He was an old man by snake-eater standards—forty—and didn't exactly have the appearance of a hardy action stud, but the diminutive Tet Caylé—Bonehead—was an impression maker, clearly an artist of disarming presentation. His skull shaved down to the corpuscles, feet bare as a beach bum's, he greeted us with the same coyote smile that seemed to have been patented by endearing naughty boys. If any Green Beret deployed to Haiti had a congenital disposition to assimilate, it had to be this officer, and you could easily imagine him up in the mythic backcountry, the *blanc* warlord running camps for Stone Age tribesmen.

"Knew you were coming," he said, drawing us through the door with that grin, its dangerous appeal.

"We call first these days," I said. "I can't handle being unwanted."

"Oh, the sensitive type."

The compound was invisible from the road, tucked far back in the bush; we had to push a buzzer at a chained gate on Route Nationale One and wait for an escort. The SF high life, fruit of countless broken promises to ODA 311, here at the Hotel Bonehead. Those days in Limbé's casern were finished. At the top of the military's troublemaker list, Limbé had received an infusion of Justice Department–trained cops from the academy's first graduating class, and the casern itself was in the process of an extraordinary makeover, its decrepit, sin-stained buildings being transformed into a complex of modern air-conditioned offices and barracks.

We fixed ourselves coffee, sat down at the kitchen table overlooking the empty blue bay where Columbus had anchored. Tet Caylé propped his pink feet up on one of the chairs, strapped his hands behind his nicked and shiny head, and there was that grin again, its irresistible all-American glibness. The captain, I was about to learn, was born to brief, to give forth sitrep shtick.

"Limbé! What a garden spot," said Tet Caylé, a former L.A. County deputy sheriff, casting cop glances at the front room. NCOs were throwing themselves down on the thin foam cushions of the living room couches—an overweight medic, a scrawny hillbilly with a malicious spark in his eyes, and the huge top sergeant, bull-necked, iron-jawed, solid as an Olympian wrestler. Duffy looked at him in awe—it was Sergeant Rock, the reincarnation of the comic book hero of his youth. The top dropped like a boulder next to the team's interpreter—a Haitian-American servicewoman from the Twenty-fifth Infantry—and began bugging her. *Women in the military, huh? Pain in the ass, huh?* As flirtations go, this one was particularly demeaning, and she pretended to slap his face. Gary was trapped among this motley crew, visibly unhappy. These were not the guys Marks had commanded up at his former AO in Port-de-Paix, and unlike the captain, who radiated cool, his new team itself seemed uncommonly loutish and juvenile.

"How are the new Haitian police getting along?" I said to Marks. The handlers from the Justice Department, supposed to mentor the rookies for sixty days, had packed up after twenty-seven, leaving behind five vehicles, on the assumption the Limbé HNP knew how to drive them. They didn't, and right away two of the policemen had been behind the wheel in hit-and-run accidents. Now all five vehicles were mashed up and broken, and the SF were taking the cops out to the runway at the Cap Haïtien airport to give them driving lessons.

The new police had no one to emulate but the old role models—attachés—and some were strolling around in civilian clothes, pistols jammed in their belts, wearing thug sunglasses. In July, the HNP wounded a murder suspect in the chest after hot pursuit through Plaisance, then walked up and shot him several more times, fatally, as he lay on the ground. "Some of them," said the captain, pinching his nose, "are already on the take."

Limbé, otherwise, was the same old tawdry story, the goodies and the baddies just waiting to have at each other once the Americans went away. Fine, said Tet Caylé. Why, just look at us, the folks back home. We had the Emancipation Proclamation in 1863, and in 1995 whites and blacks still couldn't come to terms with one another. "Nobody should expect us to come here for one year or five years or ten years and make a significant difference upon Haitian society."

Americans were into a quick-fix mode anyway. TDY—temporary duty. One hundred seventy-nine-day problem solving. After that, the pay scale became prohibitive.

It was during the captain's time on the SOC-C staff down in Port-au-Prince that the Special Forces mission in Haiti began to evaporate in front of their eyes and command started fighting with the numbers: We've got 1200, we want to go down to 990, we want to go down to 770, down to 400. General Hill, from the Twenty-fifth Infantry Division, okayed a re-alignment of SF forces, and SOC-C identified seven towns they believed they could withdraw from without incident. Limbé, because of its proximity to Cap Haïtien, was included in the test group. So, *boom*.

After that, Limbé—no matter how quiet or active it was—was always

Limbé. Captain Marks and his team arrived in town on July 4, one week after the local electoral station had been torched by the Red Army. The team of reservists from Alabama that Marks replaced had had all the yucks their fun meters could tolerate. ("You know," Tet Caylé said, "they lived in dismal conditions down there in that casern. Absolutely zilch for morale." Yeah, I said. I'd heard that.)

When Marks came in, he was determined to crack the code on Limbé. One of the big problems, he quickly realized, was intel. Haiti had become a spook training ground, all the agencies baptizing rookies in its muddy waters, and as always, there were too many keepers of the data pie. You had the intel cell down at the LIC (Light Industrial Complex) in Port-au-Prince, you had some sneaky petes up at Cap, you had the strategic dudes with cool-guy hairlines who would come down out of the sky every once in a while, you had the Christians In Action, and you had a whole bunch of guys who weren't necessarily sharing information. When Marks spoke with the UN S-2 equivalent, the intel officer confided that the two dominant political parties in Limbé were headed by Marc Lamour on the left and Doctor Hodges on the right. Who knows where the guy got that from, but whenever he came to town, that's who he'd ask the team about—Lamour and Hodges.

The intel pie was glazed with a last bit of absurdity. Except for data collected in a threat protection mode (a loophole the size of Texas), the SF teams were prohibited by law and regulations from getting seriously involved in intelligence gathering, because Haiti was a friend, and Americans, ha ha, weren't supposed to spy on friends. Marks also had to tread lightly around Hodges and the other missionaries, because gathering information on his fellow citizens was likewise considered taboo.

The result was that many pieces of the pie seemed to have a different color, taste, and texture, and not all were interchangeable. So Marks started trying to sort out the weevils, and high on the weevil list was the Red Army—apolitical thugs: whoever filled the power vacuum, they were going to be there to support them. But since they referred to themselves as an army, the blinders were on up the chain, everybody assuming they were an insurgent force.

"Okay, where do they train at?"

"Where's who train at?"

"The Red Army."

"They're not training."

"But they're army."

"No, they're a gang. Never mind. Sorry, wrong number."

One of the many ways to create a problem in the military was to do your job too well. The UN command wanted to know who Marks was and why nobody else had reported Limbé's gang infestation. (Though 311 had, however tentatively, the intel vanished into the mist, and it was true that the gangs seemed to exist just outside the team's line of vision, something peripheral.) Tet Caylé had gotten lucky, though, looked under the right rock at the right time: Here's the Red Army, here's Thoby Frasier aka Saddam Hussein, here's this, here's that, here's their tie to Cap Haïtien, here's their tie to Port-au-Prince, here's the possibility they know some people—Marc Lamour, Bobby Lecord.

Captain Marks was in a briefing frenzy, throwing documents, sitreps, arrest warrants, wanted posters, on the table in front of me. "Slow up," I said. I hadn't responded when Tet Caylé put forth the proposition that the Central Intelligence Agency represented the pragmatic side of U.S. strategic thinking toward Haiti, but this latest tidbit of analysis was too much, and I protested that there was no such thing as an organization that could embrace both the Bobby Lecords and the Marc Lamours of the world.

"True," acknowledged the captain. "But they can be linked. They can be linked by association to third parties. I'm saying if they have mutual interests, or if they have people in their organizations who are mutually linked, there's a connection."

I thought the word "organization" far too flattering for Lamour's assemblage of peasant maroons, but the captain disagreed, sliding in front of me a document that profiled what was called the Boukam Michel gang, allegedly commanded by Lamour, between fifty and one hundred renegades making trouble in the mountains. "Legend has it," said the captain, "the boys came down in early October, *dechoukéd* the Le Borgne casern, killed six FADH, burned the houses of two macoutes. Legend has it the guy's got M-79 grenade launchers, rifles, and crew-served weapons captured from the FADH, that he conducts paramilitary training in the mountains near Le Borgne, and that he has Cuban and drug connections. We also suspect the gang of murdering a Haitian-American, a big landowner from Miami, who was up there visiting at the end of July."

Marc Lamour the murderer, Marc Lamour the guerrilla fighter: after nearly a year in-country, the army still couldn't seem to grasp the fact that such characterizations were little more than a macoute fairy tale. Even if Lamour had killed to defend his land and people against tyrants and state-sanctioned terrorists, what was he supposed to do? Besides, as any UN peacekeeper hunkered down in the Balkans could tell you, nothing so readily invites attack as powerlessness. Under similar circumstances, how would Captain Craig Marks act differently than Marc Lamour? Probably his body count, I thought, would be a quantam leap higher.

THE LEGENDARY WHATEVER

Strange things, both unexpectedly wonderful and diabolically cruel, happened every day in Haiti, yet I had trouble wrapping my mind around the likelihood that the pathologically reclusive Lamour had bonded with the admittedly seductive Tet Caylé, who had become the first American soldier to meet the mystery man from the mountains. I was highly dubious the two men would ever get together tonight for a prearranged dinner, and all morning the captain had tossed enough innuendos our way to let us know that he wanted us to tag along as leverage, symbols of an imperialist warrior's good faith. Today's crucifixion canceled, due to journalists.

In our Toyota bangabout, Duffy, Gary, and I trailed the captain's Humvee out of town and into the primitive countryside. Not long after we plunged through the first river crossing, the road bent downward into a sunny hollow and we pulled alongside two truckloads of Pakistani infantrymen, stopped to urinate. The convivial zone commander, a colonel, was there, as smartly appointed as a mustachioed regimental officer of the raj. "Where they headed?" I asked Marks, as we stepped out of our vehicles for road-trip badinage with the UN troops.

"Le Borgne."

There goes dinner, I had to conclude. Guerrilla garden party etiquette abhors the implicit deception of a show of force.

"Hey," said the captain, "the guy's the zone commander. He invited himself. What was I supposed to do—tell him no?"

Our noontime arrival on Le Borgne's dusty, salt-blown streets was unheralded except by drowsy children, delighted to have their boredom knocked aside by the always riveting sight of *blancs*. We drove down to the center of town with the captain and his interpreter for a meeting with the new mayor, a follow-up on an OAS report that he was "in hiding" because the two most influential families in the north—the Simons and the Bennetts, Lamour's most animated foes—had hired a gang to kill him. It was a Simon, Orel Simon from Miami, whom Lamour was now accused of murdering. Indeed, the mayor was "hiding," a condition that so often in Haiti constituted a self-imposed degree of house arrest. He lived in a peeling clapboard house on one corner of the town square and invited us anxiously into his parlor. We sat on vinyl couches around a rickety coffee table ornamented with artificial flowers. On the stuccoed wall hung his wedding picture and an enlarged photograph of a mullah at prayer in Mecca.

Like so many of his compatriots who had somehow survived the barbarities of the regime and were now resurfacing in Aristide's government, the youthful mayor was a wisp of a man, a stick figure lost in baggy trousers and the white, long-sleeved permanent-press shirt that was as close as you could come to an outward symbol of civil authority here in the provinces. Yes, he confirmed, the elites were trying to kill him.

"Here's what I'm going to do," said the captain. What Marks was going to do, however, was essentially nothing, and whatever the mayor felt about the American officer's bromides of encouragement and resolve, he rose to his feet like a condemned man, smiled weakly, and thanked the Green Beret for coming.

"What about Marc Lamour?" I asked as he ushered us to the door.

"Oh," he answered sanguinely, "Marc Lamour is on his way right now from Le Cap to meet with you. He will be here within an hour."

This of course was a lie, one that I later imagined brought the mayor the single pleasure of his day.

"Is there anything else you can think of that I should do?" said Captain Marks, and since I did not yet know about what had occurred between Le Borgne's judge and the team's gladiatorial top sergeant, who recently had been banned by the captain from going into the mountains, I thought Marks was being naturally kind and solicitous to the mayor.

"No," said the mayor, miserable, offering us each the token of a moist but lifeless handshake. "*Merci*, no." As if to say we'd done enough harm already.

▫   ▫   ▫

Now began the tedious intrigue and fatuous stall. Out on the road, we came upon Lamour's emissaries, four men crammed into the cab of a shiny new red pickup. One of them recognized me, with some measure of bonhomie, from the year before, a short kid in a porkpie hat cradling a boom box in his lap as if it were packed with explosives. *Ah, oui, Lamour,* they said, with grimacing, exaggerated smiles. *He's coming, he'll be here soon.*

Lamour was either already in Le Borgne, we figured, or an hour west in Bassin Caiman, waiting for whatever prearranged assurance he required from his men to show himself. For more than an hour, Gary and I continued chipping away at the bluff, until the captain took me aside to say maybe the sizing-up ritual might go better if he left and he climbed back into the Humvee and pulled back.

"The captain smiles too much," sneered the driver, changing his disingenuous tune. "*Mil fois* the soldiers harass the people. A thousand times."

"What captain?" I said. "What soldiers?"

These guys seemed like the Secret Service, said Duffy, but without the earphones. I sat down on a stone wall, weary with impatience and questioning my obsession—everybody's obsession—with this man Lamour, the pointlessness of his mystery of self, one more survivor among Haiti's culture of survival. The quest had stopped making sense long ago, and there was no grand view from the summit of the guerrilla leader's reputation.

Then, as if the schools had been let out, the top of the street filled with gay children, Tet Caylé at their center, his shaved dome broiled by fierce sunlight, laughing children clinging to him, everybody trying to hold the hand of the American officer with the coyote smile, a scenario something like Colonel Kurtz does Mary Poppins. When I summoned the courage to say we had sold him short, that no one could find his name on the guest list anymore, he remained the unruffled cop–commando–do-gooder, beaming down at his sudden wealth of children—he was going to show them a movie, a *romantique,* a love story; no Bruce Lee for the captain's kids—and kept walking with his flock, the future. An hour later, with the sun about to set, Duffy, Gary, and I waded into the river.

▫   ▫   ▫

There was cheering ahead in the cooling twilight of the upper valley, uproarious yelling—not the sort of heart-quickening noise of a *manifestation* but the sound you hear when people anywhere in the world come together to celebrate. Still, we worried until we were sure of its source, which became apparent as we topped a knoll where the river turned and there, up a side valley, was a large bamboo-and-branch fence built to enclose an icon of peace and normalcy—a soccer field. The villages of Lamour's valley were holding a soccer tournament, and our arrival had been timed to the game's final goal.

Out flowed the whooping crowd through the makeshift gate, led by Lamour, whom, in his happiness, it took me a moment to recognize. He had shaved his revolutionary's beard and was dressed like the ultimate fan of civilized competition—blue and orange athletic shorts, a striped soccer jersey, a soft yellow cap like a sports car dandy's, a gold wristwatch. Duffy, shaking the hand of this small, wiry man, seemed surprised.

"*You're* Marc Lamour?" he said, having expected someone martial and unpleasant, spouting archaic, platitudinous slogans.

With the twilight deepening, we sat, turning slowly into silhouettes, in the grass above the river, the soccer crowd quietly surrounding us to hear what their champion would tell the *blancs.* Ah, the soldiers, sighed Lamour, who had been appointed vice delegate for his region. Yes, he said, unembarrassed, he had agreed to meet with Tet Caylé this afternoon, but "the darkness gave me advice." The Americans weren't sincere, the captain disrespected civilian authority, and in Le Borgne the Special Forces were acting like macoutes, so why bother meeting them? he said.

"First of all," explained Lamour, "when Orel Simon was killed, the Americans came to Le Borgne and all they wanted to know was, where was Marc Lamour? The judge refused to tell them." The big master sergeant on Marks's team lost his patience, said Lamour, slapping the back of one hand into the palm of the other in the emblematic Haitian gesture that essentially means "fucked up." The top sergeant took a bullet from his M-16 clip and gave it to the judge, said something to the effect of *This one's for you, pal.* The judge still wouldn't respond, so the Green Beret unsheathed his bayonet—which, the story goes, was dirty—and wiped it on the judge's shirt.

Oh, all right, that's not cricket. A regrettable lapse in the captain's grip-and-grin Snoop Doggy Dogg street dance motif. But when Lamour quietly weighed his words and said with all the gravity he could summon that, as a Haitian, even the old FADH could not have humiliated him any worse, I had to reconsider momentarily where being forced, literally, to eat your own shit or watch your daughter being raped fit into the local hierarchy of shame. Surely, then, I thought, he wanted the soldiers to leave Haiti.

"First of all," said the legendary whatever-he-was, "the situation is very complex." So much for American inconstancy. I supposed this was about the most convincing endorsement the military could ever hope for: Marc Lamour wanted the troops to stick around. "Their presence," he said after numerous qualifications, "is important in this country."

The moon rose full, spilling milky blue light into the valley, and in each village tucked back into the forested hills, the *vodou* drums were beating. "Last question," I said to Lamour. I pointed to the lingering crowd, the soccer fans and athletes. "Did your team win?"

They did not, but there was no real point to my question. Some games it hardly mattered if you lost.

LIMBÉ, FINÉ

"Well, I blew it," Captain Marks said, looking genuinely sad, a man misunderstood in ways most avoidable and unfortunate. He had believed he was destined to be friends, comrades, with his alter ego in the mountains, but now it was never going to happen. "I'm going to send Lamour a note, an apology," said Marks the next morning when we came to the team house, "and after that I'm leaving him alone."

It was a moment, one of those awful moments, when assigned roles are everything, friendships mean nothing, and words destroy or repair in seconds. I felt my own sense of regret, obligated to hold the captain accountable for the misbehavior of his NCO. A charge of malfeasance could readily end careers and visit scandal upon the brethren, as similar accusations would, with other correspondents, other soldiers, other incidents, in the months ahead.

"Hey, you gotta do what you gotta do," said the captain, turning up his palms in flat-faced acceptance. Duty and honor, honor and duty—no hard feelings, brah. "But first let me tell you the whole story. Back then, when Orel Simon, a 'possible' U.S. citizen, got himself whacked, was a different time. We're not the sheriff anymore. But clearly the sergeant did step over the line, and he was wrong, totally wrong. But I'm not going to crucify him upside down at the entrance to Le Borgne."

As described by a young female observer with the OAS civilian mission, the team's archetypal top sergeant was "a red-meat-eating warmonger," and her organization tried to put the incident on the front burner for a couple of weeks, but the Pakistani zone commander considered the matter closed after Captain Marks issued a formal letter of reprimand to the NCO—"You treated [the local magistrate in Le Borgne] in a contemptible manner and caused him great anxiety and fear"—and ordered the sergeant to write a letter of apology to the judge. Notwithstanding the amends made, perception is reality, said Marks, and for the longest time it seemed the team couldn't go anywhere without being dogged by international observers, waiting for the Americans to commit further abuses.

When the sergeant walked in, the giant just back from rappelling and close-quarter combat drills, he looked at the captain, looked at me, and nobody had to tell him what was going on. But he didn't withdraw into himself, didn't swagger or posture or become ingratiating. Neither contrite nor defiant nor menacing, he eased his immense weight down on the groaning couch, leaned his rifle against the armrest, and wearily accepted whatever judgment fell his way.

"Hey, I was wrong, I lost my patience."

This wasn't, couldn't be, it—the line the American public was not willing to let its soldiers cross. "The man's a superb warrior," allowed Captain Marks. "Diplomacy is not his forte."

The gangs were all Ton Ton Macoute wannabes, according to Marks. Drugs, extortion, you name it. Thoby Frasier, the head of the Red Army, a thug named Zoué, Bobby Lecord, all were prime suspects in the killing of Lieutenant Antoine and five or six other ex-FADH who had never been seen since. Lecord was supplying the Red Army—they had about two hundred fifty male members and fifty females—with guns smuggled in bags of flour from the Dominican Republic. The gang ran ops in Limbé, Plaisance, Le Borgne, but the new government wasn't too interested in catching FADH killers. The police commissioner in Limbé, Jean Moise, wouldn't support the investigation into Frasier, who HNP investigators believed was a CIA asset, and Thoby's father took him down to PAP to get a visa to Miami. Reports were, said the captain, that he got that visa. "I guess it doesn't matter that he's on the UN's ten most wanted list."

The Haitian National Police garrison at Limbé was corrupt, in collusion with the Red Army, and had probably committed at least one murder since arriving in June. Red Army files in the Cap and Limbé police stations were destroyed, no one knew how. An HNP lieutenant in Cap Haïtien, Ti Paul Coton, had been telling the Red Army they could count on protection from the SF and UN CIVPOL. "And another thing," said the captain. All the mothers in town were complaining about the new cops going after their daughters. "The mothers are mad, let me tell you. So, like, what are you gonna do? ICITAP set them up for failure."

As for the Hodges family, two months earlier the hospital's funding was cut off by the Baptist Convention, although the doctor still received donations from individual churches. "Do you know what David Hodges asked me the other day?" said Marks. " 'How many days is it till you guys leave?' " He and his brother got a real kick out of spreading anti-imperialist propaganda against the team. Fearing there'd be retribution against them if they associated with Americans, they pretended to remain apolitical. But then you had Paul Hodges up there in Cap managing the airport, refusing to cooperate with the Marines when they first came in, wouldn't give them the keys to the cargo containers lying around, and when the troops shoot the locks off, what's inside? Drugs? Weapons?

"Some charity the Hodges are running there," said the captain.

Earlier that morning, I had dispatched Gary in search of the Bossman. Now he was back to pick us up, buzzing the front gate, and his news of Jean Moulin was unsurprisingly baffling. Bossman wasn't in town, but it seemed he had been elected or appointed to office, some platform of irresponsibility. We headed into town for an audience with the now deposed mayor, Madame Bruno, who welcomed us into her modest parlor with a heaving sigh of disillusionment. We sat on plastic-covered furniture, and Madame, who looked like Idi Amin with a wig, jabbed the side of her head with her finger—somehow this was meant to demonstrate her anger and humiliation—and closed her eyes when she spoke. She'd been spending a lot of time in the capital lately, she said, and that's where she learned that Aristide had removed her from office. Bad times, said Madame Bruno, drilling the side of her head. Bad times. She had never wanted to be mayor anyway but preferred to stay where she was, as director of Limbé's national school, but the people wanted her, and now look how everything had turned out.

The people thought the SF had come to protect them against the FADH. "I'm going to get the *blanc* for you," people would threaten a troublemaker at the beginning, but then everyone realized how hollow these words were. Then came the attack on the casern. She was in her house; she heard shooting in the marketplace but didn't know what it was.

"What about the volunteer police?" I asked.

"According to me," said Madame Bruno, her hand flying out from her head as if to swat a fly, "the soldiers were wrong to think that the volunteers were qualified to take over already."

"But where are they? I want to talk to them."

From Madame Bruno's point of view, I had asked an ignorant question. The young civil police were still hiding out in the countryside or in the bigger cities. The Americans had forgotten to tell anybody that the volunteers had fallen off the baddies list, as if their names had been inscribed there in disappearing ink. They were guilty of being stupid but not of being murderers, and nobody cared about them anymore.

We drove back to Cap Haïtien to get our gear and return south to the capital. The city's blue skies were marbled with thick tendrils of coal-black smoke, tires burning in the streets at a half-dozen locations. A company of Pakistani troops in battle gear gushed over the tailgates of cattle trucks while the HNP stood by impassively, and a single American soldier in a brown T-shirt, holding his M-16 in one hand, walked toward the flames like Mr. Fixit, until he was swaddled in greasy smoke. I'd return twice more to the north, but to all intents and purposes, I had been paroled from the never-ending story of the 53rd District, and my days in Limbé were over.

MADONNA AND CHILD IN HELL

We were lost, but still in sight of the chalky unpaved road, a line of shanties no more substantial than heaps of trash, walking where nobody walked, Gary, Duffy, and I, on a weedy, sucking, forgotten path that led you nowhere through an ecology hospitable only to land crabs and vultures, here along the inside perimeter of Fort Dimanche's walls. The mud turned foul, smelly as a hog farm, and when it seeped over the tops of our boots, I said, Enough, we had to circle back to the road before I choked in disgust, take the long way around through the shanty wasteland to reach the interior walls of the fort, its courtyard and compound, its profane expanse of once forbidden grounds where laborers now worked to clear the scrubby overgrowth from a mass grave. The forensic anthropologists were coming to town.

We approached the main entrance, its gates ripped from their hinges. "Fort Dimanche," Gary explained for Duffy's benefit, "was just built to kill people."

Out here on the marshy flats between the slums and the sea, Fort Dimanche was to the Duvaliers and the macoutes what Auschwitz was to Hitler and the SS. Now it had been liberated—actually, reliberated, since it had been shut down briefly after the *dechoukaj*—and reinhabited by over three thousand squatters, burned out of Cité Soleil by FRAPH in the summer before the invasion, cramming into its cells and its stacks of airless kennel-size tiger cages, erecting shanties on its killing grounds out of scraps of tin and cardboard. Graffiti splashed across the wall facing into its courtyard—HERE IS THE CITY OF DEMOCRACY BECAUSE OF USA. Like movie extras, the dispossessed were milling around outside the former prison with an air of great expectancy, waiting to be directed to their assigned places. Nothing would happen, ever, until someone came and told them what to do, but no one was coming except us, emissaries of disappointment, and even that was somehow propitious, preferable to despair.

But where was the apathy, the sag of defeat? The people, young and old, but especially the young, wore their pathos like campaign ribbons, proud of their inexplicable survival, the terrible obstacles they had surmounted, the daily persecution, the most horrible kind of brutalities, manmade and God-made, and they were ready to climb aboard this bus of American democracy, cling to its slippery roof if no seats were available, and ride to a better world.

Here was the barefoot Guy Gilvert, twenty-five years old, like all youth in the slums a frontliner in Haiti's long war against her people, who welcomed us with a sunbeam smile, pumping our hands with gratitude for bothering to imagine that his life might hold some interest or value. He and his fellow squatters had renamed the infamous prison Village Demokrasi; they'd organized a letter-writing campaign to Aristide, asking the president to help them with their problems, but there was never any response from the palace. "It's as if we don't exist," said Gilvert, but his own irrepressible spirit seemed to me to be the very soul of Haiti's existence, and it would be more true to say it was the government, not him, that didn't exist, the government whose very being was remote from life.

He had never had a job in his life but collected rocks from the otherwise barren landscape of the prison yard to try to sell, because there was nothing else to do. "I feel I am strong," he said passionately, "and I could work with my hands, I want to work, and as long as I am alive I have hope." He was optimistic because the Americans had brought "security *à go-go*," and because of that you didn't have to see pigs eating the corpses of your friends or family anymore. Here in the most unlivable of slums, if you needed a measure for progress, this one worked pretty well.

That the animals—free-ranging swine, dogs, rats—so recently prevailed over the dead and their disposal attested to two essential truths in Haiti during the time of the tyrants, and you couldn't really say the first truth was less cruel than the second, or that both truths were less inhumane than the circumstances the dead found themselves in during the barbaric reign of the Duvaliers. Proper interment was expensive in Haiti, especially during the embargo—a few hundred dollars, about a year's wages for most peasants or slum dwellers. *We can't work for life; we work for cemetery,* a Haitian friend once told me. *We work all our lives only to have enough money to pay to be buried.* Sometimes the municipality might purchase a pine-box coffin for such destitute souls; more often they were tossed into paupers' graves, atop the bones of their neighbors, or if they had the misfortune to die in the national hospital, their bodies lay bloated in the morgue, one of its rooms reserved for babies and children, the doll-size corpses stacked like cordwood, until a dump truck was requisitioned to haul the dead out to Tintayen and scatter them like fertilizer in the swamps.

Nonburial quickly became a facet of the style of the de factos, a macabre trademark, an extension of their diseased minds. They liked it better when their victims remained on the surface among the living, on-stage in the streets and alleys and yards, in your face, in your nose, no-body's secret, everybody's fear. They liked it so much that cleaning up the dead became an act of opposition against the state. Only the animals were free to perform this mercy, which of course was the end of mercy, day after day as your loved ones watched, the last morsels of human dig-nity transformed into the excrement of scavengers and then dispersed throughout the city on the boot heels of assassins. If you were an enemy of the generals, they weren't finished with you until they had turned you into shit.

The by no means circumspect Duvaliers had taken a somewhat more conventional approach to the sowing of mass terror, less vulgar, less fla-grant, but no less taxing to the spirit of the population. Who did the killing? Except for a handful of all-star murderers like Fort Dimanche's warden, Madame Max, no one would say. Nothing could be established, documented. Whole families, entire neighborhoods, disappeared into the maw of Fort Dimanche. What happened to them, these tens of thousands, year after year? No one would say, the authorities knew nothing, but al-most always, whoever was taken away was never seen again. I suppose it was a matter of taste, an aesthetic proclivity for the pretensions of the Du-valiers, this preference for the unknown as the servitor of horror, rather than the military de factos' more literal-minded methodology, which staged the presentation of death. The imagination versus reality, not-seeing versus seeing, the disappearance of your wife into an unmarked mass grave versus the artistic presentation of your brother's trussed-up body in the gutter.

Across rotten planks and stepping-stones lodged in the putrid mud, Guy Gilvert led us into the quagmire behind the prison. It was the rainy sea-son again, and the water had collected in pools as black and thick as crude oil, mixing with whatever vileness was seeping through from below the surface. Ahead, near a cluster of shacks that seemed to be nothing more than abandoned toolsheds, I could see four or five men clearing the dese-crated earth with hoes and machetes. Like the unassuming fort itself, the square hole the workers had scraped away wasn't much to look at—about the size of a kitchen garden and not yet deep enough for the scientists to begin quarrying the bones. One of the laborers used a bucket to drain the puddles of dark, greasy, muck-smelling liquid that oozed into the depression—the diggers had chopped into hell's aquifer.

I lit a cigarette, then lit another, as if the smoke might be an antidote to all this. Duffy felt his lungs compress like bagpipes, and thought, *When will it hit me?* The aperture of our consciousness opened just enough to recompose the scene, and Duffy and I gasped simultaneously. So close by we had almost stepped on her, her feet only inches away from the precipice of the grave, sat a voluptuous young woman on the dirt threshold of the shack that was her home, a woman beautiful enough to be a fashion model, to conquer faraway worlds with the sensuality of her eyes, the angle of her cheekbones, the straightness of her nose and fullness of her lips, but here, next to the bottomless obscenity of the grave, her beauty seemed like an affront—far worse than an affront, it seemed mocking and insane.

She held a naked infant in her arms, a five-month-old boy with angry skin, red and peeling as if he'd been dipped in lye. The infant pawed her exposed breast, gumming the black swollen nipple as he nursed. Humanity's most cherished tableau, mother and child, deformed into a perversion: mother and child on the banks of the River Styx, the unseen dead hushed in approval under our feet.

The blast of sun made me nauseous. My emotions were topsy-turvy, backward, as if I stood like a blind man in a room of hot, bright lights. Moral dehydration, Duffy called it. In my imagination, up came the bones, burying the woman and her son in their eruption. It's what's beautiful in the world that most easily breaks our hearts, but the vision of this woman was like sandpaper drawn across my exasperation with Haiti, and I felt an irrational bloody rash of outrage at the living. I wanted to shout at the young woman, *Your baby is dying, your baby is dead!* as surely he would be before long, born in unspeakable filth and suckled with poison here in this mortal dump. The juxtaposition was unbearable, but where was she going to go? what was she going to do? how were you ever going to make room for her in the house of your own life, even if she had already claimed for her own the emptiness in its corners? And then what about the others? A whole nation cannot emigrate.

Duffy took pictures of the beautiful young woman and her doomed infant and stuffed money into her hand. Turning back toward the grave, I was jolted out of my morbid reverie by Gary, who stood glassy-eyed and stricken, hypnotized by the abominable hole, his breathing torturous, strangled.

"*Oh, shit.*"

I grabbed his heavy arm and pulled him back from the edge, back across the rotten planks laid over the putrefaction, back through Village Demokrasi to the road and our car, apologizing all the way for ever having brought him here. I had forgotten about Gary's father, a sergeant in François Duvalier's army who had disappeared into Fort Dimanche's chambers of horror, accused of knowing someone who knew someone who was a friend of someone who had plotted against the dictator.

After a year in Haiti, I had seen Gary cry only once, when a photographer we were working with jokingly accused him of swiping his shampoo. It was a tease that belonged to another place, another culture, a light-hearted jab. But Gary had put his head in the bowl of his hands and wept, and when he had finished weeping, he looked over the edge of his secret but now exposed misery at me, his friend, a white man who loved him.

"You don't know, you can never know," he said, "what it is to be a Haitian."

It was the shampoo—an imaginary crime, the inescapable assignation of guilt—that had broken his spirit and made him feel lost to the world, unknown by humanity.

Sometimes the men who came to kill you, the men following orders, were the only ones who saw into your soul, because they knew there was a chance, however small, you might be innocent, that even as you died, perhaps you deserved to live. But, as with the men who came to save you, to save Haiti, you never knew why.

HAPPY ANNIVERSARY

Approaching October 15, 1995, the first anniversary of Aristide's return to power, you had to search out the more recalcitant MREs or one of the more fossilized Capitol Hill xenophobes to find someone to talk dirty to you about what was happening on the island. Even the media were sending prose bouquets of roses to celebrate the Clinton administration's rub-your-eyes foreign-policy triumph. *Wow,* the popular sentiment ran, *it's working!*

No rivers of blood, no necklacing, no Marxist enclaves, applauded the October 16 *Time* magazine, under the lead "Rising from Ruin: Since returning to power, Aristide has surprised his critics and inspired a nation." A head of state with a learning curve like a ski lift. An "epidemic of elections" had given Lavalas control of eighty percent of the seats in parliament and nearly every local government in the countryside. Yet October, November, and December were infernal months, for the Special Forces especially, in Haiti. The democratic momentum was being sucked back down into its roiling undertow of voices, the vortex of Aristide's power seemed to atrophy in a cratering blast of inertia, and the mission was in peril, increasingly scorned from the outside, dry-rotting on the inside.

Economic reform—the privatization of eight or nine decrepit state-owned monopolies—was a pill no one in Haiti wanted to swallow, neither the peasants nor the president, except for a few dozen of the island's elites, bona fide wonks and aspiring CEOs, including the prime minister, who was out stumping for privatization with religious fervor, as if he thought all Haitians were yuppies and he was offering them stock options in AT&T. Whatever the merits of the reforms, the masses were convinced the government—which in their sense of it somehow excluded Aristide and his coy silence on the issue—was trying to auction off their sovereign wasteland to the multinationals. *Haiti is not for sale!* became the season's war cry, to be replaced by the more familiar, and infinitely more volatile, *Desarmé macoutes!*

Bad blood leaked from every orifice of the Haitian corpus, and the umbilical cord between Washington and Port-au-Prince stank with the infection of distrust. A disastrous tit-for-tat flurry of threat and assassination began on October 3, with the execution by unknown assailants of one of the bungling generals Cédras had left behind—one of two dozen of Aristide's high-profile opponents murdered since September 1994. A month later, on November 7, Jean Hubert Feuillé, a newly elected legislative deputy, who was a cousin, close friend, and former bodyguard of Aristide, was gunned down in a commando-style hit by right-wing forces, one of more than sixty well-known Aristide supporters killed in political attacks since the president had been restored to power.

Aristide had been infuriated earlier that fall to learn that, in a secret cable leaked to the *Washington Post*, Secretary of State Warren Christopher advised Ambassador Swing that one of the vampires still well rooted in Port-au-Prince, General Prosper Avril, erstwhile strongman in the interim between the *dechoukaj* and Aristide's election, was planning a terror and assassination campaign, to start in early December.

Why wasn't this vital intelligence directly affecting our security shared with the Haitian government? Aristide rightfully demanded. The United States was also refusing to return sixty thousand pages of documents confiscated by the Special Forces and the Tenth Mountain Division when the troops took over FRAPH and FADH headquarters, documents ripe with the names of victims, human rights abusers, CIA and DIA assets. The Americans, however, claimed that the Aristide government would exploit the documents to launch a war of revenge against the former regime.

The night following Feuillé's assassination, Aristide ordered the HNP to raid Prosper Avril's house and arrest him for plotting against the government. By the time the police arrived, the former military dictator had fled to asylum in the Colombian embassy, tipped off hours earlier by a political officer from the U.S. embassy, who had shown up at his door.

In the tempestuous years since the *dechoukaj*, Aristide had survived five assassination attempts, had watched his church burn and his congregation of slum dwellers be slaughtered before his eyes, had watched from afar in the feverish solitude of exile while his countrymen were shot for uttering his name, while the mothers and sons of his nation drowned beneath the waves of desperation, and even his return on the shoulders of a superpower couldn't seem to quiet death or appease its appetite.

In the stagnant misery and impotent hope that was the myth of his successful return to the palace, Aristide had finally been pressed hard enough against the wall of hypocrisy to make a mistake, and at the funeral of Jean Hubert Feuillé, in the face of his international cadre of duplicitous handlers, he brandished the only true power that was ever his, the wrath of a downtrodden people. Aristide's eulogy flamed into heresy. He ordered the national police to do what the United States and the United Nations would not, to disarm the remnants of the ancien régime and their paramilitary allies.

If the UN troops got in the way, he warned, they would be "sent back home to their parents." "If those who have weapons, those who have big armored tanks, those who have much power, wanted to help us, the disarmament would have been done," said Aristide, glaring at the *blancs* seated in the front row of the chapel—Lakhdar Brahimi, the civilian head of the UN mission; General Kinzer; Ambassador Swing—unable to restrain himself from swiping at their harsh expressions. "Until further notice, there are not two or three heads of state," lectured the ex-priest, "but just one. The head of state has spoken." Then, lapsing into furious emotion, he voiced the unforgivable and seemed to summon chaos upon the country.

"Here is what I am asking of the Haitian people. Don't sit back and wait with your arms crossed. Accompany the Haitian police when they are going to enter the home of those who have big weapons. Give them information, don't be afraid. When you do that, tell the policemen not to go only to the poor neighborhoods but to go to the neighborhoods where there are big houses and heavy weapons.

"This is the first time I have spoken to you like this since my return to Haiti. I need you, you need me."

True, but what Haiti needed was not this. Despite Aristide's clear and lawful delegation of authority to police, his words were taken out of context and distorted by everybody—the media and the masses, the elites, the international community. "I told you so," said a smug John Kambourian, visiting the embassy from Langley two weeks later. "I told you so," said a gleeful Lieutenant Colonel Lovasz in the Defense Attaché's Office. "I told you so," cried the MREs up the mountainside: Aristide is a demagogue, a madman. No crusader of enlightenment but an angel of darkness.

Titid second-guessed himself and tried to blunt his call to action, asking people to calm down, but to little effect; nor did it help matters that the television and radio stations seized upon the president's speech and replayed it again and again. Barely had the funeral ended before roadblocks of burning tires appeared throughout the capital. Crowds of vigilantes stopped vehicles, tearing them apart in a frenzied search for weapons. Mobs looted the houses of dozens of coup supporters, and by morning the nation was once again fractured by panic and widespread violence, and bodies lay in the streets.

Gonaïves exploded, Nepalese troops firing over the heads of a pro-Aristide mob, and more bodies lay in the streets before it was over. Limbé exploded, a mob attacking the Hodges family compound, on the road to

Bas Limbé, where twenty-one relief workers had taken refuge. A caretaker was sliced up with a machete, another man killed and beheaded, two men were burned to death in Plaine du Nord, another two murdered in the countryside.

Fueled by Aristide's incendiary words, the assault began as both an attempt to search Paul Hodges's estate for weapons and a continuing protest against the death of Jean Moulin, the Bossman, a month earlier. The HNP in Limbé claimed that Moulin had died of a heart attack; the SF said he had died of AIDS; the people of Limbé were convinced the Bossman had died of a voodoo curse placed on his life by an ally of the Hodges family. The night of the attack on their Bas Limbé estates, there was enough of a lull in the action for the Hodges retinue to chance a high-speed caravan back to the security of the hospital and its walled grounds, where again they were attacked by the angry mob until the Special Forces arrived and exchanged gunfire with the crowd. The fighting spasmed on and off for four days—the ugliest days that Captain Craig Marks would spend in Haiti, shooting illumination rounds with star clusters straight down the street at head level.

Where were the national police? Cowering behind the walls of their renovated casern. "Is Limbé really Haiti?" one of them asked me the last time I visited Limbé; all of them had gathered round to tell me that the town was a bad, bad place. What about the Red Army? I wondered. "We never heard of the Red Army," they said. "That's a story." I didn't know the young policeman who had the last word, but I recognized the irreconcilable contempt of his expression, the same expression I had witnessed on the FADH and the IPSF, his predecessors in the casern, when they had unhesitatingly shared with me their identical opinion.

"The people in Limbé have an animal behavior," said the cop. Three generations of security forces in Limbé, united only in their hatred for the people.

The Americans were caught in a dilemma. They were naturally afraid to breathe too much power into Haiti's new police force, but the result was a lack of organization and leadership. In July 1995, the HNP shot to death a half-dozen people in "displays of unwarranted violence." "An inept and trigger-happy bunch," observed one diplomat. The third week in November, an off-duty cop shot and killed a taxi driver in Saint-Marc in a dispute over a seven-cent fare. The following week, the people of Cité Soleil, who had smothered the HNP in love when they established a substation in the squalid slum in June, *dechoukéd* the entire twenty-four-man unit after one of the cops, during an argument with a bus driver, pulled his gun and accidentally shot and killed a six-year-old schoolgirl. Cité Soleil's residents refused to allow an ambulance to enter the neighborhood; the schoolgirl's body lay in the street all day. We're waiting, said the slum dwellers, for Aristide to come and see what his police have done.

And yet, throughout the country, I visited station after station where callow young officers struggled to keep the peace, to hold Haiti together, to keep it from tumbling into the civil war that seemed to be its destiny once the foreign troops were no longer around to rescue them. There had been no redistribution of wealth on the island, but here was a change worthy of attention—during the first month of the intervention, there had been a significant redistribution of weapons.

"The next couple of years here are going to be ugly," said Stanley Schrager. "Officially, we're leaving and we gave them their chance. Unofficially, it's going to be a great tragedy. Why did we even bother?"

IT ALWAYS ENDS THIS WAY

The SF had begun to turn out the lights on the mission. The presidential elections in December were basically anticlimactic, peaceful, mostly because people never showed up. Command realized that, well, this country's a helluva lot more stable than anybody thought it was, especially throughout the hinterlands, where Special Forces were posted.

On January 15, 1996, Master Sergeant Frank Norbury's team, ODA 344 in Saint-Marc, one of the last of the SF outstations, pulled back into Port-au-Prince for redeployment. Everybody was rolling out, everything was going fine, until General Kinzer received a report that the A-teams had brought in about two hundred eighty weapons with them from the countryside, mostly old IPSF weapons or bolt-action rifles guys had held on to as souvenirs; but it looked bad, it clicked with the rumors in the mainstream press that Special Forces personnel might be caching weapons, possibly to rearm the FADH and the FRAPH, and the general raised hell. Then a vehicle, traced to the Special Operations Joint Task Force, was found wrecked and abandoned in Pétionville, and suddenly the SF found itself unable to account for about twenty other vehicles, lost in the baroque chain of custody. All the snafus prompted Special Operations Command at Fort Bragg to dispatch a full-bird colonel and Third Group's sergeant major to Port-au-Prince to find out what was going on and ride herd on the two dozen troopers who remained.

ODA 343, tasked with training the presidential guards, was supposed to be the last A-team in the country, scheduled for redeployment on February 29, but two days before the inauguration of René Préval, Aristide's hapless successor as chief of state, the zone commander of the 101st Infantry prohibited the Special Forces from being at or anywhere near the palace during the February 7 ceremony. You're not welcome at the inauguration, the conventional army told ODA 343, which had been one of the teams responsible for training and re-forming the palace guard since early in the operation.

The hell with it, said the SF—if they weren't needed at the palace, they weren't needed anywhere. General Kinzer had seen the Green Berets as a necessary evil, a political liability that he had no choice but to tolerate until now. Without the A-teams, who were the eyes and ears of the zone commanders, the United Nations couldn't have controlled the countryside, but the image-conscious UN was determined to downplay SF's responsibilities, and now it was time to pull those troops in, palletize them, process them out, and send them home. Again, the redeployment plan accelerated.

"They can't afford for anything to go wrong now," Frank Norbury was telling me on the veranda of the Hotel Oloffson. "The inauguration is the capstone event, and Lord help us if we do anything wrong."

Throughout the past months, I had visited the master sergeant and his ODA in Saint-Marc. Now the team was back in North Carolina, but Frank had stayed behind, working for SOC-C over at headquarters with a handful of other noncommissioned officers and brass, logistical guys, closing down the shop. It was Thursday night at the Oloffson—party night, RAM night—and I had invited Norbury and two of his fellow sergeants for dinner, although from the expressions on their faces, the soldiers looked as if I had dragged them off to be hanged. Ski, the master sergeant from ODA 343, the team that had been kicked out of the palace, lowered his head over his plate in utmost dejection. All of them felt betrayed, sold

out by their own generals back at Fort Bragg, left to fend for themselves
in a conventional environment where they could be persecuted beyond
measure for trifles.

"What's with Ski?" I finally had to ask Frank. He wouldn't eat, drink,
talk, wouldn't eyeball the beautiful women crowding onto the veranda for
the RAM concert—nothing. Deep inside himself, Ski wasn't there.

His buddy Ski, Frank confided solemnly, his voice muffled by the hub-
bub of arriving revelers, had come to that moment of destiny-altering truth
in life that everybody had to face sooner or later, and it steamrolled right
over him. During the past three years, Haiti had become Ski's life; he believed in the people, their culture. He believed that their country needed
men like him to give their hearts to it. A Creole-speaker, he was in it from
the beginning with Haiti, had seen so many commanders and so many different clouds—same surface, different clouds—and had blood-and-sweat
equity in the mission. He was there on the *Harlan County*, he was there
in Gitmo, there for Operation Uphold Democracy, Restore Democracy,
Maintain Democracy, he had seen them all and spent more time in Haiti
than any other Green Beret, period. Nobody had to order a guy like Ski,
said Frank, to reach out his hand to Haitians. But now he was being ordered home. Booted out, with the door slamming behind him.

"This is his last hurrah," said Frank.

At lunch in the Joint Task Force mess hall, Ski had been told by the
sergeant major of the 101st Infantry to get a haircut. ODA 343 had just
come out of the field after months in Gonaïves. Was his hair a bit long?
Yes. Was it within army standards? Yes. Was it within the 101st's high-and-
tight standards? No. All Ski had to do was answer, *Yes, Sergeant Major,* and
move on, but that wasn't what he did. Now the issue wasn't a haircut but
was Ski's reaction to being told to get a haircut: giving lip to the sergeant
major—who told the US/ACOM sergeant major that he had a problem
with a Special Forces commando disrespecting him. The US/ACOM
sergeant major tells his boss, General Sheehan, who had replaced Admiral Miller at Atlantic Command in Norfolk. Sheehan calls General Downing, head of Special Operations in Tampa. Downing calls General Scott in
Fort Bragg, Scott calls Boyatt at Third Group HQ, who had done his very
best to protect his men in Haiti from the narrow-minded, anally challenged to old school headmasters in the conventional forces, but it was too
late to save Ski.

"And before you fucking know it," said Frank, "man, this huge maelstrom comes smoking back down about Special Forces guys out of control. The entire command's involved with a team sergeant needing a haircut. Before you know it, man, the thing has built to this huge fucking avalanche, and it just slid down on Ski, *whomp,* like that, and tomorrow he's on the black deuce, taking the A-train back to the States.

"Generals talk to generals: 'Yeah, I had problems with the SF guys down in Haiti. Look at all the trouble they caused me, look at this list of incidents. They wrecked vehicles, they lost vehicles, they hoarded weapons, they did all these things, look at this.' That's the way it happens," said Frank. "So we'll sacrifice our people, we'll kill our people and bury them in shallow graves, if that's what it takes to preserve our image and our support.

"We're bitter," said Frank. "It always ends this way."

The three sergeants got up from the table and left before the music started, walking unaffected through the revelry, the Oloffson crowd, to which they were a spectacle, exotic beings from the self-obliterating world outside the gates. Green Berets.

A few days later, I visited Sergeant Norbury at the LIC's Camp Democracy, where a sign on the front gate read, NO JOB HERE, DO NOT ASK. It was document-burning day, thousands of pages containing the prosaic mind of the military fed into the flames of fifty-five-gallon drums by celebrating soldiers of the Joint Task Force. A few days after that, Frank Norbury and Rick Douglas, the operations sergeant, got a call in the middle of the night. "Hey, you two guys are the last SF down there. You be at the airport at seven o'clock in the morning. You're leaving." The two sergeants grabbed their duffel bags, humped them over to the tarmac, a C-141 showed up, three CA and psy ops guys got on the plane with them, and together the five of them took a lonely ride straight to Bragg. That was it, the mission was over.

It always ends this way, Frank had said, but his bitterness was not unexpected. He couldn't think of a decent withdrawal from any campaign the Special Forces had been involved with. Vietnam. Seventh Group in El Salvador, where the sergeant realized he had not, after all, worked to free the oppressed. The Gulf War, where Fifth Group loathed the spoiled Kuwaitis and could almost understand why the Iraqis wanted to kill them. Northern Iraq, where the SF had encouraged Kurdish resistance against Saddam Hussein and then slid out the back door. Somalia, every man for himself running to the beach to get the hell out of there. Since the advent of the atomic age, there had been enough time, enough campaigns, enough wars big and small, for a truth to emerge. Soldiers weren't obsolete, only victory, and when you sipped from its battered cup, your mouth soured. Conrad Aiken's advice on Vietnam was still operative: *Declare success and go home.*

"There's never really been a graceful withdrawal from anywhere," said Master Sergeant Frank Norbury, and Haiti was no different. But it came with the territory, it was something you had to prepare yourself for. "So what do we do? We come back, we get to know our families again, what's left of them, and then get on with some training and wait for the next thing to come up."

The C-141 landed at Pope Air Force Base in the middle of a long holiday weekend, Presidents' Day, a cold Sunday, and not a soul, it seemed, within a hundred miles. Finally, one of Third Group's sergeant majors arrived at the ramp. The soldiers heaved their gear into his vehicle and went home.

EPILOGUE

A despot may go away, but no dictatorship comes to a complete end with his departure. A dictatorship depends for its existence on the ignorance of the mob; that's why all dictators take such pains to cultivate that ignorance. It requires generations to change such a state of affairs, to let some light in. Before this can happen, however, those who have brought down a dictator often act, in spite of themselves, like his heirs, perpetuating the attitudes and thought patterns of the epoch they themselves have destroyed. This happens so involuntarily and subconsciously that they burst into righteous ire if anyone points it out to them.... It is one of the most difficult things in the world to cross such boundaries, to change the past.

—Ryszard Kapuscinski

TALKING HEADS: GENERAL DICK POTTER

BS: General Potter, you hit [FRAPH] hard those first weeks, then somebody told Mark Boyatt to tell his guys to back off . . . and he gave this inspired homily about democracy and that it needs a loyal opposition.

GP: Well, I think FRAPH was an opposition, but I think to call it a loyal opposition was to give them more credit than you wanted to give them.

BS: That's what he called them, but maybe he was just being inspired. Maybe you or somebody else had given him an order saying, Back off the FRAPH and just start treating them the way you treat Lavalas. And he put his own spin on that and started talking about what a democracy is—multiparty systems, et cetera, although there's no multiparty system in Haiti.

GP: No.

BS: It's one-party rule. The sides don't coexist, and I don't know if Colonel Boyatt was simply inspired that moment or what.

GP: Well, you know, I don't know what the genesis of that was. I've talked to Mark about this previously, I mean since we've been back, and you know, basically it's, uh [long pause] . . . As far as I'm concerned, we had no charter to round up the FRAPH. No one said to us, Go and incarcerate the FRAPH.

BS: All you had was this strategic precedent: If you come in hard, they're the enemy.

GP: Yeah, but we didn't come in that way.

BS: I know, but enemies don't really change so easily.

GP: No, no, but we—and of course we had some real difficulties in policing people up who had done criminal acts, bringing them to Port-au-Prince and either statements not filed [or] people refusing to testify against them. And of course, you couldn't have rounded them all up anyway.

BS: No, you couldn't, but I'm not sure that's as important as this shift in emphasis that ended up sanitizing the FRAPH. And they were not the type of organization you wanted to be spending your efforts whitewashing.

GP: Oh, I don't think anybody whitewashed them.

BS: Well, that's not true. Boyatt did. And it went out into the AOs until you had people dutifully repeating that, again and again.

GP: There came a point where you had to treat everybody the same. Uh, I guess I don't know where you're coming from on this.

BS: Well, you weren't calling the FADH a loyal opposition, or a legitimate force in society. It was just the FRAPH, and FRAPH was a terrorist organization.

GP: No, no, I— Nobody ever called them legitimate.

BS: Let's go back to— I'm not sure where you came from on October 8 [1994], but you came out of a meeting, perhaps at the embassy with your peer group of commanders, and Ambassador Swing, I guess, and came and briefed Boyatt and told him—this is a paraphrase of what you told him—FRAPH is now a registered political party, and now this is a quote, "but I still think they are a bunch of thugs."

GP: I thought they were thugs.

BS: Sure, but where did this "registered political party" notion come from?

GP: I don't think I said that, but that's, you know . . .

BS: That's from somebody at the [staff] meeting who did take notes.

GP: But I— You know, I don't remember saying that.

BS: Where could that have come from, if in fact . . . ? Well, I've heard Boyatt say it myself. Here's somebody who heard you say it at a meeting. Where could that have come from?

GP: I don't know. I don't know. I don't know.

BS: Why does Swing say, "In regards to FRAPH, the military did their own thing, and for four months I was frustrated"?

GP: I don't know. As far as I'm concerned, the policies that we followed in the field were approved by the entire chain of command. Miller, Shelton, Meade.

BS: The issue is not, Well, did you arrest these guys or not? or, Well, did you treat them the same as everybody else or not? You treated them the same. But to me it's a policy decision, that all of a sudden a clearly identified terrorist organization is being called the loyal opposition.

GP: No, but I don't see— I don't like the term loyal opposition.

BS: Right, but how about "legitimate political party"? They were called a legitimate political party.

GP: No, they were never a political party either.

BS: These are the Special Forces' terms. Nobody else was saying this in Haiti except the Special Forces.

GP: Yeah.

SANDY'S SLIDE

How the politics of moral equivalency had contaminated Boyatt and his Green Berets was still not entirely clear to me, and when, in early December 1995, the media excoriated the performance of the U.S. Special Forces in Haiti, the tone of the criticism seemed distressingly reminiscent of Vietnam, a time when so many Americans seemed incapable of distinguishing between policymakers and foot soldiers.

"When we first came, in September [1994], we went after FRAPH real hard. We knew they were the bad boys in town. What we were told was our aggression was causing problems," Colonel Boyatt had explained to me in Fort Bragg, "and we were told to back off, we were told not to go after them but to treat them as a political party." The order, Boyatt had said obliquely, came through the chain of command. That order, needless to say, had contributed to the ongoing destabilization of Haiti and, more to the point there in North Carolina, had potentially and gratuitously endangered the lives of his men.

It was a familiar story for the Green Berets, squeezed between unsavory political machinations and the deep blue sea of duty. For the most part, the commandos' visceral bewilderment never evolved beyond a state of frustrated impartiality and ethical confusion. Which is not to say there weren't problems, deliberate misunderstandings, subversions, however isolated and seemingly inconsequential.

"FRAPH exemplified everything gone bad in the [American] military," said an SF master sergeant as we sat in a bar back in Fayetteville, trying to make sense of things after the mission was finally over. "The initial connection between SF and FRAPH was comrades in arms. The military can only understand military." The sergeant talked about how General Potter, who as commander of American forces in Germany had been given George Patton's desk, had tried to apply a European solution to a Caribbean problem. "Potter could easily connect Nazis and FRAPH and think, Okay, we can work with this. But then," said the sergeant, "your whole premise for going down there is now corrupted. I really believe there were a lot of guys down in Haiti who were not fully indoctrinated in what we do. We're not just a military force, we have a moral cause. Who are the oppressed? Who's oppressing them? Certain elements in the SF lost sight of that.

"The whole thing is, why are you there? To liberate the oppressed. They needed direction. What do you want us to do? FRAPH is a political party? Okay. They don't know, so they just follow the policy blindly. The strategic and political guidance, the leadership, failed at key times. FRAPH was a cancer, it was a key time to rid Haiti of that cancer, and the leadership, political or otherwise, failed. You can rest assured that if the leadership said FRAPH is bad, FRAPH would be dead and gone. If they said FRAPH is good and bad, then everybody's just confused."

This was January 1996. Boyatt's campaign to void Captain Barton's commission in the army had achieved its denouement, and I had been summoned to Fort Bragg by the captain's attorney to testify at his Officers Elimination Board hearing—a benign form of court-martial. I sat in Colonel Boyatt's office, waiting to be called before the panel of military judges, trying to use the media cloud that had fallen over the Third Group commander and his men as leverage to pry open the colonel's clamshell, but he was shut tight, wouldn't say a word, no matter that he and his soldiers were being painted as villains for their mission in Haiti. Besides, he was miffed at me for my defense of Barton and felt I was determined to make an inept team leader "look like a saint."

A staff officer came to escort me into the hearing room, and for the remainder of the morning I told the three high-ranking officers sitting in judgment of Barton what I knew about the conduct of the captain in Limbé. "I didn't know the military was a personality contest," I said. "Captain Barton's men didn't like him, but so what? Do you relieve officers because enlisted men don't like them?" As I left the proceeding, there in the hallway was the team, ODA 311—Top Miatke, JC the medic, Ernie Brown, Bob Fox, Commo Jim, Walt the Punisher. Our reunion was, as always, a good one, but they were not happy to be there, waiting to be called before the board. They had cold feet, they never truly imagined their conflict with their former team leader would get this far, and now they regretted the whole affair. The next day, Ed Barton was acquitted of all charges against him, reinstated as an A-team captain, and transferred to Seventh Group, out of Boyatt's sight.

For the most part, these men had wanted to play fair, to resist the uniformed impulse to throw their weight around, help those who couldn't yet help themselves, stymie the bad guys. Americans, it has always seemed to me, cannot prevent themselves from behaving as if they were responsible for the planet, as if they contained the power and the will to mend all that had been broken, or just simply made wrong, by themselves as well as others throughout the centuries, and yet however hubristic and self-deluding the impulse, the troubled world called on them again and again, inviting trespass, ambivalence, inviting scorn and failure.

Two images stay in my mind from my reunion with ODA 311, that spring of '95 in North Carolina, when they had first returned from Limbé:

Jim Pledger lived with his wife and kids on a sandy unpaved road he shared with his neighbors. When he reached home from Haiti, the road was in disrepair, so on his first day of leave he took his children's red wagon, threw a shovel into it, and went to work, filling in the potholes and the gullies between the county road and his house, waving howdy to the neighbors.

And Top, Top and the Dalmatian pup he named Bella. As I sat in Top's family room late one night, the pup chewed on our shoes, chewed on the furniture, tore into whatever caught her attention, while Top, with seemingly endless patience, sat in his recliner, reciting the master's mantra of discipline: *No, Bella. No, Bella. No no no.*

Jim was going to fix that road, Top was going to train that dog. They would fill in the holes and tame the wildness and make their world better. They were happy.

◻   ◻   ◻

With a winter storm blowing in from the Blue Ridge Mountains, I walked from Third Group headquarters back to Special Operations Command, to badger the colonel in charge of SF Public Affairs to convince the now retired General Potter—a hero sitting atop a lifetime of still classified missions; shot up all to hell on the Cambodian border in 1966; one of the founding officers of Delta Force, the army that doesn't exist—to speak with me. For months, nothing came of the request, then one day in the spring of 1996, I found myself on the phone with the general, getting directions to his home at the army's War College in Carlisle, Pennsylvania. "If somebody objects to something I did, okay," said Potter, "but I don't want it to fall on Boyatt and the lads."

I flew to Pennsylvania in April, but the stout, white-haired general seemed incapable, though not ostensibly unwilling, of standing fast in support of his Third Group commander, or even of erecting a fence between the High Command and the political tailors who had dressed FRAPH in a three-piece suit of legitimacy. Early in the occupation, at a meeting attended by Generals Potter and Shelton, Admiral Miller, and Ambassador Swing, Swing stated that "all parties should be treated equally." Shelton later remarked in a speech, "Everyone must be free to participate in the process." I asked Potter if he had ever attended a meeting with Ambassador Swing and Admiral Miller and Shelton or Meade where FRAPH, and the military's posture toward the terrorists, was discussed.

"I don't think with Swing," said the general.

"So Swing's more or less right when he says the military was doing their own thing."

"No," said the general. He had never attended a meeting where there seemed to be any disagreement about what the Special Forces were doing. There were entire days when Potter would travel around Port-au-Prince or the countryside with the ambassador or embassy people or the chief of station, and nobody ever raised the subject. "You know, you think if there was such a great concern, somebody would have said something."

It appeared that somebody did say something, but the message expressed an altogether different concern. "Someone at the White House" called the Joint Chiefs of Staff, requesting that the SF lower the heat on

FRAPH. The chiefs of staff called Potter, and Potter passed the word along to his field commander, Boyatt.

"You told him this after that initial period when you came in, when the U.S. came in and they rough-assed with everybody?" I asked. "You told him to relax?"

"Yeah, I would say that," Potter agreed. He had told Boyatt to treat everyone the same and made sure the colonel was clear about the priorities of the mission. "I'm telling you what I know and what I sincerely believe. I don't have any problems accepting responsibility for my own actions, you know."

I asked Potter if he knew whether FRAPH had pretty good political connections in Washington.

"Don't know," he said.

"I'm just wondering again: Is this how it all came down—from Washington through the embassy into Mark Boyatt's lap?"

"Well, I assume that Mark Boyatt only took his orders from me."

I assumed that as well, but at this point in every conversation I had about FRAPH, the chain-of-command frequency became garbled. I had heard Boyatt infer that he had been set up by the embassy on FRAPH, and if that was so, we weren't talking chain of command anymore.

"I think Boyatt was being coached," I speculated. "After it was more or less established that you were going to relax about FRAPH, he was coached by the embassy to say whatever it was he said."

"First of all," cautioned Potter, "I don't know how much contact the embassy had with Mark."

"On FRAPH, perhaps quite a bit. You were there when they stood up Emmanuel Constant for his press conference?"

"Yeah. I didn't."

"The military did."

"Yeah, yeah," said the general. "I mean I wouldn't, I wouldn't."

"Meade did it," I said.

"I wouldn't. Well, I was not placed in that position. Certainly that had the blessing of the embassy."

"They say it didn't. They say they went along with it."

"Aw, wait a minute."

◻   ◻   ◻

We had talked throughout the afternoon, the general and I, and although I believed Potter was a thoroughly moral man, a man who, unlike Meade, could walk into a Haitian prison and with genuine outrage clean the place out, our conversation had concentrated both light and shadow, and I never heard the general say what needed to be said. As I left that afternoon, he followed me, I thought forlornly and somewhat abashedly, to my car, once again expressing his wish that I unpin Colonel Boyatt from the controversy.

"General Potter, that's why I came all this way. I was hoping you would do that, but it doesn't seem to me that you have." Opening the car door, I paused—perhaps there was something more to say—but the general never replied.

Boyatt was sealed tight down at Fort Bragg, and that summer, fall, and winter, my repeated requests for a final audience with the colonel were met by silence. The colonel was the good soldier, the loyal comrade, taking a bullet for the team, but duty has a threshold crossed only by madmen or martyrs, and Boyatt was neither of those. No one was going to step up for the Third Group commander, and acting as a heat shield for his men in Haiti had kept a star off his shoulder. He was a man who only wanted "the record to speak for itself," as he said when we eventually spoke again, one winter morning early in 1997.

Meade was very political, said Boyatt. Policy came down from Potter or through Meade. "I got the impression from Ambassador Swing," said the colonel, "that he had been told about us backing off and found it very distasteful."

"So the embassy had nothing to do with this?" I asked.

"The hell they didn't," said Boyatt. Someone at the embassy—Boyatt said he couldn't remember who—had sent "that slide" over to SF headquarters in Port-au-Prince. That, and command's directives, was where the spin had come from—*legit political party, loyal opposition*—amplified by the colonel's own unconventional warfare philosophy, the tactical subterfuge of co-opting your enemy. That, said Boyatt, was why he had always figured the embassy was behind policy toward FRAPH.

"What slide are you talking about?" I said.

"That seesaw slide. FRAPH at one end, Lavalas at the other." Sandy Berger's slide.

There wasn't a chief of state in the world in control of every single element in his administration, but surely one could reasonably expect the Clinton White House to have a clear idea of what sort of policy imperatives the President's own National Security Council was batting around, its latest exercise in the accommodation of terrorists. Before the invasion, Sandy Berger, the deputy national security adviser, came to the embassy in Port-au-Prince to deliver a graphic-arts slide show briefing on The Players. Out went the lights; the staff directed its attention toward the screen at the front of the room:

> Cédras . . . Aristide—*Chiefs of State*
> FRAPH . . . Lavalas—*Political Parties*

Half the audience nodded and concurred. The other half threw up its hands, unable to persuade Berger and his like-minded colleagues at State and DOD that Cédras and Aristide and FRAPH and Lavalas were not, and never had been, moral or political equivalents and that a terrorist group that could boast of a trophy wall pasted with photographs of its victims, an organization that had vowed to assassinate American soldiers, was inherently undeserving of this sort of leg up on joining the legitimate political arena, let alone the human race.

What was the true relationship between the government of the United States and the terrorist organization called FRAPH? Had the CIA and the DIA interfered with the execution of American foreign policy in Haiti, or fortified that policy's more risky aspects? However the White House chooses to answer those questions, it's hard to dismiss the probability that if you clip FRAPH out of this picture, the *Harlan County* docks, there's no invasion, and no American soldiers are placed in harm's way.

Not long after his ludicrous, American-sponsored press conference at the embassy, Toto Constant fled Haiti, slipping into the United States on a tourist visa that the Port-au-Prince consulate had conveniently forgotten to invalidate. Secretary of State Warren Christopher asked Attorney General Janet Reno to detain and deport Constant on the grounds that his presence in the U.S. "compromise[d] a compelling United States foreign policy interest." At Christopher's request, the Immigration and Naturalization Service tracked down and arrested the tall, goateed FRAPH chieftain in New York in May 1995.

In late October, fearing imminent deportation into the hands of people with a big score to settle, Toto found his voice and began talking to the papers and to *60 Minutes*. "I'm the fall guy," he bleated from his cell in a Maryland detention center, a U.S. prostitute, someone good enough to bed down with at night but not fit to be seen with in broad daylight. "Everyone else is free and I'm the only one in jail," he cried to reporters. "I was Mr. Nice Guy. I was too nice. That's why I ended up where I am, because I should have made a deal with the U.S. Army. I feel like I imagine my slave ancestors would feel when they disagreed with the master."

For a while, it looked as though Constant's handlers were taking the little monster for a ride. But despite repeated requests from the Haitian government to the U.S. to deport Emmanuel Constant back to Port-au-Prince to stand trial on charges of murder, torture, and rape, National Security Adviser Anthony Lake persuaded the secretary of state and the INS to set Toto free. The former FRAPH leader now resides in Brooklyn, living the exemplary life of a retired terrorist, his brain packed in an electric fog of cocaine. His erstwhile band of thugs remain scattered through Haitian society, popping up every so often to commit robbery and homicide.

As for John Kambourian, in October 1994 he was rotated out of the embassy in Port-au-Prince back to Langley, to direct the Haiti working group at the CIA. He returned, briefly, to the island toward the end of November 1995, when Anthony Lake paid a visit to the national palace to assure himself that Aristide had no plans to retrieve the three stolen years of his presidency.

Nominated to direct the CIA by President Clinton, Mr. Lake withdrew from the appointment before ever being confirmed by Congress, protesting he was being manhandled by the process. Lake's seat as national security adviser was filled by Sandy Berger, who in 1998 told Nelson Mandela and the South Africans, in defense of U.S. policy toward Libya and Iran, that victims of terrorism want and deserve answers, and that it's difficult to forgive and go on without justice. Principles the National Security Council never seemed able to apply to Haiti.

Colonel Boyatt's revelation reminded me of a joke, reportedly Aristide's favorite: *Why will there never be a coup d'état in Washington, D.C.?* Answer: *Because there's no American embassy there.*

But the joke missed a more central truth, that despite what one hopes are our best intentions to change the world in our own image, we are clumsy sponsors of freedom, proud but graceless and self-subverting. The White House had done the right thing, cleansing Haiti of the tyrants du jour, and then it was business as usual.

My final week in Port-au-Prince, I blindly stumbled into an argument with a woman, a newspaper editor from the States. We had just returned from a trip to Cap Haïtien, where we had hiked up into the mountains to visit Henri Christophe's fortress, and were having dinner on the veranda of the Oloffson. On the walk down from the Citadel, she said, she had observed me discreetly slipping money into selected pockets. She thought this behavior was misguided. That was not the way to help anybody. It only made matters worse, she said, this personalizing of macroproblems; the most meaningful way to change things was to pay your taxes and lobby for legislative reform.

You're absolving yourself of any face-to-face responsibility, I replied hotly. Your sense of altruism is a comfortable abstraction. You detach yourself from individuals as if they were sorry apparitions, congenitally nameless.

Gary looked on, dismayed, as two more *blancs,* in a centuries-long procession of *blancs,* squabbled over the methods and mechanisms they might best apply, like bandages, when they were intermittently inspired to repair the world.

BIG EATERS

On the Haitian calendar, February 7 was a day of great importance. Jean-Claude Duvalier had been forced into exile on February 7, 1986. Jean-Bertrand Aristide had been inaugurated as Haiti's first democratically elected president on February 7, 1991. February 7, 1995, was the anniversary of that inauguration, and of the end of Duvalier. The kids from Famni C'est La Vie, Aristide's orphanage, crawled over the national palace like a screaming plague of spiders, peeing on the floors. Outside on the lawn, a thousand students were fighting over sandwiches, ball caps, and T-shirts tossed scattershot into the crowd by presidential aides. People were packed onto the palace grounds; beyond the bars of the fence, an ocean of citizens filled the Champs du Mars. Aristide appeared on the bunting-draped portico, released ten white doves, and the ocean roared.

Aristide stepped up to the podium, encased in bulletproof panels of glass, and asked the people if they should bring justice for everyone.

Justice first, before reconciliation, the crowd shouted back.

"Both at the same time," Aristide suggested. Three doves lingered at his feet. Aristide's metaphor for unity was strange (if you weren't a Haitian)— a rat sticking its tail in "the syrup bottle of democracy," then inviting all the other rats to come have a lick. He talked for a minute about handing over the presidency when his term would be up next year, and the schoolchildren screamed, *No!*

"When we are one, we are weak. When we are together, we are strong. When we are everybody, we are Lavalas," the president concluded, and the entire nation cheered its little priest, medals were draped around his neck, a robed choir atop a soundstage constructed in the center of the lawn burst into the "Hallelujah" Chorus. Dignitaries and diplomats and military officers in the reviewing stands swatted at red and blue balloons dropped from the balconies above. In front of the palace steps, young men and women were pressed together into one dense lump of overheated humanity. "If you keep bugging me I will slap you," said a student to the guy on his back. "Is that the meaning of democracy for you?" the other boy demanded.

At the security checkpoint out on the street, Argentinian IPMs were beating up and arresting two Haitian journalists who had insisted too loudly that they had the right to pass. The Twenty-fifth Infantry kept busy pulling drunks off the fence. A *raboday* street band inched its way through the crowd, a locomotive of sound in a swirl of people, singing over and over again, *We are having fun.* "Please tell Clinton we want Aristide for twenty-five years," a euphoric dancer insisted to any *blanc* she saw.

Back inside the fence, on the stage facing the front of the palace, Boukman Eksperyans, Haiti's most acclaimed band, had begun to play, shattering the pomp and circumstance of political ceremony with *racine* vibrations. Finally, RAM took over for the last set, the women dancing so beautifully it made your eyes sting. Richard Morse mounted the stage, swarmed by schoolchildren reaching to touch his single braid of hair, his skull wrapped in a scarlet bandanna.

"Mr. President," Richard's voice boomed into the microphone, "this song is for you," and then Lunise sang "Fey." The palace rocked. People danced in the dignitaries' box, danced in the tall windows on the second story, danced on the balconies. Boys fell to the lawn, humping the earth, doing handstands. Richard came off the stage with his *raboday* trumpeters, a Pied Piper working a conga line through the crowd. A girl stopped her dance abruptly, panting and stunned. "Never in my wildest dreams," she gasped. "Not only did I never think my president would be here, but I never thought one day I would be singing this song at the palace." In an upstairs window, a pair of doves sat where only seconds before a woman had been cutting loose with joy.

The following month, during Haiti's first real carnival in three years, RAM would inch its way through the ecstatic crowds atop President Aristide's float, *petro* drums thundering.

In June 1995, with the advent of municipal elections, the political staff at the American embassy were laying two-to-one odds that their man, the elegant, articulate, impeccably dressed Evans Paul would be reelected mayor of Port-au-Prince and then—the boys were just calling it as they saw it—elected to the presidency. Never happened—the embassy almost never won a bet. Evans Paul, one of the founding fathers of Lavalas, tripped into disfavor with the people after a quarrel with Aristide, and his opponent, the musician Manno Charlemagne, took over city hall on the crest of a landslide.

Manno was a singer, songwriter, poet, cast from the mold of revolutionary, tortured by the ancien régime, hunted into exile, a troubadour who sang only in the key of resistance to the tyrants. He was Haiti's own Bob Dylan, Bob Marley, her Pablo Neruda, and Manno set about reshaping his unmanageable, dystopic, festering metropolis with a righteous vengeance, bulldozing the macoute honky-tonks across from the Holiday Inn, banning the thousands of *marchands* and vendors who made the downtown streets and sidewalks impassable, criticizing the palace—though not Aristide personally—for being rife with corruption and drug dealing.

The people of Port-au-Prince had never seen or heard such things, a mayor cleaning up the city, a mayor saying something against the palace and walking away with his life. Manno might be wrong, he might be right, people said, but his behavior and his big mouth and his positive energy were all a healthy sign for the crucible of democracy.

Manno moved into the Hotel Oloffson, taking over the upstairs suites, coming and going with his entourage of Uzi-carrying kids. On the eve of René Préval's election, the first peaceful transition of power in Haitian history, I had watched and listened, amazed, as Mayor Charlemagne performed at a Préval campaign rally on the Champs du Mars. Guitar in hand, the T-shirted and blue-jeaned mayor approached the microphone with his sidekick, a glaring youth with an Uzi slung on his shoulder and a 9mm pistol jammed in his hip pocket, and told the thousands of battle-seasoned slum kids cheering in the night, "If there's a macoute in the crowd and he causes trouble, we'll shoot him dead right now." Then Manno began to sing, in his deep, creamy voice. The refrain was rousing, the melody simple, like something you'd sing at a hootenany:

> The macoute will have to eat shit for a long, long time.
> A long, long time.

Scenes from a revolution. Songs of victory. But finally you had to ask, What revolution? What victory?

Back at the Oloffson, Richard Morse and RAM were making their own preparations to play for the soon-to-be-elected president. The occupation, the restoration of Aristide and democracy, had brought a musical renaissance to the island—the bands, like Boukman Eksperyans, returning home from overseas, upstart groups moving onto the airwaves. RAM was there as always, the Thursday-night gigs packing the hotel, and always in favor at the palace, which, after Préval's inauguration in 1996, would once again sponsor Richard and the band during carnival.

Amid the onslaught of fresh sounds, RAM struggled to maintain its popularity. They needed a new album, and so for the next year Richard shuttled the musicians in and out of the studio, recording *Puritan Voodoo*. He lavished extra attention on the cut to be released for the upcoming carnival season. "Zanj"—angel—was one of a flurry of in-production carnival songs with lyrics that targeted the *Gran Manjé*—the big eaters, people in the splintering Lavalas government who had sold out, who had forgotten their roots among the people, who were lining their own pockets. Who had forgotten how much the people had suffered to bring them home. "Zanj," like "Fey," was a parable, full of mystical references, but its protest against hypocrisy and excess was anything but opaque, the lyrics denouncing "people who sit down and eat with you, and then try to poison you."

When "Zanj" began to air, in late January 1997, people in Port-au-Prince assumed, for several reasons, that the song was about the increasingly imperious mayor, Manno Charlemagne. Manno had alienated the *marchands,* sending the police to drive them off the streets, alienated the crowd who enjoyed the late-night sprees at the honky-tonks, alienated the elites, naturally, and continued to have a poor relationship with the palace, with the United Nations, with just about everybody, another man in city hall unwilling to listen, a stranger to compromise and intolerant of anyone who challenged his power. But since the invasion, power had shed the mystique of terror; the ones who wielded it had been chosen by the *pep,* the people. The friends of the people were running the country now, and the friends of the people were botching the job.

Richard told everybody he hadn't written "Zanj" with his friend the mayor in mind, but for more than a year Manno and his entourage had been encamped at the Oloffson without ever paying a bill, and the total bill had become astronomical, thousands of dollars. Richard kept asking the troubadour-turned-politician to pay up, Manno would slide past, smiling, trailed by his gunmen, and that went on until a few days before carnival. Manno had a pair of Canadian women, documentary filmmakers, living in his room, and Richard ordered his staff to throw them out and put a padlock on the door. "People didn't die for three years," said Richard, "so Manno could come back and behave the way he's behaving."

That Thursday night before carnival, RAM was getting ready to do its regular gig when Manno showed up, his guys frisking people for weapons at the door, fifty, sixty pistols going into a footlocker for safekeeping. Manno strapped on his guitar and performed a set, singing the song that everybody now identified with the government, the song that you couldn't go anywhere in Haiti without hearing twenty-four hours a day on the radio. "Gran Manjé":

> *Bring the rope to tie up the big eater.*
> *He's eaten so much he has indigestion.*

No one knew why the president had come, but Préval was there in the audience, a pained expression on his face, staring at his feet. "I don't know who they're talking about," he mumbled. "What names exactly are they bringing up?" Manno could have answered those questions, because Manno himself had written the song, but the mayor and the president weren't on speaking terms. The troubadour finished his set and split, RAM came onstage, the president jumped out of his seat to dance, just another man of the people having a good time, and once again it looked like the same old pissing contest to Richard and the band. For two years in a row, the palace had sponsored RAM's carnival float, but that wasn't going to happen this year, and Richard found himself dependent on the largesse of city hall, because the mayor of Port-au-Prince was responsible for funding all the bands participating in the capital's carnival, and all the bands but RAM had already received their flatbed trucks and the money to build their floats.

That was a problem, and not insignificant. Everybody in the city counting the hours until carnival talked about it, putting stories together— Manno was furious about being locked out of his digs; Manno was taking RAM's carnival song too personally, as an allegorical indictment of himself. The same way the FADH couldn't stand still when they heard "Fey," the mayor, the people's hero, went crazy when he heard "Zanj."

Carnival without RAM? People throughout Port-au-Prince objected. That was unimaginable.

The president seized the opportunity to resolve the standoff in his favor the following day. He notified the mayor that the palace was transferring to city hall a sum sufficient to cover RAM's expenses for carnival. But the truth was, without Aristide the authority of the presidency itself had dwindled to the smallest embers, and even so trifling a ploy as this from the executive branch of government could be ignored without consequence. A flatbed truck did arrive at the Oloffson, dispatched by the mayor, and Richard told his carpenters and designers to begin building the float. The crew was three-fourths finished when Manno's gunmen drove up and ordered them to take it apart.

The next morning, Manno Charlemagne, himself a victim during the coup, was on the radio, saying things like, "I'm going over to the Oloffson with my guns and see if he'll throw me out now." The phones started ringing at city hall, people calling to tell Manno he was wrong, people calling him a vagabond, telling him to get control of himself—a perennial flaw among Haiti's politicians.

RAM never played at carnival. Richard had hit a nerve, a very raw nerve, and he was frightened by his confrontation with Port-au-Prince's mayor. In the capital, again the streets thundered with frustration—drums like a deafening cascade of rocks on the tin roofs of oppression, and music like a shout to the gods, a call for justice.

It makes you wonder, Richard kept telling people. What was this thing—*the situation*—all about?

The Haitians had been given what they prayed for, what they paid for in blood—freedom—but the nation was in shambles, and what was there to hope for now? People were beginning to say, Maybe the price of democracy is too high.

Haiti had no jobs to give its sons and daughters. The government had proved incapable of either reforming or privatizing its corrupt monopolies, foreign investors had stayed away, foreign aid was frozen in escrow. Lavalas had divided like an amoeba, each cell at the other's throat. The bureaucracy was paralyzed with incompetence, elected officials were strangling on their own greed, and parliamentary elections had been dishonest. Electricity and water were still a lottery you would never win; roads remained impassable, and people were starving. The narcotraffickers were back in business, crime was ubiquitous, the elite families had hired private armies, and an epidemic of assassinations had been orchestrated by—depending on who was raking through the evidence—Aristide, the oligarchic families on the mountaintop, or the CIA. The president was a sullen drunk, and the ex-president, toasted by Anthony Lake at his wedding, had become a husband and a father, a family man who lived in a big house with a swimming pool, separated from the people by the high walls of silence.

Carnival, 1998. Fearing a repeat of last year's violence, RAM had decided not to play, but ten days before the festivities commenced, President Preval intervened, personally inviting the band to play on the presidential float. "You're not going to disappoint us, are you?" Preval chided Richard Morse. Manno Charlemagne relented and allowed RAM to join the celebration, arranging for the city's port authority to provide a driver for the band's float, which Richard had decorated with angels. For six hours, the float, atop its forty-foot flat-bed truck, inched through the crowds in the streets toward the mayor's reviewing stand, where the driver stopped momentarily, then stepped on the gas, careening into the mob of dancers. "Stop the float!" Lunise screamed into the microphone, to no avail. "Stop the float!" Gerrard Laforrest, the chief of RAM's security team, was the first person killed. The driver plowed onward through waves of celebrants, jumped the curb in an attempt to tip the float, then smashed into a tree. Equipment and people on the float were pitched into the air; a drummer broke both legs. The band's generator burst into flames; people trying to put out the fire were beaten by unknown assailants. Then the silence descended, disrupted only by sirens and the cries of the injured—dozens of victims, and eight people dead. Ten minutes later, the president's rapid deployment force arrived on the scene, forming a protective cordon around the toppled float. Hidden inside the wreckage by their friends, Richard and Lunise hopped to the ground, running for their lives through the back alleys of Port-au-Prince until they were finally safe, for the moment, inside the Oloffson. The driver was jailed for several weeks, then—so the story went—whisked away to a safe haven in Panama.

And this time, nobody could plead, *Where are the Americans?* because the Americans were already there.

> Why have you come to save me?
> Why have you come to save me?
> You, America, have saved me.
> Who will save me now?

Afterword

As I sit to write this, ten unimaginably horrific days have passed since the United States and the world cast its eyes once again upon the never-ending drama of Haiti, mesmerized by the apocalyptic devastation caused by the earthquake that transformed much of Port-au-Prince and its environs into blood-soaked rubble and, for the moment, the most visible nightmare on earth. Beyond the moment, it will be determined that the earthquake that struck the island on January 12, 2010, and its $13 billion price tag, enters history as the largest natural disaster visited upon any single nation in living memory.

North of the city, notorious godforsaken Tintayen, the old dumping ground for the victims of the dictators and putschists, rumbles anew with macabre activity, bulldozers excavating mass graves for the uncountable and forever nameless dead. The official toll will climb to two hundred fifty thousand (the entire population of Port-au-Prince a mere fifty years ago, though it is impossible to know how many souls remain interred beneath the crumpled buildings or concealed in the debris. Another hundred thousand have suffered ghastly life-threatening wounds; perhaps double that amount are at risk of infection from less serious injuries. Several thousand limbs will be amputated in conditions reminiscent of field hospitals during the American Civil War. Tens of thousands of children have joined the Dickensian ranks of Haiti's orphans. More than half of Port-au-Prince's two million people find themselves in a vertiginous limbo, unhoused and dispossessed and unfed, sleeping under the stars, which will soon enough be obscured by the rainy season. A third of Haiti's nine million people cannot exist day to day without the charity of international aid.

One out of every two structures in Port-au-Prince collapsed and many of those still standing are fractured and unsafe. Provincial cities, in particular Jacmel and Leogane, have been leveled. The wharves of the capital's central port buckled into the sea, destroyed along with Haiti's most treasured landmarks—the National Palace, National Cathedral, the National Museum of Art—and various symbols that had created the facade of a civil society and state—the Parliament, the United Nations headquarters, the swank Hotel Montana (Richard Morse and the Hotel Oloffson survived), the Palace of Justice and National Penitentiary, along with scores of police stations, municipal buildings, banks and businesses. The city's hospitals lay in shambles, as well as more than 90 percent of its schools, entire classrooms of students entombed at their desks. Supermarkets pancaked, shantytowns toppled over like the house of cards they actually were. Suffused by the ubiquitous reek of death, the roll call of destruction seems all-encompassing and, for once, without discrimination. Survivors of Hiroshima or Dresden could hardly have been more dazed.

What to make of all this suffering? Foreign commentators have invoked the vengeful hand of the Almighty or ancient pacts with the devil. The Haitians themselves gather in the unlit streets at night to sing thanks and praise to their Lord. You would be hard-pressed to find another culture on Earth that more reveres the breath of God in all of its many manifestations.

A catastrophe of biblical proportions, declared Secretary of State Hillary Clinton, and the volume of humanitarian aid streaming onto the island—bolstered by donations from more than half of American households—has been staggering. What remains to be seen, of course, is not the perseverance of the Haitians themselves—against all odds, they have always endured—but the stamina of those governments and organizations freshly committed not just to a beleaguered nation's recovery, as if putting Haiti back together as it was before would be any occasion for applause, but to the opportunity to build a Haiti that can finally and permanently transcend its centuries-long shackling to misfortune. One can only wish that the monumental task of recovery will be undertaken in the collective spirit of a barn-raising, rather than the green light we have come to expect that throws open the gates to the cattle rustlers. Regrettably, the damage wrought by the current assault of natural disasters, beginning with an enfilade of killer hurricanes in 2004 and 2008, has been magnified and deepened by profound human malfeasance, with plenty of blame to go around.

Perhaps on this occasion we can all agree that Haiti has finally found its bottom, but the descent, lubricated by man-made folly, was not inevitable, no matter how much a shifting fault line beneath the surface of the Earth might appear to underwrite a nation's destiny. The politics of predation and arrogance, coupled with the economics of heedless self-interest, aggravated by a racially charged paternalism, have proven over time to be a far greater author of Haiti's fate than the lethal caprice of nature against which all nations must test their strength and strengthen their vulnerabilities.

Like many Haitians and Americans who know the island and its star-crossed history, I had mixed feelings watching the video of former President Bill Clinton step off a plane onto the tarmac at Toussaint Loverture International airport on a Monday afternoon almost a week after the earthquake. Bill Clinton, the Second Coming of Hope. As you know from reading this book, the First Coming, adorned with twenty thousand American troops, did not turn out so well. More than a decade later, by almost every verifiable measure, Haiti was worse off than it was before Clinton had "rescued" the fledgling democracy from the illegitimate regime of General Raoul Cedras and his bloodthirsty network of paramilitary militias and terrorist enforcers. Ten years later, that network of forces was back in power again, aided and abetted by a cabal of inside-the-beltway policy makers angrily denounced as "the *chimeres* of Washington," by Ambassador Brian Dean Curran (Haiti, 2000–2003). *Chimere*, a Creole word which means a shape-shifting ghost, became synonymous with political thug, and was more commonly associated with the street gangs Jean-Bertrand Aristide was accused of arming and orchestrating against his virulent opposition.

A brief checklist tells not the story itself but rather the story's wretched consequences. Before the quake, Haiti's rank on the United Nations Development Index was 146 out of 177. Four out of five Haitians live in poverty, more than half in abject destitution. One percent of the population still stuffs its pockets with nearly half of the country's wealth. Drug trafficking —Haiti is the region's major transshipment venue for cocaine headed to the United States from South America—is a billion dollar a year enterprise on the island, hollowing out the country's judicial system and police force with the rot of corruption. An illiteracy rate hovering just under 50 percent, an unemployment rate stuck at around 70 percent. A daily wage (for the lucky few) that would not cover the cost of a regular cup of coffee at Starbucks. Although the pre-quake trend had begun to show some progress, Haiti has the highest rate of mortality for infants, under-5 children, and mothers giving birth in the Western hemisphere. In the United States, eleven women out of one hundred thousand die during childbirth; in Haiti, 670 women die.

Clinton's post-quake arrival had been preceded only months earlier by a two-day investment conference he had convened in Port-au-Prince as the United Nations special envoy for Haiti. The ex-president was trying to round up wary entrepreneurs to transfuse jobs and money into an economy that Clinton himself had played a major role in decimating when he slammed economic sanctions on the island in the early 1990s. The assembly line industry in Port-au-Prince, which then employed more than one hundred thousand people, plunged into a tail spin; more than eighty thousand of those jobs were still nowhere to be found when envoy Clinton's hopeful gathering of investors flew away mostly unimpressed and noncommittal before another year turned in Haiti's calendar of futility. Cue the earthquake.

At the investors' conference attended to a large extent by garment manufacturers, special envoy Clinton told a reporter that he "hated" enforcing economic sanctions against Haiti during his presidency. "But when you have people being burned to death with tires around their necks, that's important, too," he said. "We had to bring an end to that."

But an end to what, exactly? What initially struck me about his reference to burning tires was that it seemed to suggest Clinton had forgotten just whose side he had intervened on in Haiti in 1994. The bad guys, with a too enthusiastic wink and a nod from Aristide, were the fellows being necklaced or otherwise strung up by pro-democracy mobs. Ostensibly, Clinton sent the U.S. military ashore to support the good guys, the desperate Haitians whose hunger for their freely elected leader and rule of law exceeded their more immediate pangs for food. Then, upon further reflection, it struck me that Clinton had not forgotten at all, given his policy to deliberately blur the distinction between pro-democratic and anti-democratic forces on the stage of Haiti's political theater. Lo and behold, the illusion eventually gave birth to the reality. Which is to say, everybody became a bad guy by one template or another, thus fulfilling a suspicion the White House had certainly harbored all along. To be sure, Haiti brings out the cynic in me. Perhaps I should express that uneasy state of mind with more precision: the United States's two-faced relationship with Haiti stirs a cynicism within me that I'd rather not claim and yet there it is.

In all fairness to the enigmatic, self-deluded, politically juvenile and morally compromised Aristide, even if he could have been the type of leader that his people so desperately needed him to be, he never had a chance to succeed, given what he was up against. We Americans ruined Haiti's already feeble economy in 1994, and again in 2000, with ill-conceived sanctions and embargoes that only succeeded in punishing the guiltless masses and further eroding the feeble apparatus of Haiti's security, another slower and more sanitized version of destroying the village to save it. We whitewashed the bad guys, and encouraged the good men and women in our military to collaborate with monsters. The $3.2 billion we spent in Haiti during Clinton's tenure was the cost of intervention and occupation, not the cost of democracy, which is a bit more pricey, given the long-term investment of building the institutional firmament required to uphold the weight of such a righteous dream. We walked out on the mission, handing off to another underfunded and disorganized UN task force and then invaded again with a smaller footprint in 2004 and handed off again to a second UN Task Force that was only beginning to get its bearings in the year preceding the earthquake.

Clinton's number one legacy in Haiti is clear and its impact unrelenting. His administration wasted a perfectly good occupation, refused to engage in all but the smallest gestures of nation-building, and, just as his predecessors Ronald Reagan and Bush Pere did (remember Duvalierism without Duvalier?), left the poison in the system. Nobody afterward could flush it out. Or cared to, until the day arrived to overthrow the legitimate government of Aristide a second time, and by then the poison had contaminated everything. When the Haitian *merde* finally hit the Washington fan, our government preferred to do business with the "loyal opposition," the very same ensemble of murderers, narco-traffickers, oligarchs, and terrorists the U.S. Army Special Forces had once been tasked to run to ground. But this time around the American taxpayers weren't funding our troops—instead, our money went to support the *malfacteurs*.

*   *   *

We sent as our emissaries diplomats and bureaucrats and radical partisan apparatchiks who did not genuinely believe in the fundamental goodness and promise of Haiti's long-suffering people or agree with their elected choice of leadership, among them Timothy Carney, a Clinton-appointed ambassador who I and two other journalists had dinner with at his residence up the mountain near Petionville in 1999. When I asked Carney to share with us the story behind his appointment, he told me he was at his previous post in Africa when Strobe Talbot rang him up and asked him to go to Haiti. Puffing on a Cuban cigar ("I'm burning the crops of the enemy," he joked), Carney said to me, "I told Strobe, 'No way, the Haitians are maggots.' and Talbot said, 'Yeah, I know, but we need you there.'"

That about sums up the Clinton administration's duplicitous posture toward Haiti, and nicely foreshadows the perfidious intensification of contempt toward the island on display when Republicans took over the White House in 2001.

A month after the earthquake, National Public Radio's Deborah Amos, interviewing the former ambassador, asked him about the rebuilding of Haiti.

"I'll tell you frankly," said Carney, "the world also has to have some expectations of Haiti, and one of them is an end to this sterile politics of group and gang with an eye on personal advantage that has dominated the politics of Haiti for—well, since its independence."

Amos went on to invoke the vast amount of money the United States has spent on Haiti over the years and wondered, "Have we been taking the wrong approach here?"

"I think that's probably Monday morning quarterbacking," Carney replied. "The fact is, we haven't really known for sure what approach to take." He riffed for a moment on the vibrancy of Haiti's culture "as reflected in all the arts. On the other hand," he continued, "you have a record—in fact the most dismal imaginable record of governance, one worthless dictator after another preying upon the people to line their pockets and to luxuriate in power. How do you break that in order to put Haiti into a new mold? I don't know."

Well, now, speaking of indefensible records, here's an ideologue who could teach me a thing or two about cynicism. As I recall, Aristide broke the old mold only to have the Carneys and their agenda-driven neo-con cohorts conspire to glue it back together. Carney's disingenuous remarks to NPR and their phony tonality of concern merit a closer look at the very robust role the ambassador played in the outrageous political shenanigans that functioned as an accelerant for Haiti's tragedy.

Mr. Carney has been accurately described by one blogger as a man with "an incredible ability to be in the wrong place whenever the U.S. wanted to do the wrong thing," starting with his first foreign service officer career posting in Saigon, arriving on the same schedule as the Tet offensive. Later we find him in Cambodia with a front-row seat for the Khmer Rouge's rise to power, in South Africa at the height of the apartheid crisis, in Somalia in 1993, in Sudan in 1995, and in Haiti, where he took over from William Swing in January 1998 until December 1999, retiring from the State Department in 2000 but returning to Port-au-Prince for an encore performance as acting ambassador from August 2005 until February 2006.

In 1966, in *The Arrogance of Power*, Senator William Fullbright wrote that "power confuses itself with virtue" in U.S. foreign policy, and you'd have to flip a coin to determine who in Haiti had the more unflagging messianic complex, Tim Carney or Jean-Bertrand Aristide. Once he took up battle stations in the embassy, and even after he had left the island, Carney, a stalwart crusader for American exceptionalism and artful practitioner of Machiavellian tactics, "worked for years to undermine Haiti's security and stability," according to the Haitian Lawyers Leadership Network. Behind the embassy's curtains, the ambassador played Wizard of Oz, puppeteer for efforts to bring down the Lavalas government and rebrand the poison—former Duvalierists, Cedras's cashiered FAHD officers, FRAPH renegades, and the old oligarchical families—as "civil society," a euphemism for a sinister coalition of opposition groups lacking any true constituency, managed by anti-Aristide foundations in Washington, funded by the federal government, and championed by Carney, an impresario of Haiti's infamous "democracy enhancement" fake-out.

Thanks to the entire cast of characters, Haitians and foreigners alike, President Rene Preval's first government could mostly be defined by paralysis and deadlock, the Lavalas movement splintering into myriad factions dominated by Aristide's own political party, Famni Lavalas, an overboiling cauldron of half-cooked democracy. Legitimacy flowed upward and into the Haitian government but its translation into actual power was marginal at best. Lured into a cage of dubious economic reforms by the red-meat pledge of aid, against the protests of its populace base the National Palace acquiesced to U.S.-promoted agricultural policies that cost an estimated 830,000 rural jobs, and reluctantly agreed to begin privatizing state-owned sources of revenue. None of these structural readjustments to the crippled Haitian economy made that economy any healthier but instead knee-capped its capacity for real development. Unable to organize local and parliamentary elections on schedule for the end of 1998, the hapless government could only stand by while the tenure of Parliament's deputies expired in 1999 and wait until a majority of political parties agreed to postpone new elections until they could be conducted properly. Preval then closed Parliament's doors and ruled by (benign) decree until elections were held in May 2000 and a new Parliament called to order a few months later. A legitimate mess, muddled with dirty tricks yet peacefully resolved, but the public relations damage to the Haitian government was incalculable and, it turned out, irreversible. Once more, the extended hand of promised aid was withdrawn.

A few months before the 2000 elections I was invited to Arlington, Virginia, by the State Department to attend a symposium on Haiti, where I was again reminded that America's dedication to the unimpeachable voice of the ballot box is one of our nation's most depressing hypocrisies. The lip service on this occasion generated a melodious hum of earnestness until it was nullified by the USAID elections consultant for Haiti who explained to the gathering, with the help of a pointer and blackboard and overhead projector, some of the tactics the U.S. government and its minions would be employing to thwart Aristide's forthcoming re-election.

Under Carney's watch, crucial factors in the electoral delays were no mystery. The United States demanded photo ID cards for every voter in the country, an absurd requirement in a nation devoid of infrastructure and institutional competence. A shortage of ID cards caused a fiasco, and ballots, printed in the United States and shipped to the island, arrived late and without enough to go around. Irregularities, as you might expect, multiplied like frogs in the rainy season, and the delays were ruthlessly exploited by the opposition, who decided to boycott elections they never had the slightest chance of winning. The resulting stalemate, which Aristide blames for many of his countries woes, provoked foreign donors to withhold hundreds of millions of dollars in aid to Haiti for the next four years.

Rehabilitated and nurtured by Carney and friends—the International Republican Institute, the Haiti Democracy Project, the National Endowment for Democracy—Colonel Boyatt's "loyal opposition" had come home to roost, but in a slithering form I doubt the good colonel ever could have imagined. A private organization created by Congress to promote democracy "consistent with the broad concerns of U.S. national interest," the National Endowment for Democracy had been involved in Haiti since 1986. Its first president, Allen Weinstein, brazenly told *The Washington Post* in 1991, "A lot of what [NED] does today was done covertly twenty-five years ago by the CIA." The NED, always working hand in hand with USAID, helped fund former World Bank official Marc Bazin's candidacy against Aristide in 1990. After the coup d'etat, Bazin served as a prime minister under Cedras, the technocratic overseer of rampant corruption, violence, and repression. During the electoral delay in 1999, NED grants helped fund the creation of a faux-opposition party, Espace de Concertacion, which under further guidance from the U.S. embassy, mutated into a more virulent group named the Democratic Convergence. More about the Convergence in a moment.

Enter onto the stage another organization created by Congress, the International Republican Institute (IRI), whose mission is to "support the growth of political and economic freedom, good governance, and human rights around the world by educating people, parties, and governments on the values and practices of democracy." The IRI is loosely affiliated with the Republican Party, works closely with the National Endowment for Democracy, USAID, the State Department, with additional funding from corporate birds of a feather like Halliburton.

Investigative reporter Max Blumenthal paints a blood-chilling picture of how well the IRI's man in Haiti, Stanley Lucas, went about promoting the values and practices of democracy:

"On February 8, 2001, the federally funded International Republican Institute's senior program officer for Haiti, Stanley Lucas, appeared on the Haitian station Radio Tropicale, to suggest three strategies for vanquishing Haiti's president, Jean-Bertrand Aristide. First, Lucas proposed forcing Aristide to accept early elections and be voted out; second, he could be charged with corruption and arrested; and finally, Lucas raised dealing with Aristide the way the Congolese people had dealt with President Laurent Kabila the month before. 'You did see what happened to Kabila?' Lucas asked his audience."

Kabila had been assassinated.

Lucas, described by *The New York Times* as "an avowed Aristide opponent from the Haitian elite, [who] counseled the opposition to stand firm, and not work with Mr. Aristide, as a way to cripple his government and drive him from power," arrived at IRI in Haiti in 1992 and by 1998, around the time Carney showed up for the fun, Lucas controlled a three million dollar budget to be spent on unifying anybody with a gripe against Aristide and encourage them to become Haiti's very own Party of No, the Democratic Convergence, which Lucas midwifed into existence in 1999. Blumenthal viewed Lucas as the Haitian version of the Iraqi exile Ahmed Chalabi. "Like Chalabi," Blumenthal wrote, "Lucas ingratiated himself with powerful Republicans sympathetic to regime change in his native country and lobbied for increased funding to . . . reactionary political elements far more undemocratic than Aristide."

The Convergence, stepping aside in the 2000 elections to watch the sweep by Lavalas candidates, had proved to be a straw man until it leveled charges of fraud at the process, which the Clinton administration seized upon to block four hundred million dollars in multilateral loans to the Haitian government. Blumenthal: "As economic conditions deteriorated, Convergence changed its tactics. In addition to boycotting the 2000 presidential elections, between 2000 and 2002 Convergence rejected twenty proposed power-sharing proposals designed to ease Haiti's political crisis."

On November 19, 2002, a rather inauspicious event took place at the Brookings Institute in Washington, D.C.—the launching of something called the Haiti Democracy Project, a right-wing think tank founded by Republican officials in the State Department and Haitian elites, heavily financed by an imperious anti-Aristide doctor in Haiti named Rudolph Boulos. The head of HDP was none other than former ambassador Tim Carney, and the opening-night ceremony was attended by IRI's Stanley Lucas and a Miami-based Haitian businessman named Oliver Nadal, who just so happened to be implicated by human rights organizations in a peasant massacre in the Haitian town of Piatre. It was a distinction Nadal, the former president of Haiti's Chamber of Commerce, shared with a pair of Lucas's cousins, who arranged the slaughter of 250 peasants in 1987 in Jean Rebel, the hometown of Lucas's land-owning family. A week after the HDP's debut, Carney was quoted saying, "The big question is whether Aristide is going to understand that he has no future." For the next two years, under the auspices of the HDP, Carney was at the front of a rabid smear and disinformation campaign targeted at the removal of Aristide.

As for dead-ends ahead in anyone's future, Carney might also have said the same for the only American diplomat who retained his integrity during the Aristide era, Brian Dean Curran, a thirty-year veteran of the foreign service who took over as another Clinton-appointed ambassador in early in 2001. Curran's complaints and warnings about Lucas's activities—shuttling Convergence leaders to Washington to meet with Republican heavyweights on Capitol Hill, conducting subversive training sessions for hundreds of opposition members in the Dominican Republic—were flagrantly ignored by both the IRI and Curran's own chain of command in the State Department, stacked with discredited veterans of the Iran-Contra affair (Otto Reich and Elliot Abrams) and former protégés (Daniel Fisk, Roger Noriega) of Senator Jesse Helms (a Cedras supporter who believed Aristide was a psychopath and the next Castro), and at the National Security Council. At the time, Lucas told Haiti's current (2010) prime minister, Jean-Max Bellerive, that "there was a big plan for Haiti that came from Washington, that Aristide would not finish his mandate," and that "Curran was of no importance, that he did not fit in the big picture." When Lucas heard that Curran had called for his dismissal, he confronted and threatened the ambassador and another embassy official. The ambassador, said Lucas, would be out of a job "as soon as the real U.S. policy is implemented."

Unlike Curran, honorably pursuing the Bush White House's officially stated policy to chaperone Haiti's infant democracy by working in good faith with the elected government, Stanley Lucas knew what he was talking about. Under Lucas's tutelage, the Convergence refused to negotiate with Aristide, or accept any of the power-sharing deals that Aristide had agreed to. In the meantime, leaders of the Convergence had begun to conspire with and clandestinely fund a steadily growing assemblage of former FAHD soldiers and police, FRAPH gunmen, narco-traffickers, and assorted criminals camped in the Dominican Republic, led by Guy Phillipe, a former FAHD soldier assimilated into Lavalas, through which he reinvented himself as a fearsome, gang-slaying commander in the Haitian National Police from 1995 until 2000. In October of that year, however, he bolted into exile after his plans for a coup d'état against the Preval government were exposed.

It's worth noting that the Haitian National Police, created by the United States after the 1994 invasion, had a tendency for internecine warfare, playing assassination tag accompanied by a soundtrack of accusations and counter-accusations when they weren't otherwise busy facilitating drug lords, executing punks on the street, shaking down the general population, or doing absolutely nothing at all. A favorite pastime in Haiti's politics, the game of who-done-it often atrophied with opacity, defaulting toward head-scratching and eye-rolling, a plethora of varied suspects, and a general atmosphere of impunity.

When Aristide disbanded Haiti's worthless but nevertheless feral army in 1995, a military that had distinguished itself only in the annals of abuse, the majority of recruits into the new police force were cashiered soldiers, including the organization's top man, a former FAHD officer named Dany Toussaint, an Aristide loyalist (and alledged assassin) who, like many of the upper echelon of the HNP, would seesaw between allegiance and treachery in their posture toward both the National Palace and the rather straightforward tenets of democracy and justice. These men, responsible for their nation's security, were in fact complicit in its insecurity, and certainly no one Aristide could rely on for defense against the ever more aggressive opposition. Lavalas attempted to counterbalance the threat against its existence with what were called OPs, *organisations populaire,* the more militant among them morphing into the wild gun-toting neighborhood gangs known as *chimeres,* which functioned as attaché-like auxiliaries to the police and, like their sponsors in the HNP and the palace itself, their loyalty too was often shape-shifting.

Into this combustible heap of players, the Democratic Convergence introduced its opening gambit immediately following Aristide's second inauguration in February 2001, refusing to acknowledge the president's authority, announcing their intent to establish a parallel government, and calling for the restoration of the army. Under extreme pressure from reactionaries on the right, Aristide sought to mollify his opponents with a tainted package of diversity, padding his new cabinet with corrupt ministers with direct ties to the Duvalier and Cedras regimes and entertaining neoliberal economic reforms long rejected by his grassroots populist base in the Lavalas movement, which had become increasingly disillusioned with the graft, remoteness and in-fighting in the president's own political party, Famni Lavalas (FL), dominating Parliament. Outside the country, Aristide's cheerleaders were disheartened by Parliament's grant of immunity to FL Senator Dany Toussaint, Aristide's former security chief, indicted for the murder of Haiti's most influential and beloved journalist, the outspoken Jean Dominque.

Later that year, Aristide's political opponents began to experiment with armed insurrection, sponsoring criminal cadres of ex-soldiers in July attacks on police stations around the country, including the police academy in Port-au-Prince, and a well-planned commando-style assault on the National Palace in December by former members of FAHD and the palace guard. An OAS investigation of the attempted coup reported that the assailants who temporarily occupied the palace without resistance from its guards radioed out that Jean-Bertrand Aristide was no longer president and that Guy Phillipe was the new commander of the National Police of Haiti, although Phillipe did not participate directly in the assault and, in a 2007 interview with author Peter Hallward, implicated leaders of the Democratic Convergence as the architects of the attack.

Phillipe told Hallward that after he arrived in exile in the Dominican Republic at the end of 2000, leaders of Convergence traveled to the DR to ask Phillipe to "help them save the country" and from that point on, began plotting with Phillipe to bring down the government, eventually funneling hundreds of thousands of dollars to his camp to be spent on arms, ammunition, and salaries. In return for his help, the opposition leaders and elite businessmen promised Phillipe that he and his paramilitaries would be handed responsibility for Haiti's security in the *apre*-Aristide world. During the same time frame, Stanley Lucas was conducting his so-called Democracy 101 training sessions for Aristide's opposition, openly counseling hundreds of attendees to reject any reconciliation process, sessions that he would later transfer to a more private venue at the Hotel Santo Domingo in the Dominican Republic, where he occasionally ran into Phillipe, one of the hotel's residents. Lucas and Phillipe were also reported together at a club in Ecuador, where during the Cedras regime Phillipe and several of his comrades had once been trained as FAHD cadets by U.S. and Ecuadoran Special Forces. After Aristide's ouster, Lucas vehemently protested any attempt to connect him personally with Guy Phillipe, and Phillipe remained coy about their relationship, revealing only that he had known Stanley Lucas since he, Phillipe, was seven years old and that Lucas had taught him how to play ping-pong.

A few months before the July attacks in 2001, Phillipe began pulling together the disenfranchised ex-soldiers and outlaws from the Cedras regime and recruiting his high command of rogues, including Jodel Chamblain, cofounder of FRAPH with Toto Constant, a death squad leader convicted in abstentia and sentenced to life imprisonment for the assassination of a pro-Aristide businessman in 1993 and a massacre of Aristide supporters the following year. In 2002, the government's crackdown against the opposition after the December assault on the palace inspired equally forceful reprisals from the nascent ex-military groups taking up arms, which launched a campaign of hit-and-run attacks against government officials, most intensively across the Central Plateau in what appeared to be a revised strategy to drag Aristide into a destabilizing low-level guerilla war.

In September of 2003, new ambassadors arrived in Port-au-Prince from the United States (James Foley) and France. The tipping point for the insurrection came in the northern port of Gonaives in that same month, when the leader of a gang called the Cannibal Army, Amiot Metayer, was shot in both eyes and through the heart by an unknown gunman. The death of Metayer, a longtime Aristide supporter whose gang was fond of intimidating opposition members, shed light on the shallowness of the loyalty to the Lavalas movement claimed by many of the gangs throughout Haiti. The police arrested Metayer in May 2002 on arson charges in connection with an attack against a rival gang, house-torching a favorite activity of the Cannibal Army. In August, he broke out of prison and was soon back in Gonaives on an unchecked rampage for the next twelve months, battling with anybody who crossed him, especially Aristide opponents, until he showed up dead and mutilated on a side street twenty-five miles to the south in St. Marc.

The following day, the Cannibal Army and its sympathizers went berserk, burning tires and blocking roads to protest Metayer's murder, and no one seemed terribly surprised when Amiot's brother, Buteur, arrived from North Miami, accused Aristide of responsibility for Metayer's death, renamed the Cannibal Army the National Revolutionary Front for the Liberation of Haiti, and joined forces with the anti-Aristide opposition. On February 1, far to the north in Montreal, the Ottawa Initiative, a conference hosted by Canada and attended by U.S., French, Canadian, and Latin American officials, was convened to discuss regime change in Haiti and outline a scheme for the future of Haiti's government. For months the

Liberation Front rioted in the streets of Gonaives, skirmishing with the outgunned, outmanned police, and then on February 5, 2004, Buteur, reinforced with men and weapons supplied by the Democratic Convergence and Guy Phillipe, sacked and took control of the city, overran the police station, and burned it down after looting its weapons and vehicles. Within days a full-scale insurgency was roaring down the coast to St. Marc. By February 17 rebel gangs led by Lodel Chamblain captured the city of Hinche, and Guy Phillipe and his army of a few hundred men, the Front for National Reconstruction, had begun their march westward from the Dominican border to Cap-Haitien, which they captured and terrorized on February 22. By February 24, half the country was under control of Phillipe's thugs.

Then Phillipe began his journey south down Route National One toward Port-au-Prince, where Convergence leaders easily continued to resist insincere attempts from the French and American embassies to get the opposition to sit down and negotiate with a willing Aristide. By February 28, Phillipe had advanced within striking distance of the city and stopped to prepare an attack against the barricaded capital on March 2 or 3, its streets thronged with Aristide supporters determined to protect the president, but the dark genius of the Convergence was never more in evidence than at this moment of its leaders' brinkmanship, stalling Phillipe on the outskirts of Port-au-Prince while they convinced the Americans, Phillipe would later say in an interview with Peter Hallward, "to kidnap Aristide in order to prevent me, Guy Phillipe, from taking power and setting up a government in Haiti like the one Chavez set up in Venezuela," which is indeed what the extraordinarily naive Phillipe had expected to do. At the behest of the United States and France (a country infuriated by Aristide's demands that the French repay the $21 billion it had extorted from its former slave colony), Aristide's appeal for international peacekeeping forces had been rejected by the UN Security Council on February 26. Two days later, Colin Powell and Condoleezza Rice reversed the Bush administration's official position of support for Aristide and told Haiti's freely elected president to sign a letter of resignation, which he did, and get on a plane they were sending the next day to take him into exile, which Aristide also did, he said, to avoid a bloodbath. Within hours of Aristide's departure, a thousand American marines were on the ground in Haiti, putting the kibosh on Guy Phillipe's grand vision to be the new chief of the nation he had been duped into handing back over to his bosses, the leaders of the Convergence and their IRI-created affiliate, Group 184, a coalition of businessmen. On March 4, the men Phillipe now calls "Haiti's rotten political class and mafioso oligarchy . . . traitors, subhumans, cowards and opportunists," signed a tripartite agreement with France and the United States establishing a procedure for installing an interim government. Before long, drug kingpins associated with Aristide's government were arrested, extradited to the United States, convicted, and jailed. Drug lords allied with the opposition—Dany Toussaint, Guy Phillipe, and the nephew of the new interim prime minister, Youri Latortue—were allowed to stay in business. The narcotics shake-up resulted in what would qualify on Wall Street as a redirected cash flow. The tonnage of cocaine shipments through the island nudged upward, as it had in Panama after the drug-related ouster of General Manuel Noriega. Just to ensure clarity about what in fact was going on, the U.S.-approved interim prime minister, a Haitian businessman returned from exile in Boca Raton, Florida, made a pilgrimage to the grave side of Amiot Metayer in a suburb in Gonaives to hail Guy Phillipe and the former Cannibal Army as "freedom fighters" and thank them for their service to democracy.

U.S. troops left in June, handing off the tar baby of managing Haiti's security to a United Nations peacekeeping mission. The IRI's budget for exporting democracy, federally financed, tripled from 2003 to 2005, from $26 million dollars to $75 million. Democracy, George Bush said, was a "growth industry." Stanley Lucas, triumphant, was transferred to Afghanistan where he continued to export his special brand of human progress. The apotheosis of hubris and hypocrisy, Timothy Carney returned to his throne among the maggots, a seat that offered a bird's eye view of a human rights catastrophe greater than the one Clinton had tried to stop in 1994, the bloodbath that Aristide's departure was meant to avert, its body count during the two-year term of the interim government rising to eight thousand in the capital, according to a report in the British medical journal, *Lancet,* most of the victims Lavalas supporters. In the oh-by-the-way category, thirty-five thousand women and girls were sexually assaulted during the anarchy unleashed by Carney's dream-come-true regime change.

Once again, Haiti had become an object lesson on how to make a very bad omelette in the kitchen of democracy. Dressed up by the White House in the bogus finery of popular will, Aristide's resignation had the unpleasant distinction of being Haitian coup d'état Number 33, albeit a coup artfully finessed by the home team. Coup or abdication, the result was the same—an elected head of state that three American administrations could not abide had been snatched away by a mighty (foul) wind. Perhaps the only mystery is why it took so long.

Democracy doesn't need songbirds, it needs bricklayers. As invaders and occupiers, Presidents Clinton and Bush shared a tragic disregard for nation-building, a bipartisan reluctance to admit that the mechanisms of nation-building and the mechanisms of democracy are one and the same. Free and fair elections, in the absence of any viable infrastructure that institutionalizes the virtuous thrust of democracy, will eventually prove meaningless, a stagnant breeding pond for empty promises. The same truth goes for when you cut off international aid and loans to a country with no other resources for development or basic services. This equation is not beyond the intellectual capacities of these commanders-in-chief; each, for his own reasons, shrugged it aside in Haiti, with predictable results.

If you are a megalomaniac in Haiti, it's more or less your duty to run for president, and in the summer of 2005, the leaders of the Democratic Convergence and its henchman, Guy Phillipe, had a thrilling announcement to make: Not only were they not going to boycott the next presidential election, a decision received with grave indifference by the millions of Haitians unable to vote for these patriots in 2000, but the Convergence and its allies were going to field a generous slate of candidates as well, each running against each other for the privilege of winning the highest office in the land. Topping the list on separate tickets and representing their natural constituency of murderers, traitors, and hoodlums were Guy Phillipe (he received a thunderous 1.92 percent of the vote in the 2006 presidential race), the ex-Famni Lavalas senator and reputed assassin and narco-trafficker Dany Toussaint, who broke from Aristide just in time to help Metayer and his boys shoot up Gonaives (0.41 percent of the vote), and a motley field of scoundrels and vampires from the upper echelon of the coalition—the former FAHD colonel Himmler Rebu, one of the few big shots who seems to have actually participated directly in the armed insurrection; manufacturer Charles Baker, a member of the Group 184 who had worked tirelessly to erode his nation's sovereignty; former senator Serge Gilles, a Lucas favorite accused of organizing an attack on the Peligre dam in 2003; former Port-au-Prince mayor and Aristide back-stabber,

Evans Paul, the public spokesman for the Convergence. The good/bad guy Marc Bazin. The Macoute-loving Hubert de Ronceray and Franck Romain. Who am I forgetting? Given the breathtaking vanity of Haiti's ruling-class elite, I would not want to hurt anybody's feelings here by leaving them off the list of the bus load of unworthy candidates registered to stand for president in 2006.

The persistently underestimated Rene Preval's re-election to the National Palace in 2006 was in its way an unlikely happy ending to this story, reaffirming the durability of Lavalas as the expression of the Haitian people forever determined to be given the chance to lift themselves up out of misery. Despite his flaws, Aristide's great achievement was to persuade the world that the Haitian masses—the peasants and slum dwellers—were a political force that could join hands and hearts to alter the inconceivably cruel landscape of power on the island. The U.S.-backed opposition against Aristide never spent one second of their limitless energy, or one dime of their limitless wealth, trying to make life better for the Haitian people—better for anybody but themselves. Preval is Aristide without the baggage, shorn of the little priest's inflammatory rhetoric, Aristide's once and future proxy, both men committed to the welfare of the poor yet left with little choice but to accommodate the avarice and venality of the rich. Every politician in Haiti carries in his portfolio a vita of contradictions.

The re-election of Preval put to rest the pernicious lie that his predecessor was deposed by a popular uprising. When the earthquake struck, Jean-Bertrand Aristide petitioned Preval's government for permission to return home from his exile in South Africa to help his people during their time of endless need. Permission denied, and wisely so considering Haiti is in no shape to entertain the distraction of an unnecessary, toxic controversy, although you wouldn't lose money betting the odds on Aristide's prospects, given an opportunity to rejoin the fray, for the Haitian electorate to put him back in the palace for another tumultuous go-around.

And the bad guys know it.

Once again, the military's hospital ship, the *USS Comfort*, rides its anchor in the Bay of Gonave, its massive white hull a visible reminder that for the majority of those on shore who require it, help is nearby . . . nearby and still nearby while they writhe with grief and choke down patience. And for the third time since democracy was injected into the diseased metabolism of Haiti's body politic, American troops are on Haitian soil again in force, guarantors of a security most endangered by hyperventilating mainstream media types crying wolf and the ever more hazardous inability of the relief effort to figure out the logistics for the distribution of food, water, medication, and shelter to a traumatized and helpless population.

As I watched the de rigeur televised images of a volatile scrum of "looters" lifting bags of rice from the ruins of a downtown warehouse, Ernie called. Sergeant Ernie Brown, Third Group Special Forces, retired from the service in 2001 but rehired by the Special Operations Command at Ft. Bragg as a civilian, where he is still employed today. The last time I saw Ernie and his wife, Sandra, was shortly before Christmas 2004, when my Irish setters captured the attention of their five-year-old son; the time before that, I had ridden with Ernie and his brother in the limousine delivering the Green Beret to his wedding. We live far apart but as often as we can we make a point of being a part of each others life.

When he telephoned we discussed Haiti and the quake but spent most of our conversation talking where-are-they-now, Ernie briefing me on the Special Forces commandos we both knew who had served in Haiti. Colonel Mark Boyatt, forced into retirement not long after his command in Haiti, went to work for a defense contractor but these days you can see him back in the classrooms at Ft. Bragg's School House, the Green Beret's legendary special warfare training center. The last we heard of Captain Ed Barton, he had been moved to Seventh Group and sent to Colombia with a new Operational Detachment A-team to conduct counter-narcotic operations. Many of ODA-311's non-commissioned officers retired, although the attack on the towers of the World Trade Center brought them back into the military's orbit, working overseas for private security firms (Bob Fox in Iraq, Jim Pledger in Dubai) or as GS slot employees at United States Army Special Operations Command in Ft. Bragg (Bill Miatke, Ernie). The bald-headed Tet Cayle, Captain Craig Marks, also left the service to start, guess what, his own security company. Captains Stefanchik and Gottschalk were both promoted up the ranks to Lieutenant Colonel. Fritz Gottschalk went to Afghanistan, Mike Stefanchik worked at the Pentagon until a congenital heart defect strapped him onto an operating table to undergo surgery in 2009.

A pair of ODA 311's warriors remain on active duty—J. C. Collins and Walt Plaistad. Both became team sergeants—Tops—and J.C. is up for a promotion to sergeant major, the army's highest rank attainable for a NCO. Brothers-in-arms now for most of their adult lives, Walt and J.C. fought side by side together in Afghanistan's Helmand province in 2005, where Collins took shrapnel in his leg and Taliban bullets ripped through the scarf Walt had wrapped around his neck. One of their eleven team members and their interpreter were killed during the engagement. Four more Green Berets were wounded. That's the news from the land of the snake-eaters.

It's worth remembering that by the termination of the Vietnam War, the American military had become infected with a viral mistrust of the media, a condition still raging in the complicated relationship between journalists and soldiers by the time of the First Gulf War in 1991. That conflict appeared to balance out the relationship only in the sense that it reactivated the media's own mistrust of the military, thanks in no small measure to General Schwarzkopf's disdain for reporters in the field and his fierce obsession for controlling the narrative.

When Haiti popped up on the horizon, the Pentagon decided it was worth the risk to loosen the reigns on the media and began to allow journalists open and more intimate access to the troops, since the operational environment was already crawling with correspondents by the time the military came ashore. Upon occasion journalists simply self-embedded themselves into operations they stumbled upon. Some like myself were welcomed into this ad hoc arrangement, unknown to the chain of command but not necessarily prohibited. Naturally, the arrangement didn't always work. There were officers and enlisted men hostile to the media's unrestrained presence, constantly looking over their shoulders, eyeballing their every move, proffering judgements and opinions that were not always appreciated or well-informed.

But most soldiers cautiously welcomed the hounds into their midst, and a new generation of servicemen and women and a new generation of journalists were surprised by the result—a growing sense of mutual, if sometimes grudging, respect between the two entities for the professionalism, sacrifice, and humanity each exposed to the other. It wasn't exactly a love affair, but America was better served by a less antagonistic (though no less assertive) press and a less secretive, less insular military, a state of affairs that continued to mature throughout the conflicts in Bosnia and Kosovo and evolved into a truly symbiotic working relationship when the stakes were highest in Afghanistan and Iraq. It was a wake-up call for the military to recognize that journalists bleed for their country, too. Of course there were ample occasions you could point to where the tension and mistrust resurfaced, but the fact remained that since Haiti America's military and America's press corps have better understood and accepted each other's character, motivation, and vital obligations in a manner that had mostly been absent from the relationship since World War Two.

Because *The Immaculate Invasion* is as much about America's role in the world as it is about the Haitians, and about the complex set of challenges our military faces as it is deployed into the chaos of countries like Haiti, it strikes me as the right thing to do to let one of the soldiers who invaded the island in 1994 have the last word. Captain Tony Schwalm became Major Schwalm and, after 9/11, Lieutenant Colonel Schwalm of the U.S. Army Special Forces, stationed at Central Command in Tampa, where he was frequently called upon to brief a stunningly ignorant Secretary of Defense Rumsfeld about special operations in the Middle East and Central Asia. He retired from the military in 2009 and now works for a defense contractor in Virginia. In the aftermath of the earthquake, he sent me this e-mail, which I reproduce here with his permission.

"I heard a report on NPR saying that the Haitian government was in control of the relief effort and the security in the streets. 'Bullshit. How the fuck did that happen?' was all I could think. We have to alleviate the suffering, but my sense is that we intend to bring it back down to a tolerable level, for us, for the West. I imagine Haiti, with this earthquake, like a kid at school with intense dysfunctional social problems being crippled by an assault in the boy's room.

"I cannot comprehend the magnitude of the loss of life in Port-au-Prince. Interestingly, PAP was very full of people thanks to an effort by the previous administration to lower import tariffs on U.S. farm products. The result was the illegal immigrants of the San Joaquin Valley were used to flood the markets of Haiti with produce so cheaply that it drove the farmers off the land and into PAP to look for work. Certainly, the policy shift was not a causal factor in the loss of life, but it absolutely contributed to creating such a concentration in urban areas, PAP among the places people went looking for work.

"I've been getting e-mails from the 3rd SFG [Special Forces Group] mafia, most of us retired. No one laments the waste of our lives the invasion represents, but we all know and acknowledge we were part of a giant kabuki. My fondest memory of Haiti is from early on. We went east along the coastal road towards Belle Anse from Jacmel. We came across a private school of kindergartners. As I walked up in full kit, still carrying frag grenades, my pistol (round chambered) and my rifle (round chambered), the teacher opened the door and these little kids poured out, about thirty of them. The teacher had explained as we were parking that I, me, Tony Schwalm, had come to liberate them, to make their lives better. She recommended that they each give me a kiss. Holding the muzzle of my rifle nearly in the dirt, I bent down to let a class of five year olds kiss my cheek. It took about five minutes as they lined up to do it. They are all twenty-somethings now."

That image and its sentiment, despite the bittersweet innocence, are worth holding on to, preserved in a magic kingdom of honor and good intentions.

Acknowledgments

The author gratefully acknowledges the assistance of the U Cross Foundation in the completion of this work.

Additionally, I would like to thank several of the many people not mentioned in the text who unfailingly helped me along the way. From the beginning: Colin Harrison, Barbara Grossman, Lewis Lapham, Rick Mac-Arthur, Tom Shroder and the *Miami Herald*, Gail Hochman, and Mark Bryant. Throughout the years of the story, Joe Fischer, the historian at the John F. Kennedy School of Special Warfare, Colonel Ken McGraw, Jonathan Demme, and Ed Saxon provided invaluable guidance and fellowship. At the end of the road, Tracy Kidder, Meg Laughlin, Manish Nandy, Martha Cooley, Anna Hamilton Phelan, Bernard Diederich, Beena Kamlani, and Wendy Wolf provided lifesaving backup.

Thanks and ever thanks to Cat, for her unwavering enthusiasm and support. Amor, siempre.

Finally, blessings to the good citizens of Haiti, who have invariably treated me with generosity and kindness, and thanks to the Special Forces, particularly the men of Third Group, for what they shared with me . . . and for not shooting, when no reasonable person would have blamed them if they had.

Index

Hotel Roi Christophe in, 104, 106–8, 123, 126, 208, 255, 266–67, 292
penitentiary of, 106, 108–9, 124
Caputo, Dante, 37
Cardott, Gregory, 264, 269, 285
Carter, Jimmy, 53, 97, 292
Haitian accord brokered by, 70, 72, 74–77, 81, 115, 153
1990 election overseen by, 9
Castro, Fidel, 12, 33, 66, 201
CBS-TV, 83, 102, 138, 139, 202–3, 287
Cédras, Mrs. Raoul, 75
Cédras, Raoul, 38, 56, 71, 79, 88, 126, 131, 133, 153, 186, 280, 281
Carter's negotiations with, 74–77, 115
junta leadership of, 26–28, 52, 74–77
scheduled resignation and exile of, 30–35, 98, 154, 200, 213, 254, 365
U.S. relations with, 27–28, 52
Celano, Lee, 139
Centers for Disease Control, 7
Central Intelligence Agency (CIA), 8, 12, 25, 27, 29, 33, 35–36, 43, 56, 152, 155, 156–57, 166, 238, 335, 343, 358, 366, 385, 386, 393
Chamblain, 166
Chants du Exile (Norbert), 346
Charlemagne, Manno, 4, 389–93
Charles V, King of Spain, 21
chefs du section, 171, 183–85, 190, 219, 288
Christopher, Warren, 68, 366, 385
Cité Liberté, 99
Cité Soleil, 42, 360
Civil Affairs (CA), 26
Civil War, U.S., 144
Clark, Ramsey, 151
Clinton, Bill, 65, 129, 229, 254, 385, 388
Haitian policy of, 28, 29, 33, 38, 46, 51–52, 55, 60, 68–72, 74–75, 77, 144, 145, 146, 154, 218, 257, 365
political appointments of, 53, 386
political opposition to, 28, 145, 181
Close, General, 81, 154, 260
Club Med, 7, 17
CNN, 33, 46, 71, 74, 86, 132, 136, 140

coalition support teams (CST), 62
Cold War, 9, 13
Collins, Bill "JC," 64, 91, 121, 167, 177–78, 189, 191, 198–99, 240–41, 243, 283–84, 301–2, 304–5, 307, 310, 323, 326, 336, 381
Collins, Patrick, 29
Colon, Yves, 87–88, 98–99, 135–36, 138, 237
Columbus, Christopher, 20, 348
Comedians, The (film), 13–14, 15
Comedians, The (Greene), 6, 13, 95
Comfort, 68, 139
Commanders in Chief (CINC), 53–54, 55
Committee Commes il Faut, 47
Committee of the Young, 166, 173, 245
communism, 14, 280, 281
Congress, U.S., 29, 166, 386
Black Caucus in, 28, 38
Constant, Emmanuel "Toto," 29, 33–34, 155–56, 157–58, 166, 383, 385–86
Cosgrove, Ellen, 38
Côte de Arcadins, 17
Coton, Ti Paul, 358
Court of Appeals for the Armed Services, 151
Creole language, 7, 43, 91, 100, 103, 106–7, 176, 184, 198, 210, 239, 243, 255, 339, 371
Cuba, 12–13, 20, 55, 56, 57, 58, 64, 65, 66
Czechoslovakia, 144

Dachau, 144
Dalai Lama, 146
DAP, 67, 90
Dark Side of the Moon, The, 303–4
dechoukaj, 6–7, 8, 13, 15, 17, 100, 108, 134, 179, 194, 203, 351, 360, 366
Defense Attaché's Office (DAO), 30–31, 33, 35, 367
Defense Department (DOD), U.S., 9, 14, 29, 32, 53, 56, 63, 68, 151, 253, 284
Defense Intelligence Agency (DIA), 29, 366, 385
De Gobert, 182–85, 199, 215
Demme, Jonathan, 11